Themes

Thematic Guide to Organisations

NB This is a broad thematic guide – inevitably a number of the categories overlap.

Within each theme the organisations are listed alphabetically by key word as in the main listing.

Activity Holidays & Placements

Africa, Asia & Americas Venture

Archaeology Abroad

Backpackers Club

BAHA - British Activity Holiday Association

Brathay Exploration Group

BSES Expeditions

Calvert Trust

Camp Mohawk

CHICKS – Country Holidays for Inner City Children

Commonwealth Youth Exchange Council

Environment (Young People's Trust for the)

Farms for City Children

Forest School Camps

Girls' Venture Corps Air Cadets

IVS GB

Jubilee Sailing Trust

Lattitude Global Volunteering

Marine Leisure Association (MLA)

Mountain Leader Training England

National Trust Volunteering

National Trust Working Holidays

Outward Bound Trust

Prince's Trust – Pembrokeshire Adventure Centre

Project Trust

Quaker Voluntary Action

Raleigh

Scientific Exploration Society

Venture Trust

Volunteer Action for Peace

Waterway Recovery Group

Wind Sand & Stars

World Challenge Expeditions

WWOOF UK

Youth Cancer Trust

Youth Hostel Association (UK)

Addiction

Addaction

Addiction (Action on)

ADFAM

Al-Anon Alateen

Alcohol Concern

Alcoholics Anonymous

Blenheim CDP

Children of Alcoholics (National Association for)

Cocaine Anonymous UK

Drink Helpline (National)

Families Anonymous

Frank

Freshfield Service

Gam-Anon UK & Ireland

Gamblers Anonymous

Gamblers Anonymous Scotland

GAMCARE

Help – For a life without tobacco

London Drug & Alcohol Network

Narcotics Anonymous UK

Tranquillisers, Antidepressants and
Painkillers (Council for Information on)

Adoption/Fostering

AAA-NORCAP

Adoption and Fostering Information Line

Adoption records

Adoption UK

BAAF Adoption and Fostering (British
Association for)

Fostering Network

Intercountry Adoption Helpline

OASIS

PACT (Parents and Children Together)

Post-Adoption Centre

Register Office for Northern Ireland
(General)

Register Office for Scotland (General)

TACT

Talk Adoption

Alcohol

Addaction

Addiction (Action on)

ADFAM

Al-Anon Alateen

Alcohol Concern

Alcohol Education and Research Council

Alcohol Focus Scotland

Alcohol Studies (Institute of)

Alcoholics Anonymous

BNTL-Freeway

CADD

CAMRA

Children of Alcoholics (National Association
for)

Drink Helpline (National)

Drinkaware

London Drug & Alcohol Network

Portman Group

Roofie Foundation

Science in the Public Interest (Center for)

Tacade

Turning Point

Animals

ACT – Animal Cancer Trust
African Conservation Experience
Animal Aid
Animal Aid Youth
Animal Defenders International
Animal Health (National Office of)
Animal Health Trust
Animal Rescue (International)
Animal Rescuers (UK)
Animal Welfare Trust (National)
Anti Snaring Campaign (National)
Anti-Vivisection Society (National)
Ape Alliance
ARKive
Avicultural Society
Badger Trust
Bat Conservation Trust
Battersea Dogs Home
Bird Council (British)
Blue Cross
Born Free Foundation
Brooke
BUAV
Budgerigar Society
Butterfly Conservation
Canine Partners
Captive Animals' Protection Society
Care for the Wild International
Cat Fancy (Governing Council of the)
Cats Protection
Cinnamon Trust
City Farms & Community Gardens
   (Federation of)
Companion Animal Studies (Society for)

Compassion in World Farming Trust
Cruel Sports Ltd (League Against)
Crufts Dog Show
David Sheldrick Wildlife Trust
Deer Society (British)
Divers Marine Life Rescue (British)
Dogs for the Disabled
Dogs Trust
Donkey Breed Society
Donkey Sanctuary
Dragonfly Society (British)
Entomologists' Society (Amateur)
Environmental Investigation Agency
Eurogroup for Animals
Farm Animal Welfare Committee
Farms for City Children
Fauna & Flora International
Feline Advisory Bureau
FRAME
Freshfields Donkey Village
Froglife
Gambia Horse and Donkey Trust
Gorilla Organization
Guide Dogs for the Blind Association
Hamster Council (National)
HAPPA
Hawk and Owl Trust
Hearing Dogs for Deaf People
Hedgehog Preservation Society (British)
Horse Society (British)
Humane Slaughter Association
Hunt Saboteurs Association
IFAW
IPPL (UK)
Kennel Club
Lord Dowding Fund
Lost Doggies UK
Marine Conservation Society
Marine Life Study Society (British)
Naturewatch
Ocean Mammal Institute
Onekind

Orangutan Foundation
Ornithology (British Trust for)
PDSA
People's Trust for Endangered Species
Pet Advisory Committee
Pet Behaviour Counsellors (Association of)
Pet Care Trust
Pet Health Council
Pet Month (National)
PETA Foundation
PetLog Database (National)
Pets as Therapy
Pony Club
Rabbit Council (British)
Rare Breeds Survival Trust
Red List of Endangered Species
Redwings Horse Sanctuary
Respect for Animals
Royal College of Veterinary Surgeons
RSPB
RSPCA
Scottish SPCA
Shark Alliance
Small Animal Veterinary Association (British)
Support Dogs
Uncaged Campaigns
Understanding Animal Research
Viva!
Whale & Dolphin Conservation Society
Wildlife Aid
Wildlife Trusts (Royal Society of)
Wood Green Animal Shelters
World Horse Welfare
WSPA International
WWF-UK
ZSL London Zoo
ZSL Whipsnade Zoo

Architecture

Ancient Buildings (Society for the Protection of)
Archéire
Architects (Royal Institute of British)
Architectural Heritage Fund
Architecture Foundation
Design Council
Friends of Friendless Churches
Georgian Group
GreatBuildings
Landscape Institute
Open-City
Royal Scottish Academy
SALVO
Twentieth Century Society
Victorian Society

Arts

Access Art
Access London Theatre
Access Space
Action Transport Theatre
Age Exchange
Apples & Snakes
Arc Theatre
Architects (Royal Institute of British)
Architecture Foundation
Ariel Studios
Art and Design (National Society for Education in)

7

Arts continued

Art Fund

Art Library (National)

Art Therapists (British Association of)

Artists Against Racism

Arts (National Campaign for the)

Arts & Business

Arts Council England

Arts Council of Northern Ireland

Arts Council of Wales

Arts in Therapy & Education (Institute for)

Arts Marketing Association

Artsline

Artswork

ArtWatch UK

Ashmolean

Authors' Licensing and Collecting Society

Ballet Organization (British)

BBC Studio Audiences

Benesh Institute

Birmingham Royal Ballet

Bolshoi Ballet

Book Trust (Scottish)

Books Council (Welsh)

Booktrust

BRIT School for Performing Arts and Technology

British Film Institute

British Library Sound Archive

Brontë Parsonage Museum & Brontë Society

Cambridge Past, Present & Future

Cello Society (Internet)

Children's Literature (National Centre for Research in)

Chinese Arts Centre

Circus Sensible/Circus School

Circus Space

Classical Association

Contemporary Art Society

Courtauld Institute of Art

Crafts Council

Creative Partnerships

Creative Scotland

Dance UK

Danceconsortium

Design and Artists Copyright Society

Design and Technology Association

Disability Arts Cymru

Drama Association of Wales

Drama Schools (The Conference of)

Drama Training (National Council for)

Dramatic Need

Drawing (The Campaign for)

Edinburgh International Book Festival

Edinburgh International Festival

Engage

English National Ballet

English National Opera

English PEN

English Touring Theatre

ENYAN

European Youth Music Week

Festivals (British & International Federation of)

Finnish Institute

Folger Shakespeare Library

France: culture and communications website

Frankfurt Book Fair

Georgian Group

Headlong Theatre

Henry Moore Foundation

History of Cinema & Popular Culture (The Bill Douglas Centre for the)

Hull Truck Theatre

ICON

Imaginate

Italian Cultural Institute in London

IXIA

Live Theatre

London Charity Orchestra

London Schools Arts Service

London Theatre (Official)

London theatres: online

Lowry

Mousetrap Theatre Projects

Movie Review Query Engine

Museums (International Council of)

Music Council (National)

National Drama

National Opera Studio

National Theatre

National Youth Ballet of Great Britain

NODA

Northern Ballet

Northern Broadsides

Northern Stage

Open College of the Arts

Open-City

Out of Joint

Performing Arts Medicine (British Association for)

Poetry Library

Poetry Society

Polka Theatre

Project Gutenberg

PRS for Music

Public Monuments & Sculpture Association

Queen's House

RADA

Rambert Dance Company

Roundhouse

Royal Academy of Arts

Royal Academy of Dance

Royal Ballet

Royal Opera

Royal Scottish Academy

Royal Shakespeare Company

RSA

Science, Technology & the Arts (National Endowment for)

Scottish Ballet

Scottish Opera

Scottish Youth Theatre

SCRAN

Shakespeare Association (British)

Shakespeare at the Tobacco Factory

Shakespeare Birthplace Trust

Shakespeare Schools Festival

Shakespeare's Globe Theatre

Shared Experience

Skylight Circus Arts

Sound Sense

Southbank Centre

SPIT

Storytelling (Society for)

Student Drama Festival (National)

Studies in British Art (Paul Mellon Centre for)

Teaching of Drama (National Association for the)

Theatre Council (Independent)

Théâtre de Complicité

Theatre for Children and Young People (International Association of)

Theatre Network (The Amateur)

Theatrenet

Theatres Trust

Twentieth Century Society

UK Theatre Web

Unicorn Theatre for Children

Venice in Peril Fund

Visual Arts & Galleries Association

Voluntary Arts Network

Welsh National Opera

Women in Publishing

Writers in Education (National Association of)

Writers' Guild of Great Britain

Youth Arts Wales (National)

Youth Music Theatre (National)

Youth Opera (British)

Youth Orchestra (National of GB)

Youth Theatre of GB (National)

Youth Theatres (National Association of)

Care/Carers

4Children

Action for Children

Alzheimer Scotland

Alzheimer's Society

Anchor Trust

Anxiety Care

Assisted Dying (Healthcare Professions for)

Attend

Baby Lifeline

Breast Cancer Care

CACHE

Care Council for Wales

Care Quality Commission

Carers

Carers (The Princess Royal Trust For)

Chance UK

Childminding Association (National)

Christian Lewis Trust

CLICSargent

Contact a Family

Counsel and Care

Crossroads Care

Cruse Bereavement Care

Daycare Trust

Disability Law Service

Disabled Living Foundation

Early Years

Elder Abuse (Action on)

Epilepsy Society

Half the Sky Foundation

Help the Hospices

Home-Start

Hyperactive Children's Support Group

Learning Through Action Centre

Life

Macmillan Cancer Support

Marie Curie Cancer Care

Medical Foundation for the Care of Victims of Torture

Muslim Welfare House

PACT (Prison Advice & Care Trust)

Palliative Care (National Council for)

Pastoral Care in Education (National Association for)

Pituitary Foundation

Pre-school Learning Alliance

Pre-school Play Association (Scottish)

Pre-School Providers Association (Wales)

Sick Children (Action for)

Sickle Cell Society

Skills for Care

Social Care Association

Solicitors for the Elderly

Treloar Trust

Twins & Multiple Births Association

Voice

Who Cares? Trust

Censorship

ARTICLE 19

Film Classification (British Board of)

Freedom of Information (Campaign for)

Index on Censorship

Information Commissioner's Office

Internet Watch Foundation

Press and Broadcasting Freedom (Campaign for)

Video Standards Council

Charities (general)

Big Lottery Fund
CF Appointments
Charities Aid Foundation
CharitiesDirect.com
Charity Choice
Charity Commission for England & Wales
Children in Need Appeal
Comic Relief
Computers 4 Africa
Disasters Emergency Committee
Giving Nation
Jane Tomlinson Appeal
Justgiving
Medical Research Charities (Association of)
ShareGift
100 Black Men of London

Children/Young people

4Children
Access to Industry
Action for Children
Action Transport Theatre
Additives (Action on)
Adoption and Fostering Information Line
Adoption records
Adoption UK
Adventure Activities Licensing Authority
Afasic
Africans Unite Against Child Abuse
Al-Anon Alateen
Alone in London
Anti-Bullying Alliance

Anti-Bullying Network
Ariel Studios
Army Cadet Force
Artswork
Aspect
Athletic Association (English Schools')
BAAF Adoption and Fostering (British Association for)
Baby Milk Action
Babyworld
Baobab Centre for Young Survivors in Exile
Barnardo's
BASPCAN
Beatbullying
Big Read (The)
BNTL-Freeway
Boarding Concern
Bolton Lads & Girls Club
Boys' Brigade
Brainwave
Brandon Centre
Brazil's Children Trust (Action for)
Bully Free Zone
Bullying UK
Butterfly Project
CACHE
Cafcass
Camp Mohawk
Cardiac Risk in the Young
Cards for Little Lives
Catch22
Chain of Hope
Chance UK
Chernobyl Children's Life Line
CHICKS
Child Accident Prevention Trust
Child and Adolescent Mental Health (Association for)
Child Bereavement Charity
Child Brain Injury Trust
Child Contact Centres (National Association of)
Child Growth Foundation

Children/Young people continued

Child Poverty Action Group
Child Protection in Sport Unit
Child Soldiers
Childhood (Alliance for)
Childhood Bereavement Network
ChildHope
ChildLine
Childminding Association (National)
CHILDREN 1ST
Children are unbeatable! Alliance
Children in Need Appeal
Children in Scotland
Children of Alcoholics (National Association for)
Children with Leukaemia
Children's Commissioner for England (Office of the)
Children's Hope Foundation
Children's Legal Centre
Children's Literature (National Centre for Research in)
Children's Orchestra (National)
Children's Rights Alliance for England
Children's Society
Children's Book Groups (Federation of)
Children's Heart Federation
Children's Scrapstore
Children's Workforce Development Council
Christian Lewis Trust
Church Lads' and Church Girls' Brigade
Church of England Education Division
Cirdan Sailing Trust
CLICSargent
Clubs for Young People
Commonwealth Youth Exchange Council
Communication Trust
Council of Europe Youth
CRAC
CRIN
CyberMentors
Dad

Dad Talk
Dads House
Daneford Trust
Daycare Trust
Deaf Children's Society (National)
Depaul International
Depaul Nightstop UK
Down Syndrome Education International
Dramatic Need
Duke of Edinburgh's Award
Early Education
Early Years
Education (Department for)
Education and Culture (Directorate General for)
Education for Choice
Ellen MacArthur Cancer Trust
Endeavour Training Limited
England Athletics
ENYAN
Epilepsy (National Centre for Young People with)
ERIC – Education and Resources for Improving Childhood Continence
European Youth Card Association
European Youth Forum
European Youth Information and Counselling Agency
Every Child a Chance Trust
EveryChild
Fair Play for Children Association
Fairbridge
Families Need Fathers
Find a Parent or Child
First Light
Foundation For Peace (Tim Parry Johnathan Ball)
Foyer Federation
Free the Children
Get connected
Gifted Children (National Association for)
Gifted Children's Information Centre
Girlguiding UK

Girls' Brigade England & Wales

Girls' Venture Corps Air Cadets

Giving Nation

Grandparents Plus

Half the Sky Foundation

Handsel Trust

Headliners

Hideout

Hope UK

Hyperactive Children's Support Group

Imaginate

Include

Independent Safeguarding Authority

IntoUniversity

Jeans for Genes

Jewish Lads' & Girls' Brigade (JLGB)

Just for Kids Law

Kids Company

Kids for Kids

Kidscape

Lavender Trust

Leap Confronting Conflict

Learning Outside the Classroom (Council for)

Lesbian Information Service

Lifetracks

likeitis.org

Live Music Now

London Children's Ballet

London Youth

Marine Society and Sea Cadets

MATCH

Maternal & Childhealth Advocacy International

Mermaids

Methodist Children & Youth

Midi Music Company

Missing Children website

Montessori Centre

Motorvations Project Ltd

Mousetrap Theatre Projects

Mumsnet

Music for Youth

Mydaughter.co.uk

NABSS

National Youth Ballet of Great Britain

NBCS

NCB

NSPCC

Nurture Group Network

Ocean Youth Trust

Out of trouble

PACT (Parents & Abducted Children Together)

Parenting UK

Pastoral Care in Education (National Association for)

Philip Lawrence Awards Network

Plan UK

Play England

Play Wales

PLAYLINK

Pod Charitable Trust

Pre-school Learning Alliance

Pre-school Play Association (Scottish)

Pre-School Providers Association (Wales)

Prince's Trust – Pembrokeshire Adventure Centre

Prince's Trust (Head Office)

Pyramid

Quality in Study Support and Extended Services

Railway Children

Raw Material

React

Restless Development

reunite

Rona Sailing Project

Roundhouse

Runaway Helpline

Save the Children UK

School Food Trust

Scottish Youth Theatre

Scout Association

Sea Ranger Association

Children/Young people continued

SEBDA
Seven Stories
Shared Parenting Information Group
Sick Children (Action for)
Siobhan Dowd Trust
Skylight Circus Arts
Smallpeice Trust
SOS Children's Villages
Sparks
Tall Ships Youth Trust
Teenage Cancer Trust
Theatre for Children and Young People (International Association of)
Thesite.org
Trackoff
UK Parents Lounge
UK Youth
UNICEF UK
United Reformed Church
University of the First Age
Urban Saints
Values Education for Life (The Collegiate Centre for)
Venture Trust
Voice
Voluntary Arts Network
Voluntary Youth Services (National Council for)
What About The Children?
Whizz-Kidz
Who Cares? Trust
Willow Foundation
Winston's Wish
Wired Safety
Woodcraft Folk
Working on Wheels
WorldWide Volunteering
Year Out Group
YMCA England

Young Christian Workers
Young Concert Artists Trust
Young People in Focus
Young People with ME (Association of)
Young Scot
YoungMinds
Youth Access
Youth Advocacy Service (National)
Youth Agency (National)
Youth Arts Wales (National)
Youth at Risk
Youth Choir of Great Britain (National)
Youth Council (British)
Youth Council for N. Ireland
Youth for Christ
Youth in Action
Youth Information
Youth Music
Youth Music Theatre (National)
Youth Orchestra (National of GB)
Youth Sport Trust
Youth Theatre of GB (National)
Youth Theatres (National Association of)
Youthhealthtalk
YouthNet UK

Citizenship & Community Issues

Advocacy Resource Exchange
Arthur Rank Centre
Better Transport (Campaign for)
Bevan Foundation
Blenheim CDP
British Legion (Royal)
Business in the Community
Certificate ordering service
Changemakers
Citizens UK
Citizenship (Institute for)

Citizenship and the Law (National Centre for)

Citizenship Foundation

Citizenship Teaching (Association for)

City Farms & Community Gardens (Federation of)

Common Ground

Common Purpose

Communities and Local Government (Department for)

Communities in Rural England (Action with)

Community Composting Network

Community Dance (Foundation for)

Community Foundation Network

Community Matters

Community Media Association

Community Pubs Foundation

Community Rail Partnerships (Association of)

Community Self Build Agency

Community Service Volunteers

Courts and Tribunal Service (HM)

Crimestoppers

Crown Prosecution Service

DirectGov

Family Names Profiling (GB)

Forgiveness Project

Foundation For Peace (Tim Parry Johnathan Ball)

Friends, Families and Travellers

Get Global!

GFS Platform for Young Women

Global Ethics UK Trust (Institute for)

Groundwork UK

Gun Control Network

Gypsy Association

Habitat for Humanity Great Britain

Homeless Link

Immigrants (Joint Council for the Welfare of)

Immigration Aid Unit (Greater Manchester)

Integrated Education (N. Ireland Council for)

Intermix

Leap Confronting Conflict

Learning Through Action Centre

Legal Services Commission

Letslink UK

Local Government Association

Local Government Ombudsman (England)

Missing People

Peace Alliance

Pensioners Convention (National)

Pet Advisory Committee

Philip Lawrence Awards Network

Placement Survival Guide

Public Services Ombudsman (Scottish)

RAPt

Registering life events

Runaway Helpline

Science in the Public Interest (Center for)

Show Racism the Red Card

Skills for Justice

Social Care Association

Social Issues Research Centre

Social Workers (British Association of)

Squatters (Advisory Service for)

Transforming Conflict

UK Border Agency

UK New Citizen

Undercurrents

Voluntary and Community Action (National Association for)

Volunteers For Rural India

WRVS

Complementary Medicine

Acupuncture Council (British)
Acupuncture Society (British Medical)
Alexander Teachers (Professional Association of)
Alexander Technique (Society of Teachers of the)
Bach Centre
Chiropractic (Anglo-European College of)
Chiropractic Association (British)
Chiropractic Patients' Association
Complementary and Natural Medicine (Institute for)
Healing Organisations (Confederation of)
Herb Society
Holistic Therapists (Federation of)
Homeopathic Association (British)
Homeopaths (Society of)
Hypnotherapy Organisations (UK Confederation of)
Medical Herbalists (National Institute of)
Osteopathic Council (General)
Paul's Cancer Support Centre
Reflexology Association (British)
Shiatsu Society (UK)

Consumers, Commerce & Business

ABTA
Adbusters
Advertising Association
Advertising Standards Authority
Africa Now
Arts & Business
ATM locator
Banana Link

Bankruptcy Advisory Service Limited
Blind in Business
British Standards Institute
Building Societies Members Association
Bus Users UK
Business & Professional Women UK Ltd
Business Gateway
Business in Sport & Leisure
Buy Nothing Day (UK)
CAMRA
Chambers of Commerce (British)
Chartered Management Institute
Chartered Surveyors (Royal Institute of)
Chartered Surveyors Training Trust
Chartered Surveyors Voluntary Service
Citizens Advice
Community Pubs Foundation
Competition Commission
Consumer Credit Counselling Service
Consumer Direct
Consumer Focus
Consumer Focus Post
Consumers International
Corporate Watch
Credit Unions Ltd. (Association of British)
Crown Estates
Dairy Council (The)
Direct Marketing Association
Directors (Institute of)
Economics, Business and Enterprise Association
Education Business Excellence (Institute for)
Effective Dispute Resolution (Centre for)
Egg Information Service (British)
EIRIS
Ethical Consumer Research Association (ECRA)
European Central Bank
European Investment Bank
Facsimile Preference Service
Fair Trade Shops (British Association for)
Fair Trading (Office of)

Fairtrade Foundation

Farmers' Markets (Scottish Association of)

Farmers' Retail & Markets Association (National)

Financial Ombudsman Service

Financial Services Authority

Fiscal Studies (Institute for)

Food & Drink Federation

Food Commission (UK)

Fredericks Foundation

Freecycle

Freegle

Home Business Alliance

Homeworking

Howtocomplain.com

Information Management (Association for)

Intellectual Property Office

Lorna Young Foundation

Mailing Preference Service

Marine Stewardship Council

Mentoring and Befriending Foundation

Moneysavingexpert.com

My Supermarket

National Debtline

Naturewatch

OFCOM

Ofgem

Patent Office (European)

Payplan

Personnel & Development (Chartered Institute of)

Phonebrain

Phonepay Plus

Pipedown

Post Office

Postcode Finder

Postcomm (Postal Services Commission)

Rail Regulation (Office of)

Road Haulage Association

Shared Interest Society Ltd

Simple Free Law Advisor

Sleep Council

Small Businesses (Federation of)

Social Entrepreneurs (School for)

Stock Exchange (London)

SustainAbility

TaxAid

Telephone Directories On Web

Telephone Preference Service

Tour Operators (Association of Independent)

Trading Standards Institute

Traidcraft

Trainline

Unite

Water Services (Office of)

We Are What We Do

Which?

Women Entrepreneurs (British Association of)

Work & Pensions (Department for)

World Trade Organisation

Contraception, Pregnancy & Birth

Abortion Rights

Action of Postpartum Psychosis Network

Active Birth Centre

AIMS

ARC

Baby Lifeline

Babyworld

Birth Trauma Association

BirthChoice UK

Bliss – the premature baby charity

Bliss Scotland

Bounty Healthcare Fund

BPAS

Brandon Centre

Brook

COTS

Dad

Contraception, Pregnancy & Birth continued

Donor Conception Network
Education for Choice
Family Planning Association
Fertility Friends
Fertility UK
Gamete Donation Trust (National)
Human Fertilisation & Embryology Authority
Infertility Counselling Association (British)
Infertility Network UK
Interact Worldwide
La Leche League GB
Life
likeitis.org
Margaret Pyke Centre
Marie Stopes International
Midwives UK (Independent)
Miscarriage Association
Multiple Births Foundation
Mumsnet
National Childbirth Trust
Netmums
Newlife Foundation for Disabled Children
Nursing & Midwifery Council
Planned Parenthood Federation (International)
Post Natal Illness
Post-Natal Illness (Association for)
SANDS
Sex Education Forum
Tommy's, the baby charity
Twins & Multiple Births Association
UK Parents Lounge
Unborn Children (Society for the Protection of)
Voice for Choice
White Ribbon Alliance
Your Life

Counselling

AAA-NORCAP
AdviceUK
Advocacy Resource Exchange
Ahimsa
Albany Trust
Anxiety Care
Arbitrators (Chartered Institute of)
Barnardo's
BEAT
Befrienders Worldwide
Bereavement Network (London)
Birmingham Settlement
BPAS
Brandon Centre
Broken Rainbow UK
Brook
CALM
Carers (The Princess Royal Trust For)
Changing Faces
ChildLine
Citizens Advice
Communities Empowerment Network
Concord Media
Counsel and Care
Counselling & Psychotherapy (British Association for)
Crisis Counselling for Alleged Shoplifters
Cruse Bereavement Care
Cry-sis
Dial UK
Donor Conception Network
Down's Heart Group
Eating Problems Service
ENABLE Scotland
Everyman Project
Family Lives

Family Rights Group

Frank

Freshfield Service

Gamete Donation Trust (National)

Handsel Trust

Hereditary Breast Cancer Helpline (National)

Hideout

Infertility Counselling Association (British)

Karma Nirvana

Kids Company

Lesbian and Gay Switchboard (London)

Life

Marie Stopes International

Medical Advisory Service

Men's Advice Line

Miracles

Mosac

NHS Direct

No Panic

NSPCC

PACE

Paul's Cancer Support Centre

Post-Adoption Centre

Prisoners' Advice Service

Public Concern at Work

Rape Crisis

Relate

Relationships Scotland

Respect

RoadPeace

Roofie Foundation

Samaritans

SAMM

SANE

Seasonal Affective Disorder Association

SEBDA

Survivors of Bereavement by Suicide

SurvivorsUK

Talk Adoption

Teacher Support Network

Triumph over Phobia (TOP UK)

Victim Support

Wessex Cancer Trust

Who Cares? Trust

Youth Access

Youth Advocacy Service (National)

Dance
refer also to the section on Dance, Drama, Music & Performing Arts Schools

Ballet Organization (British)

Benesh Institute

Birmingham Royal Ballet

Bolshoi Ballet

Ceroc

Community Dance (Foundation for)

Dance Council (British)

Dance Education & Training (Council for)

Dance UK

Danceconsortium

Dancesport UK

Dancing and Kindred Arts (United Kingdom Alliance of Professional Teachers of)

English National Ballet

Festivals (British & International Federation of)

IDTA

ISTD

London Children's Ballet

Men's Morris & Sword Dance Clubs (National Association of)

Morris Federation

National Youth Ballet of Great Britain

Northern Ballet

Rambert Dance Company

Royal Academy of Dance

Royal Ballet

Scottish Ballet

Death and Bereavement

Advocacy After Fatal Domestic Abuse
Assisted Dying (Healthcare Professions for)
Bereavement Network (London)
Cardiac Risk in the Young
Care Not Killing
Child Bereavement Charity
Child Death Helpline
Childhood Bereavement Network
Compassionate Friends
Cremation Society of Great Britain
Cruse Bereavement Care
Dignity in Dying
Dying Matters
Friends at the end
Help the Hospices
Infant Deaths (Foundation for the Study of)
INQUEST
Lone Twin Network
Natural Death Centre
Palliative Care (National Council for)
React
SAMM
Survivors of Bereavement by Suicide
Winston's Wish

Developing World

ActionAid
ADD International
Afghanaid
Africa Centre
Africa Now
Africa, Asia & Americas Venture

African Initiatives
Africans Unite Against Child Abuse
Anti-Slavery International
Baby Milk Action
Banana Link
Bond
Book Aid International
Brazil's Children Trust (Action for)
Broadcasting Trust (International)
Brooke
Burma Campaign UK
CAFOD
CAMFED International
Canon Collins Trust
CARE International UK
Chain of Hope
Christian Aid
Chronic Poverty Research Centre
Comic Relief
Commonwealth Education Trust
Commonwealth Scolarship Commission in the UK
Commonwealth Society (Royal)
Computer Aid International
Computers 4 Africa
Concern Worldwide
Cross Cultural Solutions
Development Education Project
Dramatic Need
Ethiopiaid
Fair Trade Shops (British Association for)
Fairtrade Foundation
Forest Peoples Programme
Friends of Peoples Close to Nature
Gambia Horse and Donkey Trust
Global Crop Diversity Trust
Global Dimension
Global Eye
HALO Trust
HIV InSite
HIV/Aids Alliance (International)
Homeless International

International Development (Department for)
International Monetary Fund
International Service
Islamic Relief Worldwide
Jubilee Debt Campaign
Kids for Kids
Kiva
Labour Behind the Label
Lorna Young Foundation
Malaria No More UK
Mary's Meals
Médecins sans Frontières (UK)
Media for Development
Medical Trust (Britain-Nepal)
Mercy Corps
Nicaragua Solidarlty Campaign
ONE International
Operation Smile UK
Opportunity International UK
Overseas Development Institute
Oxfam
Panos Institute
People & Planet
Plan UK
Practical Action
Restless Development
Room to Read
Samaritans International
Save the Children UK
SCIAF
Shine a Light
Sightsavers
Skillshare International
SOS Children's Villages
Stakeholder Forum
Survival International
TAPOL
Tearfund
Tools for Self Reliance
Tourism Concern
Traidcraft
TRóCAIRE

UNICEF UK
United Nations Association of the UK
Vision Aid Overseas
VSO
War on Want
Water Aid
Womankind Worldwide
World Bank
World Development Movement
World Food Programme (United Nations)
World Health Organisation
World Vision UK
Y Care International

Disability/Special Needs

1 Voice – Communicating together
Access London Theatre
Accessible Environments (Centre for)
ADD International
Afasic
Artsline
Asian People's Disability Alliance
Back-up Trust
BASIC
Bibic
Bikers with a Disability (National Association for)
Blind (Royal National Institute of the)
Blind Golf Association (English)
Blind in Business
Blind of the United Kingdom (National Federation of the)
Blind People (Action for)
Blind Sport (British)
Blue Badge Network
Braille Chess Association
Calvert Trust

Disability/Special Needs continued

Camp Mohawk
Canine Partners
Carers (The Princess Royal Trust For)
Changing Faces
Child Growth Foundation
Children's Hope Foundation
CLAPA
ClearVision Project
Conductive Education (The National Institute of)
Connect
Contact a Family
CP Sport England and Wales
Crossroads Care
Cued Speech Association UK
Cycling Projects
Deaf Association (British)
Deaf Children's Society (National)
Deaf Education Through Listening and Talking
Deaf Sports Council (British)
Deafblind International
Deafblind Scotland
Deafblind UK
Deafness Research UK
Dial UK
Disability Action
Disability Alliance
Disability Arts Cymru
Disability Law Service
Disability Pregnancy & Parenthood International
Disability Snowsport UK
Disability Sport (English Federation of)
Disability Sport Events
Disabled Living Foundation
Disabled Motoring UK
Disabled Parents Network
Disabled People's Council (UK)
Disfigurement Guidance Centre

Dogs for the Disabled
Douglas Bader Foundation
Down's Syndrome Association
Down's Syndrome Scotland
Dyslexia Action
Dyslexia Association (British)
Dyspraxia Foundation
ENABLE Scotland
Equality and Human Rights Commission
Equality Britain
Freshfields Donkey Village
Gateway Award
Guide Dogs for the Blind Association
Hairline International
Handsel Trust
HEADWAY
Hearing Dogs for Deaf People
Hypermobility Syndrome Association
Inclusion (National Development Team for)
Inclusive Education (Alliance for)
Inclusive Education (Centre for Studies on)
Independent Living Alternatives
IPSEA
Jubilee Sailing Trust
Learning Disabilities (British Institute of)
Let's Face It
Limbless Association
Listening Books
Makaton Charity
Mencap
Mental Health Foundation
Multiple Sclerosis Society
Multiple Sclerosis Therapy Centres (National)
Music and the Deaf
Music Therapy (British Association for)
NBCS
Network 81
Newlife Foundation for Disabled Children
NOAH
Norwood
Operation Smile UK

Papworth Trust
Paralympic GB
Parents for Inclusion
Partially Sighted Society
People First
Phab
RADAR
Rathbone
REMAP
Remploy
Ricability
Riding for the Disabled Association
RNIB
RNIB National Library Service
RNID
Rona Sailing Project
RYA Sailability
Saving Faces
Scope
SeeAbility
Self Unlimited
Sense
Shine
Shopmobility (National Federation of)
Short Persons Support
Sibs
Sightsavers
Signature
Skills for Care
Sound Seekers
Sound Sense
Speakability
Special Educational Needs (National Association for)
Special Needs Education (European Agency for Development in)
Special Olympics Great Britain
SPIT
Sports Association for People with Learning Disability (UK)
Stammering Association (British)
Stammering Children (Michael Palin Centre for)

Support Dogs
Swimming Clubs for people with Disabilities (National Association for)
TACT
TAG
Talking Newspapers and Magazines (National)
Thalidomide Society (UK)
Thrive
Tourism for All
Transport for London
Treloar Trust
Tuberous Sclerosis Association UK
UPDATE
Voice UK
VoiceAbility
Volunteer Reading Help
WheelPower
Whizz-Kidz
Winvisible (Women with visible & invisible disabilities)
Wireless for the Blind Fund (British)

Drugs and Substance Abuse

Addaction
Addiction (Action on)
ADFAM
Advisory Council on the Misuse of Drugs
Blenheim CDP
BNTL-Freeway
CADD
Cocaine Anonymous UK
Drug Education Forum
Drugs and Crime (UN Office on)
Drugs Forum (Scottish)
DrugScope
Families Anonymous

Drugs and Substance Abuse continued

Frank
Freshfield Service
Hope UK
Know Cannabis
London Drug & Alcohol Network
Narcotics Anonymous UK
RAPt
Release
ReSolv
Roofie Foundation
Tacade
Thesite.org
Tranquillisers, Antidepressants and Painkillers (Council for Information on)
Transform Drug Policy Foundation
Turning Point

Economics

Adam Smith Institute
Audit Commission
Audit Office (National)
Bank of England
Bankruptcy Advisory Service Limited
Citizens Income Trust
CLES
Credit Unions Ltd. (Association of British)
Currency converter
Economic & Social Research (National Institute of)
Extreme Inequality
Foreign Policy Centre
HM Treasury
International Monetary Fund
Letslink UK

Local Economy Policy Unit
Monetary Justice (Christian Council for)
MyBnk
New Economics Foundation
Pensions Ombudsman
Public Management and Policy Association
Shared Interest Society Ltd
Smith Institute
Social & Economic Research (Institute for)
unbiased.co.uk

Education

100 Black Men of London
Access Art
Access to Industry
Alcohol Education and Research Council
Alexander Teachers (Professional Association of)
Alexander Technique (Society of Teachers of the)
Anne Frank Trust UK
Antidote
AQA
Art and Design (National Society for Education in)
Arvon Foundation
ASDAN
Asiatic Society of Great Britain and Ireland (Royal)
ASPE
Aspect
Associated Board of the Royal Schools of Music
Association of Colleges
Athletic Association (English Schools')
AV Foundation
Awesome Library
BBC Schools
Bibliomania
Big Bus

Big Read (The)
Bilingualism & Literacies Education Network
Bitesize: BBC revision web site
BKA
Black Training & Enterprise Group
Boarding Concern
Book Aid International
Book Power
Books Council (Welsh)
Booktrust
Brainwave
BRIT School for Performing Arts and Technology
British Council
Business in the Community
CACHE
CAFCAS
CAMFED International
Canon Collins Trust
Cards for Little Lives
Career Development Loans
Catholic Education Service
Chartered Surveyors Training Trust
Chess Association (English Primary Schools)
Children's Book Groups (Federation of)
Chinese Arts Centre
Choir Schools' Association
Christian Education/International Bible Reading Association (IBRA)
Christian Teachers (Association of)
CILT
Citizenship Foundation
Citizenship Teaching (Association for)
City and Guilds
Classical Association
Clear Vision Trust
ClearVision Project
Coleg Harlech (WEA)
CollegesWales
Common Purpose
Commonwealth Education Trust
Commonwealth Scolarship Commission in the UK

Commonwealth Society (Royal)
Communication Trust
Communities Empowerment Network
Conductive Education (The National Institute of)
Countryside Foundation for Education
CRAC
Creative Partnerships
CREST Awards
Cult Information Centre
Dance Education & Training (Council for)
Daneford Trust
Dark Skies (Campaign for)
Deaf Education Through Listening and Talking
Design and Technology Association
Development Education Project
Down Syndrome Education International
Drama Schools (The Conference of)
Drama Training (National Council for)
Drug Education Forum
Dyslexia Action
Dyslexia Association (British)
e-Learning Foundation
Early Education
Early Years
Eco-Schools
Economics, Business and Enterprise Association
Edexcel
Education (Advisory Centre for) Ltd
Education (Department for)
Education (Global Campaign for)
Education & Industry (Centre for)
Education and Culture (Directorate General for)
Education and Training (Centre for the Study of)
Education Business Excellence (Institute for)
Education Consultants (Society of)
Education for Choice

Education continued

Education Index (British)

Education of Adults (European Association for the)

Education Otherwise

Education Scotland

Education Statistics (National Center for)

Educational Psychologists (Association of)

Educational Recording Agency

EMI Music Sound Foundation

Employment & Learning (Department for) Northern Ireland

Engage

England Athletics

English and Media Centre

English Association

English Heritage

English Speaking Union

Enterprise Education Trust

Environment (Young People's Trust for the)

Erasmus

ESU

Eurodesk

Every Child a Chance Trust

Fair Access (Office for)

Fairbridge

Farming & Countryside Education

Field Studies Council

Film & Television Archive (Northern Region)

Film and Television School (National)

Film Education

Findhorn Foundation

Football Association (English Schools)

Fulbright Commission (The US-UK)

GCSE Revision

Geographical Association

Geological Society

Get Global!

Gifted Children (National Association for)

Gifted Children's Information Centre

GLE

Global Action Plan

Global Dimension

Global Ethics UK Trust (Institute for)

Global Eye

Governors' Association (National)

Headliners

Healthy Schools

Heartstone

Higher Education Funding Council for England

Historical Association

History World

HMRC Education Zone

Holocaust Educational Trust

Homework High

Hope UK

Human Rights Education Association

Human Scale Education Movement

IATEFL

IDTA

Imaginate

Include

Inclusion (National Development Team for)

Inclusive Education (Alliance for)

Inclusive Education (Centre for Studies on)

Independent Schools Council

Innovation in Mathematics Teaching (Centre for)

Integrated Education (N. Ireland Council for)

International Baccalaureate Organization

IntoUniversity

IPPL (UK)

IPSEA

ISTD

JANET

Japan Foundation, London

Kid Info

Kids in Museums

Language Awareness (Association for)

Language Learning (Association for)

Languages (Scotland's National Centre for)

learndirect

Learning (Campaign for)

Learning (Institute for)

Learning and Skills Development Agency Northern Ireland

Learning and Skills Improvement Service

Learning Disabilities (British Institute of)

Learning Outside the Classroom (Council for)

Learning Through Action Centre

Learning Zone

Left 'n' Write

Life Science Centre

Lifelong Learning

Lifetracks

Linguists (Chartered Institute of)

Listening Books

Literacy Association (National)

Literacy Association (UK)

Literacy in Primary Education (Centre for)

Literacy Trust (National)

Local History (British Association for)

London Schools Arts Service

Makaton Charity

Mathematical Association

Mentoring and Befriending Foundation

Met Office

Montessori Centre

Mousetrap Theatre Projects

Music Council (National)

Music Educators (National Association of)

Muslim Schools UK (Association of)

Mydaughter.co.uk

NAACE

NABSS

NAPE

National Drama

National Extension College

Network 81

NFER

NHS Health Scotland

NIACE

NUS

OCR/Oxford Cambridge and RSA Examinations

Ofqual

Ofsted

Open & Distance Learning Quality Council

Open College of the Arts

Open University

Orangutan Foundation

Outdoor Learning (Institute for)

Parents for Inclusion

Parliamentary Education Unit

Pastoral Care in Education (National Association for)

Personal Finance Education Group

Pharmaceutical Society (Royal)

Physical Education (Association for)

Physics (Institute of)

Placement Survival Guide

Pre-school Learning Alliance

Pre-school Play Association (Scottish)

Pre-School Providers Association (Wales)

Prospects

PTA-UK

Pyramid

Quality in Study Support and Extended Services

RADA

RE Today Services

Real Education (Campaign for)

REonline

Room to Read

Royal Academy of Arts

Royal College of Veterinary Surgeons

Royal Geographical Society

Royal Society

RSA

Ruskin College

School Councils UK

School Food Trust

School Journey Association

School Librarianship (International Association of)

School Library Association

Education continued

Schools Adjudicator (Office of the)

Schools Health Education Unit

Schools Music Association of Great Britain

SCIcentre

Science Education (Association for)

Science Education (Centre for)

Scottish Qualifications Authority

SCRAN

Sex Education Forum

Shakespeare Schools Festival

Simon Wiesenthal Centre

Skills Funding Agency

Smallpeice Trust

Social Entrepreneurs (School for)

Social Sciences (Association for the Teaching of the)

Spanish Embassy Education Office

Spartacus Educational

Special Educational Needs (National Association for)

Specialist Schools and Academies Trust

Spelling Society (The English)

State Education (Campaign for)

Steel Can Recycling Information Bureau

Steiner Waldorf Education (European Council for)

Steiner Waldorf Schools Fellowship

Stephen Lawrence Charitable Trust

Storytelling (Society for)

Student Awards Agency for Scotland

Student Drama Festival (National)

Sundial Society (British)

Surname Profiler

Swimming

Tacade

Teacher Support Network

Teachers of Mathematics (Association of)

Teachers of Religious Education (National Association of)

Teaching Council for England (General)

Teaching Council for Wales (General)

Teaching English & Other Community Languages to Adults (National Association for)

Teaching of Drama (National Association for the)

Teaching of English (National Association for the)

Teenage Cancer Trust

Telescope (Bradford Robotic)

The Sikh Way

Think Global

Third Age Trust

Topmarks

Training & Development Agency for Schools

Transforming Conflict

Treloar Trust

UCAS

UJIA

UK Islamic Education Waqf

UK Youth

UNESCO

Uni4me

Unistats

University of the First Age

Values Education for Life (The Collegiate Centre for)

Victorian Society

Voices Foundation

Volunteer Reading Help

We Are What We Do

Winston Churchill Memorial Trust

Workers Educational Association

Working Men's College for Women & Men

WorkLife Support Limited

World Challenge Expeditions

Writers in Education (National Association of)

Year Out Group

Young Engineers

Young Enterprise

Young People's Learning Agency

Youth Choir of Great Britain (National)

Youth in Action

Emergency Aid

CAFOD
Christian Aid
Concern Worldwide
Disasters Emergency Committee
ECHO
Islamic Relief Worldwide
Médecins sans Frontières (UK)
Mercy Corps
MERLIN
Oxfam
Plan UK
Red Cross (International Committee of the)
Save the Children UK
SCIAF
Tearfund
UNICEF UK
World Health Organisation
World Jewish Relief
World Vision UK

Environment and Countryside

10:10
Access Space
ACT ON CO2
AirportWatch
Allotment and Leisure Gardeners Ltd. (National Society of)
Alternative Technology (Centre for)
Aluminium Packaging Recycling Organisation

An Taisce
Ancient Tree Forum
Arthur Rank Centre
Basel Action Network (BAN)
Bat Conservation Trust
Biological Diversity (Convention on)
Black Environment Network
Body Shop Foundation
Born Free Foundation
Botanic Garden of Wales (National)
BTCV
Butterfly Conservation
Byways & Bridleways Trust
Cadw
Carbon Neutral Company
Carbon Trust
CEH
Choose Climate
Churches Conservation Trust
Civic Voice
CLA
Climate Change (Committee on)
Climate Change (Intergovernmental Panel on)
Climate Parliament
Common Ground
Communities in Rural England (Action with)
Community Composting Network
Conservation of Energy (Association for the)
Conservation of Plants & Gardens (National Council for the)
Conservation Volunteers Northern Ireland
Corporate Watch
Countryside Alliance
Countryside Council for Wales
Countryside Foundation for Education
CPRE
CTC
Cycling Campaign (London)
Dark Skies (Campaign for)
Deer Society (British)
Defra

Environment and Countryside continued

Divers Marine Life Rescue (British)

Down to Earth

Earth First! Worldwide

EarthAction

Earthquake Locator (World Wide)

Earthwatch Institute

Eco-Schools

Ecological Society (British)

Ecology Building Society

Ecotourism Society (The International)

Eden Project

Energy Association (International)

Energy Foundation (National)

Energy Saving Trust

Environment (Young People's Trust for the)

Environment Agency

Environment and Development (International Institute for)

Environment Council

Environment Protection Agency (Scottish)

Environmental Investigation Agency

Environmental Law Foundation

Environmental Noise Maps

Environmental Protection UK

Environmental Transport Association

Farming & Countryside Education

Fauna & Flora International

FIELD

Field Studies Council

Findhorn Foundation

Floodline

Forestry Commission Great Britain

Forestry Society (Royal)

Forum for the Future

Friends of the Earth

Friends of the Earth International

Froglife

Furniture Re-use Network

Future Balance

Gaia Foundation

Galapagos Conservation Trust

Garden History Society

Gardens Scheme (National)

Geographic Society (National)

Geographical Association

Geological Society

Global Action Plan

Global Witness

Go4awalk

Green Alliance

Green Mark

Green Party

GreenMoves

Greenpeace

Groundwork UK

Hawk and Owl Trust

Heat is Online

Hurricane Center (National)

Indigenous Tribal Peoples of the Tropical Forests (International Alliance of)

INK

Inland Waterways Association

IPPL (UK)

IUCN

Joint Nature Conservation Committee

Keep Britain Tidy

Lake District (Friends of the)

Lake District National Park Authority

Lake District Weather Line

Landlife

Landmark Trust

Landscape Institute

Living Earth Foundation

Living Streets

London Green Belt Council

Marine Conservation Society

Marine Stewardship Council

Maritime & Coastguard Agency

Met Office

Meteorological Organization (World)

Meteorological Society (Royal)

Millennium Seed Bank

Mongabay.com
National Energy Action
National Forest Company
National Parks (Campaign for)
National Tidal and Sea Level Facility
National Trust
National Trust for Scotland
National Trust Working Holidays
Natural Death Centre
Natural England
Natural Environment Research Council
Natural Heritage (Scottish)
Noise Abatement Society
Northern Ireland Environment Link
Nuclear Society (European)
Nuclear Tourist (Virtual)
Open Spaces Society
Orangutan Foundation
Ordnance Survey
Our Dynamic Earth
People & Planet
People's Trust for Endangered Species
Permaculture Association (Britain)
Pesticide Action Network UK
Pipedown
Plantlife
Port of London Authority
Preservation Trusts (UK Association of)
Protection of Rural Wales (Campaign for the)
Rainforest Concern
Rainforest Foundation
Re-Cycle
Recycle for London
recycle more
RecycleNow
Recycling Appeal
Red List of Endangered Species
RenewableUK
Rising Tide
Royal Geographical Society
Royal Horticultural Society

Royal Parks
Rural Communities (Commission for)
Rural Research (Centre for)
Rural Scotland (Association for the Protection of)
Schumacher UK
Scientific Exploration Society
Scottish Environment LINK
Shark Alliance
Snow and Ice Data Center (National)
Soil Association
Stakeholder Forum
State of the Ocean (International Programme on the)
Steel Can Recycling Information Bureau
STEPS Centre
Stop Climate Chaos
Surfers Against Sewage
SustainAbility
Telework Association
Think Global
Thrive
Town & Country Planning Association
Town Planning Institute (Royal)
Transport (Department for)
Transport & Environment (European Federation for)
Tree Council
UK Climate Projections
United Nations Environment Programme
Wales Environment Link
WalkScotland
Waste Watch
Waterways (British)
We Are What We Do
Weather Centre (BBC Online)
Whale & Dolphin Conservation Society
Wild Flower Society
Wildfowl & Wetlands Trust (WWT)
Wildlife and Countryside Link
Wildlife Trusts (Royal Society of)
Wind Energy Association (European)

Environment and Countryside continued

Women's Environmental Network
Woodland Trust
World Land Trust
World Monuments Fund Britain
WRAP
WSPA International
WWF-UK

Equality issues

Black Training & Enterprise Group
Citizens Income Trust
Education (Global Campaign for)
Equality and Human Rights Commission
Equality Britain
Extreme Inequality
Fawcett Society
Friends, Families and Travellers
Left 'n' Write
ManKind Initiative
Migration Policy Group
Minority Rights Group International
Peace & Freedom (Women's International League for)
Race Equality Foundation
Racism in Europe (Youth Against)
Room to Read
Runnymede Trust
Short Persons Support
Stonewall
Tall Persons Club (GB & Ireland)
UKRC
UNLOCK

Europe

AIRE Centre
Council of Europe
Council of Europe Youth
Education of Adults (European Association for the)
Erasmus
ESU
EU in the United Kingdom
Eurodesk
Europa
Europe in the UK
European Central Bank
European Commission Agriculture and Rural Development
European Investment Bank
European Movement UK
European Parliament Information Office in Edinburgh
European Parliament Information Office in the United Kingdom
European Parliamentary Labour Party
European Trade Union Confederation
European Union (Court of Justice of the)
European Union Committee of the Regions
European Youth Card Association
European Youth Forum
European Youth Information and Counselling Agency
European Youth Music Week
France: culture and communications website
Franco British Council
Franco-Scottish Society of Scotland
Freedom Association
Friedrich Ebert Foundation
Golf Association (European)
Rail Europe
Special Needs Education (European Agency for Development in)
Wind Energy Association (European)

Family

4Children

Action for Children

Adoption and Fostering Information Line

Adoption records

Afasic

Ahimsa

ARC

BAAF Adoption and Fostering (British Association for)

Barnardo's

Birth Trauma Association

Bounty Healthcare Fund

Certificate ordering service

Chance UK

Child Contact Centres (National Association of)

CHILDREN 1ST

Compassionate Friends

Contact a Family

Cry-sis

Dad

Dad Talk

Dads House

Daycare Trust

Disability Pregnancy & Parenthood International

Disabled Parents Network

Donor Conception Network

Donor Family Network

Down's Heart Group

Elder Abuse (Action on)

Families Need Fathers

Family Action

Family and Parenting Institute

Family Holiday Association

Family Lives

Family Planning Association

Family Rights Group

Family Search

Family Therapy (Institute of)

Fatherhood Institute

Fathers4justice Ltd

Find a Parent or Child

FreeBMD

Friendship Works

Full Time Mothers

Gamete Donation Trust (National)

Gingerbread

Grandparents Plus

Grandparents' Association

Half the Sky Foundation

HELP

Home-Start

Karma Nirvana

Lone Twin Network

Lucy Faithfull Foundation

ManKind Initiative

MATCH

Mosac

Mothers' Union

Mydaughter.co.uk

National Childbirth Trust

NCB

One Plus One

PACT (Parents & Abducted Children Together)

PACT (Parents and Children Together)

Parenting UK

Planned Parenthood Federation (International)

Prisoners' Families (Action for)

Prisoners' Families & Friends Service

Register Office for Northern Ireland (General)

Register Office for Scotland (General)

Registering life events

Relate

Relationships Scotland

Resolution

Family continued

Respect

reunite

Sibs

Twins & Multiple Births Association

Working Families

Farming/Agriculture

Allotment and Leisure Gardeners Ltd. (National Society of)

City Farms & Community Gardens (Federation of)

CLA

Compassion in World Farming Trust

Countryside Alliance

Countryside Foundation for Education

Dairy Council (The)

Defra

Environment Agency

European Commission Agriculture and Rural Development

Farm Animal Welfare Committee

Farmers' Markets (Scottish Association of)

Farmers' Retail & Markets Association (National)

Farming & Countryside Education

Farms for City Children

Food & Agricultural Organisation (United Nations)

Garden Organic

Global Crop Diversity Trust

Natural England

Organic Research Centre

Rare Breeds Survival Trust

Rural Communities (Commission for)

Rural Research (Centre for)

Soil Association

Sustain

Viva!

Women's Food & Farming Union

WWOOF UK

Young Farmers' Clubs (National Federation of)

Food

Additives (Action on)

Agriculture and Horticulture Development Board

Anaphylaxis Campaign

chewonthis.org.uk

Chocolate Society

Dairy Council (The)

Defra

Dietetic Association (British)

Egg Information Service (British)

Farmers' Markets (Scottish Association of)

Farmers' Retail & Markets Association (National)

Food & Agricultural Organisation (United Nations)

Food & Drink Federation

Food & Drug Administration (US)

Food Commission (UK)

Food Standards Agency

GM Freeze

Herb Society

IFST

Mary's Meals

Nutrition Foundation (British)

Nutrition Society

Optimum Nutrition (Institute for)

Overeaters Anonymous of Great Britain

School Food Trust

Seafish

Slow Food UK

Sustain

Tea Council (UK) Ltd.

Vegan Society

Vegetarian & Vegan Foundation

Vegetarian Society

Viva!

Women's Food & Farming Union

World Food Programme (United Nations)

Government

10 Downing Street Website

Advisory Council on the Misuse of Drugs

Attorney General's Office

Audit Commission

Audit Office (National)

Business, Innovation & Skills (Department for)

Cabinet Office

Cafcass

Central Office of Information

Charity Commission for England & Wales

CIA

Climate Change (Committee on)

Climate Parliament

Communities and Local Government (Department for)

Competition Commission

COSLA

Criminal Cases Review Commission

Criminal Injuries Compensation Authority

Crown Estates

Defence (Ministry of)

DirectGov

Education (Department for)

Energy Association (International)

EU in the United Kingdom

Europa

European Parliament Information Office in the United Kingdom

Fair Access (Office for)

Fair Trading (Office of)

FBI

Financial Ombudsman Service

Foreign and Commonwealth Office

Foreign and Commonwealth Office Travel Advice

Government Actuary's Department

Greater London Authority

Health (Department of)

Health, Social Services and Public Safety (N. Ireland Department of)

Hear From Your MP

HM Revenue and Customs

HM Treasury

HMRC Education Zone

Home Office

House of Lords

Housing Ombudsman Service

Human Rights Commission (N. Ireland)

Identity & Passport Service

Intellectual Property Office

International Development (Department for)

Joint Nature Conservation Committee

Justice

Land Registry

legislation.gov.uk

Local Economy Policy Unit

Local Government Association

Local Government Improvement and Development

Local Government Information Unit

Local Government Ombudsman (England)

Low Pay Commission

Maritime & Coastguard Agency

National Archives

National Archives of Scotland (NAS)

Northern Ireland Executive

Northern Ireland Office

Northern Ireland Ombudsman

Office for National Statistics

Ofsted

Parliament

Government continued

Parliamentary and Health Service Ombudsman

Parliamentary Education Unit

Parliaments (Websites of National)

Pensions Ombudsman

Postcomm (Postal Services Commission)

Privacy International

Public Services Ombudsman (Scottish)

Public Whip

Register Office for Northern Ireland (General)

Register Office for Scotland (General)

Schools Adjudicator (Office of the)

Scotland Office

Scottish Government

Scottish Parliament

Serious Fraud Office

TheyWorkForYou.com

Trading Standards Institute

Transparency International

Transport (Department for)

UK Border Agency

US Department of State

Wales Office

Welsh Government

Work & Pensions (Department for)

WriteToThem.com

Health and Medicine

Abortion Rights

ACT

Active Birth Centre

Acupuncture Council (British)

Acupuncture Society (British Medical)

Additives (Action on)

AIDS Trust (National)

Albinism Fellowship

Alcohol Studies (Institute of)

Allergy UK

Alzheimer Scotland

Alzheimer's Research Trust

Alzheimer's Society

Anaphylaxis Campaign

Anthony Nolan

Anxiety UK

ARC

Art Therapists (British Association of)

Arthritic Association

Arthritis Care

Arthritis Research UK

Arts in Therapy & Education (Institute for)

ASH

Aspire

Assisted Dying (Healthcare Professions for)

Asthma UK

Ataxia UK

Attend

Autistic Society (National)

AVERT

Baby Lifeline

Baby Milk Action

Bach Centre

BackCare

BASIC

BBC Health

BDA Northern Ireland

BDA Scotland

BDA Wales

BEAT

Behavioural & Cognitive Psychotherapies (British Association for)

Better Seating (Campaign for)

Bibic

Bioethics (Nuffield Council on)

BirthChoice UK

Bladder and Bowel Foundation (B&BF)

Blood Pressure Association

Bob Champion Cancer Trust

Body Positive

Bounty Healthcare Fund

Bowel Cancer UK

Brain & Spine Foundation

Breakthrough Breast Cancer

Breast Cancer Care

British Heart Foundation

British Medical Association

Brittle Bone Society

Butterfly Project

Cancer Research UK

Cancer Society (American)

CancerHelp UK

Cardiac Risk in the Young

Care Quality Commission

Carers

Casualties Union

Chain of Hope

Chernobyl Children's Life Line

chewonthis.org.uk

Child Brain Injury Trust

Child Growth Foundation

Childhood Eye Cancer Trust

Children with Leukaemia

Children's Heart Federation

Chiropodists & Podiatrists (Institute of)

Chiropodists and Podiatrists (The Society of)

Chiropractic (Anglo-European College of)

Chiropractic Association (British)

Chiropractic Patients' Association

Christian Lewis Trust

Cinnamon Trust

CLAPA

Cleanair

CLICSargent

Climb

Colitis & Crohn's UK

Complementary and Natural Medicine (Institute for)

Concord Media

Connect

Core

COTS

Crossroads Care

Cystic Fibrosis Trust

Daisy Network

DebRA

Dental Association (British)

Dental Council (General)

Depression (Action on)

Depression Alliance

Dermatologists (British Association of)

Diabetes UK

Diabetes.co.uk

Dietetic Association (British)

Different Strokes

Disfigurement Guidance Centre

Don't lose the music

Donor Family Network

Down's Syndrome Association

Down's Syndrome Medical Interest Group

Down's Syndrome Scotland

Down's Heart Group

Drinking Water Inspectorate

Drinking Water Quality Regulator For Scotland

Dyspraxia Foundation

Eating Problems Service

Eczema Society (National)

Ellen MacArthur Cancer Trust

Embarrassing Problems

Endometriosis UK

Epilepsy (National Centre for Young People with)

Epilepsy Action

Epilepsy Scotland

Epilepsy Society

ERIC – Education and Resources for Improving Childhood Continence

ETCO

Eyecare Trust

Fertility Friends

Fertility UK

FirstSigns

Health continued

Fit for Travel

Food & Drug Administration (US)

Forward

Fragile X Society

Friends at the end

GASP

General Medical Council

Genetic Alliance UK

GM Freeze

Gulf Veterans & Families Association (National)

Haemochromatosis Society

Haemophilia Society

Hairline International

HEADWAY

Health (Department of)

Health & Safety Executive

Health Information Resources

Health Professions Council

Health Protection Agency

Health, Social Services and Public Safety (N. Ireland Department of)

Healthtalkonline

Healthy Schools

Heart Research UK

Help – For a life without tobacco

Help for Heroes

Help the Hospices

Hereditary Breast Cancer Helpline (National)

Herpes Viruses Association

High Blood Pressure Foundation

HIV InSite

HIV/Aids Alliance (International)

Holistic Therapists (Federation of)

Hospital Broadcasting Association

Human Fertilisation & Embryology Authority

Human Genetics Commission

Humane Research Trust

Huntington's Disease Association

Hyperactive Children's Support Group

Hypermobility Syndrome Association

IBS Network

Infant Deaths (Foundation for the Study of)

Infertility Network UK

Interact Worldwide

Jane Tomlinson Appeal

Jeans for Genes

Jo's Cervical Cancer Trust

Kidney Patient Association (British)

Kidney Research UK

King's Fund

Lavender Trust

Learning Disabilities (The Foundation for People with)

LEPRA

Let's Face It

Leukaemia and Lymphoma Research

Liver Trust (British)

Lung Foundation (British)

Lupus UK

Macmillan Cancer Support

Malaria No More UK

Marfan Association UK

Marie Curie Cancer Care

MASTA

Maternal & Childhealth Advocacy International

MDF The Bipolar Organisation

ME (Action for)

ME Association

Médecins sans Frontières (UK)

Medical Accidents (Action Against)

Medical Advisory Service

Medical Aid for Palestinians

Medical Conditions at School

Medical Foundation for the Care of Victims of Torture

Medical Helpline (General)

Medical Research Charities (Association of)

Medical Research Council

Medical Trust (Britain-Nepal)

MedicAlert Foundation

Medicines & Healthcare products Regulatory Agency

Men's Health Helpline

Meningitis Research Foundation

Meningitis Trust

Mental Health (Scottish Association for)

MERLIN

Migraine Action Association

Migraine Trust

Miscarriage Association

Motor Neurone Disease Association

Mouth Cancer Foundation

Multiple Sclerosis Society

Multiple Sclerosis Therapy Centres (National)

Multiple Sclerosis Trust

Muscular Dystrophy Campaign

Musculoskeletal Medicine (British Institute of)

Music Therapy (British Association for)

Narcolepsy UK

National Institute for Health and Clinical Excellence

NBCS

Netdoctor

Neuro Foundation UK

Newlife Foundation for Disabled Children

NHS Blood and Transplant

NHS Careers

NHS Confederation

NHS Direct

NHS Health Scotland

NHS Support Federation

NICON - Northern Ireland Confederation

Nursing & Midwifery Council

Nutrition Foundation (British)

Obesity (International Association for the Study of) & Obesity TaskForce (International)

Obesity Forum (National)

Occupational Hygiene Society (British)

Orchid Cancer Appeal

Organ Donation

Organ Donation and Transplantation (International Registry of)

Osteopathic Council (General)

Osteoporosis Society (National)

Overeaters Anonymous of Great Britain

PACE

Pain Relief Foundation

Pain Society (British)

Pain Support

Palliative Care (National Council for)

Papworth Trust

PAPYRUS

Parkinson's Disease Society

Parliamentary and Health Service Ombudsman

Patient Safety Agency (National)

Patient UK

Patients Association

Paul's Cancer Support Centre

Performing Arts Medicine (British Association for)

Personal Injury Lawyers (Association of)

Pets as Therapy

Physiotherapy (Chartered Society of)

Pilates Foundation

Pituitary Foundation

Pod Charitable Trust

Polio Fellowship (British)

Population Services International

Positively UK

Post Natal Illness

Premenstrual Syndrome (National Association for)

Prostate Cancer Charity

Psoriasis Association

Psychiatrists (Royal College of)

Psychotherapists (British Association of)

Psychotherapy (UK Council for)

Public Health Agency

PWSA (UK)

QUIT

Raynaud's & Scleroderma Association

React

Health continued

Red Cross

Relatives & Residents Association

Restricted Growth Association

Roy Castle Lung Cancer Foundation

Royal Society of Medicine

Safer Medicines Campaign

SANDS

Schools Health Education Unit

Scoliosis Association (UK)

Sexual Advice Association

Shiatsu Society (UK)

Shine

Shingles Support Society

Sick Children (Action for)

Sickle Cell Society

Sightsavers

Skills for Care

Skin Care Campaign

Skin Foundation (British)

Sleep Council

Smokefree (NHS)

Social Workers (British Association of)

Socialist Health Association

Sorted In 10

Sparks

Speakability

Speech and Language Therapists (Royal College of)

Spinal Injuries Association

St John Ambulance

Stress Management Association UK (International)

Stroke Association

SunSmart Campaign

Surgery Door

Tampon Alert (Alice Kilvert)

TB Alert

Teenage Cancer Trust

Tenovus

Terrence Higgins Trust

Thalidomide Society (UK)

Tinnitus Association (British)

Tommy's, the baby charity

Tranquillisers, Antidepressants and Painkillers (Council for Information on)

Tropical Diseases (Hospital for)

Tuberous Sclerosis Association UK

Vision Aid Overseas

Vitiligo Society

Voice for Choice

Wellbeing of Women

Wessex Cancer Trust

White Ribbon Alliance

Williams Syndrome Foundation (UK)

Willow Foundation

World AIDS Day

World Health Organisation

Yoga (Iyengar Institute)

Young People with ME (Association of)

Your Life

Youth Cancer Trust

Youthhealthtalk

Heritage

1901 Census for England & Wales

An Taisce

Ancient Buildings (Society for the Protection of)

Ancient Monument Society

Ancient Tree Forum

Antiquaries of London (Society of)

Archaeology (Council for British)

Archaeology Abroad

Archaeology Scotland

Archéire

Architectural Heritage Fund

Arms and Armour Society

Army Museum (National)

ArtWatch UK

Black History Month

Brontë Parsonage Museum & Brontë Society

Byways & Bridleways Trust

Cadw

Cambridge Past, Present & Future

Churches Conservation Trust

Civic Voice

Community Pubs Foundation

Crown Estates

Culture, Media & Sport (Department for)

Cutty Sark Trust

English Heritage

Family Names Profiling (GB)

Family Search

FreeBMD

Friends of Friendless Churches

Garden History Society

Gardens Scheme (National)

Genealogists (Society of)

Georgian Group

Heraldry Society

Heraldry Society of Scotland

Heritage Lottery Fund

Heritage Railway Association

Historic Houses Association

Historic Scotland

Historical Association

Historical Maritime Society

History World

ICON

Landmark Trust

Local History (British Association for)

Museums (International Council of)

National Archives

National Archives of Scotland (NAS)

National Churches Trust

National Trust

National Trust for Scotland

Natural Heritage (Scottish)

Open-City

Oral History Society

Preservation Trusts (UK Association of)

Public Monuments & Sculpture Association

Quilters' Guild of the British Isles

Royal Airforce Museum Cosford

Royal Airforce Museum London

Royal Naval Museum

Royal Parks

SCRAN

Sealed Knot Ltd

Shakespeare Birthplace Trust

St Fagans: National History Museum

Sundial Society (British)

Theatres Trust

Twentieth Century Society

Vatican

Venice in Peril Fund

Victorian Society

Waterfront Museum (National)

Weights & Measures Association (British)

Women's Archive of Wales

Woodland Trust

Working Class Movement Library

World Monuments Fund Britain

Homeless and Housing

Albert Kennedy Trust

Alone in London

Big Issue

Borderline

Broadway

Building & Social Housing Foundation

Centrepoint

ChildHope

CIH

Community Self Build Agency

Crisis (UK)

Depaul International

Depaul Nightstop UK

Homeless and Housing continued

Eaves
Ecology Building Society
Elderly Accommodation Counsel
Emmaus
Empty Homes Agency
GreenMoves
Habitat for Humanity Great Britain
Homeless International
Homeless Link
Housing (Confederation of Co-operative)
Housing Advice
Housing Federation (National)
Housing Justice
Housing Ombudsman Service
Housing Policy (Centre for)
HousingCare.org
Joseph Rowntree Foundation
Llamau
Nethouseprices
Poppy Project
Refuge
Salvation Army
Scarlet Centre
Shelter
Shine a Light
Simon Community
Squatters (Advisory Service for)
Tenant Participation Advisory Service for England
Town Planning Institute (Royal)

Human Rights

African Initiatives
Africans Unite Against Child Abuse
AIRE Centre
AMAR
Amnesty International UK
Anti-Slavery International
ARTICLE 19
ATD Fourth World
BIHR
Body Shop Foundation
Burma Campaign UK
CAFCAS
Canon Collins Trust
Children are unbeatable! Alliance
Children's Rights Alliance for England
Children's Society
Colombia Solidarity Campaign
Conscience
CRIN
Disability Action
Elders (The)
EveryChild
Fair Trials International
Foreign Policy Centre
Forest Peoples Programme
Free the Children
Free Tibet
Freedom of Information (Campaign for)
Friends of Peoples Close to Nature
Global Witness
Gypsy Association
Howard League for Penal Reform
Human Fertilisation & Embryology Authority
Human Rights (European Court of)
Human Rights Commission (N. Ireland)
Human Rights Education Association
Human Rights Policy (International Council on)

Human Rights Watch

Inclusive Education (Centre for Studies on)

Indigenous Tribal Peoples of the Tropical Forests (International Alliance of)

Interact Worldwide

Interights

Islamic Human Rights Commission

JUSTICE

Kurdish Human Rights Project

Laogai Research Foundation

Liberty

Lilith Research and Development

Medical Aid for Palestinians

Medical Foundation for the Care of Victims of Torture

Minority Rights Group International

Music Freedom Day

No Sweat

Ombudsman Association (British & Irish)

Overseas Development Institute

Peace & Freedom (Women's International League for)

Peace Brigades International

Peace Pledge Union

Penal Reform International

People & Planet

Poppy Project

Prisoners Abroad

Prisoners of Conscience Appeal Fund

Privacy International

Red Cross (British)

REDRESS

Refugee Council

Release

Reporters Without Borders

Simon Wiesenthal Centre

Sojourner Project

Solidar

Statewatch

Stonewall

Survival International

TAPOL

Tibet Society UK

Tibetan Nuns Project

Torture (Association for the Prevention of)

Torture (The World Organisation Against)

Transforming Conflict

UN High Commissioner for Human Rights (Office of the)

Unborn Children (Society for the Protection of)

UNHCR

United Nations Development Programme

Unlock Democracy

Volunteer Action for Peace

War Resisters League

Womankind Worldwide

Women living under Muslim laws

World Development Movement

World Land Trust

Industry and employment

ACAS

Access to Industry

Architects (Royal Institute of British)

British Standards Institute

Business, Innovation & Skills (Department for)

Centre for Economic & Social Inclusion

Certification Officer

CF Appointments

Children's Workforce Development Council

Co-operatives UK

Community and Youth Workers in Unite

Directors (Institute of)

Directory of Social Change

Education & Industry (Centre for)

Education and Training (Centre for the Study of)

Effective Dispute Resolution (Centre for)

Industry and Employment continued

Employment & Learning (Department for) Northern Ireland

Employment Research (Warwick Institute for)

Employment Rights (Institute of)

Employment Solicitors

Employment Studies (Institute for)

Endeavour Training Limited

Engineering Council

Enterprise Education Trust

European Trade Union Confederation

Fawcett Society

Fitness Industry Association

Fredericks Foundation

GLE

Homeworking

Independent Safeguarding Authority

Industrial Injuries Advisory Council

International Labour Organization

Jobcentre Plus

Labour Behind the Label

Labour Research Department

learndirect

Liberal Democrat Trade Unionists (Association of)

Lifetracks

Mechanics' Institute

Motor Manufacturers and Traders Ltd. (Society of)

NHS Careers

No Sweat

Opportunity Now

Personnel & Development (Chartered Institute of)

Practical Action

Public Concern at Work

Public Service Excellence (Association for)

Rathbone

Reach

Recycle-IT!

Remploy

Seafish

Simon Jones Memorial Campaign

Slivers of Time

Solidar

Tea Council (UK) Ltd.

Trade Union Confederation (International)

Trade Union Rights (International Centre for)

Trades Union Congress

Travel and Tourism (Institute of)

Unite

Women and Manual Trades

Women's Engineering Society

Woodworking Federation (British)

Work & Pensions (Department for)

Work Foundation

Workaholics Anonymous

Workers Educational Association

Working Families

WorkLife Support Limited

Young Engineers

Young Enterprise

Language

Alliance Française

Apples & Snakes

Arab-British Understanding (Council for)

Bilingualism & Literacies Education Network

British Council

CILT

Communication Trust

Connect

Cymdeithas yr Iaith Gymraeg

Daiwa Anglo-Japanese Foundation

English Association

English Speaking Union

Esperanto Association of Britain

Franco British Council

Franco-Scottish Society of Scotland

Gaelic Books Council

Goethe-Institut

Hispanic & Luso Brazilian Council

IATEFL

Italian Cultural Institute in London

Japan Foundation, London

Language Awareness (Association for)

Language Learning (Association for)

Languages (Scotland's National Centre for)

Linguists (Chartered Institute of)

Literacy in Primary Education (Centre for)

Makaton Charity

Plain English Campaign

Scots Language Centre

Spanish Embassy Education Office

Spanish Institute

Speakability

Speakers Clubs (Association of)

Speech and Language Therapists (Royal College of)

Spelling Society (The English)

Teaching English & Other Community Languages to Adults (National Association for)

Teaching of English (National Association for the)

Welsh Language Board (Bwrdd yr Iaith Gymraeg)

Law

Advicenow

AdviceUK

Advocacy After Fatal Domestic Abuse

Advocacy Resource Exchange

AIRE Centre

Arbitrators (Chartered Institute of)

Ask The Police

Attorney General's Office

Bar Council

Bar Pro Bono Unit

Black Police Association (National)

Cafcass

Catch22

Children are unbeatable! Alliance

Children's Legal Centre

Citizenship and the Law (National Centre for)

Courts and Tribunal Service (HM)

Crime and Justice Studies (Centre for)

Crimestoppers

Criminal Cases Review Commission

Criminal Injuries Compensation Authority

Crisis Counselling for Alleged Shoplifters

Crown Prosecution Service

Dignity in Dying

Disability Law Service

Domestic Violence (Campaign Against)

Drugs and Crime (UN Office on)

DVLA

Employment Solicitors

Environmental Law Foundation

European Union (Court of Justice of the)

Fair Trials International

Fathers4justice Ltd

FIELD

Friends at the end

Gun Control Network

Howard League for Penal Reform

Human Rights (European Court of)

Immigration & Asylum Tribunals Service

Immigration Law Practitioners' Association

Immigration Services Commissioner (Office of the)

Independent Police Complaints Commission

Interights

International Criminal Court

Interpol

Just for Kids Law

Justice

JUSTICE

Law Centres Federation

Law continued

Law Commission
Law Society of England & Wales
Legal Action Group
Legal Services Commission
legislation.gov.uk
Liberty
Magistrates' Association
Metropolitan Police
Money Claim Online
Most Wanted (UK)
Old Bailey, London (Proceedings of) 1674
to 1834
Ombudsman Association (British & Irish)
Out of trouble
PACT (Prison Advice & Care Trust)
Peace Alliance
Penal Reform International
Personal Injury Lawyers (Association of)
Police Federation (Scottish)
Police Federation of England & Wales
Prison Reform Trust
Prison Studies (International Centre for)
Prisons and Probation Ombudsman for
England and Wales
Release
Resolution
Rights of Women
Serious Fraud Office
Simple Free Law Advisor
Skills for Justice
SOCA
Solicitors for the Elderly
SOVA
Statewatch
Trackoff
UNLOCK
Voice UK
Women Solicitors (Association of)

Libraries/Books/Publishing

American Library Association
Antiquaries of London (Society of)
ARKive
Art Library (National)
Authors' Licensing and Collecting Society
Bartleby.com
Big Read (The)
Bodleian Library
Book Aid International
Book Power
Book Trust (Scottish)
BookCrossing
Books Council (Welsh)
Booktrust
British Library
British Library Sound Archive
Buddhist Society
Children's Book Groups (Federation of)
CILIP
ClearVision Project
Demos
Edinburgh International Book Festival
Editors and Proofreaders (Society for)
English PEN
Feminist Archive
Folger Shakespeare Library
Frankfurt Book Fair
Gaelic Books Council
Hay Festival
Health Information Resources
Heartstone
Indexers (Society of)
Information Management (Association for)
INK
ipl2

Libraries for Life for Londoners

Library Campaign

Library of France (National)

Listening Books

Literacy Association (UK)

London Library

Marx Memorial Library

Music Publishers Association

National Libraries (Friends of the)

National Library of Scotland

National Library of Wales

New Internationalist

Newspaper Library (British Library)

Nobel Prize Internet Archive

People's Network

Poetry Library

Project Gutenberg

Psychical Research (Society for)

Questionpoint

Read

RNIB National Library Service

School Librarianship (International
    Association of)

School Library Association

Searchlight Magazine Ltd

Seven Stories

Siobhan Dowd Trust

Storytelling (Society for)

Women in Publishing

Women's Archive of Wales

Women's Library

Working Class Movement Library

Writers' Guild of Great Britain

Media

Adbusters

Advertising Association

Advertising Standards Authority

Al Jazeera

APRS

BBC

BBC Backstage Tours

BBC News

BBC Online

BBC Schools

BBC Studio Audiences

BBC World Service

Blogger

British Film Institute

Broadcasting Trust (International)

Channel 4

Commonwealth Broadcasting Association

Community Media Association

Concord Media

Creative Scotland

Editors and Proofreaders (Society for)

Educational Recording Agency

English and Media Centre

Extreme Inequality

Film & Television Archive (Northern Region)

Film and Television School (National)

Film Classification (British Board of)

Film Education

Film London

First Light

Five

Headliners

History of Cinema & Popular Culture (The
    Bill Douglas Centre for the)

Hospital Broadcasting Association

Media continued

Index on Censorship

Indexers (Society of)

INK

ITN

Learning Zone

Media Center (Independent)

Media for Development

Media Trust

MediaWise Trust

Movie Review Query Engine

New Internationalist

Newspaper Library (British Library)

Nominet UK

OFCOM

Paperboy

Phonepay Plus

photoLondon

Press and Broadcasting Freedom
(Campaign for)

Press Association

Press Association Ireland

Press Association Scotland

Press Complaints Commission

Radio Society of Great Britain

Raw Material

Reporters Without Borders

S4C

Sky

Talking Newspapers and Magazines
(National)

Undercurrents

Video Standards Council

Voice of the Listener and Viewer

Wireless for the Blind Fund (British)

Mental Health

Action of Postpartum Psychosis Network

Albany Trust

Anxiety Care

Anxiety UK

Behavioural & Cognitive Psychotherapies
(British Association for)

Brainwave

Butterfly Project

CALM

Care Quality Commission

Child and Adolescent Mental Health
(Association for)

Combat Stress

Depression (Action on)

Depression Alliance

Down Syndrome Education International

Educational Psychologists (Association of)

Journeys

Learning Disabilities (The Foundation for
People with)

MDF The Bipolar Organisation

Mencap

Mencap Cymru

Mencap Northern Ireland

Mental Health (Scottish Association for)

Mental Health Foundation

Mental Welfare Commission for Scotland

MIND

No Panic

OCD Action

PAPYRUS

Psychological Society (British)

Psychotherapists (British Association of)

Psychotherapy (UK Council for)

Rethink

SANE

Scarlet Centre

Seasonal Affective Disorder Association

SEBDA
Triumph over Phobia (TOP UK)
Turning Point
Women's Therapy Centre
Workaholics Anonymous
YoungMinds

Money

Bank of England (Damaged and Mutilated Banknotes)
Career Development Loans
European Central Bank
Heritage Lottery Fund
HM Revenue and Customs
International Monetary Fund
Jubilee Debt Campaign
Low Pay Commission
Money Advice Service
Moneysavingexpert.com
My Supermarket
MyBnk
Nethouseprices
Personal Finance Education Group
Slivers of Time
Student Loans Company Ltd
Turn2us

Museums/Galleries

Antiquaries of London (Society of)
Apsley House Wellington Museum
Army Museum (National)
Ashmolean
BALTIC
Bank of England Museum

Barbican
Beamish
Big Pit
British Monarchy (The official website of)
British Museum
Brontë Parsonage Museum & Brontë Society
Bugatti Trust
Burrell Collection
Childhood (Museum of) V&A
Churchill War Rooms
Courtauld Institute of Art
Culture24
Cutty Sark Trust
Design Museum
Dulwich Picture Gallery
Eureka!
Exploratorium
Fitzwilliam Museum
Football Museum (National)
Football Museum (Scottish)
Gallery of Modern Art
Glasgow Museums Resource Centre
Glass Centre (National)
GreatBuildings
Hayward Gallery
Henry Moore Foundation
HMS Belfast
Imperial War Museum
Institute of Contemporary Arts
Ironbridge Gorge Museum
Jewish Museum
Jodrell Bank Observatory
Kelvingrove Art Gallery and Museum
Kids in Museums
Lady Lever Art Gallery
Life Science Centre
Liverpool (Museum of)
Liverpool (National Museums)
London (Museum of)
London Transport Museum
Lowry

Museums/Galleries continued

Magna: science adventure centre
Manchester Museum
Maritime Museum (Merseyside)
Maritime Museum (National)
Mining Museum (National)
MOSI
Museum Net
Museum of London
Museum of Scotland (National)
Museums (International Council of)
National Gallery
National Gallery (Scottish)
National Gallery of Modern Art (Scottish)
National Media Museum
National Museum Cardiff
National Portrait Gallery
National Portrait Gallery (Scottish)
Natural History Museum
Open Museum
People's History Museum
People's Palace and Winter Gardens
Provands Lordship
Queen's House
Railway Museum (National)
Riverside Museum: Scotland's Museum of Transport and Travel
Roman Legion Museum (National)
Royal Academy of Arts
Royal Airforce Museum Cosford
Royal Airforce Museum London
Royal Armouries

Royal Institution of Great Britain
Royal Naval Museum
Royal Observatory, Greenwich
Royal Scottish Academy
Science Centre (Glasgow)
Science Museum
Scotland Street School Museum

Scottish National Gallery
Scottish National Gallery of Modern Art
Seven Stories
Slate Museum (National)
Slavery Museum (International)
Space Centre (National)
St Fagans: National History Museum
St Mungo Museum of Religious Life and Art
Sudley House
Tate Britain
Tate Liverpool
Tate Modern
Tate St Ives
The Deep
Vatican Museums & Sistine Chapel
Walker Art Gallery
Waterfront Museum (National)
Waterways Museum (National)
Wool Museum (National)
World Museum
World Rugby Museum

Music
refer also to the section on Dance, Drama, Music & Performing Arts Schools

Associated Board of the Royal Schools of Music
Barbershop Singers (British Association of)
BASCA
BKA
Cello Society (Internet)
Children's Orchestra (National)
Choir Schools' Association
CoMA
Don't lose the music
EMI Music Sound Foundation
English National Opera
European Youth Music Week

Festivals (British & International Federation of)
Guitar Foundation (International)
Live Music Now
London Charity Orchestra
London Symphony Orchestra
Making Music
Midi Music Company
Music and the Deaf
Music Council (National)
Music Educators (National Association of)
Music for Youth
Music Freedom Day
Music Publishers Association
Music Therapy (British Association for)
Musicians (Incorporated Society of)
Musicians Union
Natural Voice Practitioners' Network
NODA
Orchestras (Association of British)
Passion for Jazz
Raw Material
Royal Academy of Music
Royal Opera
Schools Music Association of Great Britain
Scottish Opera
Sound and Music
Sound Sense
SoundJunction
Southbank Centre
Suzuki Institute (British)
Voices Foundation
Welsh National Opera
Young Concert Artists Trust
Youth Choir of Great Britain (National)
Youth Music
Youth Music Theatre (National)
Youth Opera (British)
Youth Orchestra (National of GB)

Older People

Age Exchange
Age UK
Anchor Trust
Contact the Elderly
Counsel and Care
Elder Abuse (Action on)
Elderly Accommodation Counsel
Grandparents Plus
HousingCare.org
Pensioners Convention (National)
Policy on Ageing (Centre for)
Relatives & Residents Association
Ricability
Solicitors for the Elderly
Third Age Trust
WRVS

Politics

10 Downing Street Website
ACTSA
Adam Smith Institute
Baobab Centre for Young Survivors in Exile
Bevan Foundation
Cabinet Office
CARF
Christian Socialist Movement
Citizenship (Institute for)
Civitas
Co-operative Party
Colombia Solidarity Campaign
Conscience
Conservative Party
Cuba Solidarity Campaign
Democracy and Electoral Assistance (International Institute for)

Politics continued

Demos

Elders (The)

Electoral Reform Services

Electoral Reform Society

European Parliamentary Labour Party

Fabian Society

Free Tibet

Freedom Association

Green Party

Hansard Society

Hear From Your MP

House of Lords

IPPR

Labour Party

Labour Research Department

Labour Women's Network

Law Society of Scotland

Liberal Democrat Trade Unionists (Association of)

Liberal Democrats

Make My Vote Count

Martin Luther King Jr. Center

Marx Memorial Library

Media Center (Independent)

Monetary Justice (Christian Council for)

Nicaragua Solidarity Campaign

No candidate deserves my vote

Operation Black Vote

Parliament

Plaid Cymru - The Party of Wales

Policy Studies (Centre for)

Policy Studies Institute

Political Studies Association

Public Whip

Schumacher UK

Searchlight Magazine Ltd

Smith Institute

SNP

Social Democratic & Labour Party

Social Market Foundation

Socialist Health Association

Socialist Labour Party

TheyWorkForYou.com

Tibet Society UK

Unborn Children (Society for the Protection of)

Unite Against Fascism

Unlock Democracy

Voice for Choice

Welsh Government

White House

WriteToThem.com

Poverty

ActionAid

Afghanaid

ATD Fourth World

Birmingham Settlement

Brazil's Children Trust (Action for)

CARE International UK

Child Poverty Action Group

Chronic Poverty Research Centre

Church Action on Poverty

Comic Relief

Concern Worldwide

e-Learning Foundation

Ethiopiaid

Family Holiday Association

International Development (Department for)

Islamic Relief Worldwide

Kiva

Maternal & Childhealth Advocacy International

National Debtline

ONE International

Practical Action

Shine a Light

Sustain

Taskforce for the Rural Poor (International)

TaxAid

Traidcraft

VSO
War on Want
Water Aid
World Bank
World Development Movement

Prisoners

Amnesty International UK
Crime and Justice Studies (Centre for)
English PEN
Hibiscus
Howard League for Penal Reform
Human Writes
INQUEST
Inside Out Trust
Nacro
New Bridge Foundation
Out of trouble
PACT (Prison Advice & Care Trust)
Penal Reform International
Prison Reform Trust
Prison Service NI
Prison Studies (International Centre for)
Prison Visitors (National Association of
Official)
Prisoners Abroad
Prisoners of Conscience Appeal Fund
Prisoners' Advice Service
Prisoners' Families (Action for)
Prisoners' Families & Friends Service
Prisons and Probation Ombudsman for
England and Wales
RAPt
SACRO
Sentencing, prison and probation
UNLOCK
Women in Prison

Race

100 Black Men of London
Anne Frank Trust UK
Artists Against Racism
Asian People's Disability Alliance
Black Environment Network
Black History Month
Black Police Association (National)
CARF
CEMVO
Equality and Human Rights Commission
Equality Britain
Ethnic Relations (Centre for Research in)
Football Unites, Racism Divides
Heartstone
Intermix
Kick It Out
Local Government Improvement and
Development
Martin Luther King Jr. Center
NABSS
Operation Black Vote
Race Equality Foundation
Race Relations (Institute of)
Racism in Europe (Youth Against)
Runnymede Trust
Show Racism the Red Card
Stephen Lawrence Charitable Trust
UK New Citizen

Refugees and Immigration

AMAR
Asylum Aid
Baobab Centre for Young Survivors in Exile
Immigrants (Joint Council for the Welfare of)
Immigration & Asylum Tribunals Service
Immigration Advice Service
Immigration Aid Unit (Greater Manchester)
Immigration Law Practitioners' Association
Immigration Services Commissioner (Office of the)
Medical Aid for Palestinians
Refugee Council
Refugees (Student Action for)
Refugees (US Committee for)
Refugees and Exiles (European Council on)
UK Border Agency
UNHCR

Relationships

Broken Rainbow UK
Dads House
Divorced & Separated (National Council for the)
Domestic Violence (Campaign Against)
Family Therapy (Institute of)
Fatherhood Institute
Grandparents' Association
Intermix
Karma Nirvana
Leap Confronting Conflict
ManKind Initiative
Men's Advice Line

Relate
Relationships Scotland
Respect
Shared Parenting Information Group
Solo Clubs (National Federation of)

Religion and Beliefs

Arthur Rank Centre
Astrological and Psychic Society (British)
Bible Society
British Jews (Board of Deputies of)
Buddhist Centre (North London)
Buddhist Information Network
Buddhist Society
Catholic Education Service
Christian Education/International Bible Reading Association (IBRA)
Christian Socialist Movement
Christian Teachers (Association of)
Christians and Jews (Council of)
Church Army
Church Mission Society
Church of England
Church of England Education Division
Churches Together in Britain and Ireland
Clear Vision Trust
Cult Information Centre
Day One Christian Ministries
Evangelical Alliance
Findhorn Foundation
Hindu Universe – Hindu Resource Center
Humanist Association (British)
Inform
Integrated Education (N. Ireland Council for)
Inter Faith Network for the UK
Islamic Human Rights Commission
Jewish Women (League of)
Methodist Children & Youth
Methodist Church

Muslim Schools UK (Association of)
Muslim Welfare House
National Churches Trust
Nil by Mouth
Pax Christi
Quakers in Britain
RE Today Services
Reform Judaism (Movement for)
REonline
Salvation Army
Secular Society (National)
Sikh Organisations (Network of)
Teachers of Religious Education (National Association of)
Tearfund
The Sikh Way
Tibetan Nuns Project
Time for God
UK Islamic Education Waqf
United Reformed Church
Urban Saints
Vatican
Women living under Muslim laws
Young Christian Workers
Youth for Christ

Research

1901 Census for England & Wales
ACT
Alcohol Education and Research Council
Atmospheric Research (National Center for)
Australian Bureau of Statistics
AVERT
Biotechnology & Biological Sciences Research Council
Bob Champion Cancer Trust
Brain & Spine Foundation
British Heart Foundation
Cancer Research UK

CEH
Childhood Eye Cancer Trust
Children with Leukaemia
Climb
Economic & Social Research (National Institute of)
Education Index (British)
Education Statistics (National Center for)
Ergonomics & Human Factors (Institute of)
Ethnic Relations (Centre for Research in)
Feminist Archive
Fiscal Studies (Institute for)
Folger Shakespeare Library
Football Industry Group
Forward
FRAME
Friedrich Ebert Foundation
Garden Organic
Government Actuary's Department
History of Cinema & Popular Culture (The Bill Douglas Centre for the)
Human Genetics Commission
Humane Research Trust
Indian Census
International Affairs (Royal Institute of)
IPPR
JANET
Jeans for Genes
Joseph Rowntree Foundation
King's Fund
Leukaemia and Lymphoma Research
Linnean Society of London
Liver Trust (British)
Lord Dowding Fund
Lucy Faithfull Foundation
Marine Life Study Society (British)
Medical Research Charities (Association of)
Medical Research Council
Meningitis Research Foundation
Mouth Cancer Foundation
Mycological Society (British)
National Archives

Research continued

National Archives of Scotland (NAS)

Natural Environment Research Council

New Economics Foundation

NFER

NOAH

Nobel Prize Internet Archive

Ocean Mammal Institute

Office for National Statistics

Old Bailey, London (Proceedings of) 1674 to 1834

Optimum Nutrition (Institute for)

Orchid Cancer Appeal

Organic Research Centre

Overseas Development Institute

Pain Relief Foundation

PETA Foundation

Policy Studies (Centre for)

Policy Studies Institute

Political Studies Association

Prostate Cancer Charity

Psychical Research (Society for)

Public Management and Policy Association

Royal Institution of Great Britain

Rural Research (Centre for)

Saving Faces

Snow and Ice Data Center (National)

Social & Economic Research (Institute for)

Social Issues Research Centre

Social Market Foundation

Soil Association

Stammering Children (Michael Palin Centre for)

Statistics New Zealand

Suzy Lamplugh Trust

Tenovus

Tommy's, the baby charity

Understanding Animal Research

Unistats

Vitiligo Society

Wellbeing of Women

Wessex Cancer Trust

What About The Children?

World Gazetteer

Worldometers

Young People in Focus

Safety/Accidents/Injury

Airsafe.com

Arson Prevention Bureau

Aspire

Back-up Trust

BASIC

Bibic

Bicycle Helmet Initiative Trust

Brake

Casualties Union

Child Accident Prevention Trust

Child Brain Injury Trust

Consumers International

Criminal Injuries Compensation Authority

Drinking Water Inspector – Northern Ireland

Drinking Water Inspectorate

Drinking Water Quality Regulator For Scotland

Ergonomics & Human Factors (Institute of)

Fire Brigade (London)

Fire Protection Authority

Floodline

Food Commission (UK)

Foreign and Commonwealth Office Travel Advice

Get Safe Online

HEADWAY

Health & Safety Executive

Heritage Railway Association

Industrial Injuries Advisory Council

Infant Deaths (Foundation for the Study of)

Internet Watch Foundation

Kidscape
Let's Face It
Lifeguard Skills
Lifesavers
Living Streets
London Hazards Centre
Make Roads Safe
Medical Accidents (Action Against)
Medicines & Healthcare products
Regulatory Agency
Navigation (Royal Institute of)
Occupational Safety & Health (Institution of)
Personal Injury Lawyers (Association of)
Pesticide Action Network UK
Placement Survival Guide
Refuge
RoadPeace
RoSPA
Royal National Lifeboat Institution
Safety Council (British)
Simon Jones Memorial Campaign
Spinal Injuries Association
sportscotland Avalanche Information
Service
Surf Life Saving GB
Sustrans
Sustrans Cymru
Sustrans Northern Ireland
Sustrans Scotland
Suzy Lamplugh Trust
Traffic Statistics (Global)
Transport Safety (Parliamentary Advisory
Council for)

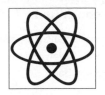

Science

Animal Health Trust
Anthropological Institute of Great Britain
and Ireland (Royal)
Astronomical Association (British)
Atmospheric Research (National Center for)
BCS – Chartered Institute for IT
Bioethics (Nuffield Council on)
Biological Diversity (Convention on)
Biology (Society of)
Biotechnology & Biological Sciences
Research Council
Botanical Society of the British Isles
CaSE - Campaign for Science &
Engineering in the UK
Chemistry (Royal Society of)
Climate Change (Intergovernmental Panel
on)
Computing Centre (National)
CREST Awards
Earthwatch Institute
Eden Project
Energy Foundation (National)
FRAME
Genetic Alliance UK
Geological Survey (British)
Geological Survey (US)
Geologists Association
GM Freeze
Heat is Online
Human Genetics Commission
Intellect
Jodrell Bank Observatory
Life Science Centre
Linnean Society of London
Magna: science adventure centre
Met Office

Science continued

Meteorological Organization (World)
Meteorological Society (Royal)
Millennium Seed Bank
Mongabay.com
MOSI
Mycological Society (British)
Nuclear Society (European)
Nuclear Tourist (Virtual)
Nutrition Society
Our Dynamic Earth
Pharmaceutical Society (Royal)
Physics (Institute of)
Popular Astronomy (Society for)
Psychical Research (Society for)
Royal Botanic Garden Edinburgh
Royal Botanic Gardens, Kew
Royal Institution of Great Britain
Royal Observatory, Greenwich
Royal Society
SCIcentre
Science Association (British)
Science Centre (Glasgow)
Science Education (Association for)
Science Education (Centre for)
Science in the Public Interest (Center for)
Science Museum
Science, Technology & the Arts (National Endowment for)
Scientists for Global Responsibility
Solar Energy Society
Space Agency (European)
Space Agency (UK)
Space Centre (National)
STEPS Centre
Telescope (Bradford Robotic)
UK Climate Projections
UNESCO
Weights & Measures Association (British)
Women Into Science & Engineering (WISE)
World Space Week

Sexual Issues

AIDS Trust (National)
Albany Trust
Albert Kennedy Trust
AVERT
BASPCAN
Beaumont Society
Body Positive
Child Protection in Sport Unit
ChildLine
Crossroads Women's Centre
HIV/Aids Alliance (International)
Justin Campaign
Lesbian and Gay Switchboard (London)
Lesbian Information Service
Lesbians & Gays (Families & Friends of)
likeitis.org
Lucy Faithfull Foundation
Mankind UK
Marie Stopes International
Mermaids
PACE
Positively UK
Sexual Advice Association
Sorted In 10
Stonewall
SurvivorsUK
Terrence Higgins Trust
Thesite.org
Your Life

Sport and Leisure

Adventure Activities Licensing Authority

Aikido Board (British)

Allotment and Leisure Gardeners Ltd.
(National Society of)

Amateur Boxing Association of England Ltd.

Amateur Boxing Scotland Ltd.

Angling Trust

Archery GB

Arms and Armour Society

Army Cadet Force

Artistic Roller Skating (Federation of)

Athletic Association (English Schools')

Athletics Federations (International
Association of)

Backpackers Club

Badminton England

BAHA

Balloon and Airship Club (British)

Basketball Association (English)

BBC Backstage Tours

Bike Events

Bike Express (European)

Blind Golf Association (English)

Blind Sport (British)

Bowling Association Ltd (English Indoor)

Bowling Federation (English)

Boys' Brigade

Braille Chess Association

British Rowing

Business in Sport & Leisure

Camping and Caravanning Club

Canoe Association (Scottish)

Canoe Association of Northern Ireland

Canoe Union (British)

Canoe Wales

Caravan Club

Caving Association (British)

Ceroc

Chess Association (English Primary
Schools)

Chess Federation (English)

Chess Scotland

Chess Union (Ulster)

Chess Union (Welsh)

Child Protection in Sport Unit

Church Lads' and Church Girls' Brigade

Circus Sensible/Circus School

Circus Space

Cirdan Sailing Trust

Clubs for Young People

Commonwealth Games Federation

Countryside Alliance

CP Sport England and Wales

Cricinfo

Cricket Board (England & Wales)

Croquet Association

Crown Green Bowling Association (British)

Crufts Dog Show

Cruising Association

CTC

Culture, Media & Sport (Department for)

Cyclenation

Cycling (British)

Cycling Association (Welsh)

Cycling Centre (National)

Cycling Projects

Cycling Union (International)

Cyclists' Federation (European)

Dancesport UK

Deaf Sports Council (British)

Disability Snowsport UK

Disability Sport (English Federation of)

Disability Sport Events

Elastic Rope Sports Association (British)

Ellen MacArthur Cancer Trust

EMDP

England Athletics

Sport and Leisure continued

England Hockey

England Netball

England Squash & Racketball

Family Holiday Association

Fell Runners Association

Fencing (British Academy of)

Fencing Association (British)

Fields in Trust – FIT

FIFA

Fitness Industry Association

Fitness League

Fitness Northern Ireland

Flower Arrangement Societies (National Association of)

Football Association

Football Association (English Schools)

Football Association (Irish)

Football Association (Scottish)

Football Foundation

Football Industry Group

Football League

Football League (Scottish)

Football Museum (National)

Football Supporters' Federation

Football Unites, Racism Divides

Footy4kids

Girlguiding UK

Girls' Brigade England & Wales

Girls' Venture Corps Air Cadets

Glasgow Life

Gliding Association (British)

Go4awalk

Golf Association (European)

Gymnastics (British)

Handball Association (England)

Handball Association (Scottish)

Hang Gliding and Paragliding Association (British)

HELP

Hostelling International

Hostelling International (N. Ireland)

Hostels.com

Human Power Club (British)

Ice Hockey UK

Ice Skating Association of Great Britain and N.I. (National)

International Olympic Committee

Jewish Lads' & Girls' Brigade (JLGB)

Ju Jitsu Association GB National Governing Body (British)

Judo Association (British)

Judo Scotland

Justin Campaign

Karate and Kickboxing Association (World)

Karate Board (N. Ireland)

Karate England

Karate Governing Body Ltd (Welsh)

Keep Fit Association

Kennel Club

Kick It Out

Kite Society of Great Britain

Lacrosse Association (English)

Ladies' Golf Union

Lake District Weather Line

Lawn Tennis Association

Lifesavers

London Marathon (Virgin)

Long Distance Walkers Association

Marine Leisure Association (MLA)

Marine Society and Sea Cadets

Martial Association (Amateur)

MCC

Medau

Mountain Leader Training England

Mountaineering Council (British)

Mountaineering Council of Scotland

NAKMAS

National Trust Holiday Cottages

Ocean Youth Trust

Olympic Association (British)

Orienteering Federation (British)

Outdoor Learning (Institute for)

Outward Bound Trust

Parachute Association (British)

Paralympic GB
Photographic Society (Royal)
Physical Education (Association for)
Pilates Foundation
Play England
PLAYLINK
Plus
Pony Club
Pool Association (English)
Professional Footballers Association
Professional Golfers' Association
Quilters' Guild of the British Isles
Ramblers
Riding for the Disabled Association
Rifle Association (National) of United Kingdom
Road Runners Club
Roller Hockey (England)
Rona Sailing Project
Royal Botanic Garden Edinburgh
Royal Botanic Gardens, Kew
Royal Mint (British)
Rugby Football League
Rugby Football Union
Rugby Football Union for Women
RYA Sailability
Sand & Land Yacht Clubs (British Federation of)
Scottish Cycling
scottishathletics
Scout Association
Scrum.com
Sea Ranger Association
Sealed Knot Ltd
Show Jumping Association (British)
Show Racism the Red Card
Ski Club of Great Britain
Skylight Circus Arts
Sparks
Speakers Clubs (Association of)
Special Olympics Great Britain
Sport & Recreation Alliance

Sport England
Sport Northern Ireland
Sport Wales
Sports Association for People with Learning Disability (UK)
Sports Centre (Lilleshall National)
Sports Coach UK
Sports Leaders UK
SportsAid
sportscotland
sportscotland Avalanche Information Service
Sub Aqua Club (British)
Surf Life Saving GB
Surfers Against Sewage
Swimming
Swimming Clubs for people with Disabilities (National Association for)
SYHA Hostelling Scotland
Table Tennis Association (English)
Tai Chi Finder
Tai Chi Union for Great Britain
Tall Ships Youth Trust
Tandem Club
Tour de France
Tourism for All
Triathlon Association (British)
UEFA
UK Sport
UK Youth
Universities and Colleges Sport (British)
Venuemasters
Volleyball Association (English)
Volleyball Association (Scottish)
Walking Federation (British)
Walkit
WalkScotland
Water Ski & Wakeboard (British)
Welsh Athletics
WheelPower
Wimbledon
Wind Sand & Stars
Windsurfing Association (UK)

Sport and Leisure continued

Women's Bowling Federation (English)

Women's Golf Association (English)

Women's Sports & Fitness Foundation

Woodcraft Folk

World Cup

World Ju-Jitsu Federation (Ireland)

World Travel & Tourism Council

Yachting Association (Royal)

YMCA England

Yoga (British Wheel of)

Yoga (Iyengar Institute)

Young Farmers' Clubs (National Federation of)

Youth Hostel Association (UK)

Youth Sport Trust

Technology

Access Art

Access Space

Alternative Technology (Centre for)

APRS

BCS – Chartered Institute for IT

Bibliomania

Blogger

Computer Aid International

Computers 4 Africa

Computing Centre (National)

CyberMentors

Design and Technology Association

e-Learning Foundation

Get Safe Online

Information Commissioner's Office

Intellect

Internet Watch Foundation

ipl2

JANET

Jodrell Bank Observatory

My Supermarket

Nominet UK

OFCOM

People's Network

Popular Astronomy (Society for)

Science, Technology & the Arts (National Endowment for)

Scientists for Global Responsibility

Space Agency (European)

Space Centre (National)

Specialist Schools and Academies Trust

STEPS Centre

TAG

Telescope (Bradford Robotic)

Telework Association

Wired Safety

World Space Week

Transport

Aeronautical Society (Royal)

AirportWatch

Airsafe.com

Automobile Association (AA)

Balloon and Airship Club (British)

Better Transport (Campaign for)

Bicycle Helmet Initiative Trust

Bikers with a Disability (National Association for)

Blue Badge Network

Brake

Bus Users UK

CAA

CADD

Choose Climate

Community Rail Partnerships (Association of)

Community Transport Association UK

Cyclenation
Cycling Campaign (London)
Cycling Projects
Disabled Motoring UK
DVLA
Environmental Transport Association
Heritage Railway Association
Human Power Club (British)
Inland Waterways Association
Liftshare.com Ltd
Light Rail Transit Association
Living Streets
Logistics and Transport in the UK
  (Chartered Institute of)
Make Roads Safe
Motorvations Project Ltd
Navigation (Royal Institute of)
Passenger Focus
Passenger Transport UK (Confederation of)
Port of London Authority
RAC
Rail Enquiries (National)
Rail Europe
Rail Regulation (Office of)
Railfuture
Road Haulage Association
RoadPeace
School Journey Association
Shopmobility (National Federation of)
Sustrans
Sustrans Cymru
Sustrans Northern Ireland
Sustrans Scotland
Traffic Statistics (Global)
Trainline
Transport & Environment (European
  Federation for)
Transport for London
Transport Safety (Parliamentary Advisory
  Council for)
WalesRails
Waterway Recovery Group
Working on Wheels

Travel & Tourism

ABTA
Berlin info
Berlin International
Bike Express (European)
Brathay Exploration Group
CHICKS
Choose Climate
Couch Surfing
Currency converter
Cycling Union (International)
Ecotourism Society (The International)
Fit for Travel
Foreign and Commonwealth Office Travel
  Advice
Geographic Society (National)
Hostelling International
Hostelling International (N. Ireland)
Hostels.com
Identity & Passport Service
Journeywoman.com
MASTA
Ordnance Survey
Royal Parks
SYHA Hostelling Scotland
Tour Operators (Association of Independent)
Tourism Concern
Tourism Offices Worldwide Directory
Transport for London
Travel and Tourism (Institute of)
Travel Warnings (US State Department)
Tropical Diseases (Hospital for)
Visit London
Visit Wales
VisitBritain
VisitEngland
VisitScotland
WalesRails
Winston Churchill Memorial Trust

Travel & Tourism continued

World Tourism Organization
World Travel & Tourism Council
Youth Hostel Association (UK)

Volunteers

Africa, Asia & Americas Venture
African Conservation Experience
An Taisce
Army Cadet Force
AV Foundation
Bond
BTCV
Casualties Union
CEMVO
Chartered Surveyors Voluntary Service
Children in Need Appeal
Cinnamon Trust
Community Service Volunteers
Community Transport Association UK
Conservation Volunteers Northern Ireland
Contact the Elderly
Couch Surfing
Cross Cultural Solutions
Depaul Nightstop UK
Directory of Social Change
Do-it
Friendship Works
Get connected
Girlguiding UK
Habitat for Humanity Great Britain
International Service
IVS GB
Jewish Lads' & Girls' Brigade (JLGB)
Jewish Women (League of)
Lattitude Global Volunteering
Lesbians & Gays (Families & Friends of)
Mercy Corps

National Trust Volunteering
NOAH
Pets as Therapy
Prince's Trust – Pembrokeshire Adventure Centre
Prince's Trust (Head Office)
Prison Visitors (National Association of Official)
Project Trust
Quaker Voluntary Action
Reach
REMAP
Restless Development
Retired and Senior Volunteer Programme
Royal National Lifeboat Institution
Scottish Environment LINK
Self Unlimited
Simon Community
SOVA
Time for God
Toc H
Tools for Self Reliance
United Nations Volunteers
Voluntary Agencies (International Council of)
Voluntary and Community Action (National Association for)
Voluntary Arts Network
Voluntary Organisations (National Council for) (NCVO)
Voluntary Organisations (Scottish Council for)
Voluntary Youth Services (National Council for)
Volunteer Action for Peace
Volunteer Development Scotland
Volunteer Now
Volunteer Reading Help
Volunteering England
Volunteers For Rural India
VSO
Waterway Recovery Group
WCVA

Women's Institutes (National Federation of)

Working For A Charity

WorldWide Volunteering

WRVS

WWOOF UK

Year Out Group

Young Enterprise

Youth Council (British)

Youth Council for N. Ireland

Youth in Action

War & Conflict

Abolition of War (Movement for the)

Aegis Trust

Army (British)

British Legion (Royal)

Campaign Against Arms Trade

Child Soldiers

Churchill War Rooms

CND

Combat Stress

Conscience

Control Arms

Defence (Ministry of)

E-MINE

ECHO

Elders (The)

Forgiveness Project

Gulf Veterans & Families Association (National)

HALO Trust

Help for Heroes

Imperial War Museum

International Criminal Court

Landmine Action

Landmines (International Campaign to Ban)

Mines Advisory Group

Miracles

Navy (US)

Pax Christi

Peace Brigades International

Peace Pledge Union

Royal Air Force

Royal Navy

Saferworld

War Resisters League

Women

Abortion Rights

Action of Postpartum Psychosis Network

AIMS

Birth Trauma Association

Black Women for Wages for Housework

Black Women's Rape Action Project

Bowling Association Ltd (English Indoor)

Breakthrough Breast Cancer

Breast Cancer Care

Business & Professional Women UK Ltd

CAMFED International

Crossroads Women's Centre

Daisy Network

Eaves

Endometriosis UK

Feminist Archive

Forward

Full Time Mothers

GFS Platform for Young Women

Hibiscus

Jewish Women (League of)

Jo's Cervical Cancer Trust

Journeywoman.com

Labour Women's Network

Ladies' Golf Union

Lavender Trust

Lilith Research and Development

Llamau

Margaret Pyke Centre

MATCH

Women continued

Mothers' Union

Netmums

Opportunity Now

Peace & Freedom (Women's International League for)

Platform 51

Poppy Project

Positively UK

Post-Natal Illness (Association for)

Premenstrual Syndrome (National Association for)

Rape Crisis

Refuge

Rights of Women

Rugby Football Union for Women

Scarlet Centre

Sea Ranger Association

Sojourner Project

Tampon Alert (Alice Kilvert)

White Ribbon Alliance

Winvisible (Women with visible & invisible disabilities)

Womankind Worldwide

Women (National Assembly of)

Women and Manual Trades

Women Entrepreneurs (British Association of)

Women in Prison

Women in Publishing

Women Into Science & Engineering (WISE)

Women living under Muslim laws

Women of Great Britain (National Council of)

Women Solicitors (Association of)

Women Working Worldwide

Women's Aid (Scottish)

Women's Aid Federation of England

Women's Clubs (National Association of)

Women's Engineering Society

Women's Environmental Network

Women's Institutes (National Federation of)

Women's Register (National)

Women's Therapy Centre

Women's Aid (Welsh)

Women's Aid Federation (N. Ireland)

Women's Archive of Wales

Women's Bowling Federation (English)

Women's Food & Farming Union

Women's Golf Association (English)

Women's Library

Women's Resource Centre

Women's Sports & Fitness Foundation

Organisations

Before contacting an organisation, check first whether your library has information. Most organisations which include British, National, International, Association, Society etc in their names have been placed in order by the key word in the name except where such a change would make the name unfamiliar or more difficult to find.

1 Voice – Communicating together
PO Box 559 Halifax HX1 2XT
Tel: 0845 330 7862
Info@1voice.info
www.1Voice.info
Network and support for children and families using communication aids

10 Downing Street Website
www.number10.gov.uk
Interactive information from Prime Minister's Department

10:10
PO Box 64749 London NW1W 8HE
Tel: 020 7388 6688
hello@1010uk.org
www.1010global.org
www.1010uk.org
A movement of people, schools, businesses and organisations cutting their carbon – 10% at a time

100 Black Men of London
The Bridge 12-16 Clerkenwell Road
London EC1M 5PQ
Tel: 08701214100
info@100bmol.org.uk
www.100bmol.org.uk
Charity dedicated to the education, development and uplifting of our youth and the wider community

1901 Census for England & Wales
www.1901censusonline.com

24 hour museum now see Culture24

4Children
City Reach 5 Greenwich View Place
London E14 9NN
Tel: 020 7512 2112
info@4children.org.uk
www.4children.org.uk
National charity that promotes out of school hours child care

A

AAA-NORCAP
112 Church Rd Wheatley Oxon OX33 1LU
Tel: 01865 875000
enquiries@norcap.org
www.norcap.org.uk
Supporting adults affected by adoption. Home to the UK's longest established Contact Register: finding, making contact, making it work

ABA see Amateur Boxing Association of England Ltd.

ABCUL see Credit Unions Ltd. (Association of British)

Abolition of War (Movement for the)
11 Venetia Road London N4 1EJ
Tel: 01908 511948
email via website
www.abolishwar.org.uk

Abortion see also ARC – Antenatal Results & Choices, BPAS, Education for Choice, Life, Marie Stopes International, Unborn Children (Society for the Protection of), Voice for Choice

Abortion Campaign (National) now see Abortion Rights

Abortion Law Reform Association now see Abortion Rights

Abortion Rights
18 Ashwin Street London E8 3DL
Tel: 020 7923 9792
email via website
www.abortionrights.org.uk
The national pro-choice campaign. Campaigns for equal access to safe, legal, free abortion on request

ABSA now see Arts & Business

ABTA The Travel Association
30 Park Street London SE1 9EQ
Consumer Affairs: 0901 201 5050
email via website
www.abta.com
Aims to ensure high standards of trading practice for the benefit of the travel industry and the consumers that they serve

ACAS Advisory, Conciliation and Arbitration Service
Euston Tower 286 Euston Road London NW1 3JJ
Helpline: 08457 47 47 47
Customer services: 08457 38 37 36
Text Relay: 18001 08457 47 47 47
www.acas.org.uk
Industrial relations and employment enquiries

Access Art
www.accessart.org.uk
Online workshops & arts educational
activities for all ages

Access London Theatre
www.officiallondontheatre.co.uk/

Access Space
Unit 1, AVEC Building 3-7 Sidney Street
Sheffield S1 4RG
Tel: 0114 249 5522
http://access-space.org/doku.php
Sustainable free, open access media lab.
People interested in art, design, computers,
recycling, music, electronics, photography
and more meet like minded people, share
and develop skills and work on creative,
enterprising and technical projects

Access to Industry Reducing barriers to
further education and employment
156 Cowgate Edinburgh EH1 1RP & 15
Blair Street Edinburgh EH1 1QR
Tel: 0131 260 9721
Tel: 0131 226 3006
mail@accesstoindustry.co.uk
www.accesstoindustry.co.uk
To move excluded people into education
and onto employment across the South East
of Scotland

Accessible Environments (Centre for)
CAE
70 South Lambeth Road London SW8 1RL
Tel: 020 7840 0125
info@cae.org.uk
www.cae.org.uk
Advise on access to the built environment/
inclusive design

ACRE see Communities in Rural England
(Action with)

ACT Animal Cancer Trust
5 Flag Business Exchange Vicarage Farm
Road Peterborough Cambridgeshire PE1
5TX
Tel: 08701 644225
info@animalcancertrust.org.uk
www.animalcancertrust.org.uk
Fighting cancer in our pets

ACT ON CO2
Energy saving advice line: 0800 512012
Email via website
http://actonco2.direct.gov.uk/home.html

Action for Children
3 The Boulevard Ascot Road Watford
WD18 8AG
Tel: 01923 361500
www.actionforchildren.org.uk
Supports and speaks out for the most
vulnerable children and young people in the UK

Action for ME see M.E. (Action for)

Action for Sick Children see Sick Children
(Action for)

Action for Southern Africa see ACTSA

Action for Victims of Medical Accidents
A see Medical Accidents (Action Against)

Action of Postpartum Psychosis Network
FREEPOST RSGT-YJEY-ZRREE Room 225
Monmouth House University Hospital of
Wales Heath Park Cardiff CF14 4XW
Tel: 0292 074 2038
app@app-network.org
www.app-network.org
Provides up to date research information
to women and their families on Postpartum
Psychosis – a severe mental illness which
has a sudden onset in the first few weeks
following childbirth

Action on Addiction see Addiction (Action
on)

Action on Disability and Development
now see ADD International

Action on Elder Abuse see Elder Abuse
(Action on)

Action Transport Theatre
Whitby Hall Stanney Lane Ellesmere Port
CH65 9AE
Tel: 0151 357 2120
info@actiontransporttheatre.org
www.actiontransporttheatre.org
Action Transport Theatre Company is an arts
and ideas company creating work for, by
and with young people

ActionAid
Chataway House Leach Rd Chard
Somerset TA20 1FR
Tel: 01460 238000
supportercare@actionaid.org
www.actionaid.org.uk
Help and support for the poorest and most
vulnerable people worldwide

Active Birth Centre
25 Bickerton Rd London N19 5JT
Tel: 020 7281 6760
info@activebirthcentre.com
www.activebirthcentre.com
Education for active birth, professional
training, water birth pool hire & sales

ACTSA Action for Southern Africa
231 Vauxhall Bridge Road London SW1V
1EH
Tel: 020 3263 2001
actsa@actsa.org
www.actsa.org
Campaigns for peace, democracy and
development in Southern Africa

Acupuncture Council (British)
63 Jeddo Road London W12 9HQ
Tel: 020 8735 0400
email via website
www.acupuncture.org.uk
Self-regulatory body for acupuncturists in the UK

Acupuncture Society (British Medical) BMAS
BMAS House 3 Winnington Court
Northwich Cheshire CW8 1AQ
Tel: 01606 786782
admin@medical-acupuncture.org.uk
www.medical-acupuncture.co.uk
Professional organisation

Adam Smith Institute
23 Great Smith St London SW1P 3BL
Tel: 020 7222 4995
info@adamsmith.org
www.adamsmith.org
Free market think-tank

Adbusters
www.adbusters.org
Website providing a critical look at advertising

ADD International
Vallis House 57 Vallis Rd Frome Somerset
BA11 3EG
Tel: 01373 473064
Email via website
www.add.org.uk
Charity working in Africa and Asia to help people with disabilities

Addaction
67-69 Cowcross St London EC1M 6PU
Tel: 020 7251 5860
info@addaction.org.uk
www.addaction.org.uk
Helping individuals and communities manage the effects of drug and alcohol misuse

Addiction (Action on)
East Knoyle Salisbury Wiltshire SP3 6BE
Tel: 0845 126 4130
email via website
www.actiononaddiction.org.uk
Charity seeking out the causes of nicotine, alcohol and drug addiction

Additives (Action on)
94 White Lion Street
London N1 9PF London N1 9PF
info@actiononadditives.com
www.actiononadditives.com
Aims to list all the foods, drinks and medicines which contain the additives linked to hyperactivity in susceptible children

ADFAM
25 Corsham Street London N1 6DR
Tel: 020 7553 7640
admin@adfam.org.uk
www.adfam.org.uk
National charity working with families affected by drugs & alcohol

Adolescent and Children's Trust see TACT

Adoption and Fostering Information Line
www.adoption.org.uk

Adoption records
www.direct.gov.uk/en/
Governmentcitizensandrights/
Registeringlifeevents/index.htm
Adoption certificates & access to birth records. Contact Register for adoptions in England and Wales

Adoption UK
Linden House 55 The Green South Bar
Street Banbury Oxon OX16 9AB
Helpline: 0844 848 7900
Tel: 01295 752240 (Admin)
email via website
www.adoptionuk.org
Supporting adoptive families before, during and after adoption

Adult Continuing Education (National Institute of) see NIACE

Adult Education see also NIACE,
learndirect, Open University, Third Age
Trust, Workers Educational Association

Advancing Gender Equality in Science, Engineering and Technology see UKRC

Adventure Activities Licensing Authority
44 Lambourne Cres Llanishen Cardiff CF14
5GG
Tel: 029 20 755 715
info@aala.org.uk
www.aala.org.uk
Inspects providers of adventure activities as per The Adventure Activities Licensing Regulations 1996

Advertising Association
7th Floor North Artillery House 11-19
Artillery Row London SW1P 1RT
Tel: 020 7340 1100
aa@adassoc.org.uk
www.adassoc.org.uk
Federation of trade bodies. Promoting and protecting the role, rights and responsibilities of advertising

Advertising Standards Authority
Mid City Place 71 High Holborn London
WC1V 6QT
Tel: 020 7492 2222
email via website
www.asa.org.uk
Regulates content of non-broadcast
advertisements

Advice see thematic guide - Counselling

Advice on Individual Rights in Europe
see AIRE Centre

Advicenow
www.advicenow.org.uk
Comprehensive legal information from a
variety of leading services

AdviceUK
6th Floor 63 St Mary Ave London EC3A
8AA
Tel: 020 7469 5700
mail@adviceuk.org.uk
www.adviceuk.org.uk
Umbrella organisation. Membership
organisation of independent social welfare
law advice centres

Advisory Council on the Misuse of Drugs
Home Office 3rd Floor Seacole Building 2
Marsham Street London SW1P 4DF
020 7035 0454
ACMD@homeoffice.gsi.gov.uk
www.homeoffice.gov.uk/agencies-public-
bodies/acmd/
Independent expert body that advises
government on drug related issues in the UK

Advocacy After Fatal Domestic Abuse
AAFDA
PO Box 3636 Swindon SN3 9BG
Helpline: 07768 386922 if you need
immediate assistance
Domestic violence Helpline: 0808 2000 24 7
(24 hr Freephone)
www.aafda.org.uk
Practical and emotional support after fatal
domestic abuse incidents

Advocacy Resource Exchange ARX
Portman House 53 Millbrook Road East
Southampton SO15 1HN
Tel: 02380 234 904
enquiries@advocacyresource.org.uk
www.advocacyresource.org.uk
A resource agency supporting local
advocacy schemes by providing training,
information and advice

Advocates for Animals see Onekind

Aegis Trust
4 Pinchin Street London E1 1SA
Tel: 020 7481 1011
office@aegistrust.org

www.aegistrust.org
Campaigns against crimes against humanity
and genocide

AENA now see England Netball

Aeronautical Society (Royal)
4 Hamilton Place London W1J 7BQ
Tel: 020 7670 4300
raes@aerosociety.com
www.aerosociety.com
A professional institution dedicated to the
Global Aerospace Community

Afasic
1st Floor, 20 Bowling Green Lane London
EC1R 0BD
Helpline: 0845 355 5577
Tel: 020 7490 9410
email via website
www.afasic.org.uk
Representing children & young adults with
speech, language and communication
impairments

Afghanaid
56 - 64 Leonard Street London EC2A 4LT
Tel: 020 7065 0825
info@afghanaid.org.uk
www.afghanaid.org.uk
UK based charity working alongside Afghan
communities

Africa Centre
Tel: 020 7836 1973
info@africacentre.org.uk
www.africacentre.org.uk
Promoting African arts, culture, opinion
and business. Planning to move but details
unavailable at time of going to press. See
website for details

Africa Now
The Old Music Hall 106-108 Cowley Road
Oxford OX4 1JE
Tel: 01865 403265
info@africanow.org
www.africanow.org
Tackles poverty in Africa by helping small-
scale businesses and promoting ethical
trade

Africa, Asia & Americas Venture
10 Market Place Devizes Wiltshire SN10
1HT
Tel: 01380 729009
av@aventure.co.uk
www.aventure.co.uk
UK-based volunteering organisation
specialising in volunteering opportunities
and gap year projects for 18 - 25 year olds
in the developing world

African Conservation Experience
Unit 1, Manor Farm Churchend Lane
Charfield Wotton-under-edge GL12 8LJ
Tel: 01454 269 182
email via website
www.conservationafrica.net
Gives volunteers the opportunity to
experience conservation work in Southern
Africa and to provide financial support and
information for conservation projects

African Initiatives
Brunswick Court Brunswick Square Bristol
BS2 8PE
Tel: 0117 915 0001
info@african-initiatives.org.uk
www.african-initiatives.org.uk
Promotes right to participate in decisions
affecting communities in Africa

Africans Unite Against Child Abuse
Unit 3D/F Leroy House 436 Essex Road
London N1 3QP
Tel: 0844 660 8607
email via website
www.afruca.org
Promoting the rights and welfare of African
children

Age Concern Now see Age Cymru, Age
UK, Age NI, Age Scotland

Age Cymru
Ty John Pathy 13-14 Neptune Court
Vanguard Way Cardiff CF24 5PJ
Age UK Advice line: 0800 169 6565
Tel: 029 20 431555
enquiries@agecymru.org.uk
www.ageuk.org.uk/cymru

Age Exchange
The Reminiscence Centre 11 Blackheath
Village London SE3 9LA
Tel: 020 8318 9105
administrator@age-exchange.org.uk
www.age-exchange.org.uk
Works with older people to improve their
quality of life by valuing their reminiscences

Age NI
3 Lower Cres Belfast BT7 1NR
Age UK Advice line: 0800 169 6565
Tel: 028 9024 5729
info@ageni.org
www.ageuk.org.uk/northern-ireland

Age Scotland
Causewayside House 160 Causewayside
Edinburgh EH9 1PR
Age UK Advice line: 0800 169 6565
Tel: 0845 125 9732
enquiries@
ageconcernandhelptheagedscotland.org.uk
www.ageuk.org.uk/scotland

Age UK
Tavis House 1-6 Tavistock Square London
WC1H 9NA
Advice: 0800 169 6565
Tel: 0800 169 8787
contact@ageuk.org.uk
www.ageuk.org.uk
Age UK is the new force combining Age
Concern and Help the Aged

Ageing (Centre for Policy on) see Policy
on Ageing (Centre for)

Ageing (Research Info) now see Age
Cymru, Age UK, Age NI, Age Scotland

**Agriculture and Horticulture
Development Board**
Stoneleigh Park Kenilworth Warwickshire
CV8 2TL
Tel: 0247 669 2051
Info@ahdb.org.uk
www.ahdb.org.uk
Helps improve the efficiency and
competitiveness of various agriculture and
horticulture sectors within the UK

Ahimsa Safer Families
1 Bridge Court Kingsmill Road Saltash
PL12 6LS
Tel: 01752 848248
mail@ahimsa-saferfamilies.co.uk
www.ahimsasaferfamilies.co.uk
Specialist help for men with a history of
violence. Support for their partners

AIDS Trust (National)
New City Cloisters 196 Old St London
EC1V 9FR
Tel: 020 7814 6767
info@nat.org.uk
www.nat.org.uk
The UK's leading independent policy and
campaigning voice on HIV and AIDS

AIDS/HIV see also AVERT, Body
Positive North West, HIV/Aids Alliance
(International), HIV InSite, ONE
International, PACE, Positively UK, Terrence
Higgins Trust

Aikido Board (British) BAB
general@bab.org.uk
www.bab.org.uk
Governing body for Aikido in the United
Kingdom

AIMS Association for Improvements in the
Maternity Services
Helpline: 0300 365 0663
helpline@aims.org.uk
www.aims.org.uk
Advice and information network for parents'
choices in childbirth

Air Cadets see Girls' Venture Corps Air Cadets

Air Transport Users' Council now see CAA

AIRE Centre Advice on Individual Rights in Europe
3rd Floor 17 Red Lion Square London WC1R 4QH
Advice Line: 020 7831 3850
Tel: 020 7831 4276
info@airecentre.org
www.airecentre.org

AirportWatch
Broken Wharf House 2 Broken Wharf London EC4V 3DT
Tel: 020 7248 2227
info@airportwatch.org.uk
www.airportwatch.org.uk
Opposes airport expansion across the UK

Airsafe.com Safety information for the airline passenger
www.airsafe.com

AITO see Tour Operators (Association of Independent)

Al Jazeera
http://english.aljazeera.net
English language web site of the Arab news service, based in Qatar

Al-Anon Alateen Family Groups (UK & Eire)
61 Great Dover St London SE1 4YF
Confidential Helpline: 020 7403 0888
Tel: 020 7407 0215
enquiries@al-anonuk.org.uk
www.al-anonuk.org.uk
Al-Anon offers understanding & support for families & friends of problem drinkers. Alateen is for 12 & 20 year olds who have been affected by someone else's drinking, usually that of a parent

&

Al-Anon Information Centre Mansfield Park Building Unit 6 22 Mansfield Street Patrick Glasgow G11 5QP
Helpline: 0141 339 8884
enquiries@al-anonuk.org.uk
www.al-anonuk.org.uk

&

Al-Anon Information Centre Room 5, 5 Capel Street Dublin 1 Republic of Ireland
Helpline: 01 873 2699
enquiries@al-anonuk.org.uk
www.al-anonuk.org.uk

&

Al-Anon Information Centre Peace House 224 Lisburn Road Belfast BT9 6GE Northern Ireland

Helpline: 02890 68 2368
enquiries@al-anonuk.org.uk
www.al-anonuk.org.uk

Albany Trust
239a Balham High Road London SW17 7BE
Tel: 020 8767 1827
info@albanytrust.org
www.albanytrust.org.uk
A professional therapy service offering emotional, sexual and/or psychological help

Albert Kennedy Trust
Unit 203 Hatton Square Business Centre 16/16a Baldwins Gardens London EC1N 7RJ
Tel: 020 7831 6562 (London)
Tel: 0161 228 3308 (Manchester)
contact@akt.org.uk
www.akt.org.uk
Supporting lesbian, gay and bisexual young people who are homeless or living in hostile environments

Albinism see also NOAH - National Organization for Albinism and Hypopigmentation

Albinism Fellowship
PO Box 77 Burnley BB11 5GN
Tel: 01282 771900
info@albinism.org.uk
www.albinism.org.uk
Advice and support

Alcohol & Drug Education (Advisory Council for) see Tacade

Alcohol Concern
64 Leman Street London E1 8EU
National Drink Helpline: 0800 917 8282
Tel: 020 7264 0510
email via website
www.alcoholconcern.org.uk
Provides information and comment on alcohol issues

Alcohol Education and Research Council AERC
Willow House 4th Floor 17-23 Willow Place London SW1P 1JH
Tel: 0207 821 7880
email via website
www.aerc.org.uk
Develops research based evidence to inform and influence policy and practice and help people and organisations to address alcohol issues

Alcohol Focus Scotland
2nd Floor 166 Buchanan Street Glasgow G1 2LW
Tel: 0141 572 6700
enquiries@alcohol-focus-scotland.org.uk
www.alcohol-focus-scotland.org.uk

Dedicated to raising awareness of, and reducing the significant health and social harm caused by alcohol

Alcohol Studies (Institute of)
Alliance House 12 Caxton St London SW1H 0QS
Tel: 020 7222 4001
info@ias.org.uk
www.ias.org.uk

Alcoholics Anonymous
PO Box 1 10 Toft Green York YO1 7ND
Helpline: 0845 7697 555
Tel: 01904 644026 (office hours only)
help@alcoholics-anonymous.org.uk
www.alcoholics-anonymous.org.uk

Alexander Teachers (Professional Association of)
Room 706 The Big Peg 120 Vyse St Birmingham B18 6NF
Tel: 01743 236 195
info@paat.org.uk
www.paat.org.uk

Alexander Technique (Society of Teachers of the)
1st Floor Linton House 39-51 Highgate Rd London NW5 1RS
Tel: 020 7482 5135
office@stat.org.uk
www.stat.org.uk

Alice Kilvert Tampon Alert see Tampon Alert (Alice Kilvert)

Allergies see also Anaphylaxis Campaign

Allergy UK
Planwell House LEFA Business Park Edgington Way Sidcup DA14 5BH
Tel: 01322 619898
info@allergyuk.org
www.allergyuk.org
Medical charity for people with allergy, food intolerance and chemical sensitivity

Alliance for Inclusive Education see Inclusive Education (Alliance for)

Alliance Française
1 Dorset Square London NW1 6PU
Tel: 020 7723 6439
email via website
www.alliancefrancaise.org.uk
French classes/diplomas in French as a foreign language & language skills consultancy, some social and cultural activities

Allotment and Leisure Gardeners Ltd. (National Society of)
O'Dell House Hunters Road Corby NN17 5JE
Tel: 01536 266 576
natsoc@nsalg.org.uk

www.nsalg.org.uk
National representative body for the allotment movement in the UK. Managed and funded by its members to protect, promote and preserve allotments for future generations to enjoy

Alone in London
Unit 6 48 Provost Street N1 7SU
Tel: 020 7278 4224
enquiries@als.org.uk
www.als.org.uk
Assists the single young homeless under 26 in London

Alopecia see Hairline International

Alternative Technology (Centre for)
Machynlleth Powys SY20 9AZ
Tel: 01654 705950
www.cat.org.uk
Environmental demonstration centre open to visitors

Aluminium Packaging Recycling Organisation
1 Brockhill Court Brockhill Lane Redditch B97 6RB
Tel: 01527 597757
info@alupro.org.uk
www.alupro.org.uk
Info packs, educational materials

Alzheimer Scotland
22 Drumsheugh Gardens Edinburgh EH3 7RN
Helpline: 0808 808 3000
Tel: 0131 243 1453
alzheimer@alzscot.org
www.alzscot.org
Helping people with dementia and their carers and families in Scotland

Alzheimer's Research Trust Defeating Dementia
The Stables Station Road Great Shelford Cambridge CB22 5LR
Tel: 01223 843899
enquiries@alzheimersresearchuk.org
www.alzheimers-research.org.uk
Leading UK research charity for Alzheimer's disease and related dementias. Provides free information on dementia

Alzheimer's Society Leading the fight against dementia
Devon House 58 St Katharine's Way London E1W 1LB
Helpline: 0845 300 0336
Tel: 020 7423 3500
enquiries@alzheimers.org.uk
www.alzheimers.org.uk
Provide local information and services across England, Wales & N. Ireland to

people affected by dementia in their communities. Provides day care and home care for people with dementia, as well as support and befriending services to help partners and families cope with the demands of caring

AMAR International Charitable Foundation
Hope House 45 Great Peter Steet London SW1P 3LT
Tel: 020 7799 2217
london@amarfoundation.org
www.amarfoundation.org
Works to create and to sustain professional services in medicine, public health, education and basic need provision within refugee and other communities living under stress in war zones or in areas of civil disorder and disruption

Amateur Boxing Association of England Ltd. ABA
The English Institute of Sport Coleridge Road Sheffield S9 5DA
Tel: 0114 223 5654
email via website
www.abae.co.uk
National governing body

Amateur Boxing Scotland Ltd.
5 Nasmyth Court Houston Industrial Estate Livingston EH54 5EG
Tel: 0845 241 7016
enquiries@abs-ltd.org.uk
www.amateurboxingscotland.co.uk
Promotes boxing as physical exercise for boys and girls

Amateur Theatre Network see Theatre Network (The Amateur)

American Library Association
www.ala.org

Amnesty International UK
17-25 New Inn Yard London EC2A 3EA
Tel: 020 7033 1500
Textphone 020 7033 1664
sct@amnesty.org.uk
www.amnesty.org.uk
Campaigns for prisoners of conscience, against the use of torture & the death penalty

An Taisce National Trust for Ireland
Tailor's Hall Back Lane Dublin 8
Tel: 00 353 1 454 1786
admin@antaisce.org
www.antaisce.org
An environmental voluntary organisation concerned with the preservation of buildings, landscapes and natural heritage

Anaphylaxis Campaign
PO Box 275 Farnborough Hants GU14 6SX
Helpline: 01252 542029
Tel: 01252 546100
info@anaphylaxis.org.uk
www.anaphylaxis.org.uk/
Fighting for people with life-threatening allergies, providing education, information and support

Anchor Trust
2nd Floor 25 Bedford Street London WC2E 9ES
Tel: 0845 140 2020
email via website
www.anchor.org.uk
Working with older people and providing residential care homes

Ancient Buildings (Society for the Protection of) SPAB
37 Spital Sq London E1 6DY
Tel: 020 7377 1644
info@spab.org.uk
www.spab.org.uk
Campaigns to save threatened buildings, gives advice on repair and runs courses

Ancient Monument Society
St Ann's Vestry Hall 2 Church Entry London EC4V 5HB
Tel: 020 7236 3934
office@ancientmonumentssociety.org.uk
www.ancientmonumentssociety.org.uk
Study and conservation of historic buildings of all ages and types

Ancient Tree Forum
c/o Woodland Trust Autumn Park Dysart Road Grantham NG32 6LL
Tel: 01476 581135
ancient-tree-forum@woodland-trust.org.uk
www.woodland-trust.org.uk/ancient-tree-forum

Angling Trust
Eastwood House 6 Rainbow Street Leominster Herefordshire HR6 8DQ
Tel: 0844 7700616
admin@anglingtrust.net
www.anglingtrust.net
Represent all game, coarse and sea anglers and angling in England

Animal Aid
The Old Chapel Bradford St Tonbridge Kent TN9 1AW
Tel: 01732 364546
info@animalaid.co.uk
www.animalaid.org.uk
Campaigns against animal abuse and for a cruelty-free lifestyle

Animal Aid Youth
www.animalaid.org.uk/h/n/YOUTH/HOME/
Youth section of Animal Aid

Animal Defenders International
Millbank Tower Millbank London SW1P
4QP
Tel: 020 7630 3340
info@ad-international.org
www.ad-international.org
Works globally with the National Anti-
Vivisection Society and the Lord Dowding
Fund for Humane Research for the
protection of animals

Animal Health (National Office of)
3 Crossfield Chambers Gladbeck Way
Enfield EN2 7HF
Tel: 020 8367 3131
noah@noah.co.uk
www.noah.co.uk
Represents the UK animal medicines
industry

Animal Health Trust
Lanwades Park Kentford Newmarket
Suffolk CB8 7UU
Tel: 01638 751000
info@aht.org.uk
www.aht.org.uk
Registered charity that aims to advance
veterinary science

Animal Rescue (International)
Lime House Regency Close Uckfield East
Sussex TN22 1DS
Tel: 01825 767688
info@internationalanimalrescue.org
www.iar.org.uk
Charity for the rescue and rehabilitation of
suffering animals

Animal Rescuers (UK)
www.animalrescuers.co.uk
Directory of UK rescue centres

Animal Research (Understanding) see
Understanding Animal Research

Animal Welfare Trust (National)
Tyler's Way Watford-By-Pass Watford
Herts WD25 8WT
Tel: 020 8950 0177
email via web
www.nawt.org.uk/
Operates rescue centres for unwanted, ill-
treated and abandoned animals and birds.
No healthy animal is ever put to sleep

**Animals in Medical Experiments (Fund
for the Replacement of)** see FRAME

Anne Frank Trust UK
Star House 104-108 Grafton Road London
NW5 4BA
Tel: 020 7284 5858

info@annefrank.org.uk
www.annefrank.org.uk
Exhibitions and educational programmes
on citizenship and social responsibility to
counter bigotry and racism. Organises the
Anne Frank Awards for Moral Courage

Antenatal Results and Choices see ARC

Anthony Nolan
2 Heathgate Place 75-87 Agincourt Rd
London NW3 2NU
Tel: 0303 303 0303
email via website
www.anthonynolan.org.uk
Co-ordinates donation of bone marrow for
treatment of disease

**Anthropological Institute of Great Britain
and Ireland (Royal)** RAI
50 Fitzroy St London W1T 5BT
Tel: 020 7387 0455
admin@therai.org.uk
www.therai.org.uk
World's longest-established scholarly
association dedicated to the study of
humankind

Anti Snaring Campaign (National) NASC
PO BOX 3058 Littlehampton West Sussex
BN16 3LG
Tel: 05601 716524
email via website
www.antisnaring.org.uk
Campaigns against the sale and
manufacture of animal snares in the UK

Anti-Bullying Alliance
National Children's Bureau 8 Wakley Street
London EC1V 7QE
aba@ncb.org.uk
www.anti-bullyingalliance.org.uk
The ABA brings together over 130
organisations into one network. Promotes
annual Anti-Bullying Week

Anti-Bullying Network
Simpson House 52 Queen Street Edinburgh
EH2 3NS
info@antibullying.net
www.antibullying.net
Network set up by The Scottish Executive
so that teachers, parents and young people
in Scotland could share ideas about how
bullying should be tackled

Anti-Nazi League now see Unite Against
Fascism

Anti-Slavery International Today's fight for tomorrow's freedom
Thomas Clarkson House The Stableyard Broomgrove Road London SW9 9TL
Tel: 020 7501 8920
info@antislavery.org
www.antislavery.org
Campaigns for the elimination of slavery, child labour, debt bondage, forced labour, trafficking people. Educational materials available

Anti-Vivisection Society (National)
Millbank Tower Millbank London SW1P 4QP
Tel: 020 7630 3340
email via website
www.navs.org.uk
Campaigns to end all animal experiments

Antidote Promising Progress
3rd Floor, Cityside House 40 Adler St London E1 1EE
Tel: 020 7247 3355
admin@antidote.org.uk
www.antidote.org.uk
Developed The PROGRESS Programme to help schools shape dynamic learning environments

Antiquaries of London (Society of)
Burlington House Piccadilly London W1J 0BE
Tel: 020 7479 7080
Tel: 020 7479 7084 (Library – to make appointments)
Tel: 020 7479 7088 (Museum - collection enquiries)

admin@sal.org.uk
www.sal.org.uk
Fellowship of antiquaries. Has a library for scholars to which access is by appointment

Anxiety Care
Cardinal Heenan Centre 326 High Rd Ilford IG1 1QP
Helpline: 020 8478 3400
Tel: 020 8262 8891
enquiries@anxietycare.org.uk
www.anxietycare.org.uk
Deals with anxiety, phobias and obsessive compulsive disorders

Anxiety UK
Zion Community Resource Centre 339 Stretford Rd Hulme Manchester M15 4ZY
Tel: 0844 4775 774
Tel: 0161 226 7727
info@anxietyuk.org.uk
www.anxietyuk.org.uk
Provides information & support for people suffering from anxiety disorders

Ape Alliance
www.4apes.com
An international coalition of organisations and individuals, working for the conservation and welfare of apes

Aphasia see Connect, Speakability

Apples & Snakes
The Albany Douglas Way Deptford London SE8 4AG
Tel: 0845 521 3460
info@applesandsnakes.org
www.applesandsnakes.org
Promotes performance poetry as a social and cross-cultural activity

APRS see Rural Scotland (Association for the Protection of)

APRS The professional recording association
PO Box 22 Totnes TQ9 7YZ
Tel: 01803 868600
email via website
www2.aprs.co.uk
Representing audio professionals

Apsley House Wellington Museum
Hyde Park Corner 149 Piccadilly London W1J 7NT
Tel: 020 7499 5676
www.apsleyhouseguide.co.uk/
One of London's finest Georgian buildings, former home of the Duke of Wellington

AQA Assessment and Qualifications Alliance
31-33 Springfield Av Harrogate HG1 2HW
Exam support: 0844 209 6614
Tel: 01423 840 015
mailbox@aqa.org.uk
www.aqa.org.uk
Largest A-level and GCSE awarding body in the UK

&
Devas St Manchester M15 6EX
Tel: 0161 953 1180
www.aqa.org.uk

&
Stag Hill House Guildford GU2 7XJ
Tel: 01483 506 506
www.aqa.org.uk

Arab-British Understanding (Council for)
CAABU
1 Gough Square London EC4A 3DE
Tel: 020 7832 1321
info@caabu.org
www.caabu.org

Arbitration see ACAS

Arbitrators (Chartered Institute of) CIArb
CIArb 12 Bloomsbury Square London
WC1A 2LP
Tel: 020 7421 7444
info@ciarb.org
www.ciarb.org
Professional organisation for arbitrators,
mediators and adjudicators

ARC Antenatal Results and Choices
73 Charlotte St London W1T 4PN
Helpline: 020 7631 0285
Tel: 020 7631 0280
info@arc-uk.org
www.arc-uk.org
Information and support to parents
throughout antenatal testing

Arc Theatre
1st Floor, The Malthouse Studios 62-76
Abbey Road Barking IG11 7BT
Tel: 020 8594 1095
email via website
www.arctheatre.com
Specialise in creating and performing theatre
that challenges assumptions and causes
real change in the way that people relate to
one another at work, at school and in the
community

Archaeology (Council for British)
St Mary's House 66 Bootham York YO30
7BZ
Tel: 01904 671417
email via website
www.britarch.ac.uk

Archaeology Abroad
31-34 Gordon Sq London WC1H 0PY
Tel: 020 8537 0849
arch.abroad@ucl.ac.uk
www.britarch.ac.uk/archabroad
Information about fieldwork opportunities
outside the UK

Archaeology Scotland
Suite 1a Stuart House Station Road
Eskmills Musselburgh EH21 7PB
Tel: 0845 872 3333
info@archaeologyscotland.org.uk
www.archaeologyscotland.org.uk

Archéire
www.archeire.com
Archéire is a website dedicated to the
promotion of Irish architecture

Archery GB
Lilleshall National Sports Centre Nr Newport
Shropshire TF10 9AT
Tel: 01952 677 888
enquiries@archerygb.org
www.archerygb.org
The governing body for the sport of archery
in Great Britain and Northern Ireland

Architects (Royal Institute of British)
RIBA
66 Portland Place London W1B 1AD
Tel: 020 7580 5533
info@inst.riba.org
www.architecture.com

Architectural Heritage Fund
Alhambra House 27-31 Charing Cross Road
London WC2H 0AU
Tel: 020 7925 0199
ahf@ahfund.org.uk
www.ahfund.org.uk
Loans and grants to charities to preserve
historic buildings

Architecture Foundation
Ground Floor East 136-148 Tooley Street
London SE1 2TU
Tel: 020 7084 6767
email via website
www.architecturefoundation.org.uk
Aims to promote the importance of high
quality contemporary architecture & urban
design

Ariel Studios
Mullacott Cross Ilfracombe Devon EX34
8ND
Tel: 01271 862701
www.ariel.org.uk
Studio/rehearsal space and digital recording
studio

ARKive
Wildscreen Ground Floor
  The Rackhay Queen Charlotte Street
Bristol BS1 4HJ
Tel : 0117 328 5950
arkive@wildscreen.org.uk
www.arkive.org
Images of life on earth. The world's
centralised digital library of films,
photographs and associated recordings of
species

Arms and Armour Society
PO Box 10232 London SW19 2ZD
armsandarmour.soc@btinternet.com
www.armsandarmour.net
A learned society for the study and
preservation of arms and armour

Army (British)
www.army.mod.uk

Army Cadet Force
www.armycadets.com
National voluntary youth organisation

Army Museum (National)
Royal Hospital Road Chelsea London SW3
4HT
Tel: 020 7881 6606 (information line)
Tel: 020 7730 0717 (switchboard)
info@nam.ac.uk
www.national-army-museum.ac.uk

Arson Prevention Bureau
www.arsonpreventionbureau.org.uk
Funded by UK insurers to reduce the
incidence and costs of arson

**Art and Design (National Society for
Education in)**
3 Masons Wharf Potley Lane Corsham
Wiltshire SN13 9FY
Tel: 01225 810134
info@nsead.org
www.nsead.org
For gallery educators, artists in residence,
parents and all those with an interest in arts
education

Art Fund
Millais House 7 Cromwell Place London
SW7 2JN
Tel: 020 7225 4800
info@artfund.org
www.artfund.org
The UK's leading art charity, it enriches
museums and galleries with works of art

Art Library (National)
Victoria and Albert Museum South
Kensington Cromwell Road London SW7
2RL
Tel: 020 7942 2000
vanda@vam.ac.uk
www.vam.ac.uk/nal/
A major public reference library & the V&A's
curatorial department for the art, craft &
design of the book

Art Therapists (British Association of)
24-27 White Lion Street London N1 9PD
Tel: 020 7686 4216
info@baat.org
www.baat.org

Arthritic Association
One Upperton Gardens Eastbourne East
Sussex BN21 2AA
Tel: 01323 416550
Freephone: 0800 652 3188
info@arthriticassociation.org.uk
www.arthriticassociation.org.uk
Offers a natural drug free Home Treatment
programme to help arthritis sufferers

Arthritis Care
18 Stephenson Way London NW1 2HD
Helpline: 0808 800 4050
Tel: 020 7380 6500
info@arthritiscare.org.uk
www.arthritiscare.org.uk
Supporting people with arthritis

Arthritis Research UK
Copeman House St Mary's Gate
Chesterfield Derbyshire S41 7TD
Tel: 0300 790 0400
enquiries@arthritisresearchuk.org
www.arthritisresearchuk.org
Aims to advance the understanding,
prevention and treatment of arthritis &
related conditions

Arthur Rank Centre
Stoneleigh Park Warwickshire CV8 2LG
Tel: 024 7685 3060
admin@arthurrankcentre.org.uk
www.arthurrankcentre.org.uk
National rural resources unit for the churches

ARTICLE 19 The Global Campaign for Free
Expression
Free Word Centre 60 Farringdon Road
London EC1R 3GA
Tel: 020 7324 2500
info@article19.org
www.article19.org
Human rights organisation which campaigns
globally for freedom of expression and
information

Artistic Roller Skating (Federation of)
10 The Broadway Thatcham Berks RG19
3JA
Tel: 01635 877322
office@fars.co.uk
www.fars.co.uk

Artists Against Racism
www.artistsagainstracism.com

Arts (National Campaign for the)
1 Kingly Street London W1B 5PA
Tel: 0207 287 3777
nca@artscampaign.org.uk
www.artscampaign.org.uk

Arts (Royal Academy of) see Royal
Academy of Arts

Arts & Business
Nutmeg House 60 Gainsford St Butler's
Wharf London SE1 2NY
Tel: 020 7378 8143
contactus@artsandbusiness.org.uk
www.artsandbusiness.org.uk
Helps business people support the arts &
the arts inspire business people

Arts Council England
14 Great Peter Street SW1P 3NQ
Tel: 0845 300 6200
Textphone: 020 7973 6564
Email via website
www.artscouncil.org.uk
National development agency for the arts in England, distributing public money from government & the national lottery

& East
Eden House 48-49 Bateman St Cambridge CB2 1LR
Tel: 0845 300 6200
Email via website
www.artscouncil.org.uk

& East Midlands
St Nicholas Ct 25-27 Castle Gate Nottingham NG1 7AR
Tel: 0845 300 6200
Email via website
www.artscouncil.org.uk

& North East
Central Square Forth St Newcastle upon Tyne NE1 3PJ
Tel: 0845 300 6200
Email via website
www.artscouncil.org.uk

& North West
The Hive 49 Lever Street Manchester M1 1FN
Tel: 0845 300 6200
Email via website
www.artscouncil.org.uk

& South East
Sovereign House Church St Brighton BN1 1RA
Tel: 0845 300 6200
Email via website
www.artscouncil.org.uk

& South West
Senate Court Southernhay Gardens Exeter EX1 1UG
Tel: 0845 300 6200
Email via website
www.artscouncil.org.uk

& West Midlands
82 Granville St Birmingham B1 2LH
Tel: 0845 300 6200
Email via website
www.artscouncil.org.uk

& Yorkshire
21 Bond St Dewsbury WF13 1AX
Tel: 0845 300 6200
Email via website
www.artscouncil.org.uk

Arts Council of Northern Ireland
77 Malone Road Belfast BT9 6AQ
Tel: 028 9038 5200
info@artscouncil-ni.org
www.artscouncil-ni.org

Arts Council of Wales Cyngor Celfyddydau Cymru
Bute Plate Cardiff CF10 5AL
Tel: 0845 8734 900
Minicom: 029 2045 1023
info@artswales.org.uk
www.artswales.org.uk

&
6 Gardd Llydaw Jackson Lane Carmarthen SA31 1QD
Tel: 01267 234248
info@artswales.org.uk
www.artswales.org.uk
The Arts Council of Wales is the organisation responsible for distributing Welsh Assembly Government and National Lottery funding to the arts in Wales

&
36 Prince's Drive Colwyn Bay LL29 8LA
Tel: 01492 533440
info@artswales.org.uk
www.artswales.org.uk

&
Bute Place Cardiff CF10 5AL
Tel: 02920 441 360
info@artswales.org.uk
www.artswales.org.uk

Arts in Therapy & Education (Institute for)
2-18 Britannia Row London N1 8PA
Tel: 020 7704 2534
info@artspsychotherapy.org
www.artspsychotherapy.org
Qualification in integrative arts psychotherapy and child therapy

Arts Marketing Association
7a Clifton Court Clifton Rd Cambridge CB1 7BN
Tel: 01223 578078
info@a-m-a.co.uk
www.a-m-a.org.uk
Works to improve professional development and the status of arts professionals

Artsline
21 Pine Court Wood Lodge Gardens Bromley BR1 2WA
Tel: 020 7388 2227
ceo@artsline.org.uk
www.artsline.org.uk
Advice service for disabled people on access to the arts and entertainment

Artswork National Youth Arts Development Agency
23 Basepoint Anderson Road Southampton SO14 5FE
Tel: 02380 682 535
info@artswork.org.uk
www.artswork.org.uk
National, independent youth arts development agency, committed to making a difference to the lives of young people at risk

ArtWatch UK
Tel: 0208 216 3492
artwatch.uk@gmail.com
www.artwatch.org.uk
Campaigning body of artists & art historians opposed to the damaging effects of modern, invasive restorations on our artistic heritage

Arvon Foundation The Foundation for Writing
Free Word Centre 60 Farringdon Road London EC1R 3GA
Tel: 020 7324 2554
london@arvonfoundation.org
www.arvonfoundation.org
Runs residential creative writing courses for adults and groups of young people at centres in Devon, Shropshire, W. Yorkshire and Inverness

ASBAH now see Shine

ASDAN
Wainbrook House Hudds Vale Rd St George Bristol BS5 7HY
Tel : 0117 941 1126
info@asdan.org.uk
www.asdan.org.uk
Curriculum development organisation and internationally recognised awarding body, offering programmes and qualifications that explicitly grow skills for learning, skills for employment and skills for life

ASH Action on Smoking and Health
First Floor 144-145 Shoreditch High Street London E1 6JE
Tel: 0207 739 5902
enquiries@ash.org.uk
www.ash.org.uk

ASH Scotland Action on Smoking and Health
8 Frederick St Edinburgh EH2 2HB
Tel: 0131 225 4725
ashscotland@ashscotland.org.uk
www.ashscotland.org.uk
Working for a tobacco-free Scotland

ASH Wales Action on Smoking and Health
2nd Floor, 8 Museum Place Cardiff CF10 3BG
Tel: 029 2064 1101
email via website
www.ashwales.org.uk
Towards a tobacco free Wales

Ashmolean Museum of Art and Archaeology
Beaumont St Oxford OX1 2PH
Tel: 01865 278002
www.ashmolean.org/

Asian People's Disability Alliance APDA
Suite 1A, 3rd Floor Alperton House Bridgewater Road Wembley Middlesex HA0 1EH
Tel: 020 8 902 2113
apdmcha@aol.com
www.apda.org.uk

Asiatic Society of Great Britain and Ireland (Royal)
14 Stephenson Way London NW1 2HD
Tel: 020 7388 4539
email via website
www.royalasiaticsociety.org
Provides a forum for those who are interested in the history, languages, cultures and religions of Asia to meet and exchange ideas. It offers lectures and seminars and it provides facilities for research and publishing

Ask The Police
www.askthe.police.uk/content
Access to the Police National Legal Database with an a-z of frequently asked questions including intended to reduce the number of non-emergency calls to police forces by providing the answers direct to the public via the Internet

Aslib see Information Management (Association for)

ASPE Association for the Study of Primary Education
The Swallow Barn Brandon Court Station Road Long Marston Herts HP23 4RA
mary@swallowbarn.fsnet.co.uk
www.aspe-uk.eu
Aims to promote and foster the development of informed and reflective study of Early Years and Primary Education

Aspect The Association of Professionals in Education and Children's Trusts
Woolley Hall Woolley Wakefield West Yorkshire WF4 2JR
Tel: 01226 383 428
info@aspect.org.uk
www.aspect.org.uk
Professional association and trade union

Aspire Supporting people with spinal injury
National Training Centre Wood Lane
Stanmore HA7 4AP
Tel: 020 8954 5759
info@aspire.org.uk
www.aspire.org.uk
Offers practical support to people living
with a spinal cord injury in the UK so that
they can lead fulfilled and independent lives
in their homes, with their families, in work
places and in leisure time

Assessment and Qualifications Alliance
see AQA

**Assisted Dying (Healthcare Professions
for)** HPAD
www.hpad.org.uk
Supporting greater patient choice at the end
of life

**Associated Board of the Royal Schools
of Music**
24 Portland Place London W1B 1LU
Tel: 020 7636 5400
Email via website
www.abrsm.org

**Association for the Protection of Rural
Scotland** see Rural Scotland (Association
for the Protection of)

Association of Colleges AOC
2-5 Stedham Place London WC1A 1HU
Tel: 020 7034 9900
enquiries@aoc.co.uk
www.aoc.co.uk
Promotes the interests of further education
colleges in England and Wales.

Asthma UK
Summit House 70 Wilson Street London
EC2A 2DB
Advice Line: 0800 121 62 44
Tel: 020 7786 4900
info@asthma.org.uk
www.asthma.org.uk
Independent UK charity

**Astrological and Psychic Society
(British)**
26 Second Avenue London W3 7RX
Tel: 0208 932 1145
email via website
www.baps.uk.com

Astronomical Association (British)
Burlington House Piccadilly London W1J
0DU
Tel: 0207 734 4145
Email via website
www.britastro.org

Astronomy see Dark Skies (Campaign for),
Popular Astronomy (Society for)

Asylum see also Immigration & Asylum
Tribunals Service

Asylum Aid
Club Union House 253-254 Upper Street
London N1 1RY
Advice line number: 0207 354 9264
Tel: 0207 354 9631
info@asylumaid.org.uk
www.asylumaid.org.uk
Free advice & legal representation to
refugees and asylum-seekers. Campaigns
for their rights

Ataxia UK
Lincoln House Kennington Park 1-3 Brixton
Road London SW9 6DE
Helpline: 0845 644 0606
Tel: 020 7582 1444
office@ataxia.org.uk
www.ataxia.org.uk
National charity working with and for
people affected by Friedreich's and other
cerebellars ataxias

ATD Fourth World
48 Addington Sq London SE5 7LB
Tel: 0207 703 3231
atd@atd-uk.org
www.atd-uk.org
Aims to eradicate extreme poverty
Organises summer volunteering
opportunities in Europe and long term
volunteer work worldwide

Athletic Association (English Schools')
ESAA
email via website
www.esaa.net
Governing body of schools athletics in
England

Athletics see also England Athletics,
scottishathletics, UK Sport, Welsh Athletics

**Athletics Federations (International
Association of)** IAAF
Email via website
www.iaaf.org

ATM locator
http://visa.via.infonow.net/locator/global/
Search facility to find ATMs worldwide

**Atmospheric Research (National Center
for)** NCAR
www.ncar.ucar.edu

ATSS see Social Sciences (Association for
the Teaching of the)

Attend
11-13 Cavendish Square London W1G 0AN
Tel: 0845 450 0285
info@attend.org.uk
www.attend.org.uk
Independent local charities which care
for and support people disadvantaged by
illness, age or disability

Attorney General's Office
20 Victoria Street London SW1H 0NF
Tel: 020 7271 2492
correspondenceunit@attorneygeneral.gsi.
gov.uk
www.attorneygeneral.gov.uk

Audit Commission
1st Floor Millbank Tower Millbank London
SW1P 4HQ
Textphone (minicom): 020 7630 0421
Tel: 020 7828 1212
Tel: 0844 798 1212
email via website
www.audit-commission.gov.uk
Helps to improve public services and
promotes the best use of public money

Audit Office (National)
157-197 Buckingham Palace Road London
SW1W 9SP
Helpdesk: 020 7798 7264
Tel: 020 7798 7000
enquiries@nao.gsi.gov.uk
www.nao.gov.uk
Monitors central government spending

Australian Bureau of Statistics
www.abs.gov.au

**Authors' Licensing and Collecting
Society**
The Writers' House 13 Haydon Street EC3N
1DB
Tel: 020 7264 5700
alcs@alcs.co.uk
www.alcs.co.uk

Autistic Society (National)
393 City Rd London EC1V 1NG
Helpline: 0808 800 4104
Tel: 020 7833 2299
nas@nas.org.uk
www.autism.org.uk
Helpline, information service and support
services

Automobile Association (AA)
www.theaa.com

AV Foundation Helping Transform Lives
Through Education
10 Market Place Devizes Wiltshire SN10
1HT
Tel: 01380 729009
av@aventure.co.uk

www.avfoundation.org
Channels funds into the rural areas to
which it sends volunteers. Objective is to
boost the quality of school education in
the communities served by AV (Africa Asia
Venture) volunteers

Avalanche Information Service see
sportscotland Avalanche Information
Service

AVERT
4 Brighton Rd Horsham West Sussex RH13
5BA
Tel: 01403 210202
info@avert.org
www.avert.org
Charity involved in HIV/AIDS education,
research and care projects worldwide

Avicultural Society
Sheraton Lodge Station Road Southminster
Essex CM0 7EW
admin@avisoc.co.uk
www.avisoc.co.uk
Covers the keeping and breeding of all types
of birds other than domesticated varieties

Award Scheme now see ASDAN

Awesome Library
www.awesomelibrary.org
American educational website

B

**BAAF Adoption and Fostering (British
Association for)**
Saffron House 6-10 Kirby Street London
EC1N 8TS
Tel: 0207 421 2600
mail@baaf.org.uk
www.baaf.org.uk

BAB see Aikido Board (British)

BABCP see Behavioural & Cognitive
Psychotherapies (British Association of)

Baby Lifeline
Empathy Enterprise Building Bramston
Crescent Tile Hill Coventry CV4 9SW
Tel: 024 7642 2135
info@babylifeline.org.uk
www.babylifeline.org.uk
Supports the care of pregnant mothers &
newborn babies

Baby Milk Action
34 Trumpington Street Cambridge CB2 1QY
Tel: 01223 464420
email via website
www.babymilkaction.org
Aims to save infant lives & end avoidable
suffering caused by inappropriate infant
feeding

Babyworld
www.babyworld.co.uk
Online magazine and discussion group

Baccalaureate see International
Baccalaureate Organization

Bach Centre
Mount Vernon Bakers Ln Brightwell-cum-
Sotwell Oxon OX10 0PZ
Consultation line: 01491 832 877
Tel: 01491 834 678
email via website
www.bachcentre.com
Home of Dr Edward Bach and the Bach
flower based remedies, information,
education & manufacture. Referral to
practitioners

Back-up Trust Transforming lives after
spinal cord injury
Jessica House Red Lion Square 191
Wandsworth High Street London SW18
4LS
Tel: 020 8875 1805
admin@backuptrust.org.uk
www.backuptrust.org.uk
Works with people paralysed through spinal
cord injury to rebuild self confidence and
independence

BackCare
16 Elmtree Rd Teddington TW11 8ST
Helpline: 0845 130 2704
Tel: 020 8977 5474
email via website
www.backcare.org.uk
National charity that aims to reduce the
impact of back pain on society. Provides
information and support

Backpackers Club
inforequest@backpackersclub.co.uk
www.backpackersclub.co.uk
A club for the lightweight camper, who
travels on foot, by bicycle, canoe or cross-
country ski

Badger Trust
PO Box 708 East Grinstead RH19 2WN
Tel: 08458 287878
email via website
www.badgertrust.org.uk
Promotes the conservation and welfare of
badgers and the protection of their setts and
habitats for the public benefit

Badminton England
National Badminton Centre Milton Keynes
MK8 9LA
Tel: 01908 268400
enquiries@badmintonengland.co.uk
www.badmintonengland.co.uk

BAHA Activity Holiday Association (British)
The Hollies Oak Bank Lane Hoole Village
Chester CH2 4ER
Tel: 01244 301342
info@baha.org.uk
www.baha.org.uk

Ballet see also Birmingham Royal Ballet,
Bolshoi Ballet, English National Ballet,
London Children's Ballet, National Youth
Ballet of Great Britain, Northern Ballet,
Royal Academy of Dance, Royal Ballet,
Scottish Ballet & see thematic guide Dance
and also section on Dance, Drama, Music &
Performing Arts Schools

Ballet Organization (British)
Woolborough House 39 Lonsdale Rd
Barnes London SW13 9JP
Tel: 020 8748 1241
info@bbo.org.uk
www.bbo.org.uk
A teaching and examining society for ballet,
jazz, modern and tap

Balloon and Airship Club (British)
Cushy Dingle Watery Lane Llanishen
Monmouthshire NP16 6QT
information@bbac.org
www.bbac.org

BALTIC The Centre for Contemporary Art
Gateshead Quays South Shore Rd
Gateshead NE8 3BA
Tel: 0191 478 1810
Text phone: 0191 440 4944
info@balticmill.com
www.balticmill.com

Banana Link
Suite 201 Sackville Place 44-48 Magdalen
Street Norwich NR3 1JU
Tel: 01603 765670
info@bananalink.org.uk
www.bananalink.org.uk
Working towards a fair and sustainable
banana industry

Bank of England
Threadneedle St London EC2R 8AH
Tel: 020 7601 4444 (switchboard)
Tel: 020 7601 4878 (public enquiries)
enquiries@bankofengland.co.uk
www.bankofengland.co.uk

**Bank of England (Damaged and
Mutilated Banknotes)**
The Manager, Dept MN, Bank of England
King Street Leeds LS1 1HT
Tel: 0113 244 1711
http://www.bankofengland.co.uk/banknotes/
damaged_banknotes.htm

Bank of England Museum
Threadneedle St London EC2R 8AH
Tel: 020 7601 5545
museum@bankofengland.co.uk
www.bankofengland.co.uk/museum
Free presentations for groups

Banking Ombudsman see Financial
Ombudsman Service

Bankruptcy Advisory Service Limited
PO Box 155 Knaresborough North
Yorkshire HG5 0UE
Tel: 01423 862114
gill@bankruptcyadvisoryservice.co.uk
www.bankruptcyadvisoryservice.co.uk

Baobab Centre for Young Survivors in Exile
6-9 Manor Gardens London N7 6LA
Tel: 020 7263 1301
email via website
www.baobabsurvivors.org
Specialises in therapeutic services to some
of the thousands of children, adolescents
and young people who arrive in Britain each
year fleeing from the trauma of political
violence

Bar Council
289-293 High Holborn London WC1V 7HZ
Tel: 020 7242 0082
ContactUs@BarCouncil.org.uk
www.barcouncil.org.uk
Regulatory & representative body for
barristers in England & Wales

Bar Pro Bono Unit
48 Chancery Lane London WC2A 1JF
Tel: 020 7092 3960
enquiries@barprobono.org.uk
www.barprobono.org.uk
Free legal advice and representation in
deserving cases where Legal Aid is not
available

Barbershop Singers (British Association of)
www.singbarbershop.com
Promoting the enjoyment of harmony singing

Barbican
Silk Street London EC2Y 8DS
Tel: 020 7638 4141 (switchboard)
Tel: 020 7382 7211 (Group Bookings)
Tel: 020 7638 8891 (Box Office &
membership)
email via website
www.barbican.org.uk

Barnardo's
Tanners Lane Barkingside Ilford IG6 1QG
Tel: 020 8550 8822
email via website
www.barnardos.org.uk

Campaigning, lobbying and research to
improve outcomes for children young people
and families. Works with families

Bartleby.com
www.bartleby.com/
Hundreds of out-of-copyright books, all
digitised and free

BASCA Songwriters, Composers and
Authors (British Academy of)
British Music House 26 Berners St London
W1T 3LR
email via website
www.basca.org.uk
Membership organisation for music writers
of all genres

Basel Action Network (BAN)
www.ban.org
Confronting the toxic trade (toxic wastes,
products and technologies) and its
devastating impacts.

BASIC Brain & Spinal Injury Centre
554 Eccles New Rd Salford M5 5AP
National Helpline: 0870 750 0000
Tel: 0161 707 6441
enquiries@basiccharity.org.uk
www.basiccharity.org.uk
Provides counselling, information and
support to patients and their families
following brain or spinal injury

Basketball Association (English)
PO Box 3971 Sheffield S9 9AZ
Tel: 0114 284 1060
info@englandbasketball.co.uk
www.englandbasketball.co.uk
Governing body

BASPCAN British Association for the Study
and Prevention of Child Abuse and Neglect
17 Priory St York YO1 6ET
Tel: 01904 613605
baspcan@baspcan.org.uk
www.baspcan.org.uk
Registered charity that aims to prevent
physical, emotional and sexual abuse
and neglect of children by promoting the
physical, emotional, and social well-being
of children. Aims to promote the rights
of children as citizens, through multi-
disciplinary collaboration, education,
campaigning etc

Bat Conservation Trust
5th Floor Quadrant House 250 Kennington
Lane London SE11 5RD
Helpline: 0845 1300 228
enquiries@bats.org.uk
www.bats.org.uk

Battersea Dogs Home
4 Battersea Park Rd London SW8 4AA
Tel: 020 7622 3626
email via website
www.battersea.org.uk

BBC
www.bbc.co.uk

BBC Backstage Tours
www.bbc.co.uk/showsandtours/tours

BBC Health
www.bbc.co.uk/health/conditions
Access to information about a wide range of
illnesses and conditions

BBC News
http://news.bbc.co.uk

BBC Online
www.bbc.co.uk
Covers all BBC programmes plus sections
on business, health, lifestyle, science

BBC Schools
Email via website
www.bbc.co.uk/schools

BBC Studio Audiences
www.bbc.co.uk/tickets/
Apply for free tickets to watch live &
recorded TV shows

BBC World Service
www.bbc.co.uk/worldservice

BCS – Chartered Institute for IT
1st Floor, Block D North Star House North
Star Ave Swindon SN2 1FA
Tel: 01793 417424
Tel: 0845 300 4417 (lo-call rate)
Email via website
www.bcs.org/
Promotes the global IT profession and the
interests of individuals engaged in that
profession for the benefit of all

BDA see Dyslexia Association (British)

BDA Northern Ireland
The Mount 2 Woodstock Link Belfast BT6
8DD
Tel: 02890 735 856
www.bda.org
National professional association for dentists

& Scotland
Forsyth House Lomond Court Castle
Business Park Stirling FK9 4TU
Tel: 01786 476040
www.bda.org

& Wales
4th Floor, 2 Caspian Point Caspian Way
Cardiff Bay CF10 4DQ
Tel: 029 2049 6174
www.bda.org

Beamish
Beamish Museum Beamish Co. Durham
DH9 0RG
Tel: 0191 370 4000
museum@beamish.org.uk
www.beamish.org.uk
Recreates Northern life in the early 1800s
and 1900s.

BEAT Beating Eating Disorders
103 Prince of Wales Rd Norwich NR1 1DW
Helpline: 0845 634 1414 & Youthline: 0845
634 7650
Tel: 01603 619090
Head Office: 0300 123 3355
help@b-eat.co.uk
fyp@b-eat.co.uk
www.b-eat.co.uk
Raises awareness & offers support to people
affected by eating disorders

Beatbullying Shaping attitudes, changing
behaviours
Rochester House Units 1, 4 & 5 4
Belvedere Road London SE19 2AT
Tel: 0208 771 3377
info@beatbullying.org
www.beatbullying.org
Empowers people to understand, recognise,
and say no to bullying, violence and
harassment by giving them the tools to
transform their lives and the lives of their
peers. Working with families, schools, and
communities

Beaumont Society
27 Old Gloucester St London WC1N 3XX
Information Line: 01582 412 220
enquiries@beaumontsociety.org.uk
www.beaumontsociety.org.uk
Transgender support group

Befrienders Worldwide with Samaritans
www.befrienders.org
Work worldwide to provide emotional
support, and reduce suicide

**Behavioural & Cognitive
Psychotherapies (British Association
for)** BABCP
Imperial House Hornby Street Bury BL9
5BN
Tel: 0161 705 4304
babcp@babcp.com
www.babcp.com

Benefits Agency see Work & Pensions
(Department for)

Benesh Institute
c/o Royal Academy of Dance 36 Battersea
Sq London SW11 3RA
Tel: 020 7326 8000
info@rad.org.uk
www.benesh.org
Training organisation and governing body of
Benesh movement notation system

Bereavement Network (London)
61 Philpot Street London E1 2JH
info@bereavement.org.uk
www.bereavement.org.uk
Forum for bereavement issues in Greater
London. Referral line for bereavement
support

Berlin info
www.berlin-info.de/en/index
Comprehensive information about Berlin

Berlin International
www.berlin.de/international/index.en.php
Berlin's official Internet site

BESO now see VSO

Better Seating (Campaign for)
www.betterseating.org
Information about the importance of chair
design

Better Transport (Campaign for)
16 Waterside 44-48 Wharf Road London
N1 7UX
Tel: 020 7566 6480
info@bettertransport.org.uk
www.bettertransport.org.uk
Sustainable transport campaign aiming to
reduce car dependence

Bevan Foundation
FREEPOST RSHC-XZZU-UTUU Innovation
Centre Festival Drive Ebbw Vale Blaenau
Gwent NP23 8XA
Tel: 01495 356 702
info@bevanfoundation.org
www.bevanfoundation.org
Radical Welsh think tank concerned with
social justice

BFI see British Film Institute

BHF see British Heart Foundation

Bibic
Knowle Hall Bridgwater Somerset TA7 8PJ
Tel: 01278 684060
info@bibic.org.uk
www.bibic.org.uk
Works to help maximise the potential of
children with conditions affecting behaviour,
sensory processing, communication, social,
motor and learning abilities.

Bible Society
Stonehill Green Westlea Swindon SN5 7DG
Tel: 01793 418 222
email via website
www.biblesociety.org.uk
Involved in translation and retranslation
projects worldwide. Work to change the
public's perception of the Bible in England
& Wales

Bibliomania
www.bibliomania.com
Literary texts (particularly those set for
exams) available online

Bibliothèque Nationale de France see
Library of France (National)

Bicycle Helmet Initiative Trust
71 Milford Rd Reading RG1 8LG
Tel: 0118 958 3585
BHIT@dial.pipex.com
www.bhit.org
Promoting and educating about the need to
wear bicycle helmets

Big Bus
Sherston Software Angel House Sherston
Wiltshire SN16 0LH
Tel: 01666 843200
support@sherston.co.uk
www.thebigbus.com
Fun interactive learning for 3-11 year-olds

Big Issue
1-5 Wandsworth Road Vauxhall
LondonSW8 2LN
Tel: 020 7526 3200
info@bigissue.coom
www.bigissue.com
Exists to offer homeless and vulnerably
housed people the opportunity to earn a
legitimate income by selling the weekly
magazine. This selling opportunity is
planned to extend to long term unemployed
and other vulnerable groups

Big Lottery Fund
1 Plough Place London EC4A 1DE
BIG advice line: 0845 410 2030
Tel: 020 7211 1800
Tel: 0300 500 5050
Textphone: 0845 602 1659
general.enquiries@biglotteryfund.org.uk
www.biglotteryfund.org.uk
Lottery distribution organisation awarding
funds for community projects

Big Pit
Blaenafon Torfaen NP4 9XP
Tel: 01495 790 311
Email via website
www.museumwales.ac.uk/en/bigpit
National Coal Museum

Big Read (The)
www.campaignforeducation.org/bigread/
Campaign against illiteracy and for a decent
education for all

BIHR British Institute of Human Rights
School of Law Queen Mary University of
London Mile End Road London E1 4NS
Tel: 020 7882 5850
info@bihr.org.uk
www.bihr.org.uk

Bike Events
PO Box 2127 Bristol BS99 7LN
Email via website
www.bike-events.com
Organises fund raising and recreational
cycle rides

Bike Express (European)
3 Newfield Lane South Cave Hull HU15
2JW
Tel: 01430 422 111
info@bike-express.co.uk
www.bike-express.co.uk
Offer bike transport for you and your bike
into Europe

Bike Links see Cycling Projects

**Bikers with a Disability (National
Association for)**
Unit 20 The Bridgewater Centre Robson
Avenue Urmston Manchester M41 7TE
Tel: 0844 415 4849
office@nabd.org.uk
www.nabd.org.uk
Helps disabled people to enjoy the freedom
and independence of motorcycling

**Bilingualism & Literacies Education
Network** blen
35 Connaught Rd London N4 4NT
Tel: 020 7281 8686
ask@blen-education.org.uk
www.blen-education.org.uk

**Bill Douglas Centre for the History of
Cinema & Popular Culture** see History of
Cinema & Popular Culture (The Bill Douglas
Centre for the)

Bioethics (Nuffield Council on)
28 Bedford Square London WC1B 3JS
Tel: 020 7681 9619
bioethics@nuffieldbioethics.org
www.nuffieldbioethics.org
Examining ethical issues around
developments in medicine and biology

Biological Diversity (Convention on)
www.cbd.int
International treaty to sustain the rich
diversity of life on Earth

Biology (Society of)
12 Roger Street London WC1N 2JU
email via website
www.societyofbiology.org
Advising Government and influencing policy;
advancing education and professional
development; supporting our members, and
engaging and encouraging public interest in
the life sciences

**Biotechnology & Biological Sciences
Research Council** BBSRC
Polaris House North Star Avenue Swindon
Wiltshire SN2 1UH
Tel: 01793 413200
email via website
www.bbsrc.ac.uk/life
Explores the science & issues of modern
biological research

Bird Council (British)
Hampstead House Condover Road West
Heath Birmingham B31 3QY
Tel: 0121 476 5999
info@britishbirdcouncil.com
www.britishbirdcouncil.com

Birmingham Royal Ballet
Thorp St Birmingham B5 4AU
Tel: 0121 245 3500
info@brb.org.uk
www.brb.org.uk

Birmingham Settlement
Units 4-7 Alma House Newtown Shopping
Centre Birmingham B19 2AB
Tel: 0121 250 3000
www.birminghamsettlement.org.uk
A multi-purpose inner city charity tackling
social disadvantage

Birth Defects Foundation see Newlife
Foundation for Disabled Children

Birth Trauma Association Helping people
traumatised by childbirth
PO Box 671 Ipswich Suffolk IP1 9AT
enquiries@birthtraumaassociation.org.uk
www.birthtraumaassociation.org.uk
Support for women suffering from Post Natal
Post Traumatic Stress Disorder (PTSD) or
birth trauma

BirthChoice UK
www.birthchoiceuk.com
To help make the right decisions about
where to have a baby

BIS see Business Innovation & Skills
(Department for)

Bitesize: BBC revision web site
www.bbc.co.uk/schools/bitesize/
For KS2, 3 & 4 / Standard Grade

BKA British Kodály Academy
c/o 10 Lapwing Close South Croydon
Surrey CR2 8TD
Tel: 020 8651 3728
enquiries@britishkodalyacademy.org
www.britishkodalyacademy.org
Musical literacy through singing

Black Environment Network
1st Floor 60 High St Llanberis LL55 4EU
Tel: 0121 643 6387
ukoffice@ben-network.org.uk
www.ben-network.org.uk
Networking organisation working for full
ethnic participation in the built & natural
environment

Black History Month
www.black-history-month.co.uk

Black Police Association (National)
PO Box 15690
  Tamworth Staffordshire B77 9HZ
Tel: 07971 162821
Email via website
www.nationalbpa.com

Black Training & Enterprise Group
2nd Floor Lancaster House 31-33 Islington
High Street London N1 9LH
Tel: 020 7843 6110
info@bteg.co.uk
www.bteg.co.uk
Seeks to ensure fair access and outcomes
for black communities in employment,
enterprise and regeneration

Black Women for Wages for Housework
contact Crossroads Women's Centre
www.allwomencount.net

Black Women's Rape Action Project
contact Crossroads Women's Centre
www.allwomencount.net

Bladder and Bowel Foundation (B&BF)
SATRA Innovation Park Rockingham Road
Kettering Northants NN16 9JH
Helpline: 0845 345 0165
Tel: 01536 533255
info@bladderandbowelfoundation.org
www.bladderandbowelfoundation.org
The UK's largest advocacy charity providing
information and support for all types of
bladder and bowel related problems,
including incontinence, prostate problems,
constipation and Diverticular Disease, for
patients, their families, carers and healthcare
professionals

Blenheim CDP The London Drug Agency
Head Office
  66 Bolton Crescent London SE5 0SE
Tel: 020 7582 2200
info@blenheimcdp.org.uk

www.blenheimcdp.org.uk
Substance misuse charity working across
London to reduce the harm caused by
drug misuse to individuals and the public.
Provides opportunity and help for people to
end their dependency on drugs

Blind see also Braille Chess Association,
ClearVision Project, Deafblind UK,
Deafblind Scotland, Guide Dogs for
the Blind Association, Listening Books,
Partially Sighted Society, Sense, RNIB,
RNIB National Library Service, SeeAbility,
Sightsavers, Talking Newspapers and
Magazines (National), Wireless for the Blind
Fund (British)

Blind (National Library for the) see RNIB
National Library Service

Blind (Royal National Institute of the)
RNIB
105 Judd St London WC1H 9NE
Helpline: 0303 123 9999
Tel: 020 7388 1266
helpline@rnib.org.uk
www.rnib.org.uk
Supporting blind and partially sighted people

Blind Golf Association (English)
email via website
www.blindgolf.co.uk

Blind in Business
4th floor 1 London Wall Buildings London
EC2M 5PG
Tel: 020 7588 1885
info@blindinbusiness.org.uk
www.blindinbusiness.co.uk
Helping blind and partially sighted people
into work

**Blind of the United Kingdom (National
Federation of the)**
Sir John Wilson House 215 Kirkgate
Wakefield WF1 1JG
Tel: 01924 291 313
nfbuk@nfbuk.org
www.nfbuk.org
Campaigning organisation for a better
quality of life for blind and partially sighted
people

Blind People (Action for)
14-16 Verney Rd London SE16 3DZ
Helpline: 0303 123 9999
Tel: 020 7635 4800
Email via website
www.actionforblindpeople.org.uk
Employment support, hotels, supported
housing, out-of-school clubs for visually
impaired children, grants, information and
advice

Blind Sport (British)
Pure Offices, Plato Close Tachbrook Park
Leamington Spa Warwickshire CV34 6WE
Tel: 01926 424247
info@britishblindsport.org.uk
www.britishblindsport.org.uk
Encourages blind and partially sighted
children and adults to take part in sport and
recreation

Bliss – the premature baby charity
9 Holyrood Street London SE1 2EL
Family Support Helpline: 0500 618 140
Tel: 020 7378 1122
RNID typetalk 018001 0500 618140
information@bliss.org.uk
www.bliss.org.uk
National charity dedicated to improving both
the survival and long-term quality of life for
babies born too soon, too small or too sick
to cope on their own

Bliss Scotland
PO Box 29198 Dunfermline KY12 2BB
Tel: 0845 157 0077
scotland@bliss.org.uk
www.bliss.org.uk

Blogger
www.blogger.com
A site to help you create and manage a
weblog

Blood Pressure Association
60 Cranmer Terrace London SW17 0QS
Blood Pressure Information Line: 0845 241
0989
Tel: 020 8772 4994
info@bpassoc.org.uk
www.bpassoc.org.uk
Information and support to the general
public on problems of high blood pressure

Blood Service (National) see NHS Blood
and Transplant

Blue Badge Network
11 Parson's Street Dudley DY1 1JJ OR
198 Wolverhampton Street Dudley DY1 1DZ
Tel: 01384 257001
headoffice@bluebadgenetwork.org.uk
www.bluebadgenetwork.org
Assists disabled people, and their families to
integrate with society to overcome access
problems. Seeks to maintain the integrity
and validity of the concessionary parking
permit

Blue Cross
Shilton Rd Burford Oxon OX18 4PF
Tel: 01993 822 651
info@bluecross.org.uk
www.bluecross.org.uk
Animal welfare charity

BMA see British Medical Association
BMAS see Acupuncture Society (British
Medical)

BNTL-Freeway British National
Temperance League
30 Keswick Road Worksop S81 7PT
Tel: 01909 477882
bntl@btconnect.com
www.bntl.org
The 'Freeway' newsletter provides drug and
alcohol resources based around the national
curriculum

Boarding Concern
www.boardingconcern.org.uk
Represents people who have concerns
about the practice of boarding education for
the young and the effect on these people
as adults. This website offers a voice
and provides information and support to
ex-boarders, current boarders and those
thinking of boarding

Boardsailing Association (UK) now see
Windsurfing Association

Bob Champion Cancer Trust
6 Old Garden House The Lanterns Bridge
Lane London SW11 3AD
Tel: 020 7924 3553
info@bobchampion.org.uk
www.bobchampion.org.uk
Aims to identify cancer genes and ultimately
eradicate male cancers

Bodleian Library
Main Enquiry Desk Bodleian Library Broad
Street Oxford OX1 3BG
Tel: 01865 277162
reader.services@bodleian.ox.ac.uk
www.bodleian.ox.ac.uk/bodley
Main research library of the University of
Oxford and copyright deposit library

Body Positive North West
39 Russell Road Whalley Range
Manchester M16 8DH
Helpline: 0161 882 2202
Tel: 0161 882 2200
info@bpnw.org.uk
www.bpnw.org.uk
Service provider for people affected and
infected by HIV/AIDS

Body Shop Foundation
Watersmead Littlehampton West Sussex
BN17 6LS
Tel: 01903 844 039
bodyshopfoundation@thebodyshop.com
www.thebodyshopfoundation.org
Human/civil rights projects, animals &
environment. No unsolicited requests for
support

Bolshoi Ballet
www.bolshoi.ru/en

Bolton Lads & Girls Club
18 Spa Road Bolton BL1 4AG
Tel: 01204 540 100
info@blgc.co.uk
www.boltonladsandgirlsclub.co.uk
The UK's biggest youth centre

Bond
Regent's Wharf 8 All Saints Street London
N1 9RL
Tel: 020 7837 8344
advocacy@bond.org.uk
www.bond.org.uk
The UK's broadest network of voluntary
organisations working in international
development

Bone Marrow donation see Anthony
Nolan, NHS Blood and Transplant

Book Aid International
39-41 Coldharbour Lane Camberwell
London SE5 9NR
Tel: 020 7733 3577
info@bookaid.org
www.bookaid.org
Works in partnership with organisations in
developing countries to support their work in
literacy, education, training and publishing

Book Fair see Frankfurt Book Fair

Book Festival see Edinburgh International
Book Festival, Hay Festival

Book Power
120 Pentonville Road London N1 9JN
Tel: 020 7843 1938
info@bookpower.org
www.bookpower.org
Making available the best, most relevant
textbooks to university and vocational
students in low-income countries at prices
which students and their institutions'
libraries can afford

Book Trust (Scottish)
Sandeman House Trunk's Close 55 High St
Edinburgh EH1 1SR
Tel: 0131 524 0160
info@scottishbooktrust.com
www.scottishbooktrust.com
Scotland's national agency for readers and
writers. Provides key services to readers,
writers and the educational sector

BookCrossing
www.bookcrossing.com
Encourages readers to leave books for
others in a public place and tracks their
progress via the web

Books Council (Welsh)
www.wbc.org.uk
www.wbc.org.uk/gwales
National body which provides a focus for the
publishing industry in Wales

Booktrust
Book House 45 East Hill London SW18
2QZ
Tel: 020 8516 2977
query@booktrust.org.uk
www.booktrust.org.uk
www.booktrustchildrensbooks.org.uk
Book information service, reading resource
centre, book prizes, projects and National
Children's Book Week

Border and Immigration Agency now see
UK Border Agency

Borderline
22 City Road London EC1Y 2AJ
Tel: 0845 456 2190
Tel: 0800 174047
email via website
www.borderline-uk.org
Advice, information & support to homeless
Scots in London

Born Free Foundation
3 Grove House Foundry Lane Horsham
RH13 5PL
Tel: 01403 240 170
info@bornfree.org.uk
www.bornfree.org.uk
Animal welfare and conservation charity.
Works to prevent individual animal suffering,
protect threatened species and keep wildlife
in the wild

Botanic Garden of Wales (National)
Llanarthne Carmarthenshire SA32 8HG
Tel: 01558 668 768
info@gardenofwales.org.uk
www.gardenofwales.org.uk

Botanic Gardens see Royal Botanic
Gardens, Edinburgh & Kew

Botanical Society of the British Isles
Botany Department The Natural History
Museum Cromwell Rd London SW7 5BD
email via website
www.bsbi.org.uk

Bounty Healthcare Fund
www.bounty.com/charity
Raises funds for good causes which make
family life easier

Bowel Cancer UK
7 Rickett St London SW6 1RU
Helpline: 0800 8 40 35 40
Tel: 020 7381 9711
admin@bowelcanceruk.org.uk or advisory@
bowelcanceruk.org.uk

www.bowelcanceruk.org.uk
National charity. Aims to save lives by raising awareness of bowel cancer, campaigning for best treatment and care and providing practical support and advice.

Bowling see also Crown Green Bowling Association (British), Women's Bowling Federations (English)

Bowling Association Ltd (English Indoor)
David Cornwell House Bowling Green Melton Mowbray LE13 0FA
Tel: 01664 481900
enquiries@eiba.co.uk
www.eiba.co.uk
National governing body for indoor level green bowls in England

Bowling Federation (English)
www.fedbowls.co.uk

Boxing see Amateur Boxing Association of England Ltd., Amateur Boxing Scotland Ltd.

Boys' Brigade
Felden Lodge Hemel Hempstead HP3 0BL
Tel: 01442 231 681
enquiries@boys-brigade.org.uk
www.boys-brigade.org.uk
Uniform youth organisation for children and young people

BPAS British Pregnancy Advisory Service
20 Timothys Bridge Road Stratford Enterprise Park Stratford-upon-Avon CV37 9BF
Actionline: 08457 30 40 30
Tel: 0870 365 5050
info@bpas.org
www.bpas.org
Non-profit making charity offering advice and treatment for unplanned pregnancy and fertility control

Braille Chess Association
customerservices@braillechess.org.uk
www.braillechess.org.uk
Promoting and supporting visually impaired chess players in the UK

Brain & Spinal Injury Centre see BASIC

Brain & Spine Foundation
3.36 Canterbury Court Kennington Park 1-3 Brixton Road London SW9 6DE
Helpline: 0808 808 1000
Tel: 020 7793 5900
info@brainandspine.org.uk
www.brainandspine.org.uk
A registered charity supporting neuroscience research projects. Offers information service and education

Brain Injuries see BASIC, BIBIC, Child Brain Injury Trust, HEADWAY

Brainwave Unlocking Children's Potential
Huntworth Gate Bridgwater Somerset TA6 6LQ
Tel: 01278 429 089
Email via website
www.brainwave.org.uk
Therapy & rehabilitation for children with special needs

Brake
PO Box 548 Huddersfield HD1 2XZ
Helpline: 0845 603 8570
Tel: 01484 559 909
helpline@brake.org.uk
www.brake.org.uk
Road safety organisation

Brandon Centre
26 Prince of Wales Rd London NW5 3LG
Tel: 020 7267 4792
reception@brandon-centre.org.uk
www.brandon-centre.org.uk
Free counselling, psychotherapy and contraceptive advice for 12-21 year olds

Brathay Exploration Group
Brathay Hall Ambleside Cumbria LA22 0HP
Tel: 015394 33942
email via website
www.brathayexploration.org.uk
Expeditions in wild parts of the world for 16-25 year olds

Brazil's Children Trust (Action for)
Level 4, 53 Frith Street London W1D 4SN
Tel: 020 7494 9344
info@abctrust.org.uk
www.abctrust.org.uk
Aims to relieve suffering, maintain and educate deprived, children, young people and their families

Breakthrough Breast Cancer
Weston House 246 High Holborn London WC1V 7EX
Freephone Info Line: 08080 100 200
Tel: 020 7025 2400
info@breakthrough.org.uk
www.breakthrough.org.uk
Research, campaigning and education – removing the fear of breast cancer

Breast Cancer Care
5-13 Great Suffolk Street London SE1 0NS
Helpline: 0808 800 6000
Textphone: 0808 800 6001
info@breastcancercare.org.uk
www.breastcancercare.org.uk
National organisation offering support and information

Breastfeeding see La Leche League GB

BRIT School for Performing Arts and Technology
60 The Crescent Croydon CR0 2HN
Tel: 020 8665 5242
admin@brit.croydon.sch.uk
www.brit.croydon.sch.uk
Britain's only FREE Performing Arts and Technology School. Dedicated to education and vocational training for the performing arts, media, art and design and the technologies that make performance possible

British Association for the Advancement of Science (BA) now see Science Association (British)

British Council
Bridgewater House 58 Whitworth Street Manchester M1 6BB
Tel: 0161 957 7755
general.enquiries@britishcouncil.org
www.britishcouncil.org/
Cultural, educational & technical co-operation between Britain & other countries

British Film Institute BFI
Belvedere Road South Bank Waterloo London SE1 8XT
Tel: 020 7928 3232
Email via website
www.bfi.org.uk

British Heart Foundation
Greater London House 180 Hampstead Road London NW1 7AW
Heart HelpLine: 0300 330 3311
Tel: 020 7554 0000
supporterservices@bhf.org.uk
www.bhf.org.uk
Leading heart research charity

British Jews (Board of Deputies of)
6 Bloomsbury Square London WC1A 2LP
Tel: 020 7543 5400
info@bod.org.uk
www.bod.org.uk
Elected representative body of the British Jewish community.

British Legion (Royal)
199 Borough High Street London SE1 1AA
Legionline: 08457 725 725
Tel: 020 3207 2100
email via website
www.britishlegion.org.uk
Safeguarding the welfare, interests and memory of those who have served in the Armed Forces

British Library
St Pancras 96 Euston Rd London NW1 2DB
Tel: 0843 2081144
Minicom: 01937 546860

Customer-Services@bl.uk
www.bl.uk
Hold 14 million books, 920,000 journal and newspaper titles, 58 million patents and 3 million sound recordings

British Library Sound Archive
96 Euston Rd London NW1 2DB
Tel: 020 7412 7831
email via website
www.bl.uk/soundarchive
Holds recordings of popular, classical & world and traditional music, oral history, drama and literature and wildlife sounds

British Medical Association BMA
BMA House Tavistock Sq London WC1H 9JP
Tel: 020 7387 4499
Email via website
www.bma.org.uk
Voluntary professional association for doctors

British Monarchy (The official website of)
email via website
www.royal.gov.uk

British Museum
Great Russell St London WC1B 3DG
Tel: 020 7323 8299
Tel: 020 7323 8000
information@britishmuseum.org
www.britishmuseum.org

British Overseas NGOs for Development see Bond

British Pregnancy Advisory Service see BPAS

British Rowing
6 Lower Mall Hammersmith London W6 9DJ
Tel: 020 8237 6700
info@britishrowing.org
www.britishrowing.org
Governing body for rowing in GB

British Standards Institute BSI
389 Chiswick High Rd London W4 4AL
Tel: 020 8996 9001
cservices@bsigroup.com
www.bsigroup.com
National body producing standards and technical regulations for industry and small businesses

Brittle Bone Society
Grant-Paterson House 30 Guthrie St Dundee DD1 5BS
Tel: 01382 204446
contact@brittlebone.org
www.brittlebone.org
Promotes research & supports people with osteogenesis imperfecta and their families

Broadcasting Standards Commission
now see OFCOM

Broadcasting Trust (International)
CAN Mezzanine 32-6 Loman Street London
SE1 0EH
Tel: 020 7922 7940
mail@ibt.org.uk
www.ibt.org.uk
Educational charity & independent TV
production company specialising in
development, environment and human rights
issues

Broadway
15 Half Moon Court Bartholomew Close
London EC1A 7H
Tel: 020 7710 0550
reception@broadwaylondon.org
http://broadway.jamkit.com
Support & rehousing services to homeless
people in London

Broken Rainbow UK
J414 Tower Bridge Business Complex 100
Clements Rd London SE16 4DG
Helpline: 0300 999 5428
Tel: 08452 60 55 60
mail@broken-rainbow.org.uk

www.broken-rainbow.org.uk/
Support for lesbian, gay, bisexual and
transgender (LGBT) people experiencing
domestic violence

Brontë Parsonage Museum & Brontë Society
Haworth Keighley West Yorkshire BD22
8DR
Tel: 01535 642 323
info@bronte.org.uk
www.bronte.info

Brook
421 Highgate Studios 53-79 Highgate Rd
London NW5 1TL
Tel: 0808 802 1234 (Free & confidential
information for under 25s)
Tel: 020 7284 6040
admin@brook.org.uk
www.brook.org.uk
Free sexual health & contraceptive advice
service for young people under 25

Brooke
30 Farringdon Street London EC4A 4HH
Tel: 0203 012 3456
Email via website
www.thebrooke.org
Dedicated to improving the lives of working
horses, donkeys and mules in some of the
world's poorest communities. Operating
across Africa, Asia and Latin America

BSES Expeditions
Royal Geographical Society 1 Kensington
Gore London SW7 2AR
Tel: 020 7591 3141
info@bses.org.uk
www.bses.org.uk
Runs adventure and research expeditions for
16-20 year olds

BSI see British Standards Institute

BTCV British Trust for Conservation
Volunteers
Sedum House Mallard Way Doncaster DN4
8DB
Tel: 01302 388883
information@btcv.org.uk
www2.btcv.org.uk
Working with people to bring about positive
environmental change

BTCV Scotland
Balallan House 24 Allan Park Stirling FK8
2QG
Tel: 01786 479697
scotland@htcv.org.uk
www2.btcv.org.uk/display/btcv_scotland

BTCV Wales
The Conservation Centre Forest Farm Road
Whitchurch Cardiff CF14 7JJ
Tel: 029 2052 0990
wales@btcv.org.uk
www2.btcv.org.uk/display/btcv_wales
Scottish environmental conservation charity

BTEC see Edexel

BUAV
16A Crane Grove London N7 8NN
Tel: 020 7700 4888
info@buav.org
www.buav.org
Campaigns peacefully to create a world
where nobody wants or believes we need to
experiment on animals

Buddhist Centre (North London)
72 Holloway Rd London N7 8JG
Tel: 020 7700 1177
email via website
www.northlondonbuddhistcentre.com

Buddhist Information Network
www.buddhanet.net

Buddhist Society
58 Eccleston Sq London SW1V 1PH
Tel: 020 7834 5858
info@thebuddhistsociety.org
www.thebuddhistsociety.org
Centre teaching Buddhism and meditation.
Also large Buddhist library and bookshop

Budgerigar Society
Spring Gardens Northampton NN1 1DR
Tel: 01604 624549
www.budgerigarsociety.com

Bugatti Trust
Prescott Hill Gotherington Cheltenham
Gloucestershire GL52 9RD
Tel: 01242 677201
Email via website
www.bugatti-trust.co.uk
To preserve and make available for study the
works of Ettore Bugatti

Building & Social Housing Foundation
BSHF
Memorial Square Coalville Leicestershire
LE67 3TU
Tel: 01530 510444
bshf@bshf.org
www.bshf.org
Carries out research into low cost housing
around the world

Building Societies see also Ecology
Building Society, Financial Ombudsman
Service

Building Societies Members Association
49 Clifford Avenue Taunton Somerset TA2
6DL
Tel: 01823 321 304
Info@building-societies-members.org.uk
www.building-societies-members.org.uk
Fighting to maintain mutuality &
accountability of the building societies to
their members

Bully Free Zone
50 Chorley New Road
  Bolton BL1 4AP
Tel: 01204 454 958
office@bullyfreezone.co.uk
www.bullyfreezone.co.uk
Provides a service for children and young
people who have issues around bullying

Bullying see also Anti-Bullying Alliance,
Anti-Bullying Network, Beatbullying,
Childline, CyberMentors, Kidscape

Bullying UK
CAN Mezzanine 49-51 East Road London
N1 6AH
Parentline: 0808 800 2222 (free)
Tel: 020 7553 3080
help@bullying.co.uk
www.bullying.co.uk
Part of Family Lives, a national charity
providing help and support in all aspects of
family life. Offers advice to young people
and parents and guidance for schools

Bungee Jumping see Elastic Rope Sports
Association (British)

Burma Campaign UK
28 Charles Square London N1 6HT
Tel: 020 73244710
info@burmacampaign.org.uk
www.burmacampaign.org.uk
Human rights & democracy in Burma

Burrell Collection
Pollok Country Park 2060 Pollokshaws Rd
Glasgow G43 1AT
Tel: 0141 287 2550
Text Phone: 0141 287 0047
museums@glasgowlife.org.uk
www.glasgowmuseums.com
A unique art collection including medieval
art, tapestries and stained glass

Bus Users UK
PO Box 119 Shepperton TW17 8UX
Tel: 01932 232574
enquiries@bususers.org
www.bususers.org
To give bus passengers a voice

Business & Professional Women UK Ltd
74 Fairfield Rise Billericay Essex CM12
9NU
Tel: 01277 623 867
hq@bpwuk.co.uk
www.bpwuk.co.uk
Lobbying training and networking
organisation for working women

**Business & Technology Education
Council (BTEC)** see Edexel

Business Gateway
Tel: 0845 609 6611
www.bgateway.com
Practical help, advice and support for new
and growing businesses in Scotland

Business in Sport & Leisure BISL
Tel: 020 8255 3782
email via website
www.bisl.org
Umbrella organisation for private sector
companies

Business in the Community
137 Shepherdess Walk London N1 7RQ
Tel: 020 7566 8650
information@bitc.org.uk
www.bitc.org.uk
Companies across the UK committed to
improving their positive impact on society

**Business, Enterprise and Regulatory
Reform (Department for)** now see
Business Innovation & Skills (Department
for)

**Business, Innovation & Skills
(Department for)** BIS
1 Victoria St London SW1H 0ET
Tel: 020 7215 5000

Minicom: 020 7215 6740
email via website
www.bis.gov.uk/

Butterfly Conservation
Manor Yard East Lulworth Wareham
Dorset BH20 5QP
Tel: 01929 400 209
info@butterfly-conservation.org
www.butterfly-conservation.org
UK charity taking action to save butterflies,
moths and their habitats

& N. Ireland
3 New Line Crossgar Downpatrick BT30
9EP
Tel: 07584 597690
bcni@btconnect.com
www.butterfly-conservation.org

& Scotland
Balallan House Allan Park Stirling FK8 2QG
Tel: 01786 447753
scotland@butterfly-conservation.org
www.butterfly-conservation.org

& Wales
10 Calvert Terrace Swansea SA1 6AR
Tel: 01792 642972
wales@butterfly-conservation.org
www.butterfly-conservation.org

Butterfly Project
Magdalen House 3 Magdalen Street Eye
Suffolk IP23 7AJ
www.recoveryourlife.com
Created for self-harmers who feel they are
ready to stop and need the motivation or
support to do so

Buy Nothing Day (UK)
www.buynothingday.co.uk
Challenges consumer culture. Takes place
on the last Saturday in November

Byways & Bridleways Trust
PO Box 117 Newcastle upon Tyne NE3 5YT
editor@bbtrust.org.uk
www.bbtrust.org.uk
Registered charity, formed to protect the
public rights that exist over the many ancient
lanes that form part the British landscape
and, our traditional means of travel

C

CAA Civil Aviation Authority
CAA House 45-59 Kingsway London
WC2B 6TE
Tel: 020 7379 7311
infoservices@caa.co.uk
www.caa.co.uk
Responsible for air safety, economic

regulation, airspace regulation, consumer
protection, environmental research and
consultancy

CAAT see Campaign Against Arms Trade

CABE now see Design Council

Cabinet Office
70 Whitehall
London SW1A 2AS
Tel: 020 7276 3000
Email via website
www.cabinetoffice.gov.uk

CACHE Council for Awards in Children's
Care and Education
Apex House 81 Camp Road St Albans
Hertfordshire AL1 5GB
Tel: 0845 347 2123
info@cache.org.uk
www.cache.org.uk

CADD Campaign Against Drinking &
Driving
PO Box 62 Brighouse West Yorkshire HD6
3YY
Helpline: 0845 123 5542
Tel: 0845 1235541
Tel: 0845 123 5543
cadd@scard.org.uk
www.cadd.org.uk
Provide support for the families of victims
killed and injured by drunk or drugged
motorists

Cadw
Welsh Assembly Government Plas Carew
Unit 5/7 Cefn Coed Parc Nantgarw Cardiff
CF15 7QQ
Tel: 01443 336000
cadw@wales.gsi.gov.uk
www.cadw.wales.gov.uk
Protects and conserves the ancient
monuments and historic buildings in Wales

CAF see Charities Aid Foundation

CAFCAS Academic Freedom & Academic
Standards (Council for)
Tel: 01932 840928
Tel: 01792 517473
email via website
www.cafas.org.uk
Dedicated to maintaining standards of
integrity and practice in academia

Cafcass Children and Family Court
Advisory and Support Service
6th Floor Sanctuary Buildings Great Smith
Street London SW1P 3BT
Tel: 0844 353 3350
webenquiries@cafcass.gsi.gov.uk
www.cafcass.gov.uk
Looks after the interests of children involved
in family proceedings. Work with children

and their families, and then advise the courts on what is considered to be in the best interests of individual children

CAFOD Catholic Overseas Development Agency
Romero House 55 Westminster Bridge Road London SE1 7JB
Tel: 020 7733 7900
cafod@cafod.org.uk
www.cafod.org.uk
The official Catholic aid agency for England and Wales

CALM Campaign Against Living Miserably
Tel: 0800 58 58 58
info@thecalmzone.net
www.thecalmzone.net
Encourages young men aged 15 to 35 in Manchester, Merseyside and Bedfordshire to open up and talk about their problems. Helpline open to all ages and sexes

Calvert Trust Kielder
Kielder Water Hexham Northumberland NE48 1BS
Tel: 01434 250232
email via website
www.calvert-trust.org.uk

& Exmoor
Wistlandpound Kentisbury Barnstaple Devon EX31 4SJ
Tel: 01598 763221
email via website
www.calvert-trust.org.uk
Activity holidays for people of all abilities

& Keswick
Little Crosthwaite Keswick Cumbria CA12 4QD
Tel/minicom: 01768 772255
email via website
www.calvert-trust.org.uk

Cambridge Past, Present & Future
Wandlebury Ring Gog Magog Hills Babraham Cambridge CB22 3AE
Tel: 01223 243830
email via website
www.cambridgeppf.org
Aims to protect the character, amenities, historic buildings and settings of Cambridge and its surroundings.

CAMFED International
22 Millers Yard Mill Lane Cambridge CB2 1RQ
Tel: 01223 362648
info@camfed.org
www.camfed.org
Supporting the education of girls in Africa

Camp Mohawk
Highfield Lane Crazies Hill Wargrave Berkshire RG10 8PU
Tel: 0118 940 4045
camp_mohawk@hotmail.com
www.campmohawk.org.uk
A unique and very caring camp offering day care for brain damaged and autistic children from all over England.

Campaign Against Arms Trade CAAT
11 Goodwin St Finsbury Park London N4 3HQ
Tel: 020 7281 0297
enquiries@caat.org.uk
www.caat.org.uk

Campaign Against Drinking & Driving see CADD

Campaign Against Living Miserably see CALM

Campaign for Nuclear Disarmament see CND, CND (Scottish)

Campaign for the Protection of Rural Wales see Protection of Rural Wales (Campaign for the)

Campaign to Protect Rural England see CPRE

Camping and Caravanning Club
Greenfields House Westwood Way Coventry CV4 8JH
Tel: 0845 130 7631
Tel: 024 7647 5448
email via website
www.campingandcaravanningclub.co.uk
The largest and longest established membership organisation for all types of camping and caravanning

CAMRA Campaign for Real Ale
230 Hatfield Rd St Albans AL1 4LW
Tel: 01727 867201
camra@camra.org.uk
www.camra.org.uk
To promote and preserve full-flavoured, distinctive beers, ciders and perries and the best features of the pub

Canals see Inland Waterways Association

Cancer see also ACT – Animal Cancer Trust, Bob Champion Cancer Trust, Bowel Cancer UK, Breakthrough Breast Cancer, Breast Cancer Care, Childhood Eye Cancer Trust, Children with Leukaemia, Christian Lewis Trust, CLICSargent, Core, Ellen MacArthur Trust, Hereditary Breast Cancer Helpline (National), Jo's Cervical Cancer Trust, Lavender Trust, Let's Face It, Leukaemia & Lymphoma Research, Macmillan Cancer Support, Marie Curie Cancer Care, Mouth Cancer Foundation,

Orchid Cancer Appeal, Paul's Cancer Support Centre, Prostate Cancer Charity, Roy Castle Lung Cancer Foundation, Saving Faces, Teenage Cancer Trust, Tenovus, Wessex Cancer Trust, World Cancer Research Fund International, Youth Cancer Trust

Cancer and Leukaemia in Childhood see CLICSargent

Cancer BACUP now see Macmillan Cancer Support

Cancer Research Fund see World Cancer Research Fund International

Cancer Research UK
Angel Building 407 St John Street London EC1V 4AD
Supporter Services: 0300 123 1861
Tel: 020 7242 0200
email via website
www.cancerresearchuk.org

Cancer Resource Centre now see Paul's Cancer Support Centre

Cancer Society (American)
www.cancer.org

Cancerbackup now see Macmillan Cancer Support

CancerHelp UK
Nurse: 0808 800 4040
email via website
www.cancerhelp.org.uk
Information website from Cancer Research UK

Canine Defence League see Dogs Trust

Canine Partners
Mill Lane Heyshott Midhurst West Sussex GU29 0ED
Tel: 08456 580 480
email via website
www.caninepartners.co.uk
Trains assistance dogs for disabled people

Canoe Association (Scottish)
Caledonia House South Gyle Edinburgh EH12 9DQ
Tel: 0131 317 7314
email via website
www.canoescotland.org
Volunteer led, membership based organisation working to support canoeing and kayaking in Scotland and the recognised Governing Body for the sport

Canoe Association of Northern Ireland
Unit 2, Rivers Edge 13-15 Ravenhill Road Belfast BT6 8DN
Tel: 02890 738884
office@cani.org.uk
www.cani.org.uk
Governing body for canoeing in Northern Ireland

Canoe Union (British)
18 Market Place Bingham Nottingham NG13 8AP
Tel: 0845 370 9500
Tel: 0300 0119 500
Info@bcu.org.uk
www.bcu.org.uk
Governing body of sport for canoe & kayak in the UK

Canoe Wales
National White Water Centre Frongoch Bala Gwynedd LL23 7NU
Tel: 01678 521199
admin@canoewales.com
www.canoewales.com
National governing body for paddle sport in Wales

Canoeing Association (Welsh) now see Canoe Wales

Canon Collins Trust Education for Southern Africa
22 The Ivories 6 Northampton St London N1 2HY
Tel: 020 7354 1462
info@canoncollins.org.uk
www.canoncollins.org.uk

Captive Animals' Protection Society
PO Box 4186 Manchester M60 3ZA
Tel: 0845 330 3911
Tel: 0161 273 3649
info@captiveanimals.org
www.captiveanimals.org
Campaigns against use of animals in circuses & zoos

Caravan Club
East Grinstead House East Grinstead West Sussex RH19 1UA
Tel: 01342 326944
enquiries@caravanclub.co.uk
www.caravanclub.co.uk

Caravanning see also Camping & Caravanning Club

Carbon Neutral Company
Bravington House 2 Bravington Walk Regent Quarter Kings Cross London N1 9AF
Tel: 020 7833 6000
email via website
www.carbonneutral.com
Plants trees to offset carbon emissions

Carbon Trust
6th Floor, 5 New Street Square London
EC4A 3BF
Tel: 0800 085 2005
email via website
www.carbontrust.co.uk
Provides specialist support to business
and the public sector to help cut carbon
emissions, save energy and commercialise
low carbon technologies

Cardiac Risk in the Young CRY
Unit 7 Epsom Downs Metro Centre
Waterfield, Tadworth Surrey KT20 5LR
Tel: 01737 363 222
cry@c-r-y.org.uk
www.c-r-y.org.uk
Raises awareness of conditions that can
lead to Young Sudden Cardiac Death
(YSCD), Sudden Death Syndrome (SDS) and
Sudden Arrhythmic Death Syndrome (SADS)

Cards for Little Lives
www.cardsforlittlelives.org.uk
Unique resource for primary schools.
Learning for well-being through prompted
discussion in PSHE

CARE now see Self Unlimited

Care Council for Wales Cyngor Gofal
Cymru
South Gate House Wood Street Cardiff
CF10 1EW
Tel: 029 2022 6257
info@ccwales.org.uk
www.ccwales.org.uk

Care for the Wild International
The Granary Tickfold Farm Kingsfold RH12
3SE
Tel: 01306 627900
email via website
www.careforthewild.com
Charity dedicated to protecting wild animals

CARE International UK
10-13 Rushworth Street London SE1 0RB
Tel: 0207 934 9334
email via website
www.careinternational.org.uk
Development charity helping world's poorest
and most vulnerable people

Care Not Killing
PO Box 56322 London SE1 8XW
Tel: 020 7234 9680
info@carenotkilling.org.uk
www.carenotkilling.org.uk
Promoting palliative care, Opposing
euthanasia and assisted suicide

Care Quality Commission
Citygate Gallowgate Newcastle upon Tyne
NE1 4PA

Tel: 03000 616161
email via website
www.cqc.org.uk/
Independent regulator of health and social
care in England. Aims to make sure better
care is provided for everyone, whether that's
in hospital, in care homes, in people's own
homes, or elsewhere

Career Development Loans
www.direct.gov.uk/cdl
A deferred repayment loan providing
individuals with help to fund vocational
education or learning

Careers Research & Advisory Centre see
CRAC

Carers see CROSSROADS Care

Carers UK
20 Great Dover Street London SE1 4LX
Adviceline: 0808 808 7777
Tel: 020 7378 4999
email via website
www.carersuk.org
Information and advice on all aspects of
caring

& Northern Ireland
58 Howard Street Belfast BT1 6JP
Adviceline: 0808 808 7777
Tel: 02890 439 843
email via website
www.carersuk.org

& Scotland
The Cottage 21 Pearce Street Glasgow
G51 3UT
Adviceline: 0808 808 7777
Tel: 0141 445 3070
email via website
www.carersuk.org

& Wales
River House Ynys Bridge Court Cardiff
CF15 9SS
Adviceline: 0808 808 7777
Tel: 02920 811 370
email via website
www.carersuk.org

Carers (The Princess Royal Trust For)
London Office
Unit 14 Bourne Court Southend Road
Woodford Green Essex IG8 8HD
Tel: 0844 800 4361
info@carers.org
www.carers.org
Information, advice and support

& Glasgow Office
Charles Oakley House 125 West Regent
Street Glasgow G2 2SD
Tel: 0141 221 5066
info@carers.org
www.carers.org

& Wales Office
Victoria House 250 Cowbridge Road East
Canton Cardiff CF5 1GZ
Tel: 02920 221788
info@carers.org
www.carers.org
Information, advice and support

CARF Racism & Fascism (Campaign Against)
BM Box 8784 London WC1N 3XX
Tel: 020 7837 1450
info@carf.org.uk
www.carf.org.uk

CaSE - Campaign for Science & Engineering in the UK
Gordon House
29 Gordon Square London WC1H 0PP
Tel: 020 7679 4994/5
info@sciencecampaign.org.uk
www.sciencecampaign.org.uk
An independent campaign for effective policies for science, engineering, technology and medicine and a proper appreciation of their cultural and economic importance

Cash Machines see ATM Locator

Casualties Union
PO Box 1942 London E17 6YU
Tel: 08700 780590
hq@casualtiesunion.org.uk
www.casualtiesunion.org.uk
Recruits volunteers to act as casualties in first aid and rescue practice

Cat Fancy (Governing Council of the)
5 King's Castle Business Park The Drove
Bridgewater Somerset TA6 4AG
Tel: 01278 427 575
info@gccfcats.org
www.gccfcats.org
Registers pedigree cats

Catch22
Churchill House 142-146 Old Street
London EC1V 9BW
Tel: 020 7336 4800
information@catch-22.org.uk
www.catch-22.org.uk
National charity that works with young people who find themselves in difficult situations

Catholic Education Service Promoting & Supporting Catholic Education in England & Wales
39 Eccleston Sq London SW1V 1BX
Tel: 0207 901 1900
general@cesew.org.uk
www.cesew.org.uk
Negotiates on behalf of all bishops, with Government, and other national bodies on legal, administrative, and religious education matters

Cats Protection
National Cat Centre Chelwood Gate
Sussex RH17 7TT
National helpline: 03000 12 12 12
Tel: 08707 708 649
helpline@cats.org.uk
www.cats.org.uk
UK's oldest and largest feline charity offering rescue, rehabilitation and rehoming services

Caving Association (British)
The Old Methodist Chapel Great Hucklow
Buxton SK17 8RG
www.british-caving.org.uk

CCETSA see Canon Collins Trust

CEH Centre for Ecology & Hydrology
Maclean Building Benson Lane Crowmarsh Gifford Wallingford Oxfordshire OX10 8BB
Tel: 01491 838800
Tel: 01491 692371 (enquiries)
enquiries@ceh.ac.uk
www.ceh.ac.uk
Environmental research

Cello Society (Internet)
www.cello.org
International cyber-community of cellists, seeks to advance the knowledge and joy of cello playing around the world

CEMVO Council of Ethnic Minority Voluntary Sector Organisations
www.cemvo.org.uk
Charity for the social regeneration of Black & Minority Ethnic Communities

Census see 1901 Census for England & Wales, Family Search, FreeBMD, Indian Census, National Archives, Office for National Statistics, Register Office for N. Ireland (General), Register Office for Scotland (General)

Central Office of Information COI
Hercules House Hercules Rd London SE1 7DU
Tel: 020 7928 2345
email via website
www.coi.gov.uk

Centre for Alternative Technology see Alternative Technology (Centre for)

Centre for Economic & Social Inclusion
3rd Floor Camelford House 89 Albert Embankment London SE1 7TP
Tel: 020 7582 7221
info@cesi.org.uk
www.cesi.org.uk
Promoting social inclusion in the labour market

Centrepoint
Central House 25 Camperdown Street
London E1 8DZ
Tel: 0845 466 3400
email via website
www.centrepoint.org.uk
Runs emergency shelters and
accommodation in Greater London for
homeless young people (16-25)

Ceroc
77 Fernhead Road London W9 3EA
Tel: 020 8969 4401
email via website
www.ceroc.com
Biggest dance club in the world. Dance style
sometimes referred to as 'Modern Jive' – a
fusion of Salsa, Ballroom, Hip Hop, Tango
and Jive

Certificate ordering service
www.gro.gov.uk/gro/content/certificates/
default.asp
General Register Office for England and
Wales online ordering service and official
information on births, marriages and deaths

Certification Officer
22nd Floor Euston Tower 286 Euston Road
London NW1 3JJ
Tel: 020 7210 3734
info@certoffice.org
www.certoffice.org
Maintains a list of trade unions and
employers' associations

CF Appointments CfA
52-54 Gracechurch Street London EC3V
0EH
Tel: 020 7220 0180
enquiries@cfappointments.com
www.cfappointments.com
Fills senior executive positions for charities
and not-for-profit organisations etc

Chain of Hope
South Parade   Chelsea London SW3 6NP
Tel: 020 7351 1978
email via website
www.chainofhope.org
Chain of Hope exists to provide children
suffering from life-threatening disease with
the corrective surgery and treatment to
which they do not have access

Chambers of Commerce (British)
65 Petty France London SW1H 9EU
Tel: 020 7654 5800
info@britishchambers.org.uk
www.britishchambers.org.uk

Chance UK
2nd Floor, London Fashion Centre 89-93
Fonthill Rd London N4 3JH

Tel: 020 7281 5858
admin@chanceuk.com
www.chanceuk.com
Early intervention in the lives of vulnerable
children, to build a brighter future. Provides
mentoring programmes for children aged
5-11 years with behavioural difficulties

Changemakers
Ground Floor Zetland House 5-25 Scrutton
Street London EC2A 4HJ
Tel: 020 7033 6970
info@changemakers.org.uk
www.changemakers.org.uk
A charity which encourages young people
to tackle issues of concern to themselves,
their community and to the world in which
they live

Changing Faces
The Squire Centre 33-37 University Street
London WC1E 6JN
Tel: 0207 391 9270
Tel: 0845 4500 275
info@changingfaces.org.uk
www.changingfaces.org.uk
www.iface.org.uk
Advice & counselling for children and adults
with disfigurements and promotion of public
awareness

Channel 4
www.channel4.com

Channel 5 see Five

Charities Aid Foundation CAF
25 Kings Hill Avenue Kings Hill West
Malling Kent ME19 4TA
Tel: 03000 123 000
enquiries@cafonline.org
www.cafonline.org
Not for profit organisation which is
committed to effective giving, providing
a range of specialist services to donors,
companies and charities in the UK and
internationally

CharitiesDirect.com
www.charitiesdirect.com
A guide to UK charities

Charity Appointments see CF
Appointments

Charity Choice
www.charitychoice.co.uk
Online Guide to Charities in the UK

**Charity Commission for England &
Wales**
PO Box 1227 Liverpool L69 3UG
Tel: 0845 300 0218
email via website
www.charity-commission.gov.uk
Registers, supervises and advises charities.

Provides free publications and runs an outreach and education programme

Charter 88 now see Unlock Democracy

Chartered Management Institute
2 Savoy Court London WC2R 0EZ
Tel: 020 7497 0580
Tel: 01536 204222
enquiries@managers.org.uk
www.managers.org.uk
Professional organisation

Chartered Surveyors (Royal Institute of)
RICS
Parliament Square London SW1P 3AD
Tel: 0870 333 1600
contactrics@rics.org
www.rics.org
Professional body for surveyors

Chartered Surveyors Training Trust
16th Floor The Tower Building 11 York Road London SE1 7NX
Tel: 0207 871 0454
cstt@cstt.org.uk
www.cstt.org.uk
Encourages young people to become chartered surveyors via other routes than university

Chartered Surveyors Voluntary Service
contact Chartered Surveyors (Royal Institute of)
Works with Citizen's Advice Bureaux when a chartered surveyor can't be afforded

Chemistry (Royal Society of)
Burlington House Piccadilly London W1J 0BA
Tel: 020 7437 8656
email via website
www.rsc.org
The largest organisation in Europe for advancing the chemical sciences

Chernobyl Children's Life Line
Courts 61 Petworth Rd Haslemere Surrey GU27 3AX
Tel: 01428 642 523
email via website
www.chernobylchildlifeline.org
Supports child victims of radioactivity and organises recuperative visits to the UK

Chess see also Braille Chess Association

Chess Association (English Primary Schools)
www.epsca.org.uk
Exists to advance the education of primary school aged children by teaching, supervising and developing the playing of chess by those children

Chess Federation (English)
The Watch Oak Chain Lane Battle East Sussex TN33 0YD
Tel: 01424 775222
office@englishchess.org.uk
www.englishchess.org.uk
Governing body for chess in England

Chess Scotland
www.chessscotland.com

Chess Union (Ulster)
www.ulsterchess.org

Chess Union (Welsh)
www.welshchessunion.org.uk

chewonthis.org.uk Honest information about the food you eat
www.chewonthis.org.uk
Committed to providing well-researched and independent information about food and health. Their campaigns and research are not funded by government or the food industry

CHICKS Country Holidays for Inner City Children
Moorland Retreat Bonnaford Brentor Tavistock Devon PL19 0LX
Tel: 01822 811020
info@chicks.org.uk
www.chicks.org.uk/
Provides free respite breaks for disadvantaged children aged between 8 and 15 regardless of race or religion

Child Abuse see also Africans Unite Against Child Abuse, Barnardo's, Chance UK, Child Protection in Sport Unit, ChildLine, Children 1st, NSPCC

Child Abuse and Neglect (British Association for the Study and Prevention of) see BASPCAN

Child Accident Prevention Trust
Canterbury Court 1-3 Brixton Road London SW9 6DE
Tel: 020 7608 3828
safe@capt.org.uk
www.capt.org.uk
Committed to reducing the number of children and young people killed, disabled or seriously injured in accidents

Child Advocacy International now see Maternal & Childhealth Advocacy International

Child and Adolescent Mental Health (Association for)
St Saviour's House 39-41 Union St London SE1 1SD
Tel: 020 7403 7458
email via website
www.acamh.org.uk
Professional organisation

Child Bereavement Charity
The Saunderton Estate Wycombe Road Saunderton Bucks HP14 4BF
Support & Info Line: 1494 568900
enquiries@childbereavement.org.uk
www.childbereavement.org.uk
Helps bereaved families by providing training, resources and support to professionals

Child Brain Injury Trust
Unit 1 The Great Barn Baynards Green Farm Nr Bicester Oxfordshire OX27 7SG
Helpline: 0845 6014939
Tel: 01869 341075
info@cbituk.org or helpline@cbituk.org
www.cbituk.org
Information, support and training to anyone affected by childhood acquired brain injury

Child Contact Centres (National Association of)
1 Heritage Mews High Pavement Nottingham NG1 1HN
Tel: 0845 4500 280
Landline (cheaper for mobiles): 0115 948 4557
contact@naccc.org.uk
www.naccc.org.uk
Supports Child Contact Centres, where children of separated families can have contact with family members

Child Death Helpline
Helpline: 0800 282 986
contact@childdeathhelpline.org
www.childdeathhelpline.org.uk
Helpline is staffed by volunteers, all of them bereaved parents. Provide support not only at times of crisis but also for ongoing needs of callers over their lifetime

Child Growth Foundation
2 Mayfield Ave Chiswick London W4 1PW
Tel: 020 8995 0257
info@childgrowthfoundation.org
www.childgrowthfoundation.org
Supports sufferers of growth disorders and their families

Child Poverty Action Group CPAG
94 White Lion St London N1 9PF
Tel: 020 7837 7979
staff@cpag.org.uk
www.cpag.org.uk
Information about low-income families and the policies that affect them. Monitor official poverty statistics and carry out research

Child Poverty Action Group Scotland
CPAG in Scotland
Unit 9, Ladywell 94 Duke Street Glasgow G4 0UW
Tel: 0141 552 3303
staff@cpagscotland.org.uk
www.cpag.org.uk

Child Protection in Sport Unit CPSU
NSPCC National Training Centre 3 Gilmour Close Beaumont Leys Leicester LE4 1EZ
Tel: 0116 234 7278
cpsu@nspcc.org.uk
www.thecpsu.org.uk
Offers advice to sports professionals, volunteers, parents and children as part of a long-term strategy for ending child abuse

& Northern Ireland
NSPCC Block 1 Jennymount Business Park North Derby Street Belfast BT15 3HN
Tel: 02890 351 135
cpsu@nspcc.org.uk
www.thecpsu.org.uk

& Cymru/Wales
Diane Engelhardt House, Treglown Court, Dowlais Road Cardiff CF24 5LQ
Tel: 0844 892 0290
cpsuwales@nspcc.org.uk
www.thecpsu.org.uk

& Scotland
CHILDREN 1ST Sussex House 61 Sussex Street Kinning Park Glasgow G41 1DY
Tel: 0141 418 5674
cpinsport@children1st.org.uk
www.thecpsu.org.uk

Child Rights Information Network see CRIN

Child Soldiers
4th Floor, 9 Marshalsea Road London SE1 1EP
Tel: 020 7367 4110/4129
info@child-soldiers.org
www.child-soldiers.org
Working to stop the use of child soldiers worldwide

Childbirth Trust see National Childbirth Trust

Childcare see Daycare Trust, Directgov

Childhood (Alliance for)
Kidbrooke Park Forest Row East Sussex RH18 5JA
Tel: 01342 827792
info@alliancechildhood.org
www.alliancechildhood.org
Partnership of individuals and organisations committed to each child's inherent right to a healthy, developmentally appropriate childhood

Childhood (Museum of) V&A
Cambridge Heath Road London E2 9PA
Tel: 020 8983 5200
Group Bookings: 020 8983 5205
moc@vam.ac.uk
www.vam.ac.uk/moc/

Childhood Bereavement Network
8 Wakley Street London EC1V 7QE
Tel: 020 7843 6309
cbn@ncb.org.uk
www.childhoodbereavementnetwork.org.uk
A national, multi-professional federation of
organisations and individuals working with
bereaved children and young people.

Childhood Eye Cancer Trust CHECT
The Royal London Hospital Whitechapel
Road London E1 1BB
Tel: 020 7377 5578
info@chect.org.uk
www.chect.org.uk
UK wide charity for families and individuals
affected by retinoblastoma. We offer support
and information, fund research and raise
public awareness of this rare cancer

ChildHope
Development House 56/64 Leonard Street
London EC2A 4LT
Tel: 0207 065 0950
info@childhope.org.uk
www.childhope.org.uk
International development charity supporting
street and working children

ChildLine
Weston House 42 Curtain Road London
EC2A 3NH
Helpline: 0800 1111
email via website
www.childline.org.uk
Confidential counselling service for children
and young people

Childlink Adoption Society now see PACT
(Parents and Children Together)

Childminding Association (National)
Helping every child reach their full potential
Royal Court 81 Tweedy Road Bromley
Kent BR1 1TG
Tel: 0845 880 0044
info@ncma.org.uk
www.ncma.org.uk
Offers help and advice on a wide range of
issues related to home-based childcare

CHILDREN 1ST Royal Scottish Society for
Prevention of Cruelty to Children
83 Whitehouse Loan Edinburgh EH9 1AT
Tel: 0131 446 2300
info@children1st.org.uk
www.children1st.org.uk

Support families under stress, protect
children from harm and neglect, help
them to recover from abuse and promote
children's rights and interests

**Children and Family Court Advisory
Support Service** see Cafcass

Children and peace see Peace Pledge
Union

Children are unbeatable! Alliance
94 White Lion Street London N1 9PF
Tel: 020 7713 0569
info@endcorporalpunishment.org
www.childrenareunbeatable.org.uk
To satisfy human rights obligations by
modernising the law on assault to afford
children the same protection as adults

& Northern Ireland
Unit 9, 40 Montgomery Road Belfast BT6
9HL
Tel: 028 9040 1290
www.childrenareunbeatable.org.uk

& Scotland
c/o ChildLine in Scotland 2nd Floor Tara
House 46 Bath St Glasgow G2 1HG
www.childrenareunbeatable.org.uk

& Wales/Cymru
Children in Wales 25 Windsor Place Cardiff
CF10 3BZ
www.childrenareunbeatable.org.uk

Children in Need Appeal BBC
www.bbc.co.uk/pudsey

Children in Scotland
Princes House 5 Shandwick Place
Edinburgh EH2 4RG
Tel: 0131 228 8484
info@childreninscotland.org.uk
www.childreninscotland.org.uk
National agency for voluntary, statutory and
professional organisations and individuals
working with children and their families in
Scotland

**Children of Alcoholics (National
Association for)** NACOA
PO Box 64 Fishponds Bristol BS16 2UH
Helpline: 0800 358 3456
Tel: 0117 924 8005
admin@nacoa.org.uk
www.nacoa.org.uk
Support and advice to children of alcoholics
and to professionals

Children with Leukaemia
51 Great Ormond St London WC1N 3JQ
Tel: 020 7404 0808
info@leukaemia.org
www.leukaemia.org
Fighting Britain's biggest childhood cancer

Children's Book Groups (Federation of)
2 Bridge Wood View Horsforth Leeds LS18 5PE
Tel: 0113 2588 910
info@fcbg.org.uk
www.fcbg.org.uk
Parents, teachers, librarians and publishers promoting good children's books

Children's Bureau (National) see NCB

Children's Care & Education (Council for Awards in) see CACHE

Children's Commissioner for England (Office of the)
33 Greycoat Street London SE1P 2QF
Tel: 020 77883 8330
info.request@childrenscommissioner.gsi.gov.uk
www.childrenscommissioner.gov.uk
Promoting the views and best interests of all children and young people

Children's Express now see Headliners

Children's Heart Federation
Level One
2-4 Great Eastern Street London EC2A 3NW
Helpline: 0808 808 5000
Tel: 020 7422 0630
Email via website
www.childrens-heart-fed.org.uk
For families of children with heart conditions

Children's Hope Foundation
15 Palmer Place London N7 8DH
Tel: 020 7700 6855
info@childrenshopefoundation.org
www.childrenshopefoundation.org.uk
Caring for children with special needs

Children's Legal Centre
University of Essex Wivenhoe Park Colchester Essex CO4 3SQ
Child Law Advice Line Freephone: 08088 020 008
Community Legal Advice: 0845 345 4345
Tel: 01206 877 910
clc@essex.ac.uk
www.childrenslegalcentre.com
www.lawstuff.org.uk
Free and confidential legal advice on issues affecting children

Children's Literature (National Centre for Research in) NCRCL
Department of English & Creative Writing
Roehampton University Roehampton Lane
London SW15 5PH
Tel: 020 8392 3000
email via website
www.roehampton.ac.uk/researchcentres/ncrcl/

Children's Medical Research Charity now see Sparks

Children's Orchestra (National)
57 Buckingham Road Weston-Super-Mare BS24 9BG
Tel: 01934 418855
mail@nco.org.uk
www.nco.org.uk
For children between the ages of 7-14 years

Children's Play Initiative now see Play England

Children's Rights Alliance for England CRAE
94 White Lion St London N1 9PF
Tel: 020 7278 8222
info@crae.org.uk
www.crae.org.uk
Promoting the fullest implementation of the UN convention on rights of the child.

Children's Scrapstore
Scrapstore House 21 Sevier Street Bristol BS2 9LB
Tel: 0117 908 5644
enquiries@childrensscrapstore.co.uk
www.childrensscrapstore.co.uk
Clean and safe waste products from industry as a resource for children's art and play activities. Directory of scrapstores.

Children's Society
Edward Rudolf House Margery St London WC1X 0JL
Tel: 020 7841 4400
Tel: 0845 300 1128
supporteraction@childrenssociety.org.uk
www.childrenssociety.org.uk
A Christian, social justice organisation concerned with children at risk on the streets, children in trouble with the law, disabled children and young refugees

Children's Workforce Development Council
2nd Floor City Exchange 11 Albion Street
Leeds LS1 5ES
Tel: 0300 123 1033
Tel: 0113 244 6311
email via website
www.cwdcouncil.org.uk
Advises and works in partnership with

organisations and people involved with children to join up the way different agencies work, and bring consistency to the way children and young people are listened to and looked after

Chinese Arts Centre
Market Buildings Thomas Street Manchester M4 1EU
Tel: 0161 832 7271
Email via website
www.chinese-arts-centre.org
UK agency for Chinese arts, culture and creativity

Chiropodists & Podiatrists (Institute of)
27 Wright St Southport PR9 0TL
Tel: 01704 546141
secretary@iocp.org.uk
www.iocp.org.uk

Chiropodists and Podiatrists (The Society of)
1 Fellmonger's Path Tower Bridge Rd London SE1 3LY
Tel: 020 7234 8620
Email via website
www.feetforlife.org
Professional Body and Trade Union for registered podiatrists. The Society represents around 10,000 private practitioners, NHS podiatrists and students

Chiropractic (Anglo-European College of)
13-15 Parkwood Rd Bournemouth BH5 2DF
Tel: 01202 436200
email via website
www.aecc.ac.uk

Chiropractic Association (British)
59 Castle Street Reading RG1 7SN
Tel: 0118 950 5950
enquiries@chiropractic-uk.co.uk
www.chiropractic-uk.co.uk

Chiropractic Patients' Association
8 Centre One Lysander Way Old Sarum Park Salisbury SP4 6BU
Tel: 01722 415 027
cpa@centreonesarum.com
www.chiropatients.org.uk
Supports chiropractic patients and seeks to make treatment more widely available

Chocolate Society
Unit 10 Lower Charlton Trading Estate Shepton Mallet Somerset BA4 5QE
Tel: 01749 342884
email via website
www.chocolate.co.uk
Promotes the consumption and enjoyment of the finest chocolates

Choir Schools' Association
The Information Officer Windrush, Church Road Market Weston Diss Norfolk IP22 2NX
Tel: 01359 221333
info@choirschools.org.uk
www.choirschools.org.uk
Provides advice to prospective pupils and bursary help where applicable

Choirs see also Youth Choir of Great Britain (National)

Choose Climate
www.chooseclimate.org
Details the science of climate change & the effects of air travel

Christian Aid
35 Lower Marsh Waterloo London SE1 7RL
Tel: 020 7620 4444
info@christian-aid.org
www.christianaid.org.uk

& Cardiff National Office
5 Station Road Radyr Cardiff CF15 8AA
Tel: 029 2084 4646
cardiff@christian-aid.org
www.christianaid.org.uk

& Glasgow National Office
Pentagon Centre 36 Washington Street Glasgow G3 8AZ
Tel: 0141 221 7475
glasgow@christian-aid.org
www.christianaid.org.uk

& Ireland
Linden House Beechill Business Park 96 Beechill Road Belfast BT8 7QN
Tel: 028 9064 8133
belfast@christian-aid.org
www.christianaid.org.uk

&
Hill View Bandon Co Cork
Tel: (+353) 238 841 468
cork@christian-aid.org
www.christianaid.org.uk

&
17 Clanwilliam Terrace Grand Canal Quay Dublin 2
Tel: (+353) 1 611 0801
dublin@christian-aid.org
www.christianaid.org.uk

Christian Education/International Bible Reading Association (IBRA)
1020 Bristol Road Selly Oak Birmingham B29 6LB
Tel: 0121 472 4242
sales@christianeducation.org.uk
www.christianeducation.org.uk
Provides Christian resources for use by individuals, families and churches

Christian Lewis Trust Children's Cancer Charity
62 Walter Road Swansea SA1 4PT
Tel: 01792 480 500
enquiries@christianlewistrust.org
www.christianlewistrust.org.uk

Christian Socialist Movement CSM
PO Box 65108 London SW1P 9PQ
Tel: 020 7783 1590
info@thecsm.org.uk
www.thecsm.org.uk

Christian Teachers (Association of)
23 Billing Road Northampton NN1 5AT
Tel: 01604 6323 046
act@christians-in-education.org.uk
www.christian-teachers.org.uk

Christians and Jews (Council of)
Godliman House
21 Godliman Street
London EC4V 5BD
Tel: 0207 015 5160
cjrelations@ccj.org.uk
www.ccj.org.uk

Chronic Poverty Research Centre
Institute for Development Policy and Management School of Environment and Development University of Manchester Humanities Bridgeford Street Manchester M13 9PL
Tel: 0161 275 2810
www.chronicpoverty.org
International partnership of universities, research institutes and NGOs which focuses on persistent or chronic poverty

Church Action on Poverty
Dale House 35 Dale Street Manchester M1 2HF
Tel: 0161 236 9321
info@church-poverty.org.uk
www.church-poverty.org.uk
Aiming to raise awareness about the causes, extent and impact of poverty in the UK

Church Army
Wilson Carlile Centre 50 Cavendish Street Sheffield S3 7RZ
Tel: 0300 123 2113
info@churcharmy.org.uk
www.churcharmy.org.uk
Sharing the gospel in a variety of situations right across the UK and Ireland

Church Lads' and Church Girls' Brigade
2 Barnsley Rd Wath-upon-Dearne Rotherham S63 6PY
Tel: 01709 876 535
brigadesecretary@clcgb.org.uk
www.clcgb.org.uk
A uniformed young people and children's organisation within the Church of England

Church Mission Society
Watlington Road Oxford OX4 6BZ
Tel: 01865 787400
info@cms-uk.org
www.cms-uk.org
Sends UK personnel to other countries, in partnership with churches

Church of England
www.churchofengland.org

Church of England Education Division
www.churchofengland.org/education.aspx

Churches Conservation Trust
1 West Smithfield London EC1A 9EE
Tel: 020 7213 0660
central@tcct.org.uk
www.visitchurches.org.uk
National charity protecting historic churches at risk

Churches Together in Britain and Ireland
39 Eccleston Square London SW1V 1BX
Tel: 0845 680 6851
info@ctbi.org.uk
www.ctbi.org.uk

Churchill War Rooms part of the Imperial War Museum
Clive Steps King Charles Street London SW1A 2AQ
Tel: 020 7930 6961
Textphone: 020 7839 4906
cwr@iwm.org.uk
http://cwr.iwm.org.uk
www.iwm.org.uk

CIA Central Intelligence Agency
www.cia.gov
Independent US Government agency responsible for providing national security intelligence to senior US policymakers

CIH
Octavia House Westwood Way Coventry CV4 8JP
Tel: 024 7685 1700
customer.services@cih.org
www.cih.org
The professional body for people working in the field of social housing

& Cymru
4 Purbeck House Lambourne Crescent Cardiff Business Park Llanishen Cardiff CF14 5GJ
Tel: 029 2076 5760
cymru@cih.org
www.cih.org

& Northern Ireland
Carnmoney House Edgewater Office Park Dargan Road Belfast BT3 9JQ
Tel: 028 9077 8222
ni@cih.org
www.cih.org

CIH Scotland
4th Floor 125 Princes Street Edinburgh
EH2 4AD
Tel: 0131 225 4544
scotland@cih.org
www.cih.org

CILIP Chartered Institute of Library and
Information Professionals
7 Ridgmount St London WC1E 7AE
Tel: 020 7255 0500
Textphone: 020 7255 0505
info@cilip.org.uk
www.cilip.org.uk
Professional body for Information Managers
and Librarians.

CILIPS Chartered Institute of Library and
Information Professionals in Scotland
1st Floor Building C Brandon Gate
Leechlee Rd Hamilton ML3 6AU
Tel: 01698 458 888
cilips@slainte.org.uk
www.cilips.org.uk

CILT National Centre for Languages
CILT Education Trust 60 Queens Road
Reading RG1 4BS
Tel: 0118 902 1000
www.cilt.org.uk

Cinema see British Film Institute, Film
Classification (British Board of), Film
Education, Film & Television Archive
(Northern Region), Film and Television
School (National), Film London, History of
Cinema & Popular Culture (The Bill Douglas
Centre for the)

Cinnamon Trust
10 Market Square Hayle Cornwall TR27
4HE
Tel: 01736 757 900
admin@cinnamon.org.uk
www.cinnamon.org.uk
National charity for the elderly, the terminally
ill and their pets

Circus see also Skylight Circus Arts

Circus Sensible/Circus School
4 The Moorings Mossley Lancs OL5 9BZ
Mobile: 07958 780246
papaclive@yahoo.com
www.circussensible.co.uk
Britain's smallest tented circus. Performance
& teaching of circus skills in schools, youth
clubs etc.

Circus Space
Coronet St London N1 6HD
Tel: 020 7613 4141
info@thecircusspace.co.uk
www.thecircusspace.co.uk
Circus training & production venue offering
the only BA circus degree in the UK

Cirdan Sailing Trust
3 Chandlers Quay Fullbridge Maldon
Essex CM9 4LF
Tel: 01621 851 433
info@cirdansailing.com
www.cirdansailing.com
Adventure sailing for groups of all abilities of
10 years+

Citizens Advice
Myddelton House 115-123 Pentonville Rd
London N1 9LZ
www.citizensadvice.org.uk
www.adviceguide.org.uk
Independent advice, policy and campaigning
charity. For local CAB, see phone book or
websites

Citizens Income Trust
37 Becquerel Court West Parkside London
SE10 0QQ
Tel: 020 8305 1222
info@citizensincome.org
www.citizensincome.org
Research and education on the feasibility of
a citizen's income: an unconditional income
for every citizen

Citizens UK
112 Cavell Street London E1 2JA
Tel: 020 7043 9881
josephine.mukanjira@citizensuk.org.uk
www.citizensuk.org
Alliance of active citizens and community
leaders organising for change

Citizenship (Institute for)
Clifford's Inn Fetter Lane London EC4A
1BZ
Tel: 020 7841 5159
info@citizen.org.uk
www.citizen.org.uk
Promotes informed, active citizenship and
greater participation in democracy

**Citizenship and the Law (National Centre
for)**
Galleries of Justice High Pavement The
Lace Market Nottingham NG1 1HN
Tel: 0115 952 0555
info@nccl.org.uk
www.nccl.org.uk/
Runs learning programmes

Citizenship Foundation
63 Gee Street London EC1V 3RS
Tel: 020 7566 4141
info@citizenshipfoundation.org.uk
www.citizenshipfoundation.org.uk
Educational charity promoting citizenship
education

Citizenship Teaching (Association for)
ACT
63 Gee Street London EC1V 3RS
Tel: 020 7566 4133
info@teachingcitizenship.org.uk
www.teachingcitizenship.org.uk
Professional subject association for those
involved in citizenship education

City and Guilds
1 Giltspur St London EC1A 9DD
Tel: 0844 543 0000
www.cityandguilds.com
Awarding body for vocational qualifications,
NVQs and GNVQs

**City Farms & Community Gardens
(Federation of)**
The GreenHouse Hereford St Bristol BS3
4NA
Tel: 01179 231 800
admin@farmgarden.org.uk
www.farmgarden.org.uk
Supports, promotes and represents city
farms and community gardens throughout
the UK

Civic Society Initiative now see Civic
Voice

Civic Voice
Unit 101 82 Wood Street The Tea Factory
Liverpool L1 4DQ
Tel: 0151 708 9920
info@civicvoice.org.uk
www.civicvoice.org.uk
National charity for the civic movement in
England. Making places more attractive,
enjoyable and distinctive and promoting
civic pride

Civil Aviation Authority see CAA

Civil Liberties see also thematic guide
Human Rights

Civil Liberties (National Council for) see
Liberty

Civitas Institute for the Study of Civil
Society
First Floor 55 Tufton Street Westminster
London SW1P 3QL
Tel: 0207 799 6677
info@civitas.org.uk
www.civitas.org.uk
Independent health, education and social
policy think tank

CLA Country Land and Business
Association
16 Belgrave Sq London SW1X 8PQ
Tel: 020 7235 0511
mail@cla.org.uk
www.cla.org.uk

A membership organisation and lobby group
representing rural land and business owners

CLAPA Cleft Lip & Palate Association
First Floor Green Man Tower 332B Goswell
Road London EC1V 7LQ
Tel: 020 7833 4883
info@clapa.com
www.clapa.com
CLAPA provides information and support for
all those with and affected by cleft lip and/
or palate

Classical Association
Senate House Malet St London WC1E 7HU
Tel: 020 7862 8706
office@classicalassociation.org
www.classicalassociation.org
To promote the development and maintain
the well-being of classical studies. Unites
the interests of all who value the study of
the languages, literature and civilisation of
ancient Greece and Rome

**Clean Air & Environmental Protection
(National Society for)** see Environmental
Protection UK

Cleanair Campaign for a Smoke Free
Environment
33 Stillness Rd London SE23 1NG
Tel: 0181 690 4649
www.ezme.com/cleanair/
Raises awareness about the dangers of
smoking

Clear Vision Trust
16-20 Turner Street Manchester M4 1DZ
Tel: 0161 839 9579
clearvision@clear-vision.org
www.clear-vision.org
Supports the teaching of Buddhism in
schools

ClearVision Project
Linden Lodge School 61 Princes Way
London SW19 6JB
Tel: 020 8789 9575
info@clearvisionproject.org
www.clearvisionproject.org
Postal lending library of children's books
suitable for sharing by sighted and visually
impaired

Cleft Lip & Palate Association see Clapa

CLES
Express Networks 1 George Leigh St
Manchester M4 5DL
Tel: 0161 236 7036
info@cles.org.uk
www.cles.org.uk
Independent think-doing organisation, with
charitable status, involved in regeneration,
local economic development and local
governance

CLICSargent
Griffin House 161 Hammersmith Rd
London W6 8SG
Child Cancer Helpline: 0800 197 0068
Tel: 0845 301 0031

helpline@clicsargent.org.uk
www.clicsargent.org.uk
Offers professional, practical and financial
help to young people up to 21 years
diagnosed with cancer, and their families

Climate see also Choose Climate, Global,
Met Office, Meteorological Organization
(World), Meteorological Society (Royal),
Rising Tide, Stop Climate Chaos Coalition

Climate Change (Committee on) CCC
4th Floor, Manning House 22 Carlisle Place
London SW1P 1JA
Tel: 0207 592 1553
enquiries@theccc.gsi.gov.uk
www.theccc.org.uk
Independent advisors to the UK Government
on tackling and preparing for climate change

**Climate Change (Intergovernmental
Panel on)** IPCC
c/o World Meteorological Organization 7bis
Avenue de la Paix C.P. 2300 CH- 1211
Geneva 2, Switzerland
Tel: 00 41 22 730 8208 / 54 / 84
ipcc-sec@wmo.int
www.ipcc.ch/
Assessment of factual information on all
aspects of climate change

Climate Parliament
www.climateparl.net
Legislators working worldwide to combat
climate change

Climate projections see UK Climate
projections

Climb Children Living with Inherited
Metabolic Diseases
Climb Building 176 Nantwich Rd Crewe
CW2 6BG
Tel: 0845 241 2173
adm.svcs@climb.org.uk
www.climb.org.uk
Support and information for families and
professionals covering over 700 metabolic
disorders

Clubs for Young People
371 Kennington Lane London SE11 5QY
Tel: 020 7793 0787
office@clubsforyoungpeople.org.uk
www.clubsforyoungpeople.org.uk
Helps young people to achieve their
potential through social and personal
development opportunities

CND Campaign for Nuclear Disarmament
Mordechai Vanunu House 162 Holloway Rd
London N7 8DQ
Tel: 020 7700 2393
enquiries@cnduk.org
www.cnduk.org
Non-political, peace educational material &
speakers

CND (Scottish)
15 Barrland St Glasgow G41 1QH
Tel: 0141 423 1222
scnd@banthebomb.org
www.banthebomb.org

Co-operative Party
77 Weston Street London SE1 3SD
Tel: 020 7367 4150
Email via website
www.party.coop
Political wing of co-operative movement

Co-operatives UK
Holyoake House Hanover St Manchester
M60 0AS
Tel: 0161 246 2900
Email via website
www.uk.coop
Information and advice on employee
ownership, innovative co-operatives, social
enterprise and mutual businesses

Coaching Foundation (National) see
Sports Coach UK

Coal Museum (National) see Big Pit

Cocaine Anonymous UK
PO Box 46920 London E2 9WF
Tel: 0800 612 0225
Tel: 800 612 0225 (From UK Mobile Phones)
info@cauk.org.uk
www.cauk.org.uk
Fellowship of men and women who share
their experience, strength and hope to help
others to recover from their addiction

COI see Central Office of Information

Coleg Harlech (WEA)
Harlech Gwynedd LL46 2PU
Tel: 01766 781900
email via website
www.harlech.ac.uk
Adult education residential college. Full time
& short courses

Colitis & Crohn's UK
4 Beaumont House Sutton Rd St Albans
Herts AL1 5HH
Tel: 0845 130 2233
Tel: 01727 844296
info@ChronsAndColitis.org.uk
www.nacc.org.uk
Aims to improve life for everyone affected by
Inflammatory Bowel Disease (IBD)

CollegesWales
7 Cae Gwyrdd, Tongwynlais Cardiff CF15 7AB
Tel: 029 2052 2500
hello@collegeswales.ac.uk
www.collegeswales.ac.uk
Raises the profile of further education with key decision-makers to improve opportunities for learners in Wales

Colombia Solidarity Campaign Fighting for peace with justice
PO Box 8446 London N17 6NZ
info@colombiasolidarity.org.uk
www.colombiasolidarity.org.uk
Campaigns for a socially just and sustainable peace in Colombia based on respect for the human rights and diversity of the Colombian people

CoMA Contemporary Music-making for Amateurs
RICH MIX 35 - 47 Bethnal Green Road London E1 6LA
Tel: 020 7739 4680
admin@coma.org
www.coma.org
Promotes participation in contemporary music through commissions, music ensembles and training

Combat Stress
Tyrwhitt House Oaklawn Road Leatherhead Surrey KT22 0BX
Tel: 01372 587000
contactus@combatstress.org.uk
www.combatstress.org.uk
Treatment and support to Ex-Service men and women with conditions such as Post Traumatic Stress Disorder (PTSD), depression and anxiety disorders

Comic Relief
89 Albert Embankment London SE1 7TP
Tel: 020 7820 2000
Minicom: 0207 820 2005
info@comicrelief.com
www.comicrelief.com

Common Ground
Gold Hill House 21 High St Shaftesbury Dorset SP7 8JE
Tel: 01747 850820
info@commonground.org.uk
www.commonground.org.uk
www.england-in-particular.info
Environmental charity; encourages people to value everyday places and local distinctiveness

Common Purpose
Discovery House 28-42 Banner St London EC1Y 8QE
Tel: 020 7608 8100

enquiries@commonpurpose.org.uk
www.commonpurpose.org.uk
Independent not-for-profit organisation that runs leadership development courses which mix people from the private, public and not-for-profit sectors

Commonwealth Broadcasting Association
17 Fleet St London EC4Y 1AA
Tel: 020 7583 5550
Email via website
www.cba.org.uk
Working for quality broadcasting throughout the Commonwealth

Commonwealth Education Trust
New Zealand House 80 Haymarket London SW1Y 4TQ
Tel: 020 7024 9822
information@cet1886.org
www.cet1886.org/
Principal objective is to advance education in the Commonwealth

Commonwealth Games Federation
2nd Floor 138 Piccadilly London W1J 7NR
Tel: 020 7491 8801
info@thecgf.com
www.thecgf.com
The organisation that is responsible for the direction and control of the Commonwealth Games – a unique, world class, multi-sports event which is held once every four years. It is often referred to as the 'Friendly Games'

Commonwealth Institute now see Commonwealth Education Trust

Commonwealth Scolarship Commission in the UK
Woburn House 20-24 Tavistock Square London WC1H 9HF
Tel: 0207 380 6700
email via website
http://cscuk.dfid.gov.uk
Offers opportunities to Commonwealth citizens to study in the UK and to identify UK citizens to study overseas

Commonwealth Society (Royal) RCS
25 Northumberland Ave London WC2N 5AP
Tel: 020 7766 9200
info@thercs.org
www.thercs.org
Promotes and educates about the Commonwealth. Provides a multicultural meeting place. Does not give out grants or sponsorship

Commonwealth Society for the Deaf see Sound Seekers

Commonwealth Youth Exchange Council
7 Lion Yard Tremadoc Road London SW4
7NQ
Tel: 020 7498 6151
ival@cyec.org.uk
www.cyec.org.uk
Promotes educational exchanges for 15-25
year olds from Britain and their partners in
the Commonwealth

Communication Trust
8 Wakley Street London EC1V 7QE
Tel: 0207 843 2526
enquiries@thecommunicationtrust.org.uk
www.thecommunicationtrust.org.uk
Highlights the importance of speech,
language and communication to enable
practitioners to access the best training and
expertise to support the communication
needs of all children

**Communities and Local Government
(Department for)**
Eland House Bressenden Place London
SW1E 5DU
Tel: 0303 444 0000
contactus@communities.gov.uk
www.communities.gov.uk
Helping to create a free, fair and responsible
Big Society by putting power in the hands of
citizens, neighbourhoods and councils

Communities Empowerment Network
Unit 104 Shakespeare Business Centre
245a Coldharbour Lane Brixton SW9 8RR
Tel: 0207 7330297
post@compowernet.org
www.compowernet.org
Provides support for people experiencing
mistreatment and disadvantage in education

**Communities in Rural England (Action
with) ACRE**
Somerford Court Somerford Rd Cirencester
GL7 1TW
Tel: 01285 653477
acre@acre.org.uk
www.acre.org.uk
A national charity supporting sustainable
rural community development

Community and Youth Workers in Unite
Transport House 211 Broad Street
Birmingham B15 1AY
Tel: 0121 643 6221
Email via website
www.cywu.org.uk
Trade union for youth, community, play
workers, mentors and personal advisers.
Part of Unite the Union, the biggest trade
union in Europe

Community Composting Network
67 Alexandra Rd Sheffield S2 3EE
Tel: 0114 258 0483
info@communitycompost.org
www.communitycompost.org
Advice & support

Community Dance (Foundation for)
LCB Depot 31 Rutland Street Leicester
LE1 1RE
Tel: 0116 253 3453
info@communitydance.org.uk
www.communitydance.org.uk
Professional organisation for anyone
involved in creating opportunities for people
to experience and participate in dance

Community Foundation Network
12 Angel Gate
320-326 City Road London EC1V 2PT
Tel: 020 7713 9326
network@communityfoundations.org.uk
www.communityfoundations.org.uk
National network linking, promoting and
supporting over 60 community foundations
throughout the UK

Community Fund see Big Lottery Fund

**Community Justice National Training
Organisation** see Skills for Justice

Community Matters
12-20 Baron St Islington London N1 9LL
Tel: 020 7837 7887
Advice: 0845 847 4253
Email via website
www.communitymatters.org.uk
National federation of community
organisations

Community Media Association
15 Paternoster Row Sheffield S1 2BX
Tel: 0114 279 5219
cma@commedia.org.uk
www.commedia.org.uk
UK representative body for the community
broadcasting sector. Committed to
promoting access to the media for people
and communities

Community Pubs Foundation
230 Hatfield Road St Albans Herts AL1
4LW
Tel: 01727 867201
communitypubs@camra.org.uk
www.communitypubs.org
Prevents the loss of, or inappropriate
alterations to, a public house of community,
architectural or historical importance

Community Rail Partnerships (Association of)
Rail and River Centre, Canal Side Civic Hall 15a New Street Slaithwaite Huddersfield HD7 5AB
Tel: 01484 847790
office@acorp.uk.com
www.acorp.uk.com
Association of organisations promoting links between railways and local communities

Community Self Build Agency
Swale Foyer Bridge Road Sheerness Kent ME12 1RH
Tel: 01795 663 073
info@communityselfbuildagency.org.uk
www.communityselfbuildagency.org.uk
Aims to create more opportunities for people to acquire the knowledge and skills to build their own homes, focusing particularly on those in housing need

Community Service Volunteers CSV
237 Pentonville Rd London N1 9NJ
Tel: 020 7278 6601
information@csv.org.uk
www.csv.org.uk
Creates opportunities for everyone to play an active part in their community

Community Transport Association UK
Central Support Office Highbank Halton St Hyde SK14 2NY
Tel: 0845 130 6195
Tel: 0161 351 1475
info@ctauk.org
www.ctauk.org
Co-ordinating body for voluntary and community transport

& London Office
CAN Mezzanine 45-51 East Road Old Street London N1 6AH
Tel: 020 7250 8362
info@ctauk.org
www.ctauk.org
Co-ordinating body for voluntary and community transport

& Northern Ireland Office
109-112 CityEast 68-72 Newtownards Road Belfast BT4 1GW
Tel: 028 9094 1661
info@ctauk.org
www.ctauk.org
Co-ordinating body for voluntary and community transport

& Scotland Office
54 Manor Place Edinburgh EH3 7EH
Tel: 0131 220 0052
info@ctauk.org
www.ctauk.org

Co-ordinating body for voluntary and community transport

& South Wales Office
Room 10, Forge Fach Hebron Road Clydach Swansea SA6 5EJ
Tel: 01792 844 290
info@ctauk.org
www.ctauk.org
Co-ordinating body for voluntary and community transport

& North Wales Office
Unit 17, Morfa Hall Church Street Rhyl Denbighshire LL18 3AA
Tel: 01745 356 751
info@ctauk.org
www.ctauk.org
Co-ordinating body for voluntary and community transport

Companion Animal Studies (Society for)
SCAS
The Blue Cross Shilton Rd Burford Oxon OX18 4PF
Tel: 01993 867214
info@scas.org.uk
www.scas.org.uk
Education charity working to support and promote the health and social benefits of interactions between people and companion animals. Works in partnership with the Blue Cross

Compassion in World Farming Trust
River Court Mill Lane Godalming Surrey GU7 1EZ
Tel: 01483 521 953
Email via website
www.ciwf.org
Campaign to end cruel factory farming

Compassionate Friends
53 North St Bristol BS3 1EN
Helpline: 0845 123 2304 (UK)
0299 77 88 016 (N Ireland)
Tel: 0845 120 3785
info@tcf.org.uk
www.tcf.org.uk
Support and friendship for bereaved parents and their families, through the loss of a child of any age and through any circumstance

Competition Commission
Victoria House Southampton Row London WC1B 4AD
Tel: 020 7271 0100
Tel: 020 7271 0243 (Public enquiries)
info@cc.gsi.gov.uk
www.competition-commission.org.uk
independent public body which conducts in-depth inquiries into mergers, markets and the regulation of the major regulated industries, ensuring healthy competition

between companies in the UK for the benefit of companies, customers and the economy

Complementary and Natural Medicine (Institute for)
Can-Mezzanine 32-36 Loman Street
London SE1 0EH
Tel: 0207 922 7980
info@icnm.org.uk
www.i-c-m.org.uk
Provides register of practitioners' names and a list of courses

Complementary Medicine Association (British)
PO Box 5122 Bournemouth BH8 0WG
Tel: 0845 345 5977
office@bcma.co.uk
www.bcma.co.uk
Umbrella organisation. Has a practitioners register

Computer Aid International
Unit 10 Brunswick Industrial Park
Brunswick Way London N11 1JL
Tel: 020 8361 5540
info@computeraid.org
www.computeraid.org
Recycles computer equipment for use in developing world

Computer Society (British) now see BCS - Chartered Institute for IT

Computers see also Intellect, NAACE, Recycle-IT!

Computers 4 Africa
Unit 4 Priory Park Mills Road Aylesford
Kent ME20 7PP
Tel: 03000 112233
Tel: 01622 808897
contact-us@computers4africa.org.uk
www.computers4africa.org.uk
Encourages schools, businesses, and individuals to give used PCs and laptops to charity for onward delivery to Africa

Computing Centre (National)
The Flint Glass Works 64 Jersey Street
Manchester M4 6JW
Tel: 0845 519 1055
info@ncc.co.uk
www.ncc.co.uk

Concern Worldwide England & Wales
13/14 Calico House Clove Hitch Quay
London SW11 3TN
Tel: 020 7801 1850
Email via website
www.concern.net
Working with the world's poorest people to transform their lives

& Republic of Ireland
52-55 Lower Camden Street Dublin 2
London SW11 3TN
Tel: ++353 1 417 7700
Email via website
www.concern.net

& Northern Ireland
47 Frederick Street Belfast BT1 2LW
Tel: ++44 28 9033 1100
Email via website
www.concern.net

& Scotland
40 St. Enoch Square Glasgow G1 4DH
Tel: ++44 141 221 3610
Email via website
www.concern.net

Concord Media (Concord Video & Film Council)
22 Hines Road Ipswich IP3 9BG
Tel: 01473 726012
sales@concordmedia.org.uk
www.concordmedia.co.uk
Hires & sells videos concerned with social welfare, counselling, health & medical education and domestic violence

Conductive Education (The National Institute of)
www.conductive-education.org.uk
Teaches children and adults with movement disabilities the skills and practical techniques they need to control their bodies

Connect The communication disability network
16-18 Marshalsea Road London SE1 1HL
Tel. 020 7367 0840
info@ukconnect.org
www.ukconnect.org
Charity for people living with aphasia, a communication disability which usually occurs after stroke or brain injury

Connect Youth now see Youth in Action

Connexions Direct now see Directgov

Conscience
Archway Resource Centre 1B Waterlow Rd
London N19 5NJ
Tel: 020 7561 1061
info@conscienceonline.org.uk
www.conscienceonline.org.uk/
Campaigns for the right for those ethically opposed to war to have the military part of their taxes spent on peace-building initiatives

Conservation see thematic guide - Environment and Countryside & Heritage

Conservation (Institute of) see ICON

Conservation of Energy (Association for the)
Westgate House 2A Prebend St London N1 8PT
Tel: 020 7359 8000
Email via website
www.ukace.org
Aims to reduce overall energy demand to ensure a secure and sustainable energy future

Conservation of Plants & Gardens (National Council for the)
Plant Heritage 12 Home Farm Loseley Park Guildford GU3 1HS
Tel: 01483 447 540
info@plantheritage.org.uk
www.nccpg.com
Charity responsible for National Plant Collection Scheme – 'living libraries' of individual species, cared for by dedicated specialist growers

Conservation Volunteers see also BTCV

Conservation Volunteers Northern Ireland (BTCV)
Beech House 159 Ravenhill Road Belfast BT6 0BP Cardiff CF14 7JJ
Tel: 028 9064 5169
cvni@btcv.org.uk
www2.btcv.org.uk/display/btcv_wales

Conservative Party
30 Millbank London SW1P 4DP
Tel: 020 7222 9000
email via website
www.conservatives.com

Consumer Affairs (Research Institute for) see Ricability

Consumer Council (National) now see Consumer Focus

Consumer Credit Counselling Service
Wade House Merrion Centre Leeds LS2 8NG
Helpline: 0800 138 1111
Email via website
www.cccs.co.uk
Charity funded by the financial services industry specialising in debt management plans

Consumer Direct
Tel: 08454 04 05 06
Welsh-speaking adviser: 08454 04 05 05
email via website
www.consumerdirect.gov.uk

Government-funded telephone and online service offering information and advice on consumer issues

Consumer Focus Campaigning for a fair deal
Fleetbank House Salisbury Square London EC4Y 8JX
Tel: 020 7799 7900
contact@consumerfocus.org.uk
www.consumerfocus.org.uk
Tackles the issues that matter to consumers, and aims to give people a stronger voice. Work with consumers and with a range of organisations to champion creative solutions that make a difference to consumers' lives.

& Scotland's Consumer Council
Royal Exchange House 100 Queen Street Glasgow G1 3DN
Consumer Direct: 08454 04 05 06
Tel: 020 7799 7900
mail@consumerfocus-scotland.org.uk
www.consumerfocus.org.uk/scotland/

& Wales' Consumer Council
Portcullis House 21 Cowbridge Road East Cardiff CF11 9SR
Consumer Direct: 08454 04 05 06
Tel: 029 2078 7100
contactwales@consumerfocus.org.uk
www.consumerfocus.org.uk/wales/

Consumer Focus Post Campaigning for a fair deal
Elizabeth House 116 Holywood Road Belfast BT4 1NY
Consumer Direct: 08454 04 05 06
Tel: 028 9067 4833
contact.post@consumerfocus.org.uk
www.consumerfocus.org.uk/northern-ireland/
Champion for postal consumers in Northern Ireland

Consumers International
24 Highbury Cres Islington London N5 1RX
Tel: 020 7226 6663
consint@consint.org
www.consumersinternational.org
Defends the rights of all consumers, especially the poorest, by international campaigning

Consumers' Association see Which?

Contact a Family
209-211 City Rd London EC1V 1JN
Helpline: 0808 808 3555
Tel: 020 7608 8700
Textphone: 0808 808 3556
helpline@cafamily.org.uk
www.cafamily.org.uk
Supporting families who care for children
with any disability or health condition
including rare disorders

Contact the Elderly
15 Henrietta St Covent Garden
London WC2E 8QG
Freephone: 0800 716543
Tel: 020 7240 0630
info@contact-the-elderly.org.uk
www.contact-the-elderly.org.uk
Links volunteers with isolated elderly people
for monthly outings

Contemporary Art Society
11-15 Emerald Street London WC1N 3QL
Tel: 020 7831 1243
info@contemporaryartsociety.org
www.contempart.org.uk
Promotes collection of contemporary art and
acquires works by living artists for gift to
public collections in UK

Continence Foundation now see Bladder
and Bowel Foundation

ContinYou Changing lives through learning
Unit C1 Grovelands Court Grovelands
Estate Longford Rd Exhall Coventry CV7
9NE
Tel: 024 7658 8440
email via website
www.continyou.org.uk
Works in education, health, economic and
community regeneration nationally and
internationally

Control Arms
www.controlarms.org
Control Arms is a campaign jointly run by
Amnesty International, IANSA and Oxfam

Core
Freepost
LON4268 London NW1 0YT
Tel: 020 7486 0341
info@corecharity.org.uk
www.corecharity.org.uk
Information for people with digestive
problems from food poisoning to bowel
cancer. Medical research

Corporate Watch
c/o Freedom Press Angel Alley 84b
Whitechapel High Street London E1 7QX
Tel: 0207 426 0005
contact@corporatewatch.org

www.corporatewatch.org.uk
Research into corporate behaviour &
structure

COSLA
Verity House 19 Haymarket Yards
Edinburgh EH12 5BH
Tel: 0131 474 9200
info@cosla.gov.uk
www.cosla.gov.uk
National voice for local government in
Scotland

Cot Death see Infant Deaths (Foundation
for the Study of)

COTS Childlessness overcome through
surrogacy
Moss Bank Manse Road Lairg IV27 4EL
Tel: 0844 414 0181
Tel: 01549 402777
info@surrogacy.org.uk
www.surrogacy.org.uk
Providing advice, help and support to
surrogates and intended parents

Cottage and Rural Enterprises Ltd. now
see Self Unlimited

Couch Surfing
www.couchsurfing.com
Helping to make connections around
the world by offering some sort of
accommodation to travellers

**Council for Advancement of
Communication with Deaf People** now
see Signature

**Council of Ethnic Minority Voluntary
Sector Organisations** see CEMVO

Council of Europe
Head Office Avenue de l'Europe F - 67075
Strasbourg Cedex
France
Tel: 00 33 3 88 41 20 00
email via website
www.coe.int

Council of Europe Youth
www.coe.int/youth
An international meeting place for youth
organisations

Counsel and Care
Twyman House 16 Bonny St London NW1
9PG
Advice Line: 0845 300 7585 (Mon-Fri 10am-
1pm)
Tel: 020 7241 8555 (Admin)
advice@counselandcare.org.uk
www.counselandcare.org.uk
Advice for older people & their carers,
research & campaigns about ageing and
quality of care in care homes

Counselling & Psychotherapy (British Association for)
BACP House 15 St John's Business Park
Lutterworth Leicestershire LE17 4HB
Client Info Helpdesk: 01455 8833316
Tel: 01455 883300
bacp@bacp.co.uk
www.bacp.co.uk
Promotion of counselling & training of
counsellors

Country Holidays for Inner City Children
see CHICKS

Country Landowners Association see
CLA

Countryside Alliance
The Old Town Hall 367 Kennington Rd
London SE11 4PT
Tel: 020 7840 9200
info@Countryside-Alliance.org
www.countryside-alliance.org.uk
Campaigning organisation on rural issues.
Defends and promotes country sports and
rural life at Parliament, in the media and on
the ground

Countryside Council for Wales
Maes y Ffynnon Penrhosgarnedd Bangor
Gwynedd LL57 2DW
Tel: 0845 1306229
email via website
www.ccw.gov.uk
Advises the government on conservation
matters in Wales

Countryside Foundation for Education
PO Box 8 Hebden Bridge West Yorkshire
HX7 5YJ
Tel: 01422 885566
info@countrysidefoundation.org.uk
www.countrysidefoundation.org.uk
Promotes an understanding of the
countryside as a living, working environment
and the problems facing those responsible
for its management

Courtauld Institute of Art
Somerset House The Strand London
WC2R 0RN
24-hour Gallery information line:
020 7848 2526
Tel: 020 7872 0220
email via website
www.courtauld.ac.uk

Courts and Tribunal Service (HM)
www.justice.gov.uk
Works with a range of Government
departments and justice agencies to ensure
access to justice is provided in the most
timely and effective way possible

CP Sport England and Wales
5 Heathcoat Building Nottingham Science
Park University Boulevard Nottingham
NG7 2QJ
Tel: 0115 925 7027
info@cpsport.org
www.cpsport.org
Provides opportunities for people with
cerebral palsy

CPRE Campaign to Protect Rural England
128 Southwark St London SE1 0SW
Tel: 020 7981 2800
info@cpre.org.uk
www.cpre.org.uk
Campaigning charity that promotes the
beauty, tranquility and diversity of rural
England

CPSU see Child Protection in Sport Unit

CPT see Passenger Transport UK
(Confederation of)

CRAC Careers Research & Advisory Centre
2nd Floor Sheraton House Castle Park
Cambridge CB3 0AX
Tel: 01223 460277
email via website
www.crac.org.uk

CRAE see Children's Rights Alliance for
England

Crafts Council
44A Pentonville Rd London N1 9BY
Tel: 0207 806 2500
email via website
www.craftscouncil.org.uk
Promotes British contemporary crafts and
provides services to craftspeople and the
public

Creative Partnerships
Great North House Sandyford Road
Newcastle upon Tyne NE1 8ND
Tel: 0844 811 2145
enquiries@cceengland.org
www.creative-partnerships.com
Supports school children in deprived areas
in developing creativity and participating
in cultural activities. Funded by The Arts
Council

Creative Scotland
Waverley Gate 2-4 Waterloo Place
Edinburgh EH1 3EG
Tel: 0845 603 6000 (enquiries)
Tel: 0330 333 2000 (office)
enquiries@creativescotland.com
www.creativescotland.com
Develop the arts, screen and creative
industries of Scotland

Credit Unions Ltd. (Association of British) ABCUL
Holyoake House Hanover St Manchester M60 0AS
Tel: 0161 832 3694
info@abcul.org
www.abcul.org
Main trade association for credit unions (financial co-operatives)

Cremation Society of Great Britain
1st Floor Brecon House 16/16a Albion Place Maidstone Kent ME14 5DZ
Tel: 01622 688292/3
info@cremation.org.uk
www.cremation.org.uk
Promotion of cremation

CREST Awards
c/o The British Science Association
Wellcome Wolfson Building 165 Queen's Gate London SW7 5HD
Tel: 0870 770 7101
email via website
www.britishscienceassociation.org/web/ccaf/CREST/
Awards for creativity in science and technology

Cricinfo
www.cricinfo.com/
Cricket information website

Cricket see also Cricinfo, MCC

Cricket Board (England & Wales) ECB
Lord's Cricket Ground London NW8 8QZ
Tel: 020 7432 1200
www.ecb.co.uk
Governing body

Crime and Justice Studies (Centre for)
2 Langley Lane London SW8 1GB
Tel: 020 7840 6110
info@crimeandjustice.org.uk
www.crimeandjustice.org.uk
Non-campaigning body for all concerned with criminal justice

Crime Concern now see Catch22

Crimestoppers
Leo House Railway Approach Wallington SM6 0DX
Tel: 0800 555 111 (for public to give info about crime anonymously)
email via website
www.crimestoppers-uk.org
Only charity in the UK helping to solve crimes

Criminal Cases Review Commission
5 St Philip's Place Birmingham B3 2PW
Tel: 0121 233 1473
info@ccrc.gov.uk
www.ccrc.gov.uk
Independent public body set up to investigate possible miscarriages of justice in England, Wales and Northern Ireland. Assesses whether convictions or sentences should be referred to a court of appeal.

Criminal Defence Service Legal Services Commission

Criminal Injuries Compensation Authority
Tay House 300 Bath Street Glasgow G2 4LN
Freephone: 0800 358 3601
email via website
www.justice.gov.uk/guidance/compensation-schemes/cica/index.htm
Government organisation that can pay money (compensation) to people who have been physically or mentally injured because they were the blameless victim of a violent crime

Criminal Justice System now see Directgov

CRIN Child Rights Information Network
East Studio 2 Pontypool Place London SE1 8QF
Tel: 020 7401 2257
info@crin.org
www.crin.org
Global network coordinating information and promoting action on child rights

Crisis (UK)
66 Commerical St London E1 6LT
Tel: 0300 636 1967
enquiries@crisis.org.uk
www.crisis.org.uk
National charity for single homeless people

Crisis Counselling for Alleged Shoplifters
PO Box 147 Stanmore Middlesex HA7 4PQ
Tel: 020 8954 8987

Croquet Association
c/o Cheltenham Croquet Club Old Bath Rd Cheltenham GL53 7DF
Tel: 01242 242318
caoffice@croquet.org.uk
www.croquet.org.uk
National governing body for the sport of Croquet in England, Wales, Northern Ireland, the Channel Islands and the Isle of Man

Cross Cultural Solutions
Tower Point 44 North Road Brighton BN1 1YR
Tel: 0845 458 2781 / 2782
Tel: 01273 666392
infouk@crossculturalsolutions.org
www.crossculturalsolutions.org
Operates international volunteer programmes

Crossroads Care
Tel: 0845 450 0350
email via website
www.crossroads.org.uk
Support for carers and the people they care
for

Crossroads Women's Centre
230a Kentish Town Road London NW5 2AB
or PO Box 287 London NW6 5QU
Tel: 020 7482 2496 (voice/minicom) (manned
Mon-Fri 1.30pm-4pm)
allwomencount@crossroadswomen.net
www.allwomencount.net
Base for a number of organisations covering
a wide range of women's issues

Crown Estates
16 New Burlington Place London W1S 2HX
Tel: 020 7851 5000
email via website
www.crownestate.co.uk
Manages land belonging to the Crown

&

6 Bell's Brae Edinburgh EH4 3BJ
Tel: 0131 260 6070
email via website
www.crownestate.co.uk
Manages land belonging to the Crown

**Crown Green Bowling Association
(British)**
94 Fishers Lane Pensby Wirral CH61 8SB
Tel: 0151 648 5740
email via website
http://talkingbowls.sports.officelive.com/
default.aspx

Crown Prosecution Service
Rose Court 2 Southwark Bridge London
SE1 9HS
Tel: 020 3357 0000
email via website
www.cps.gov.uk

Cruel Sports Ltd (League Against)
New Sparling House Holloway Hill
Godalming
 Surrey GU7 1QZ
Tel: 01483 524 250
info@league.org.uk
www.league.org.uk
Campaigning for the welfare of animals
involved in sport

Crufts Dog Show
The Kennel Club 1-5 Clarges St Piccadilly
London W1J 8AB
Tickets: 0844 444 9944
Tel: 0844 463 3980
Email via website
www.crufts.org.uk
Annual canine spectacular

Cruising Association
CA House 1 Northey St Limehouse Basin
London E14 8BT
Tel: 020 7537 2828
email via website
www.cruising.org.uk
A worldwide association of cruising boaters
with headquarters in London containing an
extensive library

Cruse Bereavement Care
PO Box 800 Richmond Surrey TW9 1RG
Helpline: 0844 477 9400
Tel: 020 8939 9530
info@cruse.org.uk
www.crusebereavementcare.org.uk
www.rd4u.org.uk
Support groups, advice & practical
information. Link to RD4U website designed
for young people by young people

CRY see Cardiac Risk in the Young

Cry-sis
BM Cry-sis London WC1N 3XX (please
send stamped addressed envelope for a
reply)
Helpline: 08451 228 669
www.cry-sis.org.uk
Support for families with excessively crying,
sleepless & demanding children

CSET see Education and Training (Centre
for the Study of)

CTC The UK's national cyclists'
organisation
Parklands Railton Rd Guildford GU2 9JX
Tel: 0844 736 8450
Direct line: 01483 238 337
cycling@ctc.org.uk
www.ctc.org.uk
Protecting and promoting the rights of
cyclists

Cuba Solidarity Campaign
c/o UNITE Woodberry 218 Green Lanes
London N4 2HB
Tel: 020 8800 0155
office@cuba-solidarity.org.uk
www.cuba-solidarity.org.uk
Campaigns in the UK against the US
blockade of Cuba

Cued Speech Association UK Complete
spoken language through vision
9 Jawbone Hill Dartmouth Devon TQ6 9RW
Tel: 01803 832 784 (voice and textphone)
info@cuedspeech.co.uk
www.cuedspeech.co.uk
Cued Speech overcomes the problems of
lip-reading and thus enables deaf children
and adults to understand full spoken
language

Cult Information Centre
BCM Cults London WC1N 3XX
Tel: 0845 4500 868
www.cultinformation.org.uk
Help and information for families and friends
of people involved in cults. Gives talks and
offers information to media and researchers

Culture, Media & Sport (Department for)
2-4 Cockspur St London SW1Y 5DH
Tel: 020 7211 6000
enquiries@culture.gov.uk
www.culture.gov.uk

Culture24
Office 4 28 Kensington Street Brighton
BN1 4AJ
Tel: 01273 623266
info@culture24.org.uk
www.culture24.org.uk
Latest news, exhibition reviews, links,
event listings and education resources
from thousands of UK museums, galleries,
archives and libraries, all in one place

Currency converter
www.xe.com/ucc/

Curvature of the spine see Scoliosis
Association (UK)

Customs and Excise see HM Revenue
and Customs

Cutty Sark Trust
2 Greenwich Church St London SE10 9BG
Tel: 020 8858 2698
enquiries@cuttysark.org.uk
www.cuttysark.org.uk
To conserve and display the clipper ship
'Cutty Sark'

CyberMentors
Beatbullying Units 1 + 4 Belvedere Road
London SE19 2AT
Tel: 0208 771 3377
admin@beatbullying.org
www.cybermentors.org.uk
Supports all young people affected by
bullying and uses social networking to allow
young people at different levels to mentor
each other.

Cyclenation
54-57 Allison Street Digbeth Birmingham
B5 5TH
email via website
www.cyclenation.org.uk
In support of cycling

Cycling see also Bike Events, Bike Express
(European), CTC, Sustrans, Tandem Club

Cycling (British)
Stuart St Manchester M11 4DQ
Tel: 0161 274 2000
info@britishcycling.org.uk

www.britishcycling.org.uk
National Governing Body for cycling in the
UK whose aim is to inspire participation
in cycling as a sport, recreation and
sustainable transport through achieving
worldwide success

Cycling Association (Welsh)
www.welshcycling.org

Cycling Campaign (London)
2 Newhams Row London SE1 3UZ
Tel: 020 7234 9310
info@lcc.org.uk
www.lcc.org.uk
The voice of cyclists in Greater London,
working to create a better city for all

Cycling Centre (National)
Stuart St Manchester M11 4DQ
Tel: 0161 223 2244
admin@nationalcyclingcentre.com
www.nationalcyclingcentre.com
Centre for training in track racing cycling
and other sports events

Cycling Projects
3 Priory Court Buttermarket Street
Warrington WA1 2NP
Tel: 01925 234 213
ian.tierney@cycling.org.uk
www.cycling.org.uk
Cycling related training, bringing cycling to
disabled people, encouraging people with
poor health to take up cycling and working
with excluded communities to help them
make cycling part of their lives. Runs Health
on Wheels and Wheels for All projects

Cycling Union (International) Union
Cycliste Internationale
International Cycling Union (UCI)
Ch. de la Mêlée 12 1860 Aigle Switzerland
Tel: 00 41 24 468 5811
admin@uci.ch
www.uci.ch
Develops and promotes all aspects of
cycling

Cyclists Touring Club now see CTC

Cyclists' Federation (European)
Rue Franklin, 28 1000 Brussels, Belgium
Tel: 0032 2 880 92 74
office@ecf.com
www.ecf.com
Promoting and encouraging cycling
throughout Europe and abroad

**Cymdeithas Clychoedd Chwarae Cyn-
ysgol Cymru** see Pre-School Providers
Association (Wales)

Cymdeithas Ddrama Cymru see Drama
Association of Wales

Cymdeithas y Cerddwyr see Ramblers Association Wales

Cymdeithas yr Iaith Gymraeg Welsh Language Society
Ystafell 5 Y Cambria Rhodfa'r Mor Aberystwyth SY23 2AZ
Tel: 01970 624501
swyddfa@cymdeithas.org
http://cymdeithas.org/

Cyngor Celfyddydau Cymru see Arts Council of Wales

Cyngor Gofal Cymru see Care Council for Wales

Cystic Fibrosis Trust
11 London Rd Bromley Kent BR1 1BY
Support helpline: 0300 373 1000
Tel: 020 8464 7211
enquiries@cftrust.org.uk
www.cftrust.org.uk

D

Dad
www.dad.info
To give dads a free and permanent source of the information they're likely to need - from pregnancy, birth and babies to financial, legal and education info - from a dad's perspective

Dad Talk
www.dadtalk.co.uk
Community of men promoting fatherhood and exploring what it is to be a dad in 21st Century Britain

Dads House
5 Kensington Square London W8 5EP
info@dadshouse.co.uk
www.dadshouse.co.uk
Homes for Fathers and Families (HOFF) project aimed at providing the same degree of support for single fathers as is available for single mothers in the UK

Dairy Council (The)
93 Baker Street London W1U 6QQ
Tel: 020 7467 2629
info@dairycouncil.org.uk
www.milk.co.uk
Provides science based information on the role of dairy foods as part of a healthy balanced diet and lifestyle and provides evidenced based information to health professionals, the media, industry and consumers

Daisy Network
PO Box 183 Rossendale BB4 6WZ
daisy@daisynetwork.org.uk

www.daisynetwork.org.uk
Nationwide support group for women who have suffered a premature menopause

Daiwa Anglo-Japanese Foundation
13/14 Cornwall Terrace London NW1 4QP
Tel: 020 7486 4348
office@dajf.org.uk
www.dajf.org.uk
Charity supporting links between Britain & Japan. Scholarships, grant-giving and cultural events

DAN see Disabled People's Council (UK)

Dance Council (British)
Terpsichore House 240 Merton Road South Wimbledon SW19 1EQ
Tel: 020 8545 0085
secretary@british-dance-council.org
www.british-dance-council.org
Governing body for ballroom dancing in Great Britain

Dance Education & Training (Council for)
Old Brewer's Yard
  17-19 Neal Street Covent Garden London WC2H 9UY
Tel: 020 7240 5703
info@cdet.org.uk
www.cdet.org.uk
Provides a list of accredited dance courses & can offer advice on obtaining grants & careers advice

Dance UK
The Urdang The Old Finsbury Town Hall Rosebery Avenue London EC1R 4QT
Tel: 020 7713 0730
info@danceuk.org
www.danceuk.org
Membership organisation for professional dancers, choreographers, teachers and dance managers

Danceconsortium
www.worldwidedanceuk.com
Group of 19 large theatres located across the UK sharing a passion for engaging people with contemporary dance from different parts of the world

Dancesport UK
www.dancesport.uk.com
Resource on competitive ballroom and Latin dancing

Dancing and Kindred Arts (United Kingdom Alliance of Professional Teachers of) UKA
Centenary House 38/40 Station Rd Blackpool FY4 1EU
info@ukadance.co.uk
www.ukadance.co.uk

Daneford Trust International Youth Exchange
45-47 Blythe St London E2 6LN
Tel: 020 7729 1928
info@danefordtrust.org
www.danefordtrust.org
Educational & working exchanges for 18-28 year olds (from London only) in Africa, Asia & the Caribbean

Dark Skies (Campaign for)
www.britastro.org/dark-skies
The British Astronomical Association's campaign explores the issues about light pollution and includes educational projects

DATA see Design and Technology Association

DATA now see ONE International

Data Protection Registrar see Information Commissioner's Office

David Sheldrick Wildlife Trust
Unit 22 Brook Willow Farm Woodlands Road Leatherhead KT22 0AN
Tel: 01372 844 608
infouk@sheldrickwildlifetrust.org
www.sheldrickwildlifetrust.org
Dedicated to the preservation and protection of Africa's wilderness and its denizens, particularly endangered species

Day One Christian Ministries
Ryelands Road Leominster Herefordshire HR6 8NZ
Tel: 01568 613740
info@dayone.co.uk
www.lordsday.co.uk

Daycare Trust
2nd Floor Novas Contemporary Urban Centre 73-81 Southwark Bridge Road London SE1 0NQ
Information line: 0845 872 6251
Tel: 0845 872 6260 (020 7940 7510)
info@daycaretrust.org.uk
www.daycaretrust.org.uk
Campaigns for quality, accessible, affordable childcare for all

Deaf see also Cued Speech Association UK, Don't lose the music, Hearing Dogs for Deaf People, Music and the Deaf, RNID, Sense, Signature, SPIT, TAG

Deaf (Commonwealth Society for the) see Sound Seekers

Deaf Association (British)
18 Leather Lane London EC1N 7SU
Tel: 0207 405 0090
bda@bda.org.uk
www.bda.org.uk

Deaf Children's Society (National) NDCS
15 Dufferin St London EC1Y 8UR
Freephone Helpline & minicom: 0808 800 8880
Tel: 020 7490 8656
Minicom: 020 7490 8656
ndcs@ndcs.org.uk
helpline@ndcs.org.uk
www.ndcs.org.uk
Campaign to break down barriers faced by deaf children and young people

& Northern Ireland
Wilton House 5 College Square North Belfast BT1 6AR
Freephone Helpline & minicom: 0808 800 8880
Tel: 028 9031 3170
Minicom: 028 9027 8177
nioffice@ndcs.org.uk
www.ndcs.org.uk

& Scotland
Second Floor Empire House 131 West Nile Street Glasgow G1 2RX
Tel: 0141 354 7850
Textphone: 0141 332 6133
ndcs.scotland@ndcs.org.uk
www.ndcs.org.uk

& Wales
4 Cathedral Road Cardiff CF11 9LJ
Tel: 029 2037 3474
Minicom: 029 2023 2739
ndcswales@ndcs.org.uk
www.ndcs.org.uk

Deaf Education Through Listening and Talking DELTA
The Con Powell Centre Alfa House Molesey Road Walton on Thames Surrey KT12 3PD
Tel: 0845 108 1437
enquiries@deafeducation.org.uk
www.deafeducation.org.uk
Members are parents of deaf children, teachers of the Deaf, etc. Provides information and advice on the Natural Aural Approach to the education of deaf children

Deaf Sports Council (British)
Suffolk House 2 Wharfedale Road Off Dales Road Ipswich IP1 4JP
email via website
www.britishdeafsportscouncil.org.uk

Deaf-Blind & Rubella Association (National) see Sense

Deafblind International Dbl
www.deafblindinternational.org
World association promoting services for deafblind people

121

Deafblind UK
National Centre for Deafblindness John
& Lucille van Geest Place Cygnet Rd
Hampton Peterborough PE7 8FD
Information and Advice Line: 0800 132 320
Tel/Minicom: 01733 358 100
info@deafblind.org.uk
www.deafblind.org.uk
Assists people who are losing their
sight and hearing and raises awareness
of deafblindness through educational
programmes
& Scotland
21 Alexandra Ave Lenzie Glasgow G66
5BG
Tel: 0141 777 6111 (voice/text)
info@deafblindscotland.org.uk
www.deafblindscotland.org.uk

Deafness Research UK
330/332 Gray's Inn Rd London WC1X 8EE
Freephone: 0808 808 2222
Tel: 020 7833 1733
Text: 020 7915 1412
contact@deafnessresearch.org.uk
www.deafnessresearch.org.uk
National medical research charity

DebRA
DebRA House 13 Wellington Business Park
Dukes Ride Crowthorne Berks RG45 6LS
Tel: 01344 771961
debra@debra.org.uk
www.debra.org.uk
Supports people living with all forms of
epidermolysis bullosa (EB) and funds
research into the condition

Deer Society (British)
The Walled Garden Burgate Manor
Fordingbridge Hampshire SP6 1EF
Tel: 01425 655434
h.q@bds.org.uk
www.bds.org.uk

Defence (Ministry of) MoD
Main Building Whitehall London SW1A 2HB
Tel: 020 7218 9000
email via website
www.mod.uk

Defra Department for Environment Food &
Rural Affairs
Nobel House 17 Smith Square London
SW1P 3JR
Tel: 08459 33 55 77
helpline@defra.gsi.gov.uk
www.defra.gov.uk/

**Delinquency (Institute for the Study
and Treatment of)** see Crime and Justice
Studies (Centre for)

Dementia see Alzheimer's Research Trust,
Alzheimer Scotland, Alzheimer's Society

**Democracy and Electoral Assistance
(International Institute for)** IDEA
Strömsborg SE-103 34 Stockholm Sweden
Tel: 00 46 8 698 3700
Email via website
www.idea.int

Demos
3rd Floor Magdalen House 136 Tooley
Street London SE1 2TU
Tel: 0845 458 5949
hello@demos.co.uk
www.demos.co.uk
Political think-tank & publisher

Dental association see also BDA Northern
Ireland, BDA Scotland, BDA Wales

Dental Association (British)
64 Wimpole St London W1G 8YS
Helpline: 0845 063 1188
Tel: 020 7935 0875
enquiries@bda.org
www.bda.org
National professional association for dentists

Dental Council (General)
37 Wimpole St London W1G 8DQ
Tel: 020 7887 3800
Tel: 0845 222 4141
email via website
www.gdc-uk.org

Depaul International
291-299 Borough High Street London SE1
1JG
Tel: 0207 939 1220
depaul@depauluk.org
www.depauluk.org
Largest charity for young homeless people in
the UK. Affiliated body for over 50 Nightstop
schemes nationwide

Depaul Nightstop UK
www.depaulnightstopuk.org
Provides safe emergency accommodation
for homeless young people aged 16-25 in
the homes of approved volunteers

Depression see also Journeys, MDF The
Bipolar Organisation

Depression (Action on)
11 Alva Street Edinburgh EH2 4PH
Helpline: 0808 802 2020
Tel: 0131 467 3050
info@dascot.org
www.dascot.org
Scotland's national charity for depression

Depression Alliance
20 Great Dover Street London SE1 4LX
Tel: 0845 1232 320
information@depressionalliance.org
www.depressionalliance.org
Information and support

Depression Alliance Cymru now see Journeys

Dermatologists (British Association of)
Willan House 4 Fitzroy Sq London W1T 5HQ
Tel: 020 7383 0266
admin@bad.org.uk
www.bad.org.uk
Professional organisation for Consultant, Trainee and Staff and Associate Specialist dermatologists in the UK and Eire

Design see also Art & Design (National Society for Education in), Better Seating (Campaign for)

Design and Artists Copyright Society
DACS
33 Great Sutton Street London EC1V 0DX
Tel: 020 7336 8811
info@dacs.org.uk
www.dacs.org.uk
By artists for artists. Not for profit visual arts rights management organisation

Design and Technology Association
DATA
16 Wellesbourne House Walton Rd
Wellesbourne Warwickshire CV35 9JB
Tel: 01789 470007
info@data.org.uk
www.data.org.uk
Professional association – inspires, develops and supports excellence in design and technology education for all

Design Council
34 Bow Street London WC2E 7DL
Tel: 020 7420 5200
info@designcouncil.org.uk
www.designcouncil.org.uk
Incorporating CABE. Provides a one stop shop for design support and advice to industry, communities, central and local government

Design Museum
Shad Thames London SE1 2YD
Tel: 020 7403 6933
info@designmuseum.org
www.designmuseum.org

Development Education Association now see Think Global

Development Education Project
Laurel Cottage 799 Wilmslow Road
Manchester M20 2RR
Tel: 0161 921 8020
info@dep.org.uk
www.dep.org.uk
Support and training to teachers

Development in Special Needs Education (European Agency for) see Special Needs Education (European Agency for Development in)

Diabetes UK
Macleod House 10 Parkway London NW1 7AA
Careline: 0845 120 2960
Tel: 020 7424 1000
info@diabetes.org.uk
www.diabetes.org.uk
Caring for those living with diabetes

& Scotland
The Venlaw 349 Bath Street Glasgow G2 4AA
Careline: 0845 120 2960
Tel: 0141 245 6380
scotland@diabetes.org.uk
www.diabetes.org.uk

& Northern Ireland
Bridgewood House Newforge Business Park Newforge Lane Belfast BT9 5NW
Tel: 028 9066 6646
n.ireland@diabetes.org.uk
www.diabetes.org.uk

& Cymru
Argyle House Castlebridge Cowbridge Road East Cardiff CF11 9AB
Tel: 029 2066 8276
wales@diabetes.org.uk
www.diabetes.org.uk

Diabetes.co.uk The global diabetes community
www.diabetes.co.uk

Dial UK
St Catherine's Tickhill Rd Doncaster DN4 8QN
Tel/Textphone: 01302 310123
informationenquiries@dialuk.org.uk
www.dialuk.info
Provides services and support to over 150 disability advice centres

Dietetic Association (British)
5th Floor Charles House 148-9 Great Charles St Queensway Birmingham B3 3HT
Tel: 0121 200 8080
info@bda.uk.com
www.bda.uk.com
Professional association and trade union for state registered dieticians

Different Strokes
9 Canon Harnett Court Wolverton Mill
Milton Keynes MK12 5NF
Tel: 0845 130 7172
Email via website
www.differentstrokes.co.uk
Charity helping stroke survivors of working age to optimise their recovery, take control of their own lives and regain as much independence as possible by offering rehabilitative services, information and advice

Digestive Disorders Foundation see CORE

Dignity in Dying
181 Oxford Street London W1D 2JT
Tel: 020 7479 7730
info@dignityindying.org.uk
www.dignityindying.org.uk/
Membership organisation campaigning nationally for greater choice and control to alleviate suffering at the end of life

DIPEx see Healthtalkonline and Youthhealthtalk

Direct Labour Organisations (Association of) see Public Service Excellence (Association for)

Direct Marketing Association
DMA House 70 Margaret St London W1W 8SS
Tel: 020 7291 3300
info@dma.org.uk
www.dma.org.uk
Trade association

DirectGov
www.direct.gov.uk
Links to all government websites

Directors (Institute of)
Tel: 020 7766 8866
enquiries@iod.com
www.iod.com

Directory of Social Change
24 Stephenson Way London NW1 2DP
Tel: 020 7391 4800
Tel: 08450 77 77 07 (Customer services team)
enquiries@dsc.org.uk
www.dsc.org.uk
Information and training for the voluntary sector

Disability Action
Portside Business Park 189 Airport Rd West
Belfast BT3 9ED
Tel: 028 9029 7880
hq@disabilityaction.org
www.disabilityaction.org

Northern Ireland organisation which works to ensure that people with disabilities attain their full rights as citizens

Disability Alliance
Universal House 88-94 Wentworth St
London E1 7SA
Tel: 020 7247 8776
office@disabilityalliance.org
www.disabilityalliance.org
Provides information on benefits through publications, training and website

Disability Arts Cymru
Sbectrwm Bwlch Rd Fairwater Cardiff CF5 3EF
Tel & textphone: 029 20 551040
post@dacymru.com
www.dacymru.com
Work with individuals and organisations to celebrate the diversity of Disabled & Deaf People's arts and culture, and develop equality across all art forms

Disability Law Service
Ground Floor 39-45 Cavell St London E1 2BP
Tel: 020 7791 9800
Minicom: 020 7791 9801
advice@dls.org.uk
www.dls.org.uk
Free and confidential legal advice to disabled people and their carers

Disability Pregnancy & Parenthood International
Unit F9 89-93 Fonthill Rd London N4 3JH
Tel: 0800 018 4730
Text: 0800 018 9949
info@dppi.org.uk
www.dppi.org.uk
National information charity on disability and parenthood

Disability Rights see RADAR

Disability Rights Commission now see Equality and Human Rights Commission

Disability Snowsport UK
Cairngorm Mountain Aviemore PH22 1RB
Tel: 01479 861272
email via website
www.disabilitysnowsport.org.uk
Providing snowsports for all disabilities. Qualified instructors and helpers attend on lessons/activity weeks

Disability Sport (English Federation of)
SportPark Loughborough University 3 Oakwood Drive Loughborough LE11 3QF
Tel: 01509 227750
federation@efds.co.uk
www.efds.co.uk

Work to identify the needs and address the issues to ensure that sport is accessible to disabled people

Disability Sport Events
Belle Vue Centre Pink Bank Lane Manchester M12 5GL
Tel: 0161 953 2499
info@dse.org.uk
www.disabilitysport.org.uk
Creates participation opportunities for disabled people with all impairments

Disabled Children (Council for) now see NCB

Disabled Living Foundation DLV
380-384 Harrow Rd London W9 2HU
Helpline: 0845 130 9177 (Textphone) 020 7432 8009
Tel: 020 7289 6111
info@dlf.org.uk
www.dlf.org.uk
Offers advice and information on equipment and daily living for people with disabilities, older people and carers

Disabled Motoring UK
Nat. HQ Ashwellthorpe Norwich NR16 1EX
Tel: 01508 489449
info@disabledmotoring.org
www.disabledmotoring.org/
To improve independence of disabled people through better mobility

Disabled Parents Network
Poynters House Poynters Road Dunstable Bedfordshire LU5 4TP
Helpline & General Enquiries: 0300 3300 639
information@disabledparentsnetwork.org.uk
www.disabledparentsnetwork.org.uk
National organisation of and for disabled people who are parents or who hope to become parents, and their families, friends and supporters

Disabled People's Council (UK)
Stratford Advice Arcade 107-109 The Grove Stratford London E15 1HP
Tel: 020 8522 7433
ceo@ukdpc.net
www.ukdpc.net
National umbrella organisation

Disablement Information see Dial UK

Disasters Emergency Committee DEC
1st Floor 43 Chalton Street London NW1 1DU
Tel: 0207 387 0200
info@dec.org.uk
www.dec.org.uk
Co-ordinates national appeals for response to major overseas disasters

Disfigurement Guidance Centre
PO Box 7 Cupar Fife KY15 4PF
Tel: 01337 870 281
Tel: 01334 839084
www.timewarp.demon.co.uk/dgc.html
www.skinlaserdirectory.org.uk
A range of services to provide support for disfigured people and their families. Also publishes directory of skin laser clinics

Dispute Resolution see Effective Dispute Resolution (Centre for)

Divers Marine Life Rescue (British)
Lime House Regency Close Uckfield East Sussex TN22 1DS
Tel: 01825 765546
info@bdmlr.org.uk
www.bdmlr.org.uk
Dedicated to the rescue and well being of all marine animals in distress around the UK

Divorce see also Families Need Fathers, Fathers4Justice, Relate

Divorced & Separated (National Council for the)
68 Parkes Hall Road Woodsetton Dudley DY1 3SR
Tel: 07041 478120
info@ncds.org.uk
www.ncds.org.uk
Helps divorced, separated and widowed people

Do-it Volunteering made easy
www.do-it.org.uk
A searchable central database about all aspects of volunteering

Dogs see also Battersea Dogs' Home, Canine Partners, Crufts Dog Show, Guide Dogs for the Blind Association, Hearing Dogs for Deaf People, Kennel Club, Lost Doggies UK, Pets as Therapy, Support Dogs

Dogs for the Disabled
The Frances Hay Centre Blacklocks Hill Banbury OX17 2BS
Tel: 01295 252600
info@dogsforthedisabled.org
www.dogsforthedisabled.org
Provides trained assistance dogs to help disabled people

Dogs Trust
17 Wakley St London EC1V 7RQ
Tel: 020 7837 0006
Email via website
www.dogstrust.org.uk
Largest dog welfare charity in the UK. Cares for dogs at a nationwide network of rehoming centres and gives educational presentations

Domain names see Nominet UK

Domestic Violence see also Advocacy After Fatal Domestic Abuse, Ahimsa, Broken Rainbow, Concord Media, Eaves Housing for Women, Family Action, Hideout, Men's Advice Line, Refuge, Women's Aid, Women's Aid Federation

Domestic Violence (Campaign Against) CADV
PO Box 2371 London E1 5NQ
Freephone 24 Hour National Domestic Violence Helpline Phone: 0808 2000 247
Tel: 020 8520 5881
enquiries@cadv.org.uk
www.cadv.org.uk
Campaigns to increase awareness of domestic violence and to improve facilities and services for women who are experiencing or have experienced domestic violence. Campaign for legal change and the recognition of domestic violence as a workplace issue

Don't lose the music
RNID   19-23 Featherstone Street London EC1Y 8SL
Telephone/Textphone: 020 7296 8142
dontlosethemusic@rnid.org.uk
www.dontlosethemusic.com
A campaign run by RNID to protect people against hearing loss caused by listening to too-loud music.

Donkey Breed Society
The Hermitage Pootings Edenbridge Kent TN8 6SD
Tel: 01732 864414
societysecretary@donkeybreed society. co.uk
www.donkeybreedsociety.co.uk

Donkey Sanctuary
Sidmouth Devon EX10 0NU
Tel: 01395 578222
email via website
www.thedonkeysanctuary.org.uk
Registered charity working worldwide for donkeys

Donor Conception Network
154 Caledonian Road London N1 9RD
Tel: 020 7278 2608
email via website
www.donor-conception-network.org/
Self-help network of over 1,300 families created with the help of donated eggs, sperm or embryos; couples and individuals seeking to found a family this way; and adults conceived using a donor

Donor Family Network
PO Box 13825 Birmingham B42 9DJ

Tel: 0845 680 1954
info@donorfamilynetwork.co.uk
www.donorfamilynetwork.co.uk
Supports donor families and promotes awareness of organ donation

Douglas Bader Foundation
45 Dundale Road Tring Herts HP23 5BU
Tel: 01442 826662
douglasbaderfdn@btinternet.com
www.douglasbaderfoundation.co.uk
Exists to advance and promote the physical, mental and spiritual welfare of persons who are without one or more limbs, or otherwise physically disabled

Down Syndrome Education International
The Sarah Duffen Centre Belmont St Southsea Hampshire PO5 1NA
Tel: 023 9285 5330
enquiries@dseinternational.org
www.dseinternational.org
Applied research and practical support improves education and transforms the lives of thousands of children worldwide

Down to Earth International Campaign for Ecological Justice in Indonesia
Greenside Farmhouse Hallbankgate Cumbria CA8 2PX
Tel: 016977 46266
dte@gn.apc.org
www.downtoearth-indonesia.org/
Works with partners in Indonesia and internationally to promote climate justice and sustainable livelihoods in Indonesia

Down's Heart Group
PO Box 4260 Dunstable Beds LU6 2ZT
Tel: 0844 288 4800
info@dhg.org.uk
www.dhg.org.uk
Support and information for families who have a member with Down's Syndrome and congenital heart defects

Down's Syndrome Association
Langdon Down Centre 2a Langdon Park Teddington TW11 9PS
Tel: 0845 2300372
info@downs-syndrome.org.uk
www.downs-syndrome.org.uk

Down's Syndrome Medical Interest Group
www.dsmig.org.uk
Essential information for healthcare professionals on 'best practice' medical care for people with Down's syndrome in the UK and Ireland. Produced by a network of doctors from the UK and Republic of Ireland

Down's Syndrome Scotland
158/160 Balgreen Road Edinburgh EH11 3AU
Tel: 0131 313 4225
info@dsscotland.org.uk
www.dsscotland.org.uk

Downing Street see 10 Downing Street Website

Dr Edward Bach see Bach Centre

Dragonfly Society (British)
23 Bowker Way Whittlesey Peterborough PE7 1PY
Tel: 01733 204286
bdssecretary@dragonflysoc.org.uk
www.british-dragonflies.org.uk

Drama see also National Drama, NODA, RADA, Student Drama Festival (National), Teaching of Drama (National Association for the), Theatre Council (Independent), Theatre for Children and Young People (International Association), Youth Theatres (National Association of)

Drama Association of Wales Cymdeithas Ddrama Cymru
The Old Library Singleton Rd Splott Cardiff CF24 2ET
Tel. 029 2045 2200
info@dramawales.org.uk
www.dramawales.org.uk
Increasing opportunities for people in the community to be creatively involved in drama. Houses the largest specialist Drama lending library in the world

Drama Schools (The Conference of)
PO Box 34252 London NW5 1XJ
info@cds.drama.ac.uk
www.drama.ac.uk
The 22 leading drama schools in UK with most courses accredited by National Council for Drama Training

Drama Training (National Council for) NCDT
249 Tooley Street London SE1 2JX
Tel: 020 7407 3686
info@ncdt.co.uk
www.ncdt.co.uk
Provides a list of accredited drama courses & can offer advice on obtaining grants & careers advice

Dramatic Need
37 Wakeman Road London NW10 5BJ
info@dramaticneed.org
www.dramaticneed.org
Sends international volunteers from the creative arts to South Africa to host workshops with children living in rural communities

Drawing (The Campaign for)
7 Gentleman's Row Enfield EN2 6PT
Tel: 020 8351 1719
admin@campaignfordrawing.org
www.campaignfordrawing.org
Organises events to promote drawing, including 'The Big Draw' in October UK-wide

Drink Helpline (National)
Drinkline: 0800 917 8282
Free confidential advice about alcohol related problems

Drinkaware
Samuel House 6 St Albans St London SW1Y 4SQ
Tel: 020 7766 9900
Email via website
www.drinkaware.co.uk
Useful information about alcohol and drinking

Drinking & Driving see CADD

Drinking Water Inspector – Northern Ireland DWINI
Tel: 028 9054 6474
EP@doeni.gov.uk
www.ehsni.gov.uk/environment/drinkWater/drinkWater.shtml

Drinking Water Inspectorate
Area 4a Ergon House Horseferry Road London SW1P 2AL
Tel: 030 0068 6400
dwi.enquiries@defra.gsi.gov.uk
www.dwi.gov.uk
Checks that the water companies in England and Wales supply safe drinking water that is acceptable to consumers and meets the standards set down in law

Drinking Water Quality Regulator For Scotland DWQR
Tel: 0131 244 0190
regulator@dwqr.org.uk
www.dwqr.org.uk/

Driver and Vehicle Licensing Agency see DVLA

Drug Education Forum
c/o Mentor UK 4th Floor 74 Great Eastern Street London EC2A 3JG
Tel: 0207 739 8494
email via website
www.drugeducationforum.com
Online forums for those involved in drug education. In particular those interested in the development of policy and practice

Drugs and Crime (UN Office on) UNODC
www.unodc.org

Drugs Forum (Scottish)
91 Mitchell Street Glasgow G1 3LN
Tel: 0141 221 1175
enquiries@sdf.org.uk
www.sdf.org.uk
National non government agency for policy
and information work

Drugs Helpline (National) now see Frank

DrugScope
Prince Consort House Suite 204 (2nd Floor)
109/111 Farringdon Road London EC1R
3BW
Tel: 020 7520 7550
info@drugscope.org.uk
www.drugscope.org.uk
Centre of expertise on drugs which works to
inform policy development and reduce drug
related risk

Duke of Edinburgh's Award
Head Office Gulliver House Madeira Walk
Windsor SL4 1EU
Tel: 01753 727400
info@DofE.org
www.dofe.org
Leading youth Charity. Gives all young
people aged 14 to 24 the chance to develop
skills for work and life, fulfil their potential
and have a brighter future

& Scotland
Thain House 226 Queensferry Road
Edinburgh EH4 2BP
Tel: 0131 343 0920
scotland@DofE.org
www.dofe.org/en/content/cms/takepart/
notice-boards/scotland/

& Northern Ireland
Unit 4 Lower Ground Floor Forestgrove
Business Park Newtownbreda Road
Belfast BT8 6AW
Tel: 028 9069 9100
nireland@DofE.org
www.dofe.org/en/content/cms/takepart/
notice-boards/northern-ireland/

& Wales
Oak House 12 The Bulwark Brecon Powys
LD3 7AD
Tel: 01874 623086
wales@DofE.org
www.dofe.org/en/content/cms/takepart/
notice-boards/northern-ireland/

Dulwich Picture Gallery
Gallery Rd London SE21 7AD
Tel: 020 8693 5254
email via website
www.dulwichpicturegallery.org.uk
England's first public art gallery

DVLA Driver and Vehicle Licensing Agency
Swansea SA6 7JL
Tel: 0300 790 6801 (Drivers enquiries)
Textphone: 0300 123 1278
email via website
www.dft.gov.uk/dvla/

Dying Matters
www.dyingmatters.org
Raising awareness of dying, death and
bereavement

Dyslexia Action
Park House Wick Rd Egham Surrey TW20
0HH
Tel: 01784 222300
email via website
www.dyslexiaaction.org.uk

Dyslexia Association (British) BDA
Unit 8, Bracknell Beeches Old Bracknell
Lane Bracknell RG12 7BW
Helpline: 0845 251 9002
Tel: 0845 251 9003
admin@bdadyslexia.org.uk helpline@
bdadyslexia.org.uk
www.bdadyslexia.org.uk

Dyspraxia Foundation
8 West Alley Hitchin Herts SG5 1EG
Tel: 01462 454 986
Tel: 01462 455 016
dyspraxia@dyspraxiafoundation.org.uk
www.dyspraxiafoundation.org.uk

E

e-Learning Foundation
3000 Hillswood Drive Hillswood Business
Park Chertsey Surrey KT16 0RS
Tel: 01932 796 036
info@e-learningfoundation.com
www.e-learningfoundation.com
Helps schools give access to IT to their most
deprived students and their families

E-MINE Electronic Mine Information
Network
www.mineaction.org
Supports planning & co-ordination of global
mine action programmes, issues, best
practice & technologies

**Early Childhood Education (British
Association for)** now see Early Education

Early Education
British Association for Early Childhood
Education 136 Cavell St London E1 2JA
Tel: 020 7539 5400
office@early-education.org.uk
www.early-education.org.uk
Works to improve educational provision for
children from birth to 8 years

Early Years The organisation for young children
6c Wildflower Way
Apollo Road Boucher Road Belfast BT12 6TA
Tel: 028 9066 2825
email via website
www.early-years.org
Provides information and training for parents, childcare providers, employers and local authorities

Earth First! Worldwide
www.earthfirst.org

EarthAction
www.earthaction.org
A global action alert network

Earthquake Locator (World Wide)
http://tsunami.geo.ed.ac.uk/local-bin/quakes/mapscript/home.pl
Website giving locations and other details of recent earthquakes

Earthwatch Institute
Mayfield House 256 Banbury Rd Oxford OX2 7DE
Tel: 01865 318 838
info@earthwatch.org.uk
www.earthwatch.org
An environmental charity supporting scientific field research

Eating Disorders see BEAT

Eating Problems Service
Tel: 020 7602 0062
post@eatingproblems.org
www.eatingproblems.org

Eaves
Unit 2.03, Canterbury Court 1-3 Brixton Rd London SW9 6DE
Tel: 020 7735 2062
post@eaveshousing.co.uk
www.eaves4women.co.uk
Support housing and refuge accommodation for homeless women and women escaping domestic violence plus other violence against women projects

ECB see Cricket Board (England & Wales)

ECHO
http://ec.europa.eu/echo
European Union's humanitarian arm, providing emergency assistance and relief to the victims of natural disaster or armed conflict worldwide

Eco-Schools
Keep Britain Tidy Elizabeth House The Pier Wigan WN3 4EX
Tel: 01942 612621
eco-schools@keepbritaintidy.org
www.eco-schools.org.uk

Promotes environmental awareness & has a scheme of awards

Ecological Society (British)
Charles Darwin House
12 Roger Street London WC1N 2JU
Tel: 0207 685 2500
info@BritishEcologicalSociety.org
www.britishecologicalsociety.org
Publishes a range of scientific literature, organises and sponsors a wide variety of meetings, funds numerous grant schemes, education work and policy work

Ecology & Hydrology (Centre for) see CEH

Ecology Building Society
7 Belton Road Silsden Keighley West Yorkshire BD20 0EE
Tel: 0845 674 5566
info@ecology.co.uk
www.ecology.co.uk
Ethical savings and green mortgages for properties in need of renovation and ecological new builds

Economic & Social Research (National Institute of)
2 Dean Trench St Smith Square Lond SW1P 3HE
Tel: 0207 222 7665
enquiries@niesr.ac.uk
www.niesr.ac.uk

Economics, Business and Enterprise Association EBEA
www.ebea.org.uk
Subject association for teachers

Ecotourism Society (The International)
www.ecotourism.org
Seeks to be the global source of knowledge and advocacy uniting communities, conservation, and sustainable travel

ECRA see Ethical Consumer Research Association

Eczema Society (National)
Hill House Highgate Hill London N19 5NA
Helpline: 0800 089 1122
Tel: 020 7281 3553
helpline@eczema.org
info@eczema.org
www.eczema.org

Eden Project
Bodelva Cornwall PL24 2SG
Tel: 01726 811911
email via website
www.edenproject.com
Centre for plants & a new scientific institute

Edexcel
190 High Holborn London WC1V 7BH
emai via website
www.edexcel.org.uk
Examining & awarding body

Edinburgh International Book Festival
5a Charlotte Square Edinburgh EH2 4DR
Tel: 0131 718 5666
admin@edbookfest.co.uk
www.edbookfest.co.uk
Organises the world's largest book festival in
Charlotte Square Gardens every August

Edinburgh International Festival
The Hub Castlehill Edinburgh EH1 2NE
Tel: 0131 473 2099
Email via website
www.eif.co.uk
A festival of the arts taking place every
August

Editors and Proofreaders (Society for)
Erico House 93–99 Upper Richmond Road
Putney London SW15 2TG
Tel: 020 8785 5617
administration@sfep.org.uk
www.sfep.org.uk

Education (Advisory Centre for) Ltd ACE
1C Aberdeen Studios 22 Highbury Grove
London N5 2DQ
General Advice Line: 0808 800 5793
Exclusion Advice Line: 0808 800 0327
Exclusion Information Line: 020 7704 9822
enquiries@ace-ed.org.uk
www.ace-ed.org.uk
Supports and advises parents whose
children aged 5-16 have problems in school

Education (Department for)
Castle View House East Lane Runcorn
Cheshire WA7 2GJ
Tel: 0370 000 2288
Typetalk: 18001 0370 000 2288
email via website
www.education.gov.uk
Responsible for education and children's
services

Education (Global Campaign for)
www.campaignforeducation.org
Aims to end the global education crisis to
provide Education for All

Education & Industry (Centre for)
University of Warwick Coventry CV4 7AL
Tel: 024 7652 3909
cei@warwick.ac.uk
www2.warwick.ac.uk/fac/soc/cei
Centre of expertise in education, especially
work related learning

**Education & Research Networking
Association (UK)** see JANET

**Education and Culture (Directorate
General for)** European Commission
http://ec.europa.eu/dgs/education_culture/
index_en.htm

**Education and Training (Centre for the
Study of)** CSET
Department of Educational Research
County South Lancaster University
Lancaster LA1 4YD
Tel: 01524 592679
d.daglish@lancaster.ac.uk
www.lancs.ac.uk/fss/centres/cset
Researches education, training & careers

**Education Business Excellence (Institute
for)** IEBE
Tel: 020 8481 3367
email via website
www.iebe.org.uk
Provides links between the worlds of
business and education to offer young
people a rewarding and realistic introduction
to the world of work

Education Consultants (Society of)
215 The Green House The Custard Factory
Gibb Street Birmingham B9 4AA
Tel: 0845 345 7932
administration@sec.org.uk
www.sec.org.uk
Network of individual consultants working
under a code of practice

Education for Choice
The Resource Centre 356 Holloway Road
London N7 6PA
Tel/fax: 020 7700 8190
efc@efc.org.uk
www.efc.org.uk/
Provides educational materials about
abortion

**Education in Art and Design (National
Society for)** see Art and Design (National
Society for Education in)

Education Index (British)
Brotherton Library University of Leeds
Leeds LS2 9JT
Tel: 0113 343 5525
bei@leeds.ac.uk
www.leeds.ac.uk/bei/
An index to the contents of 300 education
and training journals

**Education of Adults (European
Association for the)** EAEA
www.eaea.org

Education Otherwise
PO Box 3761 Swindon SN2 9GT
Helpline: 0845 478 6345
email via website

www.education-otherwise.org
For families who want to educate children outside the school system

Education Scotland
Denholm House Almondvale Business Park Livingston EH54 6GA
Tel: 0141 282 5000
Textphone:01506 600 236
enquiries@educationscotland.gov.uk
www.ltscotland.org.uk
Advice, guidance, products and services relating to the pre-school and school curriculum

Education Statistics (National Center for)
http://nces.ed.gov
Collects & analyses data about the USA & other nations. Part of the US Dept of Education

Educational Psychologists (Association of)
4 The Riverside Centre Frankland Lane Durham DH1 5TA
Tel: 0191 384 9512
enquiries@aep.org.uk
www.aep.org.uk
Trade union and professional association

Educational Recording Agency
New Premier House 150 Southampton Row London WC1B 5AL
Tel: 020 7837 3222
era@era.org.uk
www.era.org.uk
Licenses UK educational establishments to record TV & radio programmes for non commercial educational use

Educational Visits & Exchanges see British Council, Commonwealth Youth Exchange Council, Daneford Trust, Fulbright Commission, Youth in Action

Effective Dispute Resolution (Centre for)
70 Fleet Street London EC4Y 1EU
Tel: 020 7536 6000
info@cedr.com
www.cedr.com
Aims to encourage cost-effective resolution and prevention techniques

Egg Information Service (British)
52A Cromwell Road London SW7 5BE
Tel: 0207 052 8899
www.britegg.co.uk
Represents 'Lion' egg producers. Provides leaflets and information about eggs

EIRIS Experts in Responsible Investment Solutions
80-84 Bondway London SW8 1SF
Tel: 020 7840 5700
info@eiris.org

www.eiris.org
Researches the social and environmental aspects of companies. Provides general ethical investment information (non financial) to the public

Elastic Rope Sports Association (British)
BERSA
33a Canal Street Oxford OX2 6BQ
Tel: 01865 311179
info@bersa.org
www.bungeezone.com/orgs/bersa.shtml
Certification body for bungee jumping

Elder Abuse (Action on)
PO Box 60001 Streatham SW16 9BY
Helpline: 0808 808 8141
Tel: 020 8835 9280
enquiries@elderabuse.org.uk
www.elderabuse.org.uk
For anyone concerned about abuse of an older person

Elderly Accommodation Counsel
Promoting choice for older people
3rd Floor 89 Albert Embankment London SE1 7TP
Tel: 020 7820 1343
enquiries@eac.org.uk
www.eac.org.uk
Aims to help older people make informed choices about meeting their housing and care needs

Elders (The)
www.theelders.org
The Elders are an independent group of eminent global leaders, brought together by Nelson Mandela, who offer their collective influence and experience to support peace building, help address major causes of human suffering and promote the shared interests of humanity

Electoral Reform Services
The Election Centre 33 Clarendon Rd London N8 0NW
Tel: 020 8365 8909
enquiries@electoralreform.co.uk
www.electoralreform.co.uk

Electoral Reform Society
Thomas Hare House
6 Chancel St London SE1 0UU
Tel: 020 7928 1622
ers@electoral-reform.org.uk
www.electoral-reform.org.uk
Campaigns to strengthen democracy through changes to the voting system

& Scotland
111 Union Street Glasgow G1 3TA
Tel: 0141 227 3973
scotland@electoral-reform.org.uk
www.electoral-reform.org.uk

& Wales
Temple Court Cathedral Road Cardiff CF11 9HA
Tel: 029 2078 6522/3
wales@electoral-reform.org.uk
www.electoral-reform.org.uk

Electricity Regulation see Ofgem

Ellen MacArthur Cancer Trust
Cowes Waterfront - Venture Quays Castle Street East Cowes Isle of Wight PO32 6EZ
Tel: 01983 297750
info@ellenmacarthurtrust.org
www.ellenmacarthurtrust.org
Takes young people aged between 8-24 sailing to help them regain their confidence, on their way to recovery from cancer, leukaemia and other serious illness.

Embarrassing Problems
www.embarrassingproblems.com
A doctor's website that deals with health problems that can be difficult to discuss

EMDP Exercise, Movement and Dance Partnership
1 Grove House Foundry Lane Horsham West Sussex RH13 5PL
Tel: 01403 266000
info@emdp.org
www.emdp.info
Governing body

EMI Music Sound Foundation
27 Wrights Lane London W8 5SW
Tel: 020 7795 7000
enquiries@emimusicsoundfoundation.com
www.emimusicsoundfoundation.com
Independent charity providing funds for music education

Emily's List UK now see Labour Women's Network

Emmaus
76 - 78 Newmarket Road Cambridge CB5 8DZ
Tel: 01223 576103
contact@emmaus.org.uk
www.emmaus.org.uk
Emmaus Communities offer homeless men and women a home, work and the chance to rebuild their self-respect in a supportive, community environment.

Employment & Learning (Department for) Northern Ireland
Adelaide House 39-49 Adelaide Street Belfast BT2 8FD
Tel: 028 9025 7777
del@nics.gov.uk
www.delni.gov.uk

Employment Appeals Tribunal now see Justice

Employment Research (Warwick Institute for)
Social Sciences Building University of Warwick Coventry CV4 7AL
Tel: 02476 523283
ier@warwick.ac.uk
www2.warwick.ac.uk/fac/soc/ier
A leading research centre in the field of labour market analysis

Employment Rights (Institute of)
4th Floor Jack Jones House 1 Islington Liverpool L3 8EG
Tel: 0151 207 5265
office@ier.org.uk
www.ier.org.uk
Independent think tank specialising in employment and trade union law

Employment Solicitors
www.employment-solicitors.co.uk

Employment Studies (Institute for)
Sovereign House Church Street Brighton BN1 1UJ
Tel: 01273 763400
email via website
www.employment-studies.co.uk
Independent research and consultancy, employment and human resources issues

Empty Homes Agency
75 Westminster Bridge Road London SE1 7HS
Tel: 020 7921 4450
info@emptyhomes.co.uk
www.emptyhomes.com
Campaigns to bring empty buildings in the UK back into use

ENABLE Scotland
Enable Direct: 0300 0200 101
Tel: 0141 226 4541
enabledirect@enable.org.uk
www.enable.org.uk
Charity for people with learning disabilities & their families in Scotland

ENCAMS now see Keep Britain Tidy

Endeavour Training Limited
Units 5 & 6 Sheepbridge Centre Sheepbridge Lane Chesterfield S41 9RX
Tel: 01246 454 957
info@endeavour.org.uk
www.endeavour.org.uk
Providing personal development training for young people

Endometriosis UK
Suites 1 & 2 Manchester Street London W1U 7LS
Helpline: 0808 808 2227
Tel: 020 7222 2781
admin@endometriosis-uk.org

www.endometriosis-uk.org
Information and support

Energy Association (International)
www.iea.org
Intergovernmental body committed to advancing security of energy supply, economic growth and environmental sustainability

Energy Charity see National Energy Action

Energy Foundation (National)
Davy Avenue Knowlhill Milton Keynes MK5 8NG
Tel: 01908 665555
info@nef.org.uk
www.nef.org.uk
Charity providing advice and information on energy efficiency and renewable energy

Energy Saving Trust
21 Dartmouth Street London SW1H 9BP
Free energy saving advice: 0800 512 012
Tel: 020 7222 0101
Email via website
www.energysavingtrust.org.uk
UK's leading impartial organisation helping people to save energy and reduce carbon emissions

& Scotland
2nd Floor Ocean Point 1 94 Ocean Drive Edinburgh EH6 6JH
Free energy saving advice: 0800 512 012
Tel: 0131 555 7900
Email via website
www.energysavingtrust.org.uk

& Wales
1 Caspian Point Caspian Way Caspian Bay Cardiff CF10 4DQ
Free energy saving advice: 0800 512 012
Tel: 029 2046 8340
Email via website
www.energysavingtrust.org.uk

& Northern Ireland
Enterprise House 55/59 Adelaide Street Belfast BT2 8FE
Free energy saving advice: 0800 512 012
Tel: 028 9072 6007
Email via website
www.energysavingtrust.org.uk

Energywatch now see Consumer Focus

Engage The National Association for Gallery Education
35-47 Bethnal Green Road London E1 6LA
Tel: 020 7729 5858
info@engage.org
www.engage.org
Promotes understanding and enjoyment of the visual arts

Engage Scotland
Tel: 01738 787137
scotland@engage.org
www.engagescotland.org.uk

Engage Cymru
Tel: 01834 870121
cymru@engage.org
www.engagecymru.org.uk

Engineering Council
246 High Holborn London WC1V 7EX
Tel: 020 3206 0500
email via website
www.engc.org.uk
Regulates the engineering profession in the UK and runs the register of Chartered Engineers, Incorporated Engineers & Engineering Technicians

England & Wales Cricket Board see Cricket Board (England & Wales)

England Athletics
Wellington House Starley Way Birmingham International Park Solihull B37 7HB
Tel: 0121 7817271
info@englandathletics.org
www.englandathletics.org
National Governing Body for the sport, developing and promoting Athletics across the whole of the country

England Hockey
Bisham Abbey NSC Bisham Marlow Buckinghamshire SL7 1RR
Tel: 01628 897500
info@englandhockey.org
www.englandhockey.co.uk
National governing body for hockey in England

England Netball
Netball House 9 Paynes Park Hitchin SG5 1EH
Tel: 01462 442344
info@englandnetball.co.uk
www.englandnetball.co.uk

England Squash & Racketball
National Squash Centre Sportcity Manchester M11 3FF
Tel: 0161 231 4499
enquiries@englandsquashandracketball.com
www.englandsquashandracketball.com
The governing body for squash in England

English and Media Centre
18 Compton Terrace London N1 2UN
Tel: 020 7359 8080
info@englishandmedia.co.uk
www.englishandmedia.co.uk
Good practice in teaching English and media via INSET and publications and website resources.

English Association
University of Leicester University Rd
Leicester LE1 7RH
Tel: 0116 229 7622
engassoc@le.ac.uk
www.le.ac.uk/engassoc/
Aims to further knowledge, understanding
and enjoyment of the English language and
its literatures and to foster good practice in
its teaching and learning at all levels

English Heritage
1 Waterhouse Square 138-142 Holborn
London EC1N 2ST
Customer Service: 0870 333 1181
Tel: 020 7973 3000 (Head Office)
Minicom: 0800 015 0516
customers@english-heritage.org.uk
www.english-heritage.org.uk
www.english-heritage.org.uk/education
Official government agency which manages
historic buildings & ancient monuments.
Education section provides resource
material and free educational visits to
English Heritage sites

English Language see Bilingualism &
Literacies Education Network, IATEFL
(International Association of Teachers of
English as a Foreign Language), Plain
English Campaign, Teaching of English
(National Association for the)

English National Ballet
Markova House 39 Jay Mews London SW7
2ES
Tel: 020 7581 1245
comments@ballet.org.uk
www.ballet.org.uk

English National Opera
London Coliseum St Martin's Lane London
WC2N 4ES
Tel: 020 7836 0111
feedback@eno.org
www.eno.org
Performs all opera in English

English PEN
Free Word Centre 60 Farringdon Road
London EC1R 3GA
Tel: 020 7324 2535
enquiries@englishpen.org
www.englishpen.org
Promotes literature, upholds writers'
freedoms and campaigns against the
persecution of writers for stating their views

**English Schools' Athletic Association
(ESSA)** see Athletic Association (English
Schools')

English Speaking Union
Dartmouth House 37 Charles St London
W1J 5ED
Tel: 020 7529 1550
esu@esu.org
www.esu.org
Creates international understanding and
promotes human achievement through the
widening use of the English language

English Touring Theatre
25 Short St London SE1 8LJ
Tel: 020 7450 1990
admin@ett.org.uk
www.ett.org.uk
Touring productions of clarity and style
throughout the UK

ENO see English National Opera

Enterprise Education Trust
Enterprise House 1-2 Hatfields London
SE1 9PG
Tel: 020 7620 0735
info@enterprise-education.org.uk
www.enterprise-education.org.uk
Brings business to life for students, aged
14 to 19

Entomologists' Society (Amateur)
PO Box 8774 London SW7 5ZG
email via website
www.amentsoc.org
For people interested in insects

Entrepreneurs see Social Entrepreneurs
(School for)

Enuresis Resource & Information Centre
see ERIC – Education and Resources for
Improving Childhood Continence

**Environment (Young People's Trust for
the)**
3A Market Square Crewkerne Somerset
TA18 7LE
Tel: 01460 271717
info@ypte.org.uk
www.ypte.org.uk
Charity that aims to encourage young
people's understanding of the environment
and the need for sustainability

Environment Agency
National Customer Contact Centre PO Box
544 Rotherham S60 1BY
24hr Floodline: 0845 988 1188
Tel: 03708 506 506
Minicom: 08702 422 549
enquiries@environment-agency.gov.uk
www.environment-agency.gov.uk
Protects and improves environment, and
promotes sustainable development

Environment and Development (International Institute for)
3 Endsleigh St London WC1H 0DD
Tel: 020 7388 2117
info@iied.org
www.iied.org

Environment Council
www.the-environment-council.org.uk
Helps stakeholders to find sustainable solutions to environmental issues

Environment Protection Agency (Scottish) SEPA
Erskine Court Castle Business Park Stirling FK9 4TR
SEPA's Pollution Hotline - 0800 80 70 60.
SEPA's Floodline service - 0845 988 1188
Tel: 01786 457700
Email via website
www.sepa.org.uk

Environment, Food & Rural Affairs (Department for) see Defra

Environmental Investigation Agency
62/63 Upper St London N1 0NY
Tel: 020 7354 7960
ukinfo@eia-international.org
www.eia-international.org
Non-governmental organisation investigating and exposing the illegal trade in endangered species

Environmental Law & Development (Foundation for International) see FIELD

Environmental Law Foundation
2-10 Princeton Street London WC1R 4BH
Tel: 020 7404 1030
info@elflaw.org
www.elflaw.org
National UK charity linking communities and individuals to legal and technical expertise to prevent damage to the environment

Environmental Noise Maps
http://services.defra.gov.uk/wps/portal/noise
Maps of noise from roads, rail and industry in England

Environmental Protection UK
44 Grand Parade Brighton BN2 9QA
Tel: 01273 878770
admin@environmental-protection.org.uk
www.environmental-protection.org.uk
Membership based charity. Aims to promote policies and practices to reduce the negative effects on health and the environment of air pollution and greenhouses gases, manage and control noise and encourage the use and reuse of land

Environmental Transport Association
68 High St Weybridge KT13 8RS
Freephone: 0800 212 810
eta@eta.co.uk
www.eta.co.uk
Environmental breakdown company and lobby for a sustainable transport system

ENYAN Youth Arts Network (English National)
c/o Artswork Ltd No 23 Basepoint Anderson Road Southampton SO14 5FE
Tel: 023 8068 2535
hello@enyan.co.uk
www.enyan.co.uk
Aims to raise the profile and support for youth arts within England, creating more opportunities for the creative and personal development of young people, especially young people at risk.

Epidermolysis Bullosa see DEBRA

Epilepsy (National Centre for Young People with) NCYPE
St Piers Lane Lingfield Surrey RH7 6PW
Confidential enquiry line: 01342 831342
Tel: 01342 832243
enquiry@ncype.org.uk
www.ncype.org.uk
Runs courses for teachers and other education professionals.

Epilepsy Action
New Anstey House Gate Way Drive Yeadon Leeds LS19 7XY
Freephone Helpline: 0808 800 5050
Tel: 0113 210 8800
helpline@epilepsy.org.uk
epilepsy@epilepsy.org.uk
www.epilepsy.org.uk
Acting as the voice for the UK's estimated 456,000 people with epilepsy, as well as their friends, families, carers, health professionals

Epilepsy Scotland
48 Govan Rd Glasgow G51 1JL
Helpline: 0808 800 2200
Tel: 0141 427 4911
enquiries@epilepsyscotland.org.uk
www.epilepsyscotland.org.uk

Epilepsy Society
Chesham Lane Chalfont St Peter Bucks SL9 0RJ
Helpline: 01494 601400
Tel: 01494 601 300
Email via website
www.epilepsysociety.org.uk
Charity providing epilepsy research, treatment, assessment, care, info and training

Equal Opportunities Commission
now see Equality and Human Rights Commission

Equality and Human Rights Commission
Creating a fairer Britain
Offices in Manchester, London, Cardiff and Glasgow – see website
email via website
www.equalityhumanrights.com
Independent statutory body established to help promote and monitor human rights; and to protect, enforce and promote equality across the nine "protected" grounds - age, disability, gender, race, religion and belief, pregnancy and maternity, marriage and civil partnership, sexual orientation and gender reassignment

Equality Britain
Tel: 0151 707 6688
Email via website
www.equalitybritain.co.uk
Promotes opportunities for everyone regardless of race, age, disability, religion or belief, sexual orientation, gender or transgender status

Erasmus
Bridgewater House Manchester M1 6BB
Tel: 0161 957 7755
erasmus.enquiries@britishcouncil.org
www.britishcouncil.org/erasmus
European exchange programme for higher education

Ergonomics & Human Factors (Institute of)
Elms Court Elms Grove Loughborough LE11 1RG
Tel: 01509 234904
iehf@ergonomics.org.uk
www.ergonomics.org.uk
www.ergonomics4schools.com
Promoting ergonomics and supporting professionals using information about people to design for comfort, efficiency & safety. Supports a website called Ergonomics 4 Schools which provides ergonomics knowledge in a form suitable for anyone but is aimed primarily at secondary schools

ERIC – Education and Resources for Improving Childhood Continence
36 Old School House Britannia Rd Kingswood Bristol BS15 8DB
Helpline: 0845 370 8008
Tel: 0117 960 3060
info@eric.org.uk
www.eric.org.uk
Information, support and resources on childhood bedwetting and daytime wetting

ERYICA see European Youth Info. and Counselling Agency

ESAA see Athletic Association (English Schools')

Esperanto Association of Britain
Esperanto House Station Rd Barlaston Stoke-on-Trent ST12 9DE
Tel: 0845 230 1887
eab@esperanto-gb.org
www.esperanto-gb.org
Promotes the international language of Esperanto

ESU European Students' Union
Tel: 00 32 2502 23 62
Email via website
www.esib.org
Represents the 10 million students across Europe to European Institutions such as the Parliament

ETCO European Transplant Coordinators Organisation
www.europeantransplantcoordinators.org/clinical-resources/irodat/
Promotes organ and tissue donation in all member countries

Ethical Consumer Research Association (ECRA)
Unit 21 41 Old Birley St Manchester M15 5RF
Tel: 0161 226 2929
Email via website
www.ethicalconsumer.org
Publishers of ethical consumer magazine

Ethical Investment Research Service
now see EIRIS

Ethical Treatment of Animals (People for the) see PETA Foundation

Ethiopiaid
PO Box 31052 London SW1X 9WB
Tel: 020 7201 9981
ethiopiaid@reed.co.uk
www.ethiopiaid.org.uk
Aims to create lasting and positive change in Ethiopia by tackling the problems of poverty, ill health and poor education

Ethnic Relations (Centre for Research in)
University of Warwick Coventry CV4 7AL
Tel: 024 7652 4869
email via website
www2.warwick.ac.uk/fac/soc/crer
Major academic body in the UK for the research and teaching of aspects of race, migration and ethnic relations

EU in the United Kingdom European Commission Representation in the UK
Europe House 32 Smith Square London SW1P 3EU

Tel: 020 7973 1992
jonathan.scheele@ec.europa.eu
http://ec.europa.eu/unitedkingdom/index_
en.htm
Speaking for the Commission as its voice in
the UK

& European Commission Office in Northern Ireland
74 - 76 Dublin Road Belfast BT2 7HP
London SW1P 3EU
Tel: 028 9024 0708
maurice.maxwell@ec.europa.eu
http://ec.europa.eu/unitedkingdom/index_
en.htm

& European Commission Office in Scotland
9 Alva Street Edinburgh EH2 4PH
Tel: 0131 225 2058
neil.mitchison@ec.europa.eu
http://ec.europa.eu/unitedkingdom/index_
en.htm

& European Commission Office in Wales
2 Caspian Point Caspian Way Cardiff CF10 4QQ
Tel: 029 20895020
Andy.Klom@ec.europa.eu
http://ec.europa.eu/unitedkingdom/index_
en.htm

Eureka! The National Children's Museum
Discovery Road Halifax HX1 2NE
Tel: 01422 330069
Education Bookings: 01422 330012
email via website
www.eureka.org.uk
Hands on museum for children aged birth
to twelve

Eurodesk
British Council 10 Spring Gardens London SW1A 2BN
Tel: 020 7389 4030
eurodeskuk@britishcouncil.org
www.eurodesk.org.uk
Europe-wide information service on
European opportunities for young people

Eurogroup for Animals
6 rue des Patriotes 1000 Brussels Belgium
Tel: 00 32 2 740 08 20
info@eurogroupforanimals.org
www.eurogroupforanimals.org
Represents a united voice for animal welfare
organisations in Europe

Europa
http://europa.eu
Gateway to the European Union

Europe (Council of) see Council of Europe

Europe in the UK
www.europe.org.uk
EU information with sections on news,
culture, youth and education

European Central Bank
www.ecb.int
Central bank for Europe's single currency,
the euro. The ECB's main task is to maintain
the euro's purchasing power and thus price
stability in the euro area

European Commission Agriculture and Rural Development
http://ec.europa.eu/agriculture/index_en.htm

European Investment Bank
98-100, boulevard Konrad Adenauer L-2950 Luxembourg
Tel: 00 352 43 79 1
Tel: 00 352 43 79 22000 (General Information)
Email via website
www.eib.org

European Movement UK
Southbank House Black Prince Road
London SE1 7SJ
Tel: 0203 176 0543
emoffice@euromove.org.uk
www.euromove.org.uk
Pro-European campaigning

European Parliament Information Office in Edinburgh
The Tun 4 Jackson's Entry Holyrood Rd
Edinburgh EH8 8PJ
Tel: 0131 557 7866
epedinburgh@europarl.europa.eu
www.europarl.org.uk

European Parliament Information Office in the United Kingdom
32 Smith Square London SW1P 3EU
Tel: 020 7227 4300
eplondon@europarl.europa.eu
www.europarl.org.uk

European Parliamentary Labour Party
EPLP
Europe House 32 Smith Square London SW1P 3EU
Tel: 0207 222 1719
info@eurolabour.org.uk
www.eurolabour.org.uk

European Students' Union see ESU

European Trade Union Confederation
International Trade Union House (ITUH)
Boulevard Roi Albert II, 5
B-1210 Brussels Belgium
Tel: 00 32 02 224 0411
email via website
www.etuc.org

European Transplant Coordinators Organisation see ETCO

European Union (Court of Justice of the)
CURIA
http://curia.europa.eu

European Union Committee of the Regions
Bâtiment Jacques Delors Rue Belliard 99-101 B - 1040 Brussels - Belgium
Tel: 00 32 2282 2211
email via website
www.cor.europa.eu/pages/HomeTemplate.aspx
The EU's assembly of regional and local representatives

European Youth Card Association
www.euro26.org
Non-profit organisation that represents 40 youth card organisations in 38 countries issuing the European Youth Card which provides young people with benefits in the fields of culture, mobility, accommodation, services and products

European Youth Forum
www.youthforum.org
Brings together tens of millions of young people from all over Europe, organised in order to represent their common interests

European Youth Information and Counselling Agency ERYICA
26 Place de la Gare   L-1616 Luxembourg
Tel: 00 352 248 73992
email via website
www.eryica.org
European umbrella organisation for national youth info & counselling networks

European Youth Music Week
www.eymw.org
Summer course for advanced young instrumentalists aged 16-26, offering the chance to play a great repertoire and meet like-minded people from across the continent

Euthanasia see Care Not Killing, Dignity in Dying

Evangelical Alliance Uniting to change society
Whitefield House 186 Kennington Park Rd London SE11 4BT
Tel: 020 7207 2100
info@eauk.org
www.eauk.org

& Northern Ireland
Downview House 440 Shore Road Newtownabbey BT37 9RU
Tel: 028 9029 2266
nireland@eauk.org
www.eauk.org/northern-ireland/index.cfm

& Wales
20 High Street Cardiff CF10 1PT
Tel: 02920 229822
cymru@eauk.org
www.eauk.org/wales/index.cfm

& Scotland
Challenge House 29 Canal Street Glasgow G4 0AD
Tel: 0141 332 8700
scotland@eauk.org
www.eauk.org/scotland/index.cfm

Every Child a Chance Trust
The KPMG Foundation 15 Canada Square London E14 5GL
Tel: 020 7311 8039
email via website
www.everychildachancetrust.org
Aims to unlock the educational potential of socially disadvantaged children through the development and promotion of evidence-based, early intervention programmes.

Every child matters see Department for Education

EveryChild
4 Bath Place Rivington St London EC2A 3DR
Tel: 020 7749 2468
email via website
www.everychild.org.uk
international development charity working to stop children growing up vulnerable and alone

Everyman Project
1a Waterlow Road London N19 5NJ
Adviceline: 0207 263 8884
everymanproject@btopenworld.com
www.everymanproject.co.uk
Counselling programme for men who wish to change violent behaviour, and helpline for anyone affected by abuse or violence from men

Exchanges see British Council, Commonwealth Youth Exchange Council, Daneford Trust, Fulbright Commission, Youth in Action

Exclusion see also Communities Empowerment Network, Include

Exercise, Movement and Dance Partnership see EMDP

Expeditions see Brathay Exploration Group, BSES Expeditions, Raleigh, Scientific Exploration Society, Wind Sand & Stars

Exploratorium
www.exploratorium.edu
Museum of science, art and human perception

Extension College see National Extension College

Extreme Inequality
http://extremeinequality.org
Network of journalists trying to look beyond
conventional economics

Eyecare Trust
PO Box 804 Aylesbury Bucks HP20 9DF
Tel: 0845 129 5001
info@eyecaretrust.org.uk
www.eyecaretrust.org.uk

F

Fabian Society
11 Dartmouth St London SW1H 9BN
Tel: 020 7227 4900
info@fabians.org.uk
www.fabians.org.uk
Left of centre think tank

Facial Disfigurement see Changing Faces,
Disfigurement Guidance Centre, Let's Face
It, Operation Smile UK, Saving Faces

Facsimile Preference Service
DMA House
70 Margaret Street LondonW1W 8SS
FPS Registration line: 0845 070 0702
Tel:020 7291 3330 (Complaints Department)
fps@dma.org.uk
www.fpsonline.org.uk
Set up to help people being bothered by
unwanted and commercial sales faxes

Fair Access (Office for)
Northavon House Coldharbour Lane Bristol
BS16 1QD
Tel: 0117 931 7171
enquiries@offa.org.uk
www.offa.org.uk
Helps people from poor backgrounds go
to university. October 2010: Future under
consideration

Fair Play for Children Association
32 Longford Road Bognor Regis PO21 1AG
Tel: 0843 289 2578
administration@fairplayforchildren.net
www.fairplayforchildren.org
Advice & information on play issues &
protecting children at play

**Fair Trade Shops (British Association
for)** BAFTS
66 Longstomps Avenue   Chelmsford CM2
9LA
Tel: 07866 759201
info@bafts.org.uk
www.bafts.org.uk
Campaigns for fair trade. List of shops and
info leaflet on receipt of sae

Fair Trading (Office of)
Fleetbank House 2-6 Salisbury Square
London EC4Y 8JX
Tel: 020 7211 8000
Public enquiries: 08457 22 44 99
enquiries@oft.gsi.gov.uk
www.oft.gov.uk
UK's consumer and competition authority
– aims to make markets work well for
consumers

Fair Trials International
3/7 Temple Chambers Temple Avenue
London EC4Y 0HP
Tel: 0207 822 2370
email via website
www.fairtrials.net
Working for a world where every person's
right to a fair trial is respected, whatever
their nationality, wherever they are accused

Fairbridge
207 Waterloo Rd London SE1 8XD
Tel: 020 7928 1704
info@fairbridge.org.uk
www.fairbridge.org.uk
Gives disadvantaged young people the
confidence, skills and motivation to change
their lives

Fairtrade Foundation
3rd Floor Ibex House 42-47 Minories
London EC3N 1DY
Tel: 020 7405 5942
email via website
www.fairtrade.org.uk
Awards Fairtrade Mark

Families Anonymous
Doddington & Rollo Community Assoc.
Charlotte Despard Avenue Battersea
London SW11 5HD
Helpline: 0846 1200 660
office@famanon.org.uk
www.famanon.org.uk
Support for the families and friends of drug
users

Families Need Fathers
134 Curtain Rd London EC2A 3AR
National helpline: 0300 0300 363
Tel: 020 7613 5060
fnf@fnf.org.uk
www.fnf.org.uk
Maintaining a child's contact with both
parents after family break-up

Family Action
501-505 Kingsland Road London E8 4AU
Tel: 020 7254 6251
email via website
www.family-action.org.uk
UK's leading family charity, supporting over
45,000 families every year. Tackle some of
the most complex and difficult issues facing
families today – including domestic abuse,
mental health problems, learning disabilities
and severe financial hardship

Family and Parenting Institute
430 Highgate Studios 53-79 Highgate Rd
London NW5 1TL
Tel: 020 7424 3460
info@familyandparenting.org
www.familyandparenting.org
Independent charity working to support
parents in bringing up their children, to
promote the well-being of families and to
make society more family friendly

Family Holiday Association
3 Gainsford Street London SE1 2NE
Tel: 020 3117 0650
info@FamilyHolidayAssociation.org.uk
www.fhaonline.org.uk
Addresses issues of poverty and
disadvantage through increasing access to
holidays and other recreational activities

Family Lives
CAN Mezzanine 49-51 East Road London
N1 6AH
Parentline Advice & Support: 0808 800 2222
Tel: 020 7553 3080
parentsupport@familylives.org.uk
http://familylives.org.uk
Providing help and support in all aspects of
family life

Family Lives
CAN Mezzanine 49-51 East Road London
N1 6AH
Parentline: 0808 800 2222 (free)
Tel: 020 7553 3080
parentsupport@familylives.org.uk
http://familylives.org.uk
National charity providing help and support
in all aspects of family life

Family Mediation Scotland now see
Relationships Scotland

Family Names Profiling (GB)
http://gbnames.publicprofiler.org
Maps the distribution of surnames in Great
Britain, both current and historic, showing
patterns of population movement, social
mobility, regional economic development
and cultural identity. Link to world family
name maps via website

Family Planning Association
50 Featherstone Street London EC1Y 8QU
Helpline England: 0845 122 8690
Helpline Northern Ireland: 0845 122 8687
general@fpa.org.uk
www.fpa.org.uk
The UK's leading sexual health charity
working to improve the sexual health and
reproductive rights and choices of people
throughout the UK

Family Records Centre now see National
Archives

Family Rights Group
Second Floor The Print House 18 Ashwin
St London E8 3DL
Free confidential advice service: 0808 801
0366
Tel: 020 7923 2628
office@frg.org.uk
www.frg.org.uk
Advice by letter or telephone to families
whose children are involved with social
services

Family Search
www.familysearch.org
Internet genealogy service run by The
Church of Jesus Christ of Latter Day Saints

Family Therapy (Institute of)
24-32 Stephenson Way London NW1 2HX
Tel: 020 7391 9150
email via website
www.instituteoffamilytherapy.org.uk
Training in family & couple therapy and
clinical services

Family Welfare Association now see
Family Action

Faramir Sailing Trust see Cirdan Sailing
Trust

Farm Animal Welfare Committee FAWC
FAWC Secretariat Area 8B, 9 Millbank c/o
17 Smith Square London SW1P 3JR
Tel: 020 7238 5016 / 5124/ 6340
fawcsecretariat@defra.gsi.gov.uk
www.defra.gov.uk/fawc/
Provides independent advice to Defra on the
welfare of farmed animals and necessary
improvements

Farmers' Markets (Scottish Association of)
www.scottishfarmersmarkets.co.uk
Information on markets in Scotland

**Farmers' Retail & Markets Association
(National)** FARMA
12 Southgate Street Winchester SO23 9EF
Tel: 0845 45 88 420
info@farma.org.uk
www.farma.org.uk
Information on where and when markets are
held

Farming & Countryside Education FACE
Arthur Rank Centre Stoneleigh Park
Warwickshire CV8 2LG
Tel: 0845 838 7192
enquiries@face-online.org.uk
www.face-online.org.uk
A one-stop shop for all information and
educational materials about food, farming
and the countryside

Farms for City Children
Bridge House 25 Fore Street Okehampton
Devon EX20 1DL
Tel: 01837 55876
email via website
www.farmsforcitychildren.co.uk
Aims to provide young children from urban
areas with a week in which they work
actively and purposefully on a farm

Fatherhood Institute
Unit 1 Warren Courtyard Savernake
Marlborough Wiltshire SN8 3UU
Tel: 0845 634 1328
mail@fatherhoodinstitute.org
www.fatherhoodinstitute.org
Seeks to promote positive relationships
between men & their children

Fathers see also Dad, Dad Talk, Dads
House, Families Need Fathers

Fathers Direct now see Fatherhood
Institute

Fathers4justice Ltd
office@fathers-4-justice.org
www.fathers-4-justice.org

Fauna & Flora International
4th Floor Jupiter House Station Road
Cambridge CB1 2JD
Tel: 01223 571000
info@fauna-flora.org
www.fauna-flora.org
Conservation worldwide of threatened
species

FAWC see Farm Animal Welfare Committee

Fawcett Library see Women's Library

Fawcett Society
1-3 Berry Street London EC1V 0AA
Tel: 020 7253 2598
Email via website
www.fawcettsociety.org.uk
Campaigning for equality between women
and men at work, in the home and in public
life

FBI Federal Bureau of Investigation
www.fbi.gov
US government agency

Feline Advisory Bureau
Taeselbury High St Tisbury Wilts SP3 6LD

Tel: 01747 871 872
information@fabcats.org
www.fabcats.org

Fell Runners Association
www.fellrunner.org.uk

Female Education see CAMFED
International

Feminist Archive
www.feministarchivenorth.org.uk/
feministarchivesouth/index.htm
Holds a wide variety of material relating to
the Women's Liberation Movement (WLM)
from 1969 to the present. The Archive has
gone into storage, care of the University of
Bristol, who will eventually rehouse it

Fencing (British Academy of)
www.baf-fencing.org

Fencing Association (British)
1 Baron's Gate 33-35 Rothschild Road
London W4 5HT
Tel: 020 8742 3032
headoffice@britishfencing.com
www.britishfencing.com

Fertility see also Fertility Friends, Human
Fertilisation & Embryology Authority,
Infertility Network UK

Fertility Friends
Email via website
www.fertilityfriends.co.uk
A self help community for those
experiencing infertility

Fertility UK
Bury Knowle Health Centre 207 London Rd
Headington Oxford OX3 9JA
admin@fertilityuk.org
www.fertilityuk.org
The National Fertility Awareness & Natural
Family Planning Service

**Festivals (British & International
Federation of)**
Festivals House 198 Park Lane
Macclesfield SK11 6UD
Tel: 01625 428297 / 611578
info@federationoffestivals.org.uk
www.federationoffestivals.org.uk
Umbrella body for festivals of the performing
arts in the UK and beyond

FFLAG see Lesbians & Gays (Families &
Friends of)

FIELD Environmental Law & Development
(Foundation for International)
3 Endsleigh Street London WC1H 0DD
Tel: 020 7872 7200
field@field.org.uk
www.field.org.uk
Legal assistance in environmental and
sustainable development

Field Sports Society (British) now see Countryside Alliance

Field Studies Council
Preston Montford Montford Bridge
Shrewsbury SY4 1HW
Tel: 01743 852100
Tel: 0845 3454071 (Local rate phone call - UK only)
enquiries@field-studies-council.org
www.field-studies-council.org
Charity works with schools and individuals through network of centres to bring environmental understanding to all

Fields in Trust – FIT
15 Crinan Street London N1 9SQ
Tel: 0207 427 2110
info@fieldsintrust.org
www.fieldsintrust.org
Responsible for acquiring, protecting and improving playing fields and play space, especially for children and those with disabilities

& Cymru
Welsh Institute of Sport Sophia Gardens
Cardiff CF11 9SW
Tel: 029 20334 935
cymru@fieldsintrust.org
www.fieldsintrust.org

& Scotland
Dewar House Claverhouse Staffa Place
Dundee DD2 3SX
Tel: 01382 817 427
scotland@fieldsintrust.org
www.fieldsintrust.org

FIFA
FIFA-Strasse 20 P.O. Box 8044 Zurich
Switzerland
Tel: 0041 43 2227777
Email via website
www.fifa.com
International governing body for football

Film see also British Film Institute, Creative Scotland, History of Cinema & Popular Culture (The Bill Douglas Centre for the)

Film & Television Archive (Northern Region)
School of Arts and Media Teesside University Middlesbrough TS1 3BA
Tel: 01642 384022
enquiries@nrfta.org.uk
www.nrfta.org.uk
Collect, preserve and provide access to film, television and other moving image material related to the history & heritage of the North East of England

Film & Video Development Agency now see Film London

Film and Television School (National)
NFTS
Beaconsfield Studios Station Rd
Beaconsfield Bucks HP9 1LG
Tel: 01494 671234
info@nfts.co.uk
www.nfts.co.uk
MA/Diploma courses in professional disciplines for film and television. Short courses for freelancers

Film Classification (British Board of)
3 Soho Square London W1D 3HD
Tel: 020 7440 1570
feedback@bbfc.co.uk
www.bbfc.co.uk
Independent, non-governmental body which has classified cinema films since it was set up in 1912 and videos/ DVDs since the Video Recordings Act was passed in 1984

Film Council (UK) now see British Film Institute or Film London

Film Education
91 Berwick Street London W1F 0BP
Tel: 020 7292 7330
email via website
www.filmeducation.org
Provides award-winning teaching resources, teacher training and cinema based events which support the use of film within the curriculum

Film Institute (British) see British Film Institute

Film London
Suite 6.10 The Tea Building 56 Shoreditch High Street London E1 6JJ
Tel: 020 7613 7676
info@filmlondon.org.uk
www.filmlondon.org.uk
Regional media development agency

Financial Ombudsman Service
South Quay Plaza 183 Marsh Wall London E14 9SR
Helpline: 0800 0 234 567 free for people phoning from a fixed line 0300 123 9 123 free for mobile-phone users who pay a monthly charge for calls to numbers starting 01 or 02
Tel: 020 7964 1000
complaint.info@financial-ombudsman.org.uk
www.financial-ombudsman.org.uk
Power to settle financial complaints

Financial Services Authority
25 The North Colonnade Canary Wharf
London E14 5HS
Consumer Helpline: 0845 606 1234
Tel: 020 7066 1000
email via website

www.fsa.gov.uk
Regulatory body

Find a Parent or Child
www.findaparentorchild.co.uk
Reuniting parents and children

Findhorn Foundation
The Park Findhorn IV36 3TZ
Tel: 01309 690311
email via website
www.findhorn.org
Spiritual community, educational centre and
thriving ecovillage

Finnish Institute
35-36 Eagle St London WC1R 4AQ
Tel: 020 7404 3309
info@finnish-institute.org.uk
www.finnish-institute.org.uk
Work with artists, researchers, experts
and policy makers in the United Kingdom,
Finland and the Republic of Ireland to
promote strong networks in the fields of
culture and society

Fire Brigade (London)
169 Union Street London SE1 0LL
tel: 020 8555 1200
info@london-fire.gov.uk
www.london-fire.gov.uk
Full listings and links to all the fire brigades
in the UK

Fire Protection Authority
London Road Moreton in Marsh Glos GL56
0RH
Tel: 01608 812500
fpa@thefpa.co.uk
www.thefpa.co.uk
Organises fire protection seminars. 'Fire
Prevention' often covers school fire issues

First Light
Studio 28 Fazeley Studios 191 Fazeley
Street Birmingham B5 5SE
Tel: 0121 224 7511
info@firstlightonline.co.uk
www.firstlightonline.co.uk
Helps young people from all backgrounds
to develop their skills, talent, creativity,
confidence and entrepreneurial capabilities.
Provide opportunities for young people to
work with industry professionals on high
quality, youth led digital media projects

FirstSigns (Self-Injury Guidance & Network
Support)
info@firstsigns.org.uk
www.firstsigns.org.uk
Online, user-led voluntary organisation
founded to raise awareness about self-injury
and provide information and support to
people of all ages affected by self-injury

Fiscal Studies (Institute for)
7 Ridgmount St London WC1E 7AE
Tel: 020 7291 4800
email via website
www.ifs.org.uk
Independent research into UK public policy

Fishing see Marine Stewardship Council,
Peta Foundation, Seafish

Fit for Travel
www.fitfortravel.scot.nhs.uk
Travel health information for people travelling
abroad from the UK

Fitness Industry Association
Castlewood House 77-91 New Oxford
Street London WC1A 1PX
Tel: 020 7420 8560
email via website
www.fia.org.uk
Non-profit making trade association for the
entire health and fitness industry

Fitness League
6 Station Parade Sunningdale Berkshire
SL5 0EP
Tel: 01344 874787
info@thefitnessleague.com
www.thefitnessleague.com
Teaches rhythmic exercise to music

Fitness Northern Ireland
The Robinson Centre Montgomery Rd
Belfast BT6 9HS
Tel 028 9070 4080
fitnessni@aol.com
www.fitnessni.org
Governing body for fitness instructors

Fitzwilliam Museum
Trumpington St Cambridge CB2 1RB
Tel: 01223 332900
Education: 01223 332993
Group Bookings: 01223 332904
fitzmuseum-enquiries@lists.cam.ac.uk
www.fitzmuseum.cam.ac.uk

Five
Customer Services Five Television 10
Lower Thames Street London EC3R 6EN
Tel: 020 8612 7700
Tel: 0845 705 0505
customerservices@channel5.com
www.channel5.com

Floodline
Floodline: 0845 988 1188
Type talk: 0845 602 6340
24 hr advice & info

Flower Arrangement Societies (National Association of)
Osborne House 12 Devonshire Sq London EC2M 4TE
Tel: 020 7247 5567
flowers@nafas.org.uk
www.nafas.org.uk

Folger Shakespeare Library Advancing knowledge & the arts
www.folger.edu
Independent research library located on Capitol Hill in Washington, DC

Food & Agricultural Organisation (United Nations)
Viale delle Terme di Caracalla 00153 Rome Italy
Tel: 00 39 06 57051
FAO-HQ@fao.org
www.fao.org
Leads international efforts to defeat hunger. Helps developing countries and countries in transition modernise and improve agriculture, forestry and fisheries practices and ensure good nutrition for all

Food & Drink Federation
6 Catherine St London WC2B 5JJ
Tel: 020 7836 2460
Email via website
www.fdf.org.uk
Trade organisation for the food manufacturing industry

Food & Drug Administration (US)
www.fda.gov

Food Alliance (National) see Sustain

Food Commission (UK) Watchdog on food issues
94 White Lion Street London N1 9PF
info@foodmagazine.org.uk
www.foodmagazine.org.uk
Independent watchdog on food issues. In 2011, it will be a virtual organisation with a website and email maintained by volunteers and supported by donations and by the Food Commission Research Charity

Food Science & Technology (Institute of) see IFST

Food Standards Agency
Aviation House 125 Kingsway London WC2B 6NH
Helpline: 020 7276 8829
Tel: 020 7276 8000 (switchboard)
helpline@foodstandards.gsi.gov.uk
www.food.gov.uk
Provision of advice/information on food safety issues to consumers

Food Standards Agency (Northern Ireland)
10 A-C Clarendon Road Belfast BT1 3BG
Tel: 028 9041 7700
infosani@foodstandards.gsi.gov.uk
www.food.gov.uk

Food Standards Agency (Scotland)
St Magnus House 6th Floor 25 Guild St Aberdeen AB11 6NJ
Tel: 01224 285100
scotland@foodstandards.gsi.gov.uk
www.food.gov.uk

Food Standards Agency (Wales)
11th Floor Southgate House Wood Street Cardiff CF10 1EW
Tel: 02920 678999
wales@foodstandards.gsi.gov.uk
www.food.gov.uk

Football see also FIFA, Footy4kids, Kick It Out, Professional Footballers Association, Show Racism the Red Card, World Cup

Football Association
Wembley Stadium PO Box 1966 London SW1P 9EQ
Customer relations: 0844 980 8200
email via website
www.thefa.com
Governing body of football in England

Football Association (English Schools)
4 Parker Court Staffordshire Technology Park Stafford ST18 0WP
Tel: 01785 785970
office@esfa.co.uk
www.esfa.co.uk

Football Association (Irish)
20 Windsor Avenue Belfast BT9 6EG
Tel: 028 90 669 458
info@irishfa.com
www.irishfa.com

Football Association (Scottish) SFA
Hampden Park Glasgow G42 9AY
Tel: 0141 616 6000
info@scottishfa.co.uk
www.scottishfa.co.uk

Football Foundation
Whittington House 19-30 Alfred Place London WC1E 7EA
Tel: 0845 345 4555
enquiries@footballfoundation.org.uk
www.footballfoundation.org.uk
Funds football and other sporting facilities

Football Industry Group
www.liv.ac.uk/footballindustry
Conducts academic research into the social, economic, historical, business, cultural and political aspects of football in the UK and abroad

Football League
Edward VII Quay Navigation Way Preston
PR2 2YF
Tel: 0844 463 1888
enquiries@football-league.co.uk
www.football-league.co.uk
The central administrative office of the clubs
in The Championship, League One, League
Two and the Coca Cola Football League

Football League (Scottish) SFL
The National Stadium Hampden Park
Glasgow G42 9EB
Tel: 0141 620 4160
info@scottishfootballleague.com
www.scottishfootballleague.com

Football Museum (National)
Urbis Building Cathedral Gardens
Manchester M4 3BG
Tel: 0161 605 8200
enquiries@nationalfootballmuseum.com
www.nationalfootballmuseum.com/
Opening in early 2012

Football Museum (Scottish)
Hampden Park Glasgow G42 9BA
Tel: 0141 616 6139
email via website
www.scottishfootballmuseum.org.uk

Football Supporters' Federation
Kingsmeadow Jack Goodchild Way 422A
Kingston Road Kingston upon Thames KT1
3PB
Tel: 0330 44 000 44
info@fsf.org.uk.
www.fsf.org.uk
www.fsf.org.uk/campaigns/safestanding.php

Football Unites, Racism Divides
The Stables Connexions Centre Sharrow
Lane Sheffield S11 8AE
Tel: 0114 2553156
enquiries@furd.org
www.furd.org

Footy4kids
www.footy4kids.co.uk
Website dedicated to drills, articles, practice
plans and forums where advice from
experienced youth soccer coaches is offered

Foreign and Commonwealth Office
King Charles St London SW1A 2AH
Tel: 020 7008 1500
Email via website
www.fco.gov.uk
Provides services to British nationals and
British businesses overseas through a global
network of Embassies. Provides practical
advice, assistance and support to travellers
in emergencies

Foreign and Commonwealth Office Travel Advice
King Charles Street London SW1A 2AH
Tel: 0845 850 2829
TravelAdvicePublicEnquiries@fco.gov.uk
www.fco.gov.uk/en/travel-and-living-abroad/
travel-advice-by-country/
Advice to British Nationals on whether it is
safe to travel abroad

Foreign Policy Centre
Suite 11, 2nd Floor 23-28 Penn Street
London N1 5DL
Tel: 020 7729 7566
events@fpc.org.uk
www.fpc.org.uk
Research into business ethics, foreign
policy, human rights and international
economics

Forest Peoples Programme
1c Fosseway Business Centre Stratford
Road Moreton-in-Marsh GL56 9NQ
Tel: 01608 652893
email via website
www.forestpeoples.org
Works to assist tribal tropical forest peoples
to protect their rights and livelihood

Forest School Camps
www.fsc.org.uk
Educational charity and voluntary
organisation

Forestry Commission Great Britain
England National Office
620 Bristol Business Park Coldharbour
Lane Bristol BS16 1EJ
Tel: 0117 906 6000
fcengland@forestry.gsi.gov.uk
www.forestry.gov.uk
Government department responsible for the
protection and expansion of Britain's forests
and woodlands

& Scotland National Office
Silvan House 231 Corstorphine Road
Edinburgh EH12 7AT
Tel: 0131 334 0303
www.forestry.gov.uk

& Wales National Office
Welsh Assembly Government Rhodfa
Padarn Llanbadarn Fawr Aberystwyth
Ceredigion SY23 3UR
Tel: 0300 068 0300
www.forestry.gov.uk

Forestry Society (Royal)
102 High St Tring Herts HP23 4AF
Tel: 01442 822028
rfshq@rfs.org.uk
www.rfs.org.uk
Educational charity dedicated to promoting
the wise management of trees and woods

Forgiveness Project
3rd Floor, 38 Buckingham Palace Road
London SW1W 0RE
Tel: 0207 821 0035
info@theforgivenessproject.com
www.theforgivenessproject.com
An organisation working with grassroots
projects in the fields of conflict resolution,
reconciliation and victim support

Forum for the Future
Overseas House 19-23 Ironmonger Row
London EC1V 3QN
Tel: 020 7324 3630
info@forumforthefuture.org
www.forumforthefuture.org/
Charity with mission to achieve sustainability
taking a positive solutions orientated
approach

Forward Foundation for Women's Health
Research & Development
Suite 2.1 Chandelier Building 2nd Floor 8
Scrubs Lane London NW10 6RB
Tel: 0208 960 4000
Email via website
www.forwarduk.org.uk
International charity acting for the health,
wellbeing and rights of African women &
girls, tackling female genital mutilation, child
marriage and related rights

Fostering see also thematic guide
Adoption and Fostering

Fostering Network London Office
87 Blackfriars Road London SE1 8HA
Tel: 020 7620 6400
info@fostering.net
www.fostering.net
Charity for everyone involved in fostering

& Belfast Office
Unit 10 40 Montgomery Road Belfast BT6
9HL
Tel: 028 9070 5056
ni@fostering.net
www.fostering.net/northern-ireland

& Cardiff Office
1 Caspian Point Pierhead Street Cardiff
Bay CF10 4DQ
Tel: 029 2044 0940
wales@fostering.net
www.fostering.net/wales/

& Glasgow Office
Ingram House, 2nd Floor 227 Ingram Street
Glasgow G1 1DA
Tel: 0141 204 1400
scotland@fostering.net
www.fostering.net/scotland/

**Foundation For Peace (Tim Parry
Johnathan Ball)**
Peace Centre Peace Drive Great Sankey
Warrington WA5 1HQ
Tel: 01925 581231
info@foundation4peace.org
www.foundation4peace.org
Works nationally and internationally with:
victims and survivors of acts of terrorism
and other politically motivated conflict;
former combatants who are no longer
involved in violence and young people
whose communities are divided by faith or
racial prejudice

Foyer Federation
3rd Foor 5-9 Hatton Wall London EC1N
8HX
Tel: 020 7430 2212
inbox@foyer.net
www.foyer.net
National umbrella organisation for Foyers:
affordable accommodation, training &
support for disadvantaged young people

fPcN interCultural see Friends of Peoples
Close to Nature

Fragile X Society
Rood End House 6 Stortford Road Great
Dunmow Essex CM6 1DA
Tel: 01371 875100
info@fragilex.org.uk
www.fragilex.org.uk
Supports those affected by the most
common cause of inherited learning
disability

FRAME Fund for the Replacement of
Animals in Medical Experiments
Russell & Burch House 96-98 North
Sherwood St Nottingham NG1 4EE
Tel: 0115 958 4740
frame@frame.org.uk
www.frame.org.uk
Researches alternatives to animal testing

**France: culture and communications
website**
www.culture.fr

Franco British Council
British Section 10-11 Dacre Street London
SW1H 0DJ
Tel: 020 7976 8380
info@francobritishcouncil.org.uk
www.francobritishcouncil.org.uk
To promote better understanding
between Britain and France. A short story
prize exists to promote France and French
to a younger age group

Franco-Scottish Society of Scotland
Association Franco-Ecossaise
21 Lindsay Drive Glasgow G12 0HD
email via website
www.franco-scottish.org.uk
To foster educational, cultural and social
activities between France & Scotland

Frank National Drugs Helpline
Tel: 0800 77 66 00 (24hr freefone)
Email via website
www.talktofrank.com
Advice, information and support to anyone
affected by drugs

Frankfurt Book Fair
info@book-fair.com
http://buchmesse.de/en/fbf/index.html

Fredericks Foundation
Tel: 01276 472 722
mail@fredericksfoundation.net
www.fredericksfoundation.org
Helps disadvantaged people of any age to
realise their potential, often by helping them
to start their own business

Free the Children
www.freethechildren.com
Children under 18 years old helping children
to end abuse and exploitation

Free Tibet
28 Charles Square London N1 6HT
Tel: 020 7324 4605
mail@freetibet.org
www.freetibet.org
Campaigning for an end to the Chinese
occupation of Tibet

FreeBMD
http://freebmd.rootsweb.com
Free online access to transcribed records
of births, marriages and deaths in England
and Wales

Freecycle
www.freecycle.org
A grassroots movement of people who are
giving (& getting) stuff for free in their own
towns

Freedom Association
Richwood House 1 Trinity School Lane
Cheltenham Gloucestershire GL52 2JL
Tel: 0845 833 9626
email via website
www.tfa.net
A pressure group campaigning for limited
government & for individual freedom

Freedom of Information (Campaign for)
Suite 102 16 Baldwins Gardens London
EC1N 7RJ
Tel: 020 7831 7477

admin@cfoi.demon.co.uk
www.cfoi.org.uk

Freegle
www.ilovefreegle.org
National grassroots organisation of people
who are giving and receiving free unwanted
items in their immediate communities

Freshfield Service
Drugs advice: 0500 241952
www.freshfieldservice.co.uk
Confidential counselling & advice for drug
users & their families in Cornwall & Isles of
Scilly

Freshfields Donkey Village
The Michael Elliott Trust Freshfields Farm
Peak Forest Derbyshire SK17 8EE
Tel: 01298 79775
www.donkey-village.org.uk
Provide a sanctuary for donkeys rescued
from abandonment, abuse or neglect and
provides a safe place where special needs
children can adopt a donkey and help feed,
groom and care for it during their visit

Friedreich's Ataxia Group now see Ataxia
UK

Friedrich Ebert Foundation
London Office 66 Great Russell Street
London WC1B 3BN
Tel: 020 70250990
info@feslondon.net
www.feslondon.org.uk
Promotes better understanding of British-
German relations

Friends at the end
11 Westbourne Gardens Glasgow G12 9XD
Tel: 0141 334 3287
info@friends-at-the-end.org.uk
www.friends-at-the-end.org.uk
Friends at the End is a members' democratic
society, dedicated to promoting knowledge
about end-of-life choices and dignified
death

Friends of Friendless Churches
St Ann's Vestry Hall 2 Church Entry London
EC4V 5HB
Tel: 020 7236 3934
office@friendsoffriendlesschurches.org.uk
www.friendsoffriendlesschurches.org.uk
Campaigns for the preservation of ancient
and beautiful but redundant churches

Friends of Peoples Close to Nature
email via website
www.fpcn-global.org
A network of people concerned with survival
of savage tribal peoples especially hunter-
gatherers

Friends of the Earth
26-28 Underwood St London N1 7JQ
Tel: 020 7490 1555
Email via website
www.foe.co.uk/
Environmental pressure group and charity

& Cymru
33 Castle Arcade Balcony Cardiff CF10 1BY
Tel: 029 20229577
cymru@foe.co.uk
www.foe.co.uk/cymru_english.html

& Northern Ireland
7 Donegall Street Place BELFAST BT1 2FN
Tel: 028 9023 3488
foe-ni@foe.co.uk
www.foe.co.uk/northern_ireland_index.html

& Scotland
Thorn House 5 Rose Street Edinburgh EH2 2PR
Tel: 0131 243 2700
email via website
www.foe-scotland.org.uk
Campaigning for environmental justice, a decent environment for all and a fair share of the earth's resources

Friends of the Earth International
www.foei.org
Environmental pressure group and charity

Friends United Network now see Friendship Works

Friends, Families and Travellers
Community Base 113 Queens Rd Brighton BN1 3XG
Tel: 01273 234 777
fft@gypsy-traveller.org
www.gypsy-traveller.org
Charity working on behalf of all Gypsies and Travellers regardless of ethnicity, culture or background. Offers advice and information

Friendship Works
Studio 442 Highgate Studios 53-79 Highgate Rd London NW5 1TL
Tel: 020 7485 0900
info@friendshipworks.org.uk
www.friendshipworks.org.uk
Children's mentoring charity providing support for children across London

Froglife
2A Flag Business Exchange
Vicarage Farm Road Fengate
Peterborough PE1 5TX
Tel: 01733 558844
Tel: 01733 558960 (Wildlife Information Service)
info@froglife.org
www.froglife.org

Conservation and promotion of native reptiles & amphibians to benefit biodiversity and people

Fulbright Commission (The US-UK)
Battersea Power Station 188 Kirtling Street London SW8 5BN
Tel: 020 7498 4010
programmes@fulbright.co.uk
www.fulbright.co.uk
Awards and advice for US-UK exchange. Promotes peace and cultural understanding through educational exchange

Full Time Mothers
PO Box 43690 London SE22 9WN
http://ftmuk.wordpress.com/
Supports full time mothers and campaigns for policy changes

Fund for Animal Welfare (International)
IFAW

Fur Trade see PETA Foundation, Respect for Animals

Furniture Re-use Network
48-54 West Street St Philips Bristol BS2 0BL
donations: 0845 602 8003
Tel: 0117 954 3571
info@frn.org.uk
www.frn.org.uk
Co-ordinating body for furniture recycling projects in UK

Further Education National Training Organisation see Lifelong Learning

Future Balance
Earlsgate Lodge Livilands Lane Stirling Scotland FK8 2BG
Tel: 05600 010 560
email via website
www.forward-scotland.org.uk
Charity that provides independent expert advice for sustainability

G

Gaelic Books Council
32 Mansfield St Glasgow G11 5QP
Tel: 0141 337 6211
Email via website
www.gaelicbooks.org
Supports Gaelic publishing with grants and services and has its own bookshop

Gaia Foundation
6 Heathgate Place Agincourt Road London NW3 2NU
Tel: 020 7428 0055
info@gaianet.org
www.gaiafoundation.org

The Gaia Foundation works towards cultural and biological diversity, ecological justice and Earth democracy

Galapagos Conservation Trust
5 Derby St London W1J 7AB
Tel: 020 7629 5049
gct@gct.org
www.savegalapagos.org
UK charity set up to raise funds for, and awareness of, the conservation needs of the Galapagos Islands

Gallery of Modern Art GoMA
Royal Exchange Square Glasgow G1 3AH
Tel: 0141 287 3050
Text Phone: 0141 287 3005
museums@glasgowlife.org.uk
www.glasgowlife.org.uk/museums/our-museums/goma/Pages/home.aspx

Gam-Anon UK & Ireland
National Helpline: 08700 50 88 80
www.gamanon.org.uk
UK fellowship for those affected by compulsive gambling

Gambia Horse and Donkey Trust
Brewery Arms Cottage Stane Street Ockley Surrey RH5 5TH
Tel: 01306 627568
email via website
www.gambiahorseanddonkey.org.uk
Ensuring that the horses and donkeys on which farmers depend are well cared for

Gamblers Anonymous
c/o CVS Building 5 Trafford Court Off Trafford Way Doncaster DN1 1PN
National Public Relations Officer: 07930 557 887 London: 020 7384 3040
Manchester: 0161 976 5000 Sheffield: 0114 262 0026
Birmingham: 0121 233 1335 Ulster: 0287 135 1329
email via website
www.gamblersanonymous.org.uk
Fellowship of men and women who have joined together to do something about their own gambling problem and to help other compulsive gamblers do the same. Some meetings also have a meeting called GAMANON. This is for family and friends

Gamblers Anonymous Scotland
Central Halls 304 Maryhills Road Glasgow G20 7YE
Helpline: 0370 050 8881
www.gascotland.org

GAMCARE
2nd Floor 7-11 St John's Hill London SW11 1TR
Helpline: 0845 6000 133
Tel: 020 7801 7000
info@gamcare.org.uk
www.gamcare.org.uk
Information, advice, support and free counselling for the prevention and treatment of problem gambling

Gamete Donation Trust (National)
PO Box 2121 Gloucester GL19 4WT
Confidential helpline: 0845 226 9193
info@ngdt.co.uk
www.ngdt.co.uk
Information mainly for those considering becoming an egg or sperm donor but also for health professionals and those requiring treatment with donor eggs or sperm

Gap Activity Projects now see Lattitude Global Volunteering

Garden History Society
70 Cowcross St London EC1M 6EJ
Tel: 020 7608 2409
enquiries@gardenhistorysociety.org
www.gardenhistorysociety.org
Promotes the study of the history of gardening, landscape gardening and horticulture. Encourages conservation, advises on restoration and supports the development of parks, gardens and designed landscapes

Garden Organic
Coventry Warwickshire CV8 3LG
Tel: 02476 303517
enquiry@gardenorganic.org.uk
www.gardenorganic.org.uk
Researching and promoting organic gardening, farming and food

Gardens see also Allotment and Leisure Gardeners Ltd. (National Society of), Botanic Garden of Wales (National), City Farms & Community Gardens (Federation of), Community Composting Network, Conservation of Plants & Gardens (National Council for the), Historic Houses Association, Landscape Institute, Royal Botanic Gardens, Thrive

Gardens Scheme (National)
Hatchlands Park East Clandon Guildford GU4 7RT
Tel: 01483 211535
email via website
www.ngs.org.uk
Opening gardens of quality, character and interest to the public for charity

Gas & Electricity Markets (Office of) see Ofgem

GASP One Stop Shop for Smokefree
Solutions
Unit 9, Parkway Trading Estate St
Werburghs Bristol BS2 9PG
Tel 0117 955 0101
gasp@gasp.org.uk
www.gasp.org.uk
Educational resources and consultancy

Gateway Award
Mencap 3rd Floor Delta View 2309 -
2311Coventry Road Birmingham B26 3PG
Tel: 0121 722 5900
Gateway.award@mencap.org.uk
www.mencap.org.uk
Recreation, education resources for people
with learning disabilities

Gateway Award see Mencap

Gay Issues see thematic guide - Sexual
Issues

GCSE Revision
www.gcse.com

Genealogists (Society of)
14 Charterhouse Buildings Goswell Rd
London EC1M 7BA
Tel: 020 7251 8799
email via website
www.sog.org.uk
National library and education centre for
family history

General Medical Council GMC
Regent's Place, 350 Euston Rd London
NW1 3JN
Tel: 0161 923 6602 (general enquiries)
gmc@gmc-uk.org
www.gmc-uk.org
Governing body for doctors in UK

General Register Office see Registering
life events

Genetic Alliance UK
Unit 4D, Leroy House, 436 Essex Rd
London N1 3QP
Tel: 0207 704 3141
mail@geneticalliance.org.uk
www.geneticalliance.org.uk
Umbrella group for charities concerned with
human genetic disorders

Genetics see also Human Genetics
Commission, Jeans for Genes

Genocide see Aegis Trust

Geographic Society (National)
www.nationalgeographic.com
American non-profit scientific and
educational organisation

Geographical Association
160 Solly St Sheffield S1 4BF
Tel: 0114 296 0088

email via website
www.geography.org.uk
National subject teaching association for
geography teachers in the UK

Geographical Society (Royal) see Royal
Geographical Society

Geological Society
Burlington House Piccadilly London W1J
0BG
Tel: 020 7434 9944
Email via website
www.geolsoc.org.uk
Professional & learned society for working
geologists

Geological Survey (British)
Kingsley Dunham Centre Keyworth
Nottingham NG12 5GG
Tel: 0115 936 3100 (switchboard)
Tel: 0115 936 3143 (enquiries)
enquiries@bgs.ac.uk
www.bgs.ac.uk
Natural environment research council

Geological Survey (US)
www.usgs.gov
Provides impartial information on the health
of our ecosystems and environment, the
natural hazards that threaten us, the natural
resources we rely on, the impacts of climate
and land-use change

Geologists Association
Burlington House Piccadilly London W1J
0DU
Tel: 020 7434 9298
geol.assoc@btinternet.com
www.geologistsassociation.org.uk
Charitable organisation that exists for
all geologists and earth scientists, both
professional and amateur, bringing together
enthusiasts of all ages and backgrounds to
meet people with similar interests

Georgian Group
6 Fitzroy Sq London W1T 5DX
Tel: 087 1750 2936
info@georgiangroup.org.uk
www.georgiangroup.org.uk
Architectural group

Get connected
Helpline: 0808 808 4994
Email via website
www.getconnected.org.uk
Runaway children can call free to talk to
trained volunteers

Get Global!
www.getglobal.org.uk
Support and training for teachers involved in
global citizenship

Get Safe Online
www.getsafeonline.org/
Protect yourself against internet threats.
The site is sponsored by government and
leading businesses working together to
provide a free, public service

GFS Platform for Young Women
Unit 2, Angel Gate 326 City Road London
EC1V 2PT
Tel: 020 7837 9669
info@gfsplatform.org.uk
www.gfsplatform.org.uk
Support for young women in community
projects

Gifted Children (National Association for)
Suite 1.2 Challenge House Sherwood
Drive Bletchley Bucks MK3 6DP
Tel: 01908 646433
amazingchildren@nagcbritain.org.uk
www.nagcbritain.org.uk
Works with the whole family to support the
child who is gifted and talented

Gifted Children's Information Centre
Hampton Grange 21 Hampton Lane Solihull
B91 2QJ
Tel: 0121 705 4547
petercongdon@blueyonder.co.uk
www.dyslexiabooks.biz/
www.syntheticphonics.uk.com
Assessment, guidance and legal help
for children with special needs eg gifted
dyslexics, ADHD, Aspberger's Syndrome

Gingerbread National Council for One
Parent Families
255 Kentish Town Road
London NW5 2LX
Single parent helpline: 0808 802 0925
Tel: 020 7428 5400
email via website
www.gingerbread.org.uk
Offer advice, practical support and
campaign for single parents

Girlguiding UK
17-19 Buckingham Palace Rd London
SW1W 0PT
Freephone: 0800 1 69 59 01 (info about
recruitment into all parts of Guide
Movement)
Tel: 0207 834 6242
chq@girlguiding.org.uk
www.girlguiding.org.uk
UK's largest voluntary organisation for girls
and young women with around 600,000
members

Girls' Brigade England & Wales
PO Box 196 129 Broadway Didcot
Oxfordshire OX11 8XN
Tel: 01235 510425
gbco@girlsbrigadeew.org.uk
www.girlsb.org.uk

Girls' Venture Corps Air Cadets
1 Bawtry Gate Sheffield S9 1UD
Tel: 0114 2448405
gvcac@toucansurf.com
www.gvcac.org.uk
A uniformed organisation for girls aged
11-20 years. With interests in aviation,
adventure and travel.

Giving Nation
Citizenship Foundation 2nd Floor 63 Gee
Street London EC1V 3RS
Tel: 020 7566 4141
info@g-nation.org.uk
www.g-nation.co.uk
Works with young people throughout the
UK to show them how they can change the
world by giving

Glasgow Life
www.glasgowlife.org.uk
Encourage participation, involvement and
engagement in culture and sport for all.
Links to Sport, Museums, Libraries, Events,
Arts, Music etc

Glasgow Museums Resource Centre
200 Woodhead Road South Nitshill
Industrial Estate Glasgow G53 7NN
Tel: 0141 276 9300
Text Phone: 0141 276 9428
GMRCbookings@glasgowlife.org.uk
Store for the museums' collections when
they're not on display – accessible to the
public

Glass Centre (National)
Liberty Way Sunderland SR6 0GL
Tel: 0191 515 5555
info@nationalglasscentre.com
www.nationalglasscentre.com
Exploring ideas through glass and providing
opportunities for people to be creative, enjoy
themselves and feel inspired

GLE Greater London Enterprise
10-12 Queen Elizabeth Street London SE1
2JN
Tel: 020 7403 0300
info@gle.co.uk
www.gle.co.uk
Training & support for young people who are
thinking of starting their own business

Gliding Association (British)
8 Merus Court Meridian Business Park
Leicester LE19 1RJ
Tel: 0116 289 2956
office@gliding.co.uk
www.gliding.co.uk
National governing body

Global Action Plan Creating the climate for change
9-13 Kean Street London WC2B 4AY
Tel: 020 7420 4444
Email via website
www.globalactionplan.org.uk
Aims to engage people in practical solutions to environmental & social problems

Global Crop Diversity Trust A foundation for food security
www.croptrust.org
Organisation set up to ensure the conservation and availability of crop diversity for food security worldwide

Global Dimension
www.globaldimension.org.uk
Explores our connections with the rest of the world. With a global dimension to their education, learners can engage with complex global issues and explore the links between their own lives and people, places and issues throughout the world

Global Ethics UK Trust (Institute for)
6 Dyers Buildings Holborn London EC1N 2JT
Tel: 020 7405 5709
igeuk@globalethics.org.uk
www.globalethics.org.uk
Works in citizenship education, business ethics and public policy

Global Eye
www.globaleye.org.uk
Aims to increase awareness of development issues

Global Witness
6th Floor, Buchanan House   30 Holborn London EC1N 2HS
Tel: 0207 4925820
mail@globalwitness.org
www.globalwitness.org
Focuses on areas where profits from environmental exploitation fund human rights abuses

Globe Theatre see Shakespeare's Globe Theatre

GM see GM Freeze

GM Freeze
50 South Yorkshire Buildings Silkstone Common Barnsley S75 4RJ
Tel: 0845 217 8992
Coordinator@gmfreeze.org
www.gmfreeze.org
Campaign on GM food, crops and patenting of genetic resources

GMC see General Medical Council

Go4awalk
www.go4awalk.com
Website for walkers and hikers

Goethe-Institut London
50 Princes Gate Exhibition Rd London SW7 2PH
Tel: 020 7596 4000
info@london.goethe.org
www.goethe.de/london
Promotes German language & culture abroad

& Manchester
Churchgate House 56 Oxford St Manchester M1 6EU
Tel: 0161 237 1077
info@manchester.goethe.org
www.goethe.de/manchester

& Glasgow
3 Park Circus Glasgow G3 6AX London SW7 2PH
Tel: 0141 3322555
info@glasgow.goethe.org
www.goethe.de/glasgow

Golf see also Blind Golf Association (English), Ladies' Golf Union, Professional Golfers' Association, Women's Golf Association (English)

Golf Association (European)
Place de la Croix-Blanche 19 CH-1066 Epalinges Switzerland
Tel: 00 41 21785 70 60
info@ega-golf.ch
www.ega-golf.ch

Gorilla Organization
110 Gloucester Av London NW1 8HX
Tel: 020 7483 2681
info@gorillas.org
www.gorillas.org
International charity led by African conservationists dedicated to saving the world's last remaining gorillas from extinction

Government Actuary's Department
Finlaison House 15-17 Furnival Street London EC4A 1AB
Tel: 020 7211 2601
enquiries@gad.gov.uk
www.gad.gov.uk

Government Websites see DirectGov

Governors' Association (National) NGA
Ground Floor
  36 Great Charles Street Birmingham B3 3JY
Tel: 0121 237 3780
governorhq@nga.org.uk
www.nga.org.uk

Independent organisation that represents school governors in England. Aims to improve the well-being of children and young people by promoting high standards in schools

Grandparents Plus
18 Victoria Park Square Bethnal Green London E2 9PF
Advice & information: 0300 123 7015
Tel: 020 8981 8001
advice@grandparentsplus.org.uk
www.grandparentsplus.org.uk
Promotes the vital role of grandparents and the extended family in children's lives, particularly where parents are no longer able to care for their children.

Grandparents' Association
Moot House The Stow Harlow CM20 3AG
Helpline: 0845 434 9585
Tel: 01279 428040
Info@grandparents-association.org.uk
www.grandparents-association.org.uk

GreatBuildings
www.greatbuildings.com
Data and illustrations of many significant buildings worldwide

Greater London Authority
City Hall The Queen's Walk More London London SE1 2AA
Tel: 020 7983 4000
email via website
www.london.gov.uk
Home to the Mayor of London and the London Assembly

Greater London Enterprise see GLE

Green Alliance
36 Buckingham Palace Rd London SW1W 0RE
Tel: 020 7233 7433
ga@green-alliance.org.uk
www.green-alliance.org.uk
Promotes sustainable development by ensuring that the environment is at the heart of decision making

Green Mark
GLE Consulting New City Court 20 St Thomas Street London SE1 9RS
Tel: 020 7940 1562
green.mark@gle.co.uk
www.greenmark.co.uk
Environmental management and sustainable development. Environmental training & consultancy for the public & private sectors

Green Party
56-64 Development House Leonard Street London EC2A 4LT
Tel: 020 7549 0310
office@greenparty.org.uk
www.greenparty.org.uk
Political party committed to social justice and ecological sustainability

GreenMoves
Orchard Cottage
  Charlynch
  Somerset TA5 1BL
Tel: 0845 0944663
enquiries@greenmoves.com
www.greenmoves.com
Dedicated to advertising homes for sale that are more energy efficient than conventional home

Greenpeace
Canonbury Villas London N1 2PN
Tel: 020 7865 8100
info@uk.greenpeace.org
www.greenpeace.org.uk

Groundwork UK
Lockside 5 Scotland Street Birmingham B1 2RR
Tel: 0121 236 8565
info@groundwork.org.uk
www.groundwork.org.uk
Working in partnership to improve local environments & contribute to economic & social regeneration

Guide Dogs for the Blind Association
Burghfield Common Reading RG7 3YG
Tel: 0118 983 5555
guidedogs@guidedogs.org.uk
www.gdba.org.uk

Guitar Foundation (International) IGF
www.igf.org.uk
Arts agency dedicated to the promotion, understanding and enjoyment of the guitar, its music and artist. Stages festivals and large-scale summer schools

Gulf Veterans & Families Association (National)
Building E, Office 8
  Chamberlain Business Centre Chamberlain Road Hull HU8 8HL
Tel: 0845 257 4853
info@ngvfa.org.uk
www.ngvfa.com/

Gun Control Network
PO Box 11495 London N3 2FE
Crimestoppers: 0800 555 111
contact@gun-control-network.org
www.gun-control-network.org
Working towards a tighter control of firearms and a gun-free environment

Gutenberg see Project Gutenberg

Gymnastics (British)
Ford Hall Lilleshall National Sports Centre
Newport Shrops TF10 9NB
Tel: 0845 129 7129
information@british-gymnastics.org
www.british-gymnastics.org
Governing body

Gypsy Association
Tel: 07963 56 59 52
info@gypsy-association.com
www.gypsy-association.com
www.gypsy-association.co.uk
Information, advice, liaison & support.
Address on request

H

Habitat for Humanity Great Britain
46 West Bar Street Banbury OX16 9RZ
Tel: 01295 264240
SupporterServices@habitatforhumanity.org.uk
www.habitatforhumanity.org.uk
International development organisation that
builds homes with volunteers and people in
need

Hadley Centre for Climate Prediction and Research see Met Office

Haemochromatosis Society
Hollybush House Hadley Green Road
Barnet EN5 5PR
Tel: 0208 449 1363
info@haemochromatosis.org.uk
www.haemochromatosis.org.uk
Support for sufferers from this common
genetic iron overload disorder

Haemophilia Society
First Floor Petersham House 57a Hatton
Garden London EC1N 8JG
Support Line: 0800 018 6068
Tel: 020 7831 1020
info@haemophilia.org.uk
www.haemophilia.org.uk
National and independent organisation for all
people affected by bleeding disorders

Hairline International
Lyons Court 1668 High Street Knowle
West Midlands B93 0LY
www.hairlineinternational.com/
The Alopecia Patients Society

Half the Sky Foundation
PO Box 332 Telford TF1 9DG
Tel: 01952 261 004
contact@halfthesky.org
www.halfthesky.org
Aims to ensure that every one of China's
orphans has a caring adult in their life

HALO Trust
Carronfoot Thornhill Dumfies DG3 5BF
Tel: 01848 331100
mail@halotrust.org
www.halotrust.org
Mine clearance and bomb disposal in the
developing world

Hamster Council (National)
www.hamsters-uk.org

Handball Association (England)
The Halliwell Jones Stadium Winwick Road
Warrington WA2 7NE
Tel: 01925 246482/3
handball@englandhandball.com
www.englandhandball.com
National governing body for Handball and
Beach Handball in England

Handball Association (Scottish)
National Sports Centre Inverclyde Burnside
Road Largs Scotland KA30 8RW
Tel: 01475 687820
AnneMclaughlin@hotmail.co.uk
www.scottishhandball.com

Handsel Trust
Parks Farm Clifford Herefordshire HR3 5HH
Tel: 01497 831550
enquiries@handseltrust.org
www.handseltrust.org
Promotes effective support in the UK for all
children with disabilities and special needs
and their families

Hang Gliding and Paragliding Association (British)
8 Merus Court Meridian Business Park
Leicester LE19 1RJ
Tel: 0116 289 4316
office@bhpa.co.uk
www.bhpa.co.uk

Hansard Society
40-43 Chancery Lane London WC2A 1JA
Tel: 020 7438 1222
hansard@lse.ac.uk
www.hansardsociety.org.uk
Educational charity to promote effective
parliamentary democracy

HAPPA Horses and Ponies Protection Association
Taylor Building, Shores Hey Farm Black
House Lane Halifax Road Briercliffe Nr
Burnley Lancashire BB10 3QU
Tel: 01282 455992
www.happa.org.uk
Equine welfare

Hawk and Owl Trust
PO Box 400 Bishops Lydeard Taunton TA4
3WH

Tel: 0844 984 2824
enquiries@hawkandowl.org
www.hawkandowl.org
Protect & conserve wild birds of prey & their habitats

Hay Festival
The Drill Hall 25 Lion Street Hay-on-Wye
HR3 5AD
Tel: 01497 822 620 (admin)
admin@hayfestival.com
www.hayfestival.com
Book festival

Hayward Gallery
Southbank Centre
Belvedere Rd Belvedere Road London SE1 8XX
Tel: 020 7960 4200 (switchboard)
Ticket Office: 0844 875 0073
customer@southbankcentre.co.uk
www.southbankcentre.co.uk/venues/ hayward-gallery

Headliners
Rich Mix 35-47 Bethnal Green Road
London E1 6LA
Tel: 020 7749 9360
enquiries@headliners.org
www.headliners.org
Charity that inspires and encourages the personal development of young people through journalism. Young people are trained to research and produce stories on issues important to them for publication and broadcast in national and local newspapers, magazines, television, radio and online

Headlong Theatre
34-35 Berwick Street London W1F 8RP
Tel: 020 74780270
info@headlongtheatre.co.uk
www.headlongtheatre.co.uk

HEADWAY The Brain Injury Association
Bradbury House 190 Bagnall Road
  Old Basford Nottingham NG6 8SF
Free helpline: 0808 800 2244
Tel: 0115 924 0800
enquiries@headway.org.uk or helpline@ headway.org.uk
www.headway.org.uk
Support for brain injury survivors and their families

Healing Organisations (Confederation of)
www.confederation-of-healing-organisations.org
To make contact & distant healing available on NHS & in private medicine

Health (Department of)
Richmond House 79 Whitehall London SW1A 2NS

Tel: 020 7210 4850
Textphone: 020 7210 5025
Email via website
www.dh.gov.uk

Health & Safety Executive
Redgrave Court Merton Road Bootle
Merseyside L20 7HS
www.hse.gov.uk
The purpose of HSE is to prevent people being killed, injured or made ill by work. From September 2011 it operated mainly as an online service

Health Information Resources
www.evidence.nhs.uk

Health Professions Council
Park House 184 Kennington Park Road
London SE11 4BU
Tel: 020 7582 0866
See website for email
www.hpc-uk.org
Training, performance and conduct for 13 health professions (excluding doctors and nurses). Check online if a health professional is registered

Health Protection Agency
email via website
www.hpa.org.uk
From April 2012 the HPA will become part of Public Health England

Health Service Ombudsman now see Parliamentary and Health Service Ombudsman

Health, Social Services and Public Safety (N. Ireland Department of)
Castle Buildings Stormont Belfast BT4 3SQ
Tel: 028 9052 0500
webmaster@dhsspsni.gov.uk
www.dhsspsni.gov.uk

Healthtalkonline
DIPEx PO Box 428 Witney Oxon OX28 9EU
Tel: 01865 744209
info@healthtalkonline.org
www.healthtalkonline.org
Unique database of personal and patient experiences

Healthy Schools
www.education.gov.uk/schools/ pupilsupport/pastoralcare/a0075278/ healthy-schools
Offers support for schools to equip young people with the knowledge to make informed health choices

Hear From Your MP
www.hearfromyourmp.com
Allows constituents to sign up to get emails from their local MP about local issues

Hearing Dogs for Deaf People
The Grange Wycombe Rd Saunderton
Princes Risborough Bucks HP27 9NS
Tel: 01844 348 100
info@hearingdogs.org.uk
www.hearingdogs.org.uk
National charity and centre for training
dogs to alert their deaf owners to important
sounds and danger signals in the home,
work place and public buildings

Heart Foundation (British) see British
Heart Foundation

Heart Research UK
Suite 12D Joseph's Well Leeds LS3 1AB
Tel: 0113 234 7474
info@heartresearch.org.uk
www.heartresearch.org.uk

Heartstone
Mayfield High Street Dingwall Ross-shire
IV15 9SS
Tel: 01349 865400
info@heartstone.co.uk
www.heartstone.co.uk
Uses story, fiction and photojournalism to
challenge racism and intolerance

Heat is Online
www.heatisonline.org
Extreme weather worldwide

Hedgehog Preservation Society (British)
Hedgehog House Dhustone Ludlow
Shropshire SY8 3PL
Tel: 01584 890801
info@britishhedgehogs.org.uk
www.britishhedgehogs.org.uk

HELP Holiday Endeavour for Lone Parents
25 Brook Street Hemswell Gainsborough
DN21 5U
Tel: 01427 668717
janice@help.fslife.co.uk
www.helphols.co.uk
Offers reduced cost holidays to lone parent
families

Help – For a life without tobacco
www.help-eu.com

Help for Heroes
Unit 6 Aspire Business Centre Ordnance
Road Tidworth SP9 7QD
Tel: 0845 673 1760
email via website
www.helpforheroes.org.uk
Raises money to support members of the
armed forces who have been wounded in
the service of their country

Help the aged now see Age Cymru, Age
UK, Age NI, Age Scotland

Help the Hospices
Hospice House 34-44 Britannia St London
WC1X 9JG
Tel: 020 7520 8200
info@helpthehospices.org.uk
www.helpthehospices.org.uk
Worldwide link for information about
hospice/palliative care

Henry Doubleday Research Association
see Garden Organic

Henry Moore Foundation
Dane Tree House Perry Green Herts SG10
6EE
Tel: 01279 843 333
Email via website
www.henry-moore.org
Registered charity. Founded by the artist in
1977 to encourage public appreciation of
the visual arts, especially sculpture

Heraldry Society
PO Box 772 Guildford Surrey GU3 3ZX
Tel: 01483 237373
email via website
www.theheraldrysociety.com
Exists to increase and extend interest in
and knowledge of heraldry, armory, chivalry,
genealogy and allied subjects.

Heraldry Society of Scotland
25 Craigentinny Crescent Edinburgh EH7
6QA
Tel: 0131 5532232
info@heraldry-scotland.co.uk
www.heraldry-scotland.co.uk

Herb Society
Sulgrave Manor PO Box 946 Northampton
NN3 0BN
Tel: 0845 491 8699
info@herbsociety.org.uk
www.herbsociety.org.uk

Herbalists see Medical Herbalists (National
Institute of)

**Hereditary Breast Cancer Helpline
(National)**
Helpline: 01629 813000
canhelp@btopenworld.com
www.breastcancergenetics.co.uk/
Aims to ensure that those worried about
their family history have full access to
information on the options available to
enable them to make informed choices

Heritage Lottery Fund
7 Holbein Place London SW1W 8NR
020 7591 6000
enquire@hlf.org.uk
www.hlf.org.uk

Gives grants to support heritage: museums, parks and historic places, archaeology, natural environment and cultural traditions

Heritage Railway Association
2 Littlestone Road New Romney Kent TN28 8PL
email via website
www.heritagerailways.com
A trade organisation for heritage railways

Herpes Viruses Association
41 North Road London N7 9DP
Tel: 0845 123 2305
info@herpes.org.uk
www.herpes.org.uk
Gives help and advice to people with herpes viruses. Enclose sae for information

Hi8us First Light Now see First Light

Hibiscus Female Prisoners Welfare Project
12 Angel Gate 320 City Road London EC1V 2PT
Tel: 020 7278 7116
fpwphibiscus@aol.com
http://fpwphibiscus.org.uk
Addresses the special needs of foreign national women imprisoned in the UK.

Hideout
www.thehideout.org.uk
National website supporting children and young people living with domestic violence

High Blood Pressure Foundation
Dept. of Medical Sciences Western General Hospital Edinburgh EH4 2XU
Tel: 0131 332 9211
hbpf@hbpf.org.uk
www.hbpf.org.uk
Increasing awareness of dangers of high blood pressure

Higher Education Funding Council for England
Northavon House Coldharbour Lane Bristol BS16 1QD
Tel: 0117 931 7317
hefce@hefce.ac.uk
www.hefce.ac.uk
Distributes public funding for teaching and research and related activities in universities and colleges.

Hindu Universe – Hindu Resource Center
www.hindunet.org

Hispanic & Luso Brazilian Council
Canning House 2 Belgrave Sq London SW1X 8PJ
Tel: 020 7235 2303
enquiries@canninghouse.org
www.canninghouse.org
A focal point for the Spanish & Portuguese speaking worlds: commercial, cultural, educational and diplomatic.

Historic Houses Association
2 Chester St London SW1X 7BB
Tel: 020 7259 5688
info@hha.org.uk
www.hha.org.uk
Representative body for private owners of historic houses, parks and gardens

Historic Monuments (Welsh) see Cadw

Historic Scotland
Longmore House Salisbury Place Edinburgh EH9 1SH
Tel: 0131 668 8600
hs.website@scotland.gsi.gov.uk
www.historic-scotland.gov.uk

Historical Association
59a Kennington Park Rd London SE11 4JH
Tel: 0300 100 0223
emaiil via website
www.history.org.uk

Historical Manuscripts Commission see National Archives

Historical Maritime Society
2 Mount Zion Brownbirks Street Cornholme Todmorden OL14 8PG
Tel: 01706 819248
grog@tesco.net
www.hms.org.uk/hmshome.htm
UK based historical research and re-enactment group recreating the Royal Navy

History Museum (National): St Fagans
see St Fagans: National History Museum

History of Cinema & Popular Culture (The Bill Douglas Centre for the)
University of Exeter The Old Library Prince of Wales Rd Exeter EX4 4SB
Tel: 01392 724321
bdc@exeter.ac.uk
www.billdouglas.org
Museum & academic research centre

History World
www.historyworld.net
Site run by Bamber Gascoigne covering in 1 million words 400 separate histories and 4000 key events

HIV InSite
http://hivinsite.ucsf.edu/
Up-to-date information on HIV/AIDS treatment and prevention

HIV/AIDS see also AVERT, Body Positive North West, HIV/Aids Alliance (International), HIV InSite, ONE International, PACE, Positively UK, Terrence Higgins Trust

HIV/Aids Alliance (International)
1st and 2nd Floor Preece House 91-101
Davigdor Road Hove BN3 1RE
Tel: 01273 718900
mail@aidsalliance.org
www.aidsalliance.org
Supporting community action on AIDS in
developing countries

HM Prison Service now see Sentencing,
prison and probation

HM Revenue and Customs
www.hmrc.gov.uk
Advice on VAT, excise & customs

HM Treasury
Correspondence and Enquiries Unit 1 Horse
Guards Rd London SW1A 2HQ
Tel: 020 7270 4558
public.enquiries@hm-treasury.gov.uk
www.hm-treasury.gov.uk

HMRC Education Zone
www.hmrc.gov.uk/education-zone/index.htm

HMS Belfast part of the Imperial War
Museum
Morgan's Lane Tooley Street London SE1
2JH
Tel: 020 7940 6300
email via website
http://hmsbelfast.iwm.org.uk
www.iwm.org.uk

Holiday Care see Tourism for All

Holiday Endeavour for Lone Parents see
HELP

Holidays see also BAHA, Calvert Trust,
Family Holiday Association, Jubilee Sailing
Trust, Landmark Trust, National Trust
Holiday Cottages, National Trust Working
Holidays

Holistic Therapists (Federation of)
18 Shakespeare Business Centre Hathaway
Close Eastleigh Hampshire SO50 4SR
Tel: 023 8062 4350
info@fht.org.uk
www.fht.org.uk
Professional body representing over 20,000
professional therapists offering massage,
aromatherapy, reflexology, beauty and
fitness therapies.

Holocaust Educational Trust
BCM Box 7892 London WC1N 3XX
Tel: 020 7222 6822
email via website
www.het.org.uk

Holy See see Vatican

Home Business Alliance
Werrington Business Centre 86 Papyrus
Road Peterborough PE4 5BH

Tel: 0871 284 5100
info@homebusiness.org.uk
www.homebusiness.org.uk

Home Office Public Enquiries Unit
Direct Communications Unit 2 Marsham
Street London SW1P 4DF
Tel: 020 7035 4848
public.enquiries@homeoffice.gsi.gov.uk
www.homeoffice.gov.uk

Home-Start
8-10 West Walk Leicester LE1 7NA
Free info line: 0800 068 63 68
Tel: 0116 258 7900
info@home-start.org.uk
www.home-start.org.uk
Offers support to parents with at least one
child under 5, who are finding it difficult to
cope

Homeless International
Queens House 16 Queens Rd Coventry
CV1 3EG
Tel: 024 7663 2802
info@homeless-international.org
www.homeless-international.org
Supports community-led housing and
infrastructure related developments in Asia,
Africa and Latin America

Homeless Link
Gateway House Milverton Street, London
SE11 4AP
Tel: 020 7840 4430
Email via website
www.homeless.org.uk
Umbrella organisation for organisations
working with homeless people

Homeopathic Association (British)
29 Park St West Luton LU1 3BE
Tel: 01582 408675
info@britishhomeopathic.org
www.britishhomeopathic.org

Homeopaths (Society of)
11 Brookfield Duncan Close Moulton Park
Northampton NN3 6WL
Tel: 0845 450 6611
Info@homeopathy-soh.org
www.homeopathy-soh.org
Professional association

Homework High
www.channel4learning.com/apps/
homeworkhigh/
Channel 4's website where teachers answer
questions. Also contains a searchable bank
of questions already asked & their answers

Homeworking
www.homeworking.co.uk
Free information for those wishing to work
from home

Honour abuse see Karma Nirvana

Hope UK
25f Copperfield St London SE1 0EN
Tel: 020 7928 0848
enquiries@hopeuk.org
www.hopeuk.org
Drug education charity specialising in work
with children & young people

Horse Society (British)
Abbey Park
Stareton
Kenilworth
Warwickshire CV8 2XZ
Tel: 0844 848 1666
Tel: 02476 840500
email via website
www.bhs.org.uk

**Horses (International League for the
Protection of)** now see World Horse
Welfare

**Horses and Ponics Protection
Association** see HAPPA

Horticultural Society (Royal) see Royal
Horticultural Society

Hospices see Help the Hospices

Hospital and Community Friends now
see Attend

Hospital Broadcasting Association HBA
www.hbauk.co.uk

Hostelling International
2nd Floor, Gate House Fretherne Road
Welwyn Garden City   AL8 6RD
Tel: 01707 324170
info@hihostels.com
www.hihostels.com
Has 90 Youth Hostel Associations in 90
countries, operating 4,000 hostels

Hostelling International (N. Ireland)
22-32 Donegall Rd Belfast BT12 5JN
Tel: 028 9032 4733
info@hini.org.uk
www.hini.org.uk

Hostels.com
www.hostels.com
List of youth hostels worldwide in a
continually updated database

House of Commons Information Office
London SW1A 2TT
Tel: 020 7219 4272
Text phone: dial 18001 followed by 020 7219
4272
hcinfo@parliament.uk
www.parliament.uk/mps-lords-and-offices/
offices/commons/hcio/

House of Lords
London SW1A 0PW
Tel: 020 7219 3107
hlinfo@parliament.uk
www.parliament.uk/business/lords/

Housing (Chartered Institute of) see CIH

Housing (Confederation of Co-operative)
19 Devonshire Road Liverpool L8 3TX
Tel: 0151 726 2228
info@cch.coop
www.cch.coop
The UK organisation for housing co-
operatives, tenant-controlled housing
organisations and regional federations of
housing co-ops

Housing Advice Northern Ireland
10-12 High Street Belfast BT1 2BA
Tel: 028 9024 5640
email via website
www.housingadviceni.org
Independent housing advice

Housing Federation (National)
Lion Court 25 Procter Street London WC1V
6NY
Tel: 020 7067 1010
email via website
www.housing.org.uk
Representative organisation for registered
social landlords (mainly housing
associations)

Housing Justice
22-25 Finsbury Square London EC2A 1DX
Tel: 020 7920 6600
info@housingjustice.org.uk
www.housingjustice.org.uk
Takes practical action to prevent, and
campaigns against homelessness

Housing Ombudsman Service
81 Aldwych London WC2B 4HN
Tel: 0300 111 3000
info@housing-ombudsman.org.uk
www.housing-ombudsman.org.uk
The Ombudsman Service is free for users.
People with speech or hearing problems can
contact the service via typetalk

Housing Policy (Centre for)
University of York Heslington York YO10
5DD
Tel: 01904 321480
chp@york.ac.uk
www.york.ac.uk/inst/chp/
Research institute

HousingCare.org Information for older people
EAC FirstStop Advice 3rd Floor 89 Albert Embankment London SE1 7TP
Tel: 0800 377 7070
info@firststopadvice.org.uk
www.housingcare.org
Aims to help older people make decisions about where to live, and any support or care they need

Howard League for Penal Reform
1 Ardleigh Rd London N1 4HS
Tel: 020 7249 7373
info@howardleague.org
www.howardleague.org
Works for humane, effective and efficient reform of the penal system

Howtocomplain.com Your right to be heard
PO Box 1290 Salisbury SP1 1YN
complaints@howtocomplain.com
www.howtocomplain.com
Independent British website aimed at making complaints work for everyone

Hull Truck Theatre
50 Ferensway Hull HU2 8LB
Box Office: 01482 323638
Information: 01482 224800
boxoffice@hulltruck.co.uk
admin@hulltruck.co.uk
www.hulltruck.co.uk

Human Fertilisation & Embryology Authority
21 Bloomsbury Street London WC1B 3HF
Tel: 020 7291 8200
admin@hfea.gov.uk
www.hfea.gov.uk
A statutory body that regulates infertility treatments including IVF, the use of donated sperm or eggs, and human embryo research

Human Genetics Commission
605 Wellington House 133-155 Waterloo Rd
London SE1 8UG
Tel: 020 7972 4351
hgc@dh.gsi.gov.uk
www.hgc.gov.uk
UK Government's advisory body on new developments in human genetics and how they impact on individual lives

Human Power Club (British) BHPC
www.bhpc.org.uk
Non-conformist wheeled vehicles (recumbents). Organise races and provide information and support for those interested in all kinds of human powered vehicles (HPVs)

Human Rights (European Court of)
Council of Europe 67075 Strasbourg-Cedex France
Tel: 0033 3 88 41 20 18
www.echr.coe.int

Human Rights Commission (N. Ireland)
Temple Court 39 North St Belfast BT1 1NA
Tel: 028 9024 3987
Textphone: 028 9024 9066
info@nihrc.org
www.nihrc.org
Aims to protect and promote the human rights in law, policy and practice

Human Rights Education Association
www.hrea.org
International non-governmental organisation that supports human rights learning

Human Rights Policy (International Council on)
Rue Ferdinand-Hodler 17 CH-1207 Geneva Switzerland
Tel: 00 41 22 775 3300
ichrp@ichrp.org
www.ichrp.org
Researches into issues that present dilemmas for human rights organisations

Human Rights Watch
1st Floor Audrey House 16-20 Ely Place
London EC1N 6SN
Tel: 020 7713 1995
Email via website
www.hrw.org

Human Rights(British Institute of) see BIHR

Human Scale Education Movement
Unit 8, Fairseat Farm Chew Stoke Bristol BS40 8XF & CAN Mezzanine 49-51 East Road London N1 6AH
Tel: 01275 332516
info@hse.org.uk
www.hse.org.uk
Helps large schools find ways to work in smaller units and support parents and teachers wishing to set up their own schools

Human Writes
4 Lacey Grove Wetherby West Yorkshire LS22 6RL
humanwritesuk@yahoo.co.uk
www.humanwrites.org
Support through letter writing to those on death row

Humane Research Trust
29 Bramhall Lane South Bramhall
Stockport SK7 2DN
Tel: 0161 439 8041
info@humaneresearch.org.uk
www.humaneresearch.org.uk

Charity working to fund and promote medical research which does not involve animals or animal tissue. Aims to eliminate the need for animals in human medical research

Humane Slaughter Association
The Old School Brewhouse Hill Wheathampstead Herts AL4 8AN
Tel: 01582 831 919
info@hsa.org.uk
www.hsa.org.uk
Charity exclusively concerned with the welfare of animals during marketing, transport and slaughter

Humanist Association (British)
1 Gower St London WC1E 6HD
Tel: 020 7079 3580
info@humanism.org.uk
www.humanism.org.uk
A non-religious approach to life based on reason & common humanity

Hunt Saboteurs Association
BM HSA London WC1N 3XX
Tel: 0845 4500727
info@huntsabs.org.uk
www.huntsabs.org.uk

Huntington's Disease Association
Suite 24 Liverpool Science Park Innovation Centre 1 131 Mount Pleasant Liverpool L3 5TF
Tel: 0151 331 5444
info@hda.org.uk
www.hda.org.uk

Hurricane Center (National)
www.nhc.noaa.gov
US website

Hydrology see CEH

Hyperactive Children's Support Group
71 Whyke Lane Chichester W Sussex PO19 7PD
Tel: 01243 539966
hacsg@hacsg.org.uk
www.hacsg.org.uk
Provides information, ideas & literature for parents, carers & professionals. Focuses on non medication

Hypermobility Syndrome Association
49 Orchard Crescent Oreston Plymouth PL9 7NF
Tel: 0845 345 4465
email via website
www.hypermobility.org

Hypnotherapy Organisations (UK Confederation of)
Suite 404 Albany House 324-326 Regent Street London W1B 3HH
Tel: 0800 952 0560

petermatthews@manageyourstress.co.uk
www.ukcho.co.uk
Aims to ensure that hypnotherapists are safe and competent to practise and adhere to national standards of ethics and training

I

IAAF see Athletics Federations (International Association of)

IASO see Obesity (International Association for the Study of)

IATEFL International Association of Teachers of English as a Foreign Language)
Darwin College University of Kent Canterbury CT2 7NY
Tel: 01227 824430
generalenquiries@iatefl.org
www.iatefl.org
Educational charity supporting EFL teachers worldwide

IBS Network
Unit 5 53 Mowbray Street Sheffield S3 8EN
Helpline: 0872 300 4537
Tel: 0114 272 3253
info@theibsnetwork.org
www.theibsnetwork.org
For help with problems related to Inflammatory Bowel Disease (IBD) and Irritable Bowel Syndrome

Ice Hockey UK
www.icehockeyuk.co.uk
National governing body for ice hockey

Ice Skating Association of Great Britain and N.I. (National)
Grains Building High Cross Street Hockley Nottingham NG1 3AX
Tel: 0115 988 8060
email via website
www.iceskating.org.uk
Body overseeing amateur ice skating in UK

ICON Institute of Conservation
1.5 Lafone House The Leathermarket Weston Street London SE1 3ER
Tel: 0203 142 6799
icon@icon.org.uk
www.icon.org.uk
Lead voice for the conservation of cultural heritage in the UK. As a charity, Icon is committed to public benefit through promoting public understanding of and access to all the diverse elements of cultural heritage

ICSTIS now see Phonepay Plus

ICVA see Voluntary Agencies (International Council of)

IDeA now see Local Government Improvement and Development

Identity & Passport Service London
Globe House 89 Eccleston Square London SW1V 1PN
Passport Adviceline: 0300 222 0000
Text Relay: 18001 0300 222 0000
Text Phone: 0300 222 0222
www.ips.gov.uk/passport/contact.asp
www.direct.gov.uk/en/TravelAndTransport/Passports/index.htm
You will need to visit a Regional Passport Office if you need a passport urgently and want to apply in person using the Fast Track one-week or Premium one-day service. You must make an appointment by calling the passport advice line

& Belfast
Law Society House 90-106 Victoria Street Belfast BT1 3GN

& Glasgow regional passport office
3 Northgate 96 Milton Street Cowcaddens Glasgow G4 0BT

& Liverpool
101 Old Hall Street Liverpool L3 9BD

& Newport
Olympia House Upper Dock Street Newport Gwent NP20 1XA

& Peterborough
Aragon Court Northminster Road Peterborough PE1 1QG

& Durham
Millburngate House Durham DH97 1PA

IDTA International Dance Teachers Association
76 Bennett Rd Brighton BN2 5JL
Tel: 01273 685 652
email via website
www.idta.co.uk
An awarding body delivering qualifications in dance

IFAW Fund for Animal Welfare (International)
87-90 Albert Embankment London SE1 7UD
Tel: 020 7587 6700
info-uk@ifaw.org
www.ifaw.org
Saving animals in crisis around the world

IFST Institute of Food Science & Technology
5 Cambridge Court 210 Shepherds Bush Rd London W6 7NJ
Tel: 020 7603 6316
info@ifst.org
www.ifst.org
Professional qualifying body for food scientists and technologists and educational charity

ILO see International Labour Organization

Imaginate
45a George Street Edinburgh ES2 2HT
Tel: 0131 225 8050
info@imaginate.org.uk
www.imaginate.org.uk
Promoting and developing performing arts for children and young people in Scotland

IMF see International Monetary Fund

Immigrants (Joint Council for the Welfare of)
115 Old St London EC1V 9RT
Tel: 020 7251 8708
info@jcwi.org.uk
www.jcwi.org.uk

Immigration see also UK Border Agency

Immigration & Asylum Tribunals Service
PO Box 7866 Loughborough LE11 2XZ
Tel: 0845 6000 877
Text phone: 0845 606 0766
customer.service@tribunals.gsi.gov.uk
www.tribunals.gov.uk/ImmigrationAsylum
Hears appeals against asylum and immigration decisions

Immigration Advice Service Liverpool
Beetham House 61 Tithebarn Street Liverpool L2 2SB
Telephone advice service: 0844 887 0111
Tel: 07773399271 out of hours only
Tel: 07534813156
info@iasservices.org.uk
www.iasuk.org
Specialist immigration lawyers with over 30 years combined experience of providing advice on immigration, asylum and citizenship cases at all levels. Surgeries in Birmingham, Cardiff, Leeds, London & Preston by appointment

& Manchester
Conavon Court Blackfriars Street Manchester M3 5BQ
Telephone advice service: 0844 887 0111
Tel: 07773399271 out of hours only
info@iasservices.org.uk
www.iasuk.org

& Sheffield
Suite 2 Saville Street Sheffield S4 7UD
Telephone advice service: 0844 887 0111
Tel: 07773399271 out of hours only
info@iasservices.org.uk
www.iasuk.org

Immigration Aid Unit (Greater Manchester)
1 Delaunays Road Crumpsall Green Manchester M8 4QS
Tel: 0161 740 7722

email via website
www.gmiau.org

Immigration Law Practitioners' Association
Lindsey House 40-42 Charterhouse St.
London EC1M 6JN
Tel: 020 7251 8383
info@ilpa.org.uk
www.ilpa.org.uk

Immigration Services Commissioner (Office of the)
5th Floor Counting House 53 Tooley St
London SE1 2QN
Tel: 0845 000 0046
Tel: 020 7211 1553
info@oisc.gov.uk
www.oisc.gov.uk
Independent body committed to the elimination of unscrupulous administration advisers and the fair investigation of complaints. October 2010: Future under consideration - including possible merger.

Imperial Society of Teachers of Dancing
see ISTD

Imperial War Museum Collections
http://collections.iwm.org.uk
www.iwm.org.uk
Collection covering all aspects of twentieth and twenty-first century conflict involving Britain and the Commonwealth

Imperial War Museum Duxford
Cambridgeshire CB22 4QR
Tel: 01223 835000
School visit booking line: 020 7416 5313
duxford@iwm.org.uk
http://duxford.iwm.org.uk
www.iwm.org.uk

Imperial War Museum London
Lambeth Road London SE1 6HZ
Tel: 020 7416 5000
School visit booking line: 020 7416 5313
mail@iwm.org.uk
http://london.iwm.org.uk/
www.iwm.org.uk

Imperial War Museum North
The Quays Trafford Wharf Road
Manchester M17 1TZ
Tel: 0161 836 4000
School visit booking line: 0161 836 4064
iwmnorth@iwm.org.uk
http://north.iwm.org.uk
www.iwm.org.uk

Impotence Association see Sexual Advice Association

Include
60 Queens Rd Reading RG1 4BS
Tel: 0118 902 1000
www.cfbt.com/teach/excludedyoungpeople/include.aspx
Projects for children excluded from or not attending school and post 16 'hard to help'.

Inclusion see Centre for Economic & Social Inclusion

Inclusion (National Development Team for) NDTi
Montreux House 18a James Street West
Bath BA1 2BT
Tel: 01225 789135
office@ndti.org.uk
www.ndti.org.uk
A not-for-profit organisation concerned with promoting inclusion and equality for people who risk exclusion and who need support to lead a full life

Inclusive Education (Alliance for)
336 Brixton Road London SW9 7AA
Tel: 020 7737 6030
info@allfie.org.uk
www.allfie.org.uk
Campaigning to end segregation in education

Inclusive Education (Centre for Studies on)
The Park Daventry Road Knowle Bristol
BS4 1DQ
Tel: 0117 353 3150
admin@csie.org.uk
www.csie.org.uk
Working for inclusive education for all children and a gradual end to all segregated education, based on human rights arguments.

Incontinence see Bladder and Bowel Foundation, ERIC

Independent Advice Centres see AdviceUK

Independent Living Alternatives
Trafalgar House Grenville Place London
NW7 3SA
Tel: 020 8906 9265
PAServices@ILAnet.co.uk
www.ilanet.co.uk/
Promotes independent living for people with disabilities

Independent Midwives Association see Midwives UK (Independent)

Independent News Collective see INK

Independent Police Complaints Commission
90 High Holborn London WC1V 6BH
Tel: 08453 002 002
Text Relay: 18001 0207 166 3000
enquiries@ipcc.gsi.gov.uk
www.ipcc.gov.uk

Independent Safeguarding Authority
PO Box 181 Darlington DL1 9FA
Vetting and Barring Scheme: 0300 123 1111
Tel: 01325 953 795
isadispatchteam@homeoffice.gsi.gov.uk
www.isa-gov.org
To help prevent unsuitable people from working with children and vulnerable adults

Independent Schools Council
St Vincent House 30 Orange Street London WC2H 7HH
Tel: 020 7766 7070
email via website
www.isc.co.uk
Umbrella body representing 1,280 independent schools educating more than 500,000 children in the UK and Ireland

Independent Television Commission now see OFCOM

Independent Television News see ITN

Index on Censorship
www.indexoncensorship.org
Defends free expression

Indexers (Society of)
Woodbourn Business Centre 10 Jessell Street Sheffield S9 3HY
Tel: 0114 244 9561or 0845 872 6807
info@indexers.org.uk
www.indexers.org.uk

Indian Census
www.censusindia.net

Indian Volunteers for Community Service now see Volunteers For Rural India

Indigenous Tribal Peoples of the Tropical Forests (International Alliance of)
www.international-alliance.org

Indonesia Human Rights Campaign see TAPOL

Industrial Injuries Advisory Council
2nd Floor Caxton House Tothill Street Lonon SW1H 9NA
Tel: 020 7449 5618
iiac@dwp.gsi.gov.uk
www.iiac.org.uk

Infant Deaths (Foundation for the Study of)
11 Belgrave Road London SW1V 1RB
Helpline: 0808 802 6868
Tel: 020 7802 3200
Fundraising: 020 7802 3201
office@fsid.org.uk
www.fsid.org.uk
Funds research into sudden infant death, supports bereaving parents & disseminates baby safety information

Infertility see also Fertility Friends, Human Fertilisation & Embryology Authority

Infertility Counselling Association (British) BICA
www.bica.net
Professional association for infertility counsellors and counselling in the UK

Infertility Network UK
Charter House 43 St Leonards Rd Bexhill on Sea TN40 1JA
Tel: 0800 008 7464
admin@infertilitynetworkuk.com
www.infertilitynetworkuk.com
For those experiencing problems of infertility

Inform Information Network on Religious Movements
Houghton St London WC2A 2AE
Tel: 020 7955 7654
inform@lse.ac.uk
www.inform.ac
Help and information on new religious movements & cults

Information Commissioner's Office
Wycliffe House Water Lane Wilmslow SK9 5AF
Helpline: 0303 123 1113
Tel: 01625 545745
email via website
www.ico.gov.uk
Enforces the Data Protection Act 1998 and The Freedom of Information Act 2000

Information Management (Association for) Aslib
Howard House Wagon Lane Bingley BD16 1WA
Tel: 01274 777700
email via website
www.aslib.com
Actively promotes best practice in the management of information resources

Injuries see Safety/Accidents/Injury theme

INK Independent News Collective
F24 Acton Business Centre School Road London NW10 6TD
Tel: 020 8453 1144
inkgateway@pro-net.co.uk
www.ink.uk.com
Association of UK's alternative press - future under review, see website for details

Inland Revenue see HM Revenue and Customs

Inland Revenue Education Service now see HMRC Education Zone

Inland Waterways Association
Island House Moor Road Chesham HP5 1WA
Tel: 01494 783 453
iwa@waterways.org.uk
www.waterways.org.uk
National charity run by volunteers. Campaigns to use, maintain and restore Britain's inland waterways

Innovation in Mathematics Teaching (Centre for)
Rolle Building University of Plymouth Drake Circus Plymouth PL4 8AA
Tel: 01752 585346
www.cimt.plymouth.ac.uk
Aims to enhance the teaching and learning

INQUEST United Campaigns for Justice
89-93 Fonthill Rd London N4 3JH
Tel: 020 7263 1111
inquest@inquest.org.uk
www.inquest.org.uk
Helps the families & friends of those who die in custody, special hospitals etc or other controversial circumstances. General advice on coroners inquest system.

Inside Out Trust Restorative Justice at Work in Prisons
Hilton House 55-57a High St Hurstpierpoint West Sussex BN6 9TT
Tel: 01273 833050
info@iotrust.plus.com
www.inside-out.org.uk
Runs projects in prisons to benefit the community and to give prisoners skills

Institute for Optimum Nutrition see Optimum Nutrition (Institute for)

Institute of Contemporary Arts
12 Carlton House Terrace London SW1Y 5AH
Box office: 020 7930 3647
Switchboard: 020 7930 0493
email via website
www.ica.org.uk

Institute of Directors see Directors (Institute of)

Institute of Race Relations see Race Relations (Institute of)

Instituto Cervantes see Spanish Institute

Insurance Ombudsman see Financial Ombudsman Service

Integrated Education (N. Ireland Council for)
25 College Gardens Belfast BT9 6BS
Tel: 02890 972910
info@nicie.org.uk
www.nicie.org.uk

Intellect
Russell Square House 10-12 Russell Square London WC1B 5EE
Tel: 020 7331 2000
info@intellectuk.org
www.intellectuk.org
UK trade association for information technology, telecommunications and electronics companies

Intellectual Property Office
Concept House Cardiff Rd Newport S Wales NP10 8QQ
Tel: 0300 300 2000
Minicom (text phone): 0300 0200 015
information@ipo.gov.uk
www.ipo.gov.uk
Stimulates innovation and competitiveness via patents, trade marks, copyrights etc.

Inter Faith Network for the UK
8a Lower Grosvenor Place London SW1W 0EN
Tel: 020 7931 7766
ifnet@interfaith.org.uk
www.interfaith.org.uk
Promotes mutual respect and understanding between different faith communities

Interact Worldwide
Finsgate 5-7 Cranwood Street London EC1V 9LH
Tel: 0300 777 8500
programmes@interactworldwide.org
www.interactworldwide.org
Advancing the rights of all people to free and informed reproductive health choice and confidential sexual and reproductive health services including family planning

Intercountry Adoption Helpline
First Floor 71-73 High Street Barnet Herts EN5 5UR
Advice Line: 0208 447 4753
Tel: 020 8449 2562
Email via website
www.icacentre.org.uk

Interights
Lancaster House 33 Islington High Street London N1 9LH
Tel: 020 7278 3230
ir@interights.org
www.interights.org
Expert advice and assistance to those defending human rights through the law

Intermediate Technology see Practical Action

Intermix
9 Dunster Gardens London NW6 7NG
Tel: 07961 982 398
contact@intermix.org.uk
www.intermix.org.uk
Organisation for the benefit of mixed-race families, individuals and anyone who feels they have a multiracial identity

International Affairs (Royal Institute of)
Chatham House 10 St James's Sq London SW1Y 4LE
Tel: 020 7957 5700
contact@chathamhouse.org.uk
www.chathamhouse.org.uk
Brings together people of all nationalities from government, politics, business, the academic world and the media

International Baccalaureate Organization
Route des Morillons 15 Grand-Saconnex, Genève
 CH-1218 Switzerland
Tel: 00 41 22 791 7740
ibhq@ibo.org
www.ibo.org
Offers three programmes for students aged 3 to 19 help develop the intellectual, personal, emotional and social skills to live, learn and work in a rapidly globalising world

International Criminal Court
www.icc-cpi.int
An independent, permanent court that tries persons accused of the most serious crimes of international concern, namely genocide, crimes against humanity and war crimes. It will not act if a case is investigated or prosecuted by a national judicial system.

International Dance Teachers Association see IDTA

International Development (Department for)
1 Palace St London SW1E 5HE
Tel: 0845 300 4100
Tel: 020 7023 0000 (Switchboard)
enquiry@dfid.gov.uk
www.dfid.gov.uk
UK Government department responsible for promoting development and the reduction of poverty

International Labour Organization ILO
4 route des Morillons CH-1211 Geneva 22
Switzerland
Tel: 00 41 22 799 6111
ilo@ilo.org
www.ilo.org
UN agency which promotes fundamental principles and rights at work

International Monetary Fund
www.imf.org

International Olympic Committee IOC
Château de Vidy Case postale 356 1001 Lausanne
Switzerland
Tel: 00 41 21 621 6111
www.olympic.org

International Registry of Organ Donation and Transplantation see Organ Donation and Transplantation (International Registry of)

International Service
Hunter House 57 Goodramgate York YO1 7FX
Tel: 01904 64 77 99
email via website
www.internationalservice.org.uk
2 year placements for experienced professionals with development projects in Latin America, West Africa and Palestine

International Union for Conservation of Nature see IUCN

Internet see also ipl2, Nobel Prize Internet Archive, Nominet, People's Network, Topmarks, Wired Safety

Internet Watch Foundation
Suite 7310 First Floor Building 7300 Cambridge Research Park Waterbeach Cambridge CB25 9TN
Tel: 01223 20 30 30
admin@iwf.org.uk.
www.iwf.org.uk
To hinder potentially illegal material on the internet

Interpol
General Secretariat 200 quai Charles de Gaulle 69006 Lyon France
Email via website
www.interpol.int

IntoUniversity
95 Sirdar Road London W11 4EQ
el: 020 7243 0242
info@ntouniversity.org
www.intouniversity.org
Provides local learning centres in London where young people are inspired to achieve

Investment Ombudsman see Financial Ombudsman Service

IOC see International Olympic Committee

IOSH see Occupational Safety & Health (Institution of)

IOTF see Obesity (International Association for the Study of) & Obesity TaskForce (International)

ipl2
www.ipl.org
US website. A searchable, annotated subject directory of more than 8,500 internet resources selected & evaluated by librarians for their usefulness to users of public libraries

IPPL (UK) International Primate Protection League
Fourth Floor 63 St Mary Axe London EC3A 8AA
Tel: 020 7283 9008
enquiries@ippl-uk.org
www.ippl.org.uk
Dedicated to the rescue of monkeys and apes

IPPR Institute for Public Policy Research
4th Floor 14 Buckingham Street London WC2N 6DF
Tel: 020 7470 6100
info@ippr.org
www.ippr.org
Progressive research think-tank

IPSEA Independent Parental Special Education Advice
Hunters Court Debden Road Saffron Walden CB11 4AA
Advice Line: 0800 0184016
Tel: 01799 582030
www.ipsea.org.uk
Charity advising parents of children with special educational needs of the obligations of LEAs

Ironbridge Gorge Museum
Coach Road Coalbrookdale Telford TF8 7DQ
Education: 01952 433970
Visitor Information Centre: 01952 433424
Email via website
www.ironbridge.org.uk

ISCIS now see Independent Schools Council

Islamic Education see UK Islamic Education Waqf

Islamic Human Rights Commission
PO Box 598 Wembley HA9 7XH
Tel: 020 89044222
info@ihrc.org
www.ihrc.org

Islamic Relief Worldwide
19 Rea St South Digbeth Birmingham B5 6LB
Tel: 0121 605 5555
Email via website
www.islamic-relief.com
Brings relief & development aid to the world's poorest people

ISSUE now see Infertility Network UK

ISTD Imperial Society of Teachers of Dancing
22/26 Paul St London EC2A 4QE
Tel: 020 7377 1577
www.istd.org
Teaching and examining body

Italian Cultural Institute in London
39 Belgrave Sq London SW1X 8NX
Tel: 020 7235 1461
icilondon@esteri.it
www.icilondon.esteri.it/IIC_Londra

ITC see OFCOM

ITDG see Practical Action

ITN Independent Television News
200 Gray's Inn Rd London WC1X 8XZ
Tel: 020 7833 3000
www.itn.co.uk

IUCN International Union for Conservation of Nature
mail@iucn.org
www.iucn.org
Conservation of Nature and Natural Resources (International Union for)

IVS GB International Voluntary Service
Thorn House 5 Rose Street Edinburgh EH2 2PR
Tel: 0131 243 2745
info@ivsgb.org
www.ivsgb.org

IXIA
Unit 114 Custard Factory Gibb Street Birmingham B9 4AA
Tel: 0121 753 5301
info@ixia-info.com
www.ixia-info.com
National organisation for public art development in England

Iyengar Yoga Institute see Yoga (Iyengar Institute)

J

Jane Tomlinson Appeal
PO BOX 314 Rothwell Leeds LS26 1BY
Tel: 0113 216 2064
info@janetomlinsonappeal.com
www.janetomlinsonappeal.com
Jane undertook feats of sporting endurance
to raise money for charity and to show that
people with a terminal prognosis can still
lead an active life

JANET The UKs Education and Research
Network
Lumen House Library Ave Harwell Oxford
Didcot Oxon OX11 0SG
Tel: 01235 822 200
Service Desk: 0300 300 2212
service@ja.net
www.ja.net
A company operating and developing
JANET information networks for use in
higher education institutions

Japan Foundation, London
6th Floor Russell Square House 10-12
Russell Square London WC1B 5EH
Tel: 020 7436 6698
info.language@jpf.org.uk
www.jpf.org.uk
A support centre for teachers of Japanese

Jeans for Genes
1st Floor Macmillan House Paddington
Station London W2 1FT
Freephone: 0800 980 4800
Tel: 020 7199 3300
Email via website
www.jeansforgenes.com
Helps children with genetic disorders

Jewish Israel Appeal (United) see UJIA

Jewish Lads' & Girls' Brigade (JLGB)
Camperdown 3 Beechcroft Rd South
Woodford London E18 1LA
Tel: 020 8989 8990
getinvolved@JLGB.org
www3.jlgb.org

Jewish Museum London
Raymond Burton House 129-131 Albert St
Camden Town London NW1 7NB
Tel: 020 7284 7384
admin@jewishmuseum.org.uk
www.jewishmuseum.org.uk

Jewish Women (League of)
6 Bloomsbury Sq London WC1A 2LP
Tel: 020 7242 8300
office@theljw.org
www.theljw.org
Volunteers who provide welfare care for all
people

Jews (Board of Deputies of British) see
British Jews (Board of Deputies of)

Jo's Cervical Cancer Trust
16 Lincoln's Inn Fields London WC2A 3ED
Helpline: 0808 802 8000
Tel: 020 7936 7498
info@jostrust.org.uk
www.jostrust.org.uk
The only UK charity dedicated to women
and their families affected by cervical cancer
and cervical abnormalities

Jobcentre Plus
http://jobseekers.direct.gov.uk/homepage.
aspx?sessionid=8cfb352f-a189-4352-a140-
b7db17b65466&pid=4
Helps people without jobs to find work &
employers to fill their vacancies

Jodrell Bank Observatory
The University of Manchester Macclesfield
Cheshire SK11 9DL
Tel: 01477 571321
www.jb.man.ac.uk

Joint Nature Conservation Committee
Monkstone House City Road
Peterborough PE1 1JY
Tel: 01733 562626
comment@jncc.gov.uk
www.jncc.gov.uk
Advises Government on UK and
international nature conservation.

Joseph Rowntree Foundation
The Homestead 40 Water End York YO30
6WP
Tel: 01904 629241
info@jrf.org.uk
www.jrf.org.uk
Researches underlying causes of poverty
and supports research into housing, social
care & social policy

Journeys Toward recovery from depression
120-122 Broadway Roath Cardiff CF24 1NJ
Tel: 029 2069 2891
info@journeysonline.org.uk
www.journeysonline.org.uk/
Supporting people to find their route to
recovery from depression

Journeywoman.com
www.journeywoman.com
US site for women travellers

**Ju Jitsu Association GB National
Governing Body (British)**
5 Avenue Parade Accrington Lancashire
BB5 6PN
Tel: 01254 396806
chairman@bjjagb.com
www.bjjagb.com

Ju-Jitsu see also World Ju-Jitsu Federation (Ireland)

Jubilee Debt Campaign
The Grayston Centre 28 Charles Square London N1 6HT
Tel: 020 7324 4722
info@jubileedebtcampaign.org.uk
www.jubileedebtcampaign.org.uk
Aiming to stop poor countries paying money to the rich world and cancellation of unpayable poor country debts

Jubilee Sailing Trust
12 Hazel Road Woolston Southampton SO19 7GA
Tel: 023 8044 9108
info@jst.org.uk
www.jst.org.uk
Adventure tallship sailing holidays for able bodied & disabled

Judo Association (British)
Suite B, Loughborough Tech Park Epinal Way Loughborough LE11 3GE
Tel: 01509 631670
bja@britishjudo.org.uk
www.britishjudo.org.uk

Judo Scotland
EICA: Ratho, South Platt Hill Ratho Newbridge EH28 8AA
Tel: 0131 333 2981
info@judoscotland.com
www.judoscotland.com

Junk Mail see Facsimile Preference Service, Mailing Preference Service

Just for Kids Law JfK Law
402 Harrow Road London W9 2HU
Tel: 020 7266 7159
info@justforkidslaw.org
www.justforkidslaw.org
Runs a number of programmes aimed at providing support, advocacy and assistance to young people with a variety of needs

Justgiving
First Floor 30 Eastbourne Terrace London W2 6LA
Tel: 0845 021 2110
Email via website
www.justgiving.com
Fundraising website

Justice
www.justice.gov.uk
Encompasses online content from the YJB, Ministry of Justice, Her Majesty's Courts Service, the Prison Service, the Legal Services Commission and many other justice agencies, enabling information on the administration, regulation and scrutiny of justice to be provided by one single site

JUSTICE
59 Carter Lane London EC4V 5AQ
Tel: 020 7329 5100
admin@justice.org.uk
www.justice.org.uk
All-party law reform and human rights charity

Justin Campaign
info@thejustincampaign.com
www.thejustincampaign.com
Justin Fashanu was the world's first openly gas professional footballer – he committed suicide in 1998. The Campaign was founded to demonstrate that homophobia still exists in both grassroots and professional football

K

Karate and Kickboxing Association (World)
www.wkaworld.com

Karate and Martial Art Schools (National Association of) now see NAKMAS

Karate Board (N. Ireland)
89 Brooke Drive Belfast BT11 9NJ
Tel: 028 9061 6453 (Chairman/President)
obrunton@aol.com
www.irishkarate.com

Karate England
PO Box 490 Northwich CW9 9AU
Tel: 07931 545924
admin@karateengland.org.uk
www.karateengland.org.uk

Karate Governing Body Ltd (Welsh)
105 Queens Drive Llantwit Fardre Pontypridd CF38 2NY
Tel: 01443 203733
email via website
www.wkgb.org.uk

Karma Nirvana
PO Box 148 Leeds LS13 9DB
Honour Network Helpline: 0800 5999 247
Tel: 0113 218 0114
Email via website
www.karmanirvana.org.uk/honour-network
To support victims and survivors of forced marriage and honour based violence. Also seeks to increase the reporting of victims and also survivors many of which are disowned by their families

Keep Britain Tidy
Elizabeth House The Pier Wigan WN3 4EX
Tel: 01942 612621
email via website
www.keepbritaintidy.org
Environmental charity and the anti-
litter campaign for England. Also runs
programmes such as Eco-Schools, Blue
Flag and Quality Coast Awards for beaches,
and the Green Flag for parks to demonstrate
practical action

Keep Fit Association KFA
1 Grove House Foundry Lane Horsham
West Sussex RH13 5PL
Tel: 01403 266000
office@emdp.org
www.keepfit.org.uk

Kelvingrove Art Gallery and Museum
Argyle Street Glasgow G3 8AG
Tel: 0141 276 9599
Text Phone: 0141 276 9500
museums@glasgowlife.org.uk
www.glasgowlife.org.uk/museums/our-
museums/kelvingrove/Pages/home.aspx
22 themed, state-of-the-art galleries
displaying 8000 objects. The collections
include natural history, arms and armour, art
from many art movements and periods of
history

Kennel Club
1-5 Clarges St Piccadilly London W1J 8AB
Tel: 0844 463 3980
Email via website
www.thekennelclub.org.uk
To promote in every way the general
improvement of all dogs

Kew Gardens see Royal Botanic Gardens,
Kew

Kick It Out
PO Box 29544 London EC2A 4WR
Freephone: 0800 169 9414 (Hotline for
reporting racist abuse and incidents only)
Tel: 020 7684 4884 (General enquiries)
info@kickitout.org
www.kickitout.org
Football's anti-racism campaign

Kid Info
www.kidinfo.com/school_subjects.html
US homework and research site

Kidney Patient Association (British)
BKPA
3 The Windmills St Mary's Close Turk Street
Alton GU34 1EF
Tel: 01420 541424
info@britishkidney-pa.co.uk
www.britishkidney-pa.co.uk
Financial help, advice & literature for kidney
patients & their families

Kidney Research UK
Nene Hall
Lynch Wood Park Peterborough PE2 6FZ
Tel: 0845 070 7601
enquiries@kidneyresearchuk.org
www.kidneyresearchuk.org

Kids Company
1 Kenbury Street London SE5 9BS
Tel: 0845 644 6838
Tel: 0207 274 8378
info@kidsco.org.uk
www.kidsco.org.uk
To deliver emotional and practical support
within structures which are directly
accessible by children - and not dependent
on a carer

Kids for Kids
PO Box 456 Dorking Surrey RH4 2WS
Tel: 07957 206440
contact@kidsforkids.org.uk
www.kidsforkids.org.uk
Helps children struggling to survive in
remote villages in Darfur, Sudan

Kids in Museums
CAN Mezzanine 49-51 East Road London
N1 6AH
Tel: 020 7250 8338
getintouch@kidsinmuseums.org.uk
www.kidsinmuseums.org.uk
Guiding museums and galleries across the
country to make family visits engaging and
enjoyable.

Kids' Clubs Network now see 4Children

Kidscape
2 Grosvenor Gardens London SW1W 0DH
Parents' Anti-Bullying Helpline: 08451 205
204
General Enquiries: 020 7730 3300
email via website
www.kidscape.org.uk
Offers support and advice to parents
of bullied children. Confidence building
sessions for children who are bullied.
Provides booklets, literature, posters,
training guides and educational videos

Kilvert (Alice) see Tampon Alert (Alice Kilvert)

King's Fund
11-13 Cavendish Square London W1G 0AN
Tel: 020 7307 2400
enquiry@kingsfund.org.uk
www.kingsfund.org.uk
An independent charitable foundation working for better health, especially in London

Kite Society of Great Britain
PO Box 2274 Gt Horkesley Colchester CO6 4AY
Tel: 01206 271489
info@thekitesociety.org.uk
www.thekitesociety.org.uk

Kiva Loans that change Lives
www.kiva.org
Helps people out of poverty by direct lending from individuals to selected entrepreneurs in the developing world. Once the money is repaid it can be withdrawn or lent again

Know Cannabis
www.knowcannabis.org.uk
Website which can help you assess your cannabis use, its impact on your life and how to make changes if you want to

Kodaly see BKA

Kurdish Human Rights Project
11 Guilford Street London WC1N 1DH
Tel: 020 7405 3835
khrp@khrp.org
www.khrp.org

L

La Leche League GB
PO Box 29 West Bridgford Nottingham NG2 7NP
Helpline: 0845 120 2918
Tel: 0845 456 1855 (General enquiries)
enquiries@laleche.org.uk
www.laleche.org.uk
Breastfeeding support & information

Labour Behind the Label
THE CLEAN CLOTHES CAMPAIGN 10-12 Picton Street Bristol BS6 5QA
Tel: 0117 944 1700
Email via website
www.labourbehindthelabel.org
Campaigns for better conditions for garment workers around the world and for fair trade

Labour Party
Labour Central Kings Manor Newcastle Upon Tyne NE1 6PA

Tel: 0845 092 2299
Email via website
www2.labour.org.uk

Labour Research Department
78 Blackfriars Rd London SE1 8HF
Tel: 020 7928 3649
info@lrd.org.uk
www.lrd.org.uk

Labour Women's Network
11 Well House Road LEEDS LS8 4BS
email via website
www.lwn.org.ukk
Dedicated to supporting Labour women to play a full part in the Party, and to securing the election of more Labour women to public office at every level

Lacrosse Association (English)
The Belle Vue Centre
Pink Bank Lane Longsight Manchester M12 5GL
Tel: 0161 227 3626
info@englishlacrosse.co.uk
www.englishlacrosse.co.uk

Ladies' Golf Association (English) now see Women's Golf Association (English)

Ladies' Golf Union
The Scores St Andrews Fife KY16 9AT
Tel: 01334 475811
Email via website
www.lgu.org
Governing body of ladies' golf

Lady Lever Art Gallery
Port Sunlight Village Wirral CH62 5EQ
Tel: 0151 478 4136
email via website
www.liverpoolmuseums.org.uk/ladylever
Housing one of the UK's finest collections of fine and decorative art

Lake District (Friends of the)
Murley Moss Oxenholme Rd Kendal LA9 7SS
Tel: 01539 720788
info@fld.org.uk
www.fld.org.uk
A regional conservation charity dedicated to the protection and enhancement of the landscape and countryside of Cumbria and the Lake District

Lake District National Park Authority
Murley Moss Oxenholme Rd Kendal LA9 7RL
Tel: 01539 724555
hq@lakedistrict.gov.uk
www.lakedistrict.gov.uk

Lake District Weather Line
Tel: 0844 846 2444
www.lakedistrict.gov.uk/weatherline
Provides a weather forecast for the day. The next day's forecast is available after 5.15pm

Land Registry
Tel: 0844 892 1111
customersupport@landregistry.gsi.gov.uk
www1.landregistry.gov.uk
Register of ownership of land in England and Wales

Land Yachts see Sand & Land Yacht Clubs (British Federation of)

Landlife
National Wildflower Centre Court Hey Park Liverpool L16 3NA
Tel: 0151 737 1819
info@landlife.org.uk
www.landlife.org.uk
Environmental charity growing and selling wildflower seeds and plants, promoting new wildflower landscapes

Landmark Trust
Shottesbrooke Maidenhead Berks SL6 3SW
Tel: 01628 825920
info@landmarktrust.org.uk
www.landmarktrust.org.uk
Charity that restores buildings of historic & architectural importance, then secures their future by letting them for holidays

Landmine Action
5th Floor Epworth House 25 City Road London EC1Y 1AA
Tel: 020 7256 9500
info@landmineaction.org
www.landmineaction.org
Umbrella organisation campaigning for the elimination of landmines

Landmines see also HALO Trust, Mines Advisory Group

Landmines (International Campaign to Ban)
www.icbl.org
Key umbrella organisation for anti-landmine groups worldwide

Landscape Institute
Charles Darwin House 12 Roger Street London WC1N 2JU
Tel: 020 7685 2640
www.landscapeinstitute.org.uk
Professional body in UK for landscape architects and designers, planners and managers

Language Awareness (Association for)
www.languageawareness.org

Language Learning (Association for)
University of Leicester University Road Leicester LE1 7RH or visit at 106 New Walk Leicester LE1 7EA
Tel: 0116 229 7600
info@all-languages.org.uk
www.all-languages.org.uk
Association for teachers of modern foreign languages

Language Teaching & Research (Centre for Information on) now see CILT

Languages (Scotland's National Centre for) SCILT
Room D1.23, David Stow Building University of Strathclyde 76 Southbrae Drive Jordanhill Glasgow G13 1PP
Tel: 0141 950 3308/3369
scilt@strath.ac.uk
www.strath.ac.uk/scilt

Laogai Research Foundation
www.laogai.org
Washington DC based organisation exposing human rights abuses in China

Lattitude Global Volunteering
Tel: 0118 959 4914
email via website
www.lattitude.org.uk
International youth development charity offering volunteering and gap year placements for under 25s

Lavender Trust at Breast Cancer Care
Breast Cancer Care Helpline: 0808 800 6000
www.breastcancercare.org.uk/about-us/lavender-trust
Raises money specifically to fund Breast Cancer Care's support and information services for younger women

Law Centres Federation
PO Box 65836 London EC4P 4FX
Tel 020 7842 0720
info@lawcentres.org.uk
www.lawcentres.org.uk
Co-ordinating body for community Law Centres

Law Commission
Steel House 11 Tothill Street London SW1H 9LJ
Tel: 020 3334 0200
email via website
www.lawcom.gov.uk

Law Society of England & Wales
113 Chancery Lane London WC2A 1PL
Tel: 020 7242 1222
Email via website
www.lawsociety.org.uk
Professional body for solicitors in England and Wales.

Law Society of Scotland
26 Drumsheugh Gardens Edinburgh EH3
7YR
Tel: 0131 226 7411
email via website
www.lawscot.org.uk

Lawn Tennis Association
National Tennis Centre 100 Priory Lane
Roehampton London SW15 5JQ
Tel: 020 8487 7000
Info@LTA.org.uk
www.lta.org.uk
Governing body

League Against Cruel Sports see Cruel
Sports Ltd (League Against)

Leap Confronting Conflict
Wells House (Unit 7) 5-7 Wells Terrace
Finsbury Park London N4 3JU
Tel: 020 7561 3700
info@leapcc.org.uk
www.leaplinx.com
Provides opportunities for young people and
adults to explore creative approaches to
conflicts in their lives

learndirect
PO Box 900 Leicester LE1 6XJ
Tel: 0800 101 901
www.learndirect.co.uk
Provides adults with free advice on learning
and career opportunities

learndirect Scotland
Freepost SCO5775 PO Box 25249
Glasgow G3 8XN
Helpline: 0808 100 9000
info@learndirectscotland.com
www.learndirectscotland.com

Learning (Campaign for)
24 Greencoat Place Westminster London
SW1P 1RD
Tel: 020 7930 1111
info@cflearning.org.uk
www.campaign-for-learning.org.uk/cfl/index.
asp
Charity working to stimulate learning that will
sustain people for life

Learning (Institute for)
First Floor 49-51 East Road London N1
6AH
Tel: 0844 815 3202
enquiries@ifl.ac.uk
www.ifl.ac.uk
Professional body for teachers, trainers,
tutors, student teachers and assessors in
the further education and skills sector

Learning and Skills Council now see
Skills Funding Agency, Young People's
Learning Agency

**Learning and Skills Development Agency
Northern Ireland** LSDA Northern Ireland
2nd Floor Alfred House 19-21 Alfred Street
Belfast BT2 8ED
Tel: 02890 447700
www.lsdani.org.uk
Improvement and staff development
programmes that support specific
government initiatives

Learning and Skills Improvement Service
LSIS
Friars House Manor House Drive Coventry
West Midlands CV1 2TE
Tel: 024 7662 7900 (Switchboard)
enquiries@lsis.org.uk
www.lsis.org.uk
Formed from CEL and QIA to develop FE
provision

Learning and Teaching Scotland see
Education Scotland

Learning Disabilities (British Institute of)
Campion House Green St Kidderminster
DY10 1JL
Tel: 01562 723010
enquiries@bild.org.uk
www.bild.org.uk

**Learning Disabilities (The Foundation for
People with)**
9th Floor Sea Containers House 20 Upper
Ground London SE1 9QB
Tel: 020 7803 1100
email via website
www.learningdisabilities.org.uk
Aims to improve the quality of life for people
with learning disabilities. Part of the Mental
Health Foundation

**Learning Outside the Classroom
(Council for)**
www.lotc.org.uk

Learning Through Action Centre
High Close School Wiltshire Road
Wokingham Berkshire RG40 1TT
Tel: 0870 770 7985
Email via website
www.learning-through-action.org.uk
Workshops for children and young people,
their parents and carers on social and health
issues

Learning Zone
www.bbc.co.uk/learningzone
BBC education website

Left 'n' Write
5 Charles St Worcester WR1 2AQ
Tel: 01905 25798
info@leftshoponline.co.uk
www.leftshoponline.co.uk
Provides information and resources for left
handed people, courses for teachers on
needs of left handed children

Legal Action Group
242 Pentonville Rd London N1 9UN
Tel: 020 7833 2931
lag@lag.org.uk
www.lag.org.uk
Working with lawyers and advisers to
promote equal access to justice through
publications, training and policy work

Legal Services Commission
Legal Services Commission 4 Abbey
Orchard Street London SW1P 2BS
Helpline (Legal Aid): 0845 345 4345
Tel: 0207 783 7000
Tel: 0800 085 6643 (Customer Service)
www.legalservices.gov.uk/criminal.asp
Guarantees that people under police
investigation or facing criminal charges can
get legal advice and representation

legislation.gov.uk
www.legislation.gov.uk
Branch of the National Archive which
publishes all UK legislation. Provides online
access and regulates Crown Copyright

LEPRA Health in action
28 Middleborough Colchester Essex CO1
1TG
Tel: 01206 216700
lepra@leprahealthinaction.org
www.lepra.org.uk
Medical charity aiming to eradicate leprosy
and other diseases of poverty

Lesbian and Gay Switchboard (London)
PO Box 7324 London N1 9QS
Helpline: 0300 330 0630
Tel: 020 7837 6768
admin@llgs.org.uk
www.llgs.org.uk
Switchboard aims to operate a 24 hour
service offering support, information and
referrals to callers on any issue relating to
lesbian, gay or bisexual life

Lesbian Information Service
PO Box 8 Todmorden Lancs OL14 5TZ
Tel: 017067 817235
jan@lesbianinformationservice.org
www.lesbianinformationservice.org
Research publications concerned with
needs of lesbians and gays and can be
downloaded from website

Lesbians & Gays (Families & Friends of)
FFLAG
PO Box 495 Little Stoke Bristol BS34 9AP
Helpline: 0845 652 0311
info@fflag.org.uk
www.fflag.org.uk
A national voluntary organisation for
parents of gay sons and lesbian daughters.
It provides information and support
through confidential helplines, groups and
publications

Let's Face It
72 Victoria Ave Westgate-on-Sea Kent CT8
8BH
Tel: 01843 833 724
chrisletsfaceit@aol.com
www.lets-face-it.org.uk
For people with facial disfigurement ie
cancer, accidents, congenital acne

Letslink UK
12 Southcote Rd London N19 5BJ
Tel: 020 7607 7852
admin@letslinkuk.net
www.letslink.org
Community development - local exchange
of goods & services

Leukaemia see also Children with
Leukaemia, CLICSargent

Leukaemia and Lymphoma Research
39-40 Eagle Street London WC1R 4TH
Tel: 020 7405 0101
info@beatbloodcancers.org
www.beatbloodcancers.org

LGA see Local Government Association

**Liberal Democrat Trade Unionists
(Association of)**
30 Leigh Rd London E10 6JH
http://www.libdems.org.uk/
Exists to support Liberal Democrat members
in the trade union movement and to input
into party policy

Liberal Democrats
8-10 Great George Street London SW1P
3AE
Tel: 020 7222 7999
info@libdems.org.uk
www.libdems.org.uk

Liberty National Council for Civil Liberties
21 Tabard St London SE1 4LA
Tel: 020 7403 3888 or 0203 145 0460
email via website
www.liberty-human-rights.org.uk

Libraries for Life for Londoners
31 Milton Park London N6 5QB
Tel: 020 7607 2665
mail@librarylondon.org
www.librarylondon.org

Campaigning for a comprehensive, high quality library service for all Londoners

Library Association see CILIP

Library Association (Scottish) see CILIPS

Library Campaign
22 Upper Woburn Place London WC1H 0TB
Tel: 0845 450 5946
librarycam@aol.com
www.librarycampaign.com
Supporting friends and users of public libraries

Library of France (National)
www.bnf.fr/en/tools/lsp.site_map.html
Web page giving information about the National Library of France in French and in English

Life
1 Mill Street Leamington Spa Warwickshire CV31 1ES
Helpline: 0800 915 4600
Tel: 01926 421587
email via website
www.lifecharity.org.uk
Helping disadvantaged children and young people in the UK by supporting vulnerable pregnant mothers and young families

Life Science Centre A centre for world-class science
Times Square Newcastle Upon Tyne NE1 4EP
Tel: 0191 243 8210
info@life.org.uk
www.life.org.uk
Exhibitions, events, theatre shows and the biggest planetarium in the North

Lifeguard Skills
www.lifeguardskills.co.uk
Practical tips on water safety

Lifelong Learning
www.lifelonglearning.co.uk
Includes advice about financing study

Lifesavers The Royal Life Saving Society UK
River House High Street Broom Alcester Warwickshire B50 4HN
Tel: 01789 773994
email via website
www.lifesavers.org.uk
Dedicated to the prevention of unnecessary loss of life, transforming bystanders into lifesavers

Lifetracks
c/o YouthNet First Floor 50 Featherstone Street London EC1Y 8RT
Tel: 020 7250 5700
email via website
www.lifetracks.com

Aims to be the first place all young people turn to when they're making decisions about their work, study or training

Liftshare.com Ltd
www.liftshare.com
UK wide & web based car share scheme provider

Light Rail Transit Association
c/o 138 Radnor Avenue Welling DA16 2BY
Tel: 01179 517785
office@lrta.org
www.lrta.org

likeitis.org
www.likeitis.org
Gives young people access to information about all aspects of sex education and teenage life

Lilith Research and Development
Unit 2.03 Canterbury Court 1-3 Brixton Road London SW9 6DE
Tel: 020 7735 2062
post@eaveshousing.co.uk
www.eaves4women.co.uk
Research, campaigning and development project run by Eaves, that works on all issues of violence against women,

Lilleshall see Sports Centre (Lilleshall National)

Limbless Association
Unit 16 Waterhouse Business Centre 2 Cromar Way Chelmsford CM1 2QE
Helpline: 0800 644 0185
Tel: 216670, 01245 216671 or 01245 216672
enquiries@limbless-association.org
www.limbless-association.org
Providing information and support to UK amputees and the limb-loss community

Linguists (Chartered Institute of)
Saxon House 48 Southwark St London SE1 1UN
Tel: 020 7940 3100
info@iol.org.uk
www.iol.org.uk
Professional association and examining board for linguists, interpreters, translators, educationists and other professionals for whom a foreign language is a requirement for their daily jobs

Linnean Society of London
Burlington House Piccadilly London W1J 0BF
Tel: 020 7434 4479
info@linnean.org
www.linnean.org
For the study of natural history

Listening Books
12 Lant St London SE1 1QH
Tel: 020 7407 9417
info@listening-books.org.uk
www.listening-books.org.uk
Audio books postal library service for people who find it difficult or impossible to read due to illness or disability

Literacy Association (National)
87 Grange Road Ramsgate Kent CT11 9QB
Tel: 01843 239 952
wendy@nla.org.uk
www.nla.org.uk
Works with children and young people who are underachieving in literacy

Literacy Association (UK)
University of Leicester Leicester LE1 7RH
Tel: 0116 223 1664
admin@ukla.org
www.ukla.org
For teachers, advisers and researchers into literacy education

Literacy in Primary Education (Centre for) CLPE
Webber St London SE1 8QW
Tel: 020 7401 3382/3
Tel: 0207 633 0840
info@clpe.co.uk
www.clpe.co.uk

Literacy Trust (National)
68 South Lambeth Road London SW8 1RL
Tel: 020 7587 1842
email via website
www.literacytrust.org.uk
Works in partnership to enhance literacy standards in the UK

Live Music Now LMN UK
Music Base Kings Place 90 York Way
London N1 9AG
Tel: 01653 668551
email via website
www.livemusicnow.org
Takes live music to those who don't have easy access & offers performance opportunities to young professional musicians. See website to find out more about LMN in your area

Live Theatre
Broad Chare Quayside Newcastle upon Tyne NE1 3DQ
Box Office: 0191 232 1232
Tel: 0191 261 2694 (Admin)
www.live.org.uk

Liver Trust (British) Fighting liver disease
2 Southampton Road Ringwood Hampshire BH24 1HY
Helpline: 0800 652 7330

Tel: 01425 481 320
info@britishlivertrust.org.uk
www.britishlivertrust.org.uk
National charity working to reduce the impact of liver disease in the UK through support, information and research

Liverpool (Museum of)
Pier Head Liverpool L3 1DG
Tel: 0151 478 4545
email via website
www.liverpoolmuseums.org.uk/mol/
Tells the story of LIverpool

Liverpool (National Museums)
Collections Management Division Midland Railway Building 1 Peter Street Liverpool L1 6BL
Tel: 0151 478 4812
email via website
www.liverpoolmuseums.org.uk/conservation
Collections from living bugs to The Beatles, fine art to photography, the Titanic to ancient Egypt - holds over 4 million objects across the collections in all their museums and galleries

Living Earth Foundation Ideas into action
5 Great James Steet London WC1N 3DB
Tel: 020 7440 9750
info@livingearth.org.uk
www.livingearth.org.uk
Non-membership organisation. International, national and local environmental and community education programmes

Living Museum of the North see Beamish

Living Streets
4th Floor Universal House 88-94 Wentworth Street London E1 7SA
Tel: 020 7377 4900
info@ livingstreets.org.uk
www.livingstreets.org.uk
National charity that stands up for pedestrians. Campaigns to achieve safe, pleasant, vibrant & healthy streets for all. Organises Walk to School campaign

Living Wills see Dignity in Dying

Llamau
23 Cathedral Road Cardiff CF11 9HA
Tel: 029 2023 9585
email via website
www.llamau.org.uk
Helping vulnerable young people realise their potential

Local Authorities (Convention of Scottish) now see COSLA

Local Economic Strategies (Centre for) now see CLES

Local Economy Policy Unit
London South Bank University 103 Borough

Rd London SE1 0AA
Tel: 020 20 7815 7798
localeconomy@lsbu.ac.uk
www.lsbu.ac.uk/lepu
Centre for action on local economic development and urban regeneration

Local Government Association LGA
Local Government House Smith Square London SW1P 3HZ
Tel: 020 7664 3000
info@local.gov.uk
www.lga.gov.uk
Lobby and campaign for changes in policy, legislation and funding on behalf of their member councils and the people and communities they serve

Local Government Improvement and Development
Layden House 76-86 Turnmill St London EC1M 5LG
Tel: 020 7296 6880
ihelp@local.gov.uk
www.idea.gov.uk
Works to address issues of equality and diversity to deliver best practice in local government

Local Government Information Unit LGiU
22 Upper Woburn Place London WC1H 0TB
Tel: 020 7554 2800
info@lgiu.org.uk
https://member.lgiu.org.uk/Pages/default.aspx

Local Government Ombudsman (England)
PO Box 4771 Coventry CV4 0EH
Tel: 0300 061 0614
Tel: 0845 602 1983
email via website
www.lgo.org.uk
Investigates complaints made about maladministration by local authorities in England

Local History (British Association for) BALH
PO Box 6549 Somersal Herbert Ashbourne DE6 5WH
Tel: 01283 585947
info@balh.co.uk
www.balh.co.uk

Logistics and Transport in the UK (Chartered Institute of)
Logistics & Transport Centre Earlstrees Court Earlstrees Rd Corby Northants NN17 4AX
Tel: 01536 740104
membership@ciltuk.org.uk
www.ciltuk.org.uk

London (Museum of)
150 London Wall London EC2Y 5HN
Tel: 020 7001 9844
info@museumoflondon.org.uk
www.museumoflondon.org.uk

London Charity Orchestra
info@lco.org.uk
www.londoncharityorchestra.co.uk
Professional musicians, music students and experienced amateurs who help charitable causes

London Children's Ballet
73 St Charles Square London W10 6EJ
Tel: 020 8969 1555
info@londonchildrensballet.com
www.londonchildrensballet.com

London Citizens now see Citizens UK

London Drug & Alcohol Network
c/o DrugScope Prince Consort House Suite 204 109/111 Farringdon Road London EC1R 3BW
Tel: 020 7520 7566
info@ldan.org.uk
www.ldan.org.uk

London Environment Centre now see Green Mark

London Green Belt Council
Tel: 07794 592 924
info@londongreenbeltcouncil.org.uk
http://londongreenbeltcouncil.org.uk

London Hazards Centre
Hampstead Town Hall Centre 213 Haverstock Hill London NW3 4QP
Tel: 020 7794 5999
mail@lhc.org.uk
www.lhc.org.uk
Resource centre for Londoners fighting health & safety hazards in the workplace & community

London Library
14 St James's Square London SW1Y 4LG
Tel: 020 7930 7705
enquiries@londonlibrary.co.uk
www.londonlibrary.co.uk
Subscription library

London Marathon (Virgin)
Tel: 020 7902 0200
www.virginlondonmarathon.com

London Schools Arts Service
25 King's Terrace London NW1 0JP
Tel: 020 7387 8882
email via website
www.lonsas.org.uk
Arts projects & partnerships in schools, colleges and education settings

London Symphony Orchestra LSO
6th Floor, Barbican Centre Silk Street
London EC2Y 8DS
Box office: 020 7638 889
Tel: 020 7588 1116
email via website
www.lso.co.uk

London Theatre (Official)
www.officiallondontheatre.co.uk/access
Guide to West End Theatres

London theatres: online
www.officiallondontheatre.co.uk

London Tourist Board see Visit London

London Transport Museum
Covent Garden Piazza London WC2E 7BB
Main switchboard: 020 7379 6344
Tel: 020 7565 7298 (School visits service)
24 hour information: 020 7565 7299
Minicom: 020 7565 7310
Email via website
www.ltmuseum.co.uk

London Travel Information now see
Transport for London

London Youth Federation of London Youth
Clubs
47-49 Pitfield Street London N1 6DA
Tel: 020 7549 8800
hello@londonyouth.org.uk
www.londonyouth.org.uk

Lone Parents see also Families Need
Fathers, Friendship Works, Gingerbread,
HELP, One Plus One

Lone Twin Network
54 Ventnor Avenue Hodge Hill Birmingham
B36 8EF
info@lonetwinnetwork.org.uk
www.lonetwinnetwork.org.uk
Offers a network of contacts and support to
anyone whose twin has died

Long Distance Walkers Association
www.ldwa.org.uk

Lord Dowding Fund
Millbank Tower Millbank London SW1P
4QP
Tel: 020 7630 3340
email via website
www.ldf.org.uk
Funds and sponsors non-animal research

Lord's Day Observance Society now see
Day One Christian Ministries

Lorna Young Foundation
47 Lea Lane Netherton Huddersfield HD4
7DP
Tel: 07944 979 721
projectmanager@lyf.org.uk
www.lyf.org.uk

Internationally, the LYF supports
smallholder producers in developing
countries to build their commercial capacity,
shorten supply chains; and create local
brands and markets

Lost Doggies UK
enquiries@lost-doggies.com
www.lost-doggies.com
Website to report lost or found dogs and
to help those wanting to give a home to a
rescue dog

Lottery see Big Lottery Fund

Low Pay Commission
6th Floor Victoria House Southampton Row
London WC1B 4AD
Tel: 020 7271 0450
lpc@lowpay.gov.uk
www.lowpay.gov.uk
Independent statutory public body advising
the Government on all aspects of the
minimum wage

Lowry Art & Entertainment
Pier 8, Salford Quays Manchester M50 3AZ
Tel: 0843 208 6000
Groups: 0843 208 6003
email via website
www.thelowry.com

LSO see London Symphony Orchestra

Lucy Faithfull Foundation Working to
protect children
Bordesley Hall The Holloway, Alvechurch
Birmingham B48 7QA or Nightingale House
46-48 East Street Epsom KT17 1HB
Confidential freephone helpline: 0808 1000
900
Tel: 01527 591922
Tel: 01372 847160
email via website
http://lucyfaithfull.org
www.stopitnow.org.uk

Lung Foundation (British)
73-75 Goswell Road London EC1V 7ER
Helpline: 08458 50 50 20
Email via website
www.lunguk.org
Funds research into lung diseases, produces
information literature & has support groups

Lupus UK
St James House Eastern Road Romford
Essex RM1 3NH
Tel: 01708 731251
headoffice@lupusuk.org.uk
www.lupusuk.org.uk

M

Macmillan Cancer Support
89 Albert Embankment London SE1 7UQ
Macmillan Support Line: 0808 808 0000
Tel: 020 7840 7840
email via website
www.macmillan.org.uk
Aims to improve the lives of people
affected by cancer. Provides practical,
medical and financial support and pushes
for better cancer care

Magistrates' Association
28 Fitzroy Square London W1T 6DD
Tel: 020 7387 2353
information@magistrates-association.org.uk
www.magistrates-association.org.uk
Membership organisation representing
over 80% of serving volunteer magistrates.
Promotes the sound administration of the
law

Magna: science adventure centre
Sheffield Rd Rotherham S60 1DX
Tel: 01709 720002
www.visitmagna.co.uk

Mailing Preference Service
DMA House 70 Margaret St London W1W
8SS
Registration line: 0845 703 4599
Tel. 020 7291 3310
mps@dma.org.uk
www.mpsonline.org.uk
Allows consumers to remove their names
from mailing lists

Makaton Charity
Manor House 46 London Road Blackwater
Camberley Surrey GU17 0AA
Tel: 01276 606760
info@makaton.org
www.makaton.org
Language programme for children and
adults with communication and learning
disabilities

Make My Vote Count
www.makemyvotecount.org.uk
Campaigns on changing the way we elect
our MPs

Make Roads Safe Campaign for Global
Road Safety
www.makeroadssafe.org/Pages/home.aspx
Campaigns to stop the daily tragedy of
thousands of preventable deaths and injuries
on the world's roads

Making Music National Federation of
Music Societies
2-4 Great Eastern Street London EC2A
3NW
Tel: 020 7422 8280
info@makingmusic.org.uk
www.makingmusic.org.uk
Supports and champions voluntary and
amateur music groups and amateur
musicians

Malaria No More UK
33 Ransomes Dock 35-37 Parkgate Road
London SW11 4NP
Tel: 020 7801 3840
info@malarianomore.org.uk
http://malarianomore.org.uk/
Part of a global effort to put an end to the
suffering and death caused by malaria

Management (Institute of) see Chartered
Management Institute

Manchester Museum
University of Manchester Oxford Rd
Manchester M13 9PL
Tel: 0161 275 2634
museum@manchester.ac.uk
www.museum.manchester.ac.uk

Manic Depression Fellowship see MDF
The Bipolar Organisation

ManKind Initiative
Flook House Belvedere Road Taunton
Somerset TA1 1BT
Helpline: 01823 334 244
admin@mankind.org.uk
www.mankind.org.uk
Provides help and support for male victims
of domestic abuse and domestic violence

Mankind UK
P.O.Box 124 Newhaven East SussexBN9
9TQ
Tel: 01273 510447
admin@mankindcounselling.org.uk
www.mankindcounselling.org.uk
Support and resource service for men
who have been sexually abused, sexually
assaulted and/or raped.

Mapping see Ordnance Survey

Marathon (London) see London Marathon
(Virgin)

Marfan Association UK
Rochester House 5 Aldershot Road Fleet
Hampshire GU51 3NG
Tel: 01252 810472
contactus@marfan-association.org.uk
www.marfan-association.org.uk
Supports sufferers from disorders of the
connective tissue

Margaret Pyke Centre
73 Charlotte St London W1T 4PL
Tel: 020 33173737 (switchboard)
www.margaretpyke.org
Provides advice and treatment on
contraception, family planning, HRT, plus
pregnancy testing

Marie Curie Cancer Care
89 Albert Embankment London SE1 7TP
Free phone: 0800 716 146
supporter.services@mariecurie.org.uk
www.mariecurie.org.uk
Free practical nursing care at home and
specialist care at 10 centres. Conducts
research into the causes and treatment of
cancer

Marie Stopes International
Helpline: 0845 300 8090 (24 hours)
Tel: 020 7636 6200
services@mariestopes.org.uk
www.mariestopes.org.uk
Counselling and help with women's
sexual health, termination of pregnancy,
contraception, sterilisation, vasectomy

Marine Conservation Society
Unit 3, Wolf Business Park Alton Road
Ross-on-Wye HR9 5NB
Tel: 01989 566017
email via website
www.mcsuk.org
The UK charity dedicated to the protection
of the marine environment and its wildlife

& Scotland
11A Chester Street Edinburgh EH3 7RF
Tel: 0131 226 6360/2391
email via website
www.mcsuk.org/scotland
The UK charity dedicated to the protection
of the marine environment and its wildlife

& Wales
www.mcsuk.org/wales
The UK charity dedicated to the protection
of the marine environment and its wildlife

Marine Leisure Association (MLA)
Marine House Thorpe Lea Road
Egham
Surrey TW20 8BF
Tel: 01784 223640
info@marineleisure.co.uk
www.marineleisure.co.uk
Trade Association for Training, Charter &
Holidays

Marine Life Rescue see Divers Marine Life
Rescue (British)

Marine Life Study Society (British)
Glaucus House 14 Corbyn Cres Shoreham-
by-Sea BN43 6PQ

Tel: 01273 465433
glaucus@hotmail.com
www.glaucus.org.uk

Marine Society and Sea Cadets
202 Lambeth Rd London SE1 7JW
Tel: 020 7654 7000
info@ms-sc.org
www.ms-sc.org

Marine Stewardship Council
Marine House 1 Snow Hill London EC1A
2DH
Tel: 020 7246 8900
Email via website
www.msc.org
Promotes responsible fishing practices

Maritime & Coastguard Agency
Spring Place 105 Commercial Rd
Southampton SO15 1EG
Tel: 02380 329100
Email via website
www.dft.gov.uk/mca

Maritime Museum (Merseyside)
Albert Dock Liverpool L3 4AQ
Tel: 0151 478 4499
email via website
www.liverpoolmuseums.org.uk/maritime
Uncover objects from the Titanic, find out
about life at sea and learn about the port of
Liverpool

Maritime Museum (National)
Maritime Galleries Park Row Greenwich
London SE10 9NF
Museum switchboard: 020 8858 4422
Recorded information line: 020 8312 6565
Bookings;: 020 8312 6608
bookings@nmm.ac.uk
www.nmm.ac.uk/places/maritime-galleries/

Maritime Trust see Cutty Sark Trust

Martial Arts see thematic guide - Sport &
Leisure

Martial Association (Amateur)
169 Cotswold Crescent Walshaw Park Bury
BL8 1QL
Tel: 0161 763 5599
www.amauk.co.uk
National association of martial arts and
kickboxing

Martin Luther King Jr. Center for
nonviolent social change
www.thekingcenter.org
Set up in 1968 as a memorial to Dr Martin
Luther King Jnr to further his philosophy of
non-violence in human relations

Marx Memorial Library
37a Clerkenwell Green London EC1R 0DU
Tel: 0207 253 1485
info@marx-memorial-library.org

www.marx-memorial-library.org
Collection of books about politics, economics and social sciences with a left-wing emphasis

Mary's Meals
Craig Lodge Dalmally Argyll PA33 1AR
Tel: 01838 200605
info@marysmeals.org
www.marysmeals.org
An international movement to set up school feeding projects in communities where poverty and hunger prevent children from gaining an education.

Marylebone Cricket Club see MCC

MASTA Medical Advisory Services for Travellers Abroad
Moorfield Rd Yeadon Leeds LS19 7BN
www.masta-travel-health.com
Provider of travel vaccines and travel health advice to the NHS and many companies and organisations

MATCH Mothers Apart from Their Children
BM Box No. 6334 London WC1N 3XX
enquries@matchmothers.org
www.matchmothers.org
For mothers living apart from their children, and those mothers who have little or no contact with their children

Maternal & Childhealth Advocacy International MCAI
83 Derby Road Nottingham NG1 5BB
Tel: 0115 950 6662
office@mcai.org.uk
www.mcai.org.uk
Charity dedicated to saving the lives of seriously ill pregnant women, children and babies in countries where there is extreme poverty

Maternity Services (Association for Improvements in the) see AIMS

Mathematical Association
259 London Rd Leicester LE2 3BE
Tel: 0116 221 0013
office@m-a.org.uk
www.m-a.org.uk
Long established professional subject association devoted to the needs of classroom mathematics teachers & lecturers

Mathematics see also Innovation in Mathematics Teaching (Centre for), Teachers of Mathematics (Association of)

MCC Marylebone Cricket Club
Lord's Cricket Ground St John's Wood
London NW8 8QN
Tel: 020 7616 8500
email via web
www.lords.org
Guardian of the laws of cricket

MDF The Bipolar Organisation
11 Belgrave Road London SW1V 1RB
Tel: 020 7931 6480
mdf@mdf.org.uk
www.mdf.org.uk
Provides support for all affected by manic depression

ME see also Young People with ME (Association of)

ME (Action for)
PO Box 2778 Bristol BS1 9DJ
Tel: 0845 123 2380
Tel: 0117 927 9551
admin@actionforme.org.uk
www.afme.org.uk
Information and campaigning to support people with ME

ME Association
7 Apollo Office Court Radclive Road
Gawcott Bucks MK18 4DF
Helpline: 0844 576 5326
Tel: 01280 827070
meconnect@meassociation.org.uk
www.meassociation.org.uk
Funds and supports research and provides information and support, education and training

Meat & Livestock Commission now see Agriculture and Horticulture Development Board

Mechanics' Institute
The Mechanics Centre 103 Princess St
Manchester M1 6DD
Tel: 0161 236 9336
mailhost@mechanicsinstitue.co.uk
Conference/function centre

Medau Movement for life
1 Grove House Foundry Lane Horsham
West Sussex RH13 5PL
Tel: 01403 266000
medau@emdp.org
www.medau.org.uk
Dance based workout

Médecins sans Frontières (UK)
67-74 Saffron Hill London EC1N 8QX
Tel: 020 7404 6600
office-ldn@london.msf.org
www.msf.org.uk
International medical aid organisation

Media Center (Independent)
www.indymedia.org
Grassroots, non-corporate coverage of world news

Media for Development
16 Hoxton Square London N1 6NT
Tel: 020 7033 2170
jonathanw@mediafordevelopment.org.uk
www.mediafordevelopment.org.uk
A media consultancy specialising in the
design & implementation of public education
campaigns in the developing world and the
UK

Media Trust
4th Floor Block A, Centre House Wood
Lane London W12 7SB
Tel: 020 7871 5600
info@mediatrust.org
www.mediatrust.org
Charity building partnerships between the
media & the voluntary sector

MediaWise Trust
University of the West of England Canon
Kitson Oldbury Court Road Bristol BS16
2JP
Tel: 0117 93 99 333
info@mediawise.org.uk
www.mediawise.org.uk
Registered charity providing advice,
information and training on media matters

Medical Accidents (Action Against) AvMA
44 High Street Croydon Surrey CR0 1YB
Helpline: 0845 123 2352
www.avma.org.uk
National charity that provides independent
advice and support to anyone who has
suffered a medical accident

Medical Advisory Service
www.medicaladvisoryservice.org.uk
Various helplines on different medical
matters

**Medical Advisory Services for Travellers
Abroad** see MASTA

Medical Aid for Palestinians
33a Islington Park St London N1 1QB
Tel: 020 7226 4114
info@map-uk.org
www.map-uk.org

Medical Conditions at School
c/o Asthma UK Summit House 70 Wilson
Street London EC2A 2DB
www.medicalconditionsatschool.org.uk
Information to help schools and school
healthcare professionals support all pupils
with medical conditions

Medical Emergency Relief International
see MERLIN

**Medical Foundation for the Care of
Victims of Torture**
111 Isledon Road London N7 7JW
Tel: 020 7697 7777

email via website
www.torturecare.org.uk
Charity dedicated solely to the treatment of
torture survivors. Provides help for victims,
documentary evidence of torture, training for
professionals and education for the public

Medical Helpline (General)
Helpline: 020 8994 9874
Covers all general medical queries

Medical Herbalists (National Institute of)
Elm House 54 Mary Arches Street Exeter
EX4 3BA
Tel: 01392 426022
info@nimh.org.uk
www.nimh.org.uk

Medical Progress (Europeans for) now
see Safer Medicines Campaign

**Medical Research Charities (Association
of)**
Charles Darwin House 12 Roger Street
London WC1N 2JU
Tel: 020 20 7685 2620
www.amrc.org.uk
Membership organisation that works to
advance medical research in the UK and, in
particular, aims to improve the effectiveness
of the charitable sector in medical research

Medical Research Council MRC
14th Floor One Kemble Street London
WC2B 4AN
Tel: 01793 416200
corporate@headoffice.mrc.ac.uk
www.mrc.ac.uk

Medical Trust (Britain-Nepal)
130 Vale Rd Tonbridge Kent TN9 1SP
Tel: 01732 360 284
info@britainnepalmedicaltrust.org.uk
www.britainnepalmedicaltrust.org.uk
Works on projects within Nepal's own
developing health programme

MedicAlert Foundation
1 Bridge Wharf 156 Caledonian Rd London
N1 9UU
Tel: 0800 581 420
info@medicalert.org.uk
www.medicalert.org.uk
Emergency identification system for people
with hidden medical conditions and allergies

**Medicines & Healthcare products
Regulatory Agency**
151 Buckingham Palace Road, Victoria
London, SW1W 9SZ
Tel: 020 3080 6000.
info@mhra.gsi.gov.uk
www.mhra.gov.uk
Ensures that all medicines & healthcare
products on the UK market meet appropriate
standards of safety, quality and efficacy

Men's Advice Line
Confidential Helpline: 0808 801 0327
info@mensadviceline.org.uk
www.mensadviceline.org.uk
Advice and support for men experiencing domestic violence by a current or ex-partner. This includes all men - in heterosexual or same-sex relationships

Men's Health Helpline
Helpline: 020 8995 4448

Men's Morris & Sword Dance Clubs (National Association of)
www.themorrisring.org.uk/

Mencap
123 Golden Lane London EC1Y 0RT
Learning Disability Helpline: 0808 808 1111
or mencap Direct: 0300 333 1111
Tel: 020 7454 0454
Mencap Direct:
0300 333 1111
help@mencap.org.uk
www.mencap.org.uk

& Cymru
31 Lambourne Crescent Cardiff Business Park Llanishen Cardiff CF14 5GF
Wales Learning Disability Helpline: 0808 808 1111
Tel: 02920 747588
Mencap Direct:
0300 333 1111
helpline.wales@mencap.org.uk
www.mencap.org.uk/wales

& Northern Ireland
Segal House 4 Annadale Avenue Belfast BT7 3JH
Learning Disability Helpline:
0808 808 1111
Tel: 02890 691351
Mencap Direct:
0300 333 1111
helpline.ni@mencap.org.uk
www.mencap.org.uk/northern-ireland

Meningitis Research Foundation England & Wales
Midland Way Thornbury Bristol BS35 2BS
Helpline: 080 8800 33 44
Tel: 01454 281 811
info@meningitis.org
www.meningitis.org
Funds scientific research into meningitis & septicaemia, raises awareness of the diseases and supports those affected

& Scotland
28 Alva Street Edinburgh EH2 4PY
Helpline: 080 8800 33 44
Tel: 0131 510 2345
info@scotland-meningitis.org.uk
www.meningitis.org

& Northern Ireland
71 Botanic Avenue Belfast BT7 1JL
Helpline: 080 8800 33 44
Tel: 028 9032 1283
info@meningitis-ni.org
www.meningitis.org

& Republic of Ireland
63 Lower Gardiner Street Dublin 1
Helpline: 080 8800 33 44
Tel: 01 819 6931
info@meningitis-ireland.org
www.meningitis.org

Meningitis Trust
Fern House Bath Rd Stroud GL5 3TJ
UK Freephone: 0800 028 1828
Children's Helpline (UK only): Freephone 0808 801 0388
Tel: 01453 768000
info@meningitis-trust.org
www.meningitis-trust.org
Working towards a world that is free from meningitis where those affected by the disease receive quality care and support

& Scotland
Centrum Offices 38 Queen Street Glasgow G1 3DX
UK Freephone: 0800 028 1828
Children's Helpline (UK only): Freephone 0808 801 0388
Tel: 0845 120 2123
info@meningitis-trust.org
www.meningitis-trust.org

& Northern Ireland
Wellington Park Business Centre 3 Wellington Park Malone Road Belfast BT9 6DJ
UK Freephone: 0800 028 1828
Children's Helpline (UK only): Freephone 0808 801 0388
Tel: 0845 120 0663
info@meningitis-trust.org
www.meningitis-trust.org

& Wales/Cymru
Sophia House 28 Cathedral Road Cardiff CF11 9LJ
UK Freephone: 0800 028 1828
Children's Helpline (UK only): Freephone 0808 801 0388
Tel: 0845 120 4597
info@meningitis-trust.org
www.meningitis-trust.org

& Ireland
PO Box 102 Bray Co Wicklow
Tel: 01 276 2050
eolas@meningitis-trust.ie
www.meningitis-trust.ie

Menopause see Daisy Network

Mental Health (Scottish Association for)
SAMH
Brunswick House 51 Wlilson Street
Glasgow G1 1UZ
Tel: 0141 530 1000
enquire@samh.org.uk
www.samh.org.uk

Mental Health Act Commission now see Care Quality Commission

Mental Health Foundation
9th Floor, Sea Containers House 20 Upper Ground London SE1 9QB
Tel: 020 7803 1100
email via web
www.mentalhealth.org.uk
Covers all aspects of mental illness & learning disabilities

& Scotland
Merchants House 30 George Square
Glasgow G2 1EG
Tel: 0141 572 0125
Email via website
www.mentalhealth.org.uk

& Scotland
Scottish Development Centre for Mental Health 17a Graham Street Edinburgh EH6 5QN
Tel: 0131 555 5959
Email via website
www.mentalhealth.org.uk

& Wales
Merlin House No. 1 Langstone Business Park Priory Drive Newport NP18 2HJ
Tel: 01633 415 434
Email via website
www.mentalhealth.org.uk

Mental Welfare Commission for Scotland
Thistle House 91 Haymarket Terrace
Edinburgh EH12 5HE
Freephone: 0800 389 6809
Tel: 0131 313 8777
Textphone: dial 18001 before freephone number to access RNID relay assist
enquiries@mwcscot.org.uk
www.mwcscot.org.uk
Protects the rights and interests of people with a mental illness or learning disability in Scotland

Mentoring and Befriending Foundation
Suite 1, 4th Floor, Building 3 Universal Square Devonshire Street North
Manchester M12 6JH
Tel: 03300 882877
info@mandbf.org
www.mandbf.org.uk
Provides assistance and support for the development of mentoring

Mercy Corps
40 Sciennes Edinburgh EH9 1NJ
To give: 0800 066 5766
email via website
www.mercycorps.org.uk
To alleviate suffering, poverty and oppression by helping people all over the world

MERLIN
12th Floor, 207 Old Street London EC1V 9NR
Tel: 020 7014 1600
hq@merlin.org.uk
www.merlin.org.uk
Provides emergency healthcare to people affected by wars, epidemics and natural disasters

Mermaids
BM Mermaids London WC1N 3XX
Information line: 0208 1234819
email via website
www.mermaidsuk.org.uk
Family and individual support for teenagers and children with gender identity issues

Message Home see also Missing People and Runaway Helpline
Freefone: 0800 700 740 (confidential 24/7 service)
messagehome@missingpeople.org.uk
www.missingpeople.org.uk/areyoumissing/message-home/
Helps missing people who feel unable to make direct contact with the people they have left behind, by forwarding a message on their behalf. They will only pass on the message and will not tell the family any other information

Met Office
FitzRoy Road Exeter Devon EX1 3PB
Tel: 0870 900 0100
Tel: 01392 885680
enquiries@metoffice.gov.uk education@metoffice.gov.uk
www.metoffice.gov.uk
www.metoffice.gov.uk/education
UK's national weather service

Metabolic Diseases see Climb

Meteorological Organization (World)
7 bis, avenue de la Paix, Case Postale 2300 CH 1211 Geneva 2 Switzerland
Tel: 00 41 22 730 8111
wmo@wmo.int
www.wmo.int

Meteorological Society (Royal)
104 Oxford Rd Reading RG1 7LL
Tel: 0118 956 8500
chiefexec@rmets.org
www.rmets.org

Advancing the understanding of weather and climate, the science and its applications for the benefit of all

Meteorology see Met Office

Methodist Association of Youth Clubs see Methodist Children & Youth

Methodist Children & Youth
Discipleship & Ministries Cluster The Connexional Team Methodist Church House 25 Marylebone Road London NW1 5JR
Helpdesk: 020 7486 5502
childrenandyouthteam@methodistchurch.org.uk
www.childrenandyouth.org.uk

Methodist Church
25 Marylebone Road London NW1 5JR
Tel: 020 7486 5502
helpdesk@methodistchurch.org.uk
www.methodistchurch.org.uk

Metropolitan Police
New Scotland Yard Broadway London SW1H 0BG
Anti-Terrorist Hotline: 0800 789 321
Tel: 0300 123 1212
For Victims of Human Trafficking: 0800 783 2589
Email via website
www.met.police.uk

Michael Palin Centre see Stammering Children (Michael Palin Centre for)

Midi Music Company
77 Watsons St Deptford London SE8 4AU
Tel: 020 8694 6093
theteam@themidimusiccompany.co.uk
www.themidimusiccompany.co.uk
Uses arts to bring groups of young disadvantaged people together. Provides a range of music and midi technology activities

Midwives UK (Independent)
PO Box 539 Abingdon OX14 9DF
Tel: 0845 4600 105
information@independentmidwives.org.uk
www.independentmidwives.org.uk
Working outside the NHS to give individualised care to women

Migraine Action Association
4th Floor 27 East Street Leicester LE1 6NB
Tel: 0116 275 8317
Email via website
www.migraine.org.uk
www.migraineadventure.org.uk

Migraine Trust
52-53 Russell Square London WC1B 4HP
Tel: 020 7631 6970
info@migrainetrust.org
www.migrainetrust.org

Patient support and medical research charity providing information and support

Migration Policy Group
205 Rue Belliard, Box 1 1040 Brussels Belgium
Tel: 32 2 230 59 30
info@migpolgroup.com
www.migpolgroup.com
Independent organisation committed to policy development on mobility, migration, diversity, equality and anti-discrimination

Millennium Seed Bank
Wakehurst Place Ardingly Haywards Heath W. Sussex RH17 6TN
Tel: 01444 894066
wakehurst@kew.org
www.kew.org/science-conservation/save-seed-prosper/millennium-seed-bank/
Aims to safeguard over 24,000 plant species worldwide & to secure the future of UK native flowering plants

MIND National Association for Mental Health
15-19 Broadway Stratford London E15 4BQ
Infoline: 0300 123 3393
Tel: 020 8519 2122
contact@mind.org.uk
www.mind.org.uk
Leading mental health charity in England and Wales

Mine Action Service (UN) now see E-MINE

Mine Information Network (Electronic) see E-MINE

Mines see also HALO Trust, Landmines (International Campaign to Ban)

Mines Advisory Group MAG
68 Sackville Street Manchester M1 3NJ
Tel: 0161 236 4311
info@maginternational.org
www.maginternational.org
Mine clearance & awareness programmes

Mining Museum (National) Scotland
Lady Victoria Colliery Newtongrange Midlothian EH22 4QN
Tel: 0131 663 7519
enquiries@scottishminingmuseum.com
www.scottishminingmuseum.com

Ministry of Defence see Defence (Ministry of)

Minority Rights Group International
54 Commercial Street London E1 6LT
Tel: 020 7422 4200
minority.rights@mrgmail.org
www.minorityrights.org
Working to secure the rights of ethnic, linguistic and religious minorities and indigenous peoples worldwide

Miracles
PO Box 3003 Littlehampton West Sussex
BN16 1SY
Tel: 01903 775673
miracles@fastnet.co.uk
www.miraclesthecharity.org
Crisis funding to alleviate situations of dire
and multiple distress; positive thinking; a
listening ear, and practical support for those
with nowhere else to turn.

Miscarriage Association
17 Wentworth Terrace Wakefield WF1 3QW
Tel: 01924 200 799
Tel: 01924 200795 (admin)
email via website
www.miscarriageassociation.org.uk
Provides support and information on
pregnancy loss

Missing Children website
www.missingkids.co.uk

Missing People see also Runaway Helpline
and Message Home
284 Upper Richmond Road West London
SW14 7JE
Freefone: 0500 700 700
Tel: 020 8392 4590
info@missingpeople.org.uk
www.missingpeople.org.uk/
Search on behalf of those left behind and
provide specialised support

Mobilise now see Disabled Motoring UK

MoD see Defence (Ministry of)

Monetary Justice (Christian Council for)
Tel: 020 7207 0509
info@ccmj.org
www.ccmj.org
Campaigning for democratic control of the
monetary system

Money Advice Service
25 The North Colonnade Canary Wharf
London E14 5HS
Money Advice Line: 0300 500 5000
Tel: 020 7943 0500
enquiries@moneyadviceservice.org.uk
www.moneyadviceservice.org.uk
Work with partners from a wide range of
industries, government and other sectors to
find new ways of making money matters and
financial choices clearer for everyone

Money Claim Online
Online helpdesk: 0845 601 5935 or 01604
619 402
www.direct.gov.uk/en/
MoneyTaxAndBenefits/ManagingDebt/
Makingacourtclaimformoney/DG_195688
Electronic service can be used by
individuals, solicitors, businesses and

government departments to sue for money
owing, subject to conditions

Moneysavingexpert.com
www.moneysavingexpert.com
Tips on how to save money and get the best
deals

Mongabay.com
www.mongabay.com
Environmental science and conservation
news sites

Moniack Mhor Ltd. now see Arvon
Foundation

Monopolies and Mergers Commission
now see Competition Commission

Montessori Centre
18 Balderton St London W1K 6TG
Tel: 020 7493 8300
centre@montessori.org.uk
www.montessori.org.uk
Training college for those wishing to train in
the Montessori method of teaching young
children

Monuments see Public Monuments &
Sculpture Association

Morris Federation
www.morrisfed.org
Association of self-governing Morris clubs

Mosac
141 Greenwich High Road London SE10
8JA
Helpline: 0800 980 1958
Tel: 020 8293 9990
enquiries@mosac.org.uk
www.mosac.org.uk
Supports all non-abusing parents and carers
whose children have been sexually abused,
providing advocacy, information and advice,
befriending, counselling, play therapy and
support groups following alleged child
sexual abuse

MOSI Museum of Science & Industry
Liverpool Road Castlefield Manchester M3
4FP
Tel: 0161 832 2244
email via website
www.mosi.org.uk

Most Wanted (UK)
Crimestoppers: 0800 555 111
http://wanted.crimestoppers-uk.org
Website aimed at tracking Britain's most
wanted crime suspects

Mothers see also Full Time Mothers,
MATCH

Mothers' Union Christian care for families
Mary Sumner House 24 Tufton St London
SW1P 3RB

Tel: 020 7222 5533
email via website
www.themothersunion.org

Motor Manufacturers and Traders Ltd. (Society of)
71 Great Peter Street London SW1P 2BN
Tel: 020 7235 7000
Email via website
www.smmt.co.uk
Encouraging and promoting in the UK and abroad, the interests of the motor industry

Motor Neurone Disease Association
PO Box 246 Northampton NN1 2PR
Helpline: 08457 626262
Tel: 01604 250505
enquiries@mndassociation.org
www.mndassociation.org
Provides support and advice to people affected by Motor Neurone Disease and funds research

Motorvations Project Ltd
13-14 Maldon Road Romford Essex RM7 0JB
Tel: 01708 723733
motorvations@mail.com
www.motorvations.net
To engage young people in motor vehicle and related activities to enable them to break the cycle of social exclusion

Mountain Leader Training England
Siabod Cottage Capel Curig Conwy LL24 0ES
Tel: 01690 720314
info@mlte.org
www.mlte.org
Administers the training programme and qualifications for leaders of groups hill walking and rock climbing in mountainous country

Mountaineering Council (British)
The Old Church 177-179 Burton Rd Manchester M20 2BB
Tel: 0161 445 6111
office@thebmc.co.uk
www.thebmc.co.uk
Governing body for sport of mountaineering in Britain

Mountaineering Council of Scotland
The Old Granary West Mill St Perth PH1 5QP
Tel: 01738 493942
info@mcofs.org.uk
www.mcofs.org.uk
Representative body for mountaineers and walkers

Mousetrap Theatre Projects ...inspiring young people
23-24 Henrietta Street Covent Garden London WC2E 8ND
Tel: 020 7836 4388
info@mousetrap.org.uk
www.mousetrap.org.uk
Charity dedicated to creating theatre access and education programme for young people with limited resources or support

Mouth Cancer Foundation
P O Box 498 Wakefield WF1 9AW
Helpline: 01924 950 950
info@mouthcancerfoundation.org
www.mouthcancerfoundation.org
Supporting people with mouth, throat and other head & neck cancer

Movie Review Query Engine
www.mrqe.com
Allows access to reviews of over 30,000 film titles

MRC see Medical Research Council

MS see Multiple Sclerosis

Multiple Births see also Twins & Multiple Births Association

Multiple Births Foundation
Hammersmith House Level 4 Queen Charlotte's and Chelsea Hospital Du Cane Rd London W12 0HS
Tel: 020 3313 3519
mbf@imperial.nhs.uk
www.multiplebirths.org.uk

Multiple Sclerosis Society
MS National Centre 372 Edgware Rd London NW2 6ND
Helpline: 0808 800 8000
Tel: 020 8438 0700
helpline@mssociety.org.uk
www.mssociety.org.uk

& Scotland
Ratho Park 88 Glasgow Road Ratho Station Newbridge EH28 8PP
Helpline: 0808 800 8000
Tel: 0131 335 4050
helpline@mssociety.org.uk
www.mssociety.org.uk

& Wales/Cymru
Temple Court Cathedral Road Cardiff CF11 9HA
Helpline: 0808 800 8000
Tel: 029 2078 6676
helpline@mssociety.org.uk
www.mssociety.org.uk

Multiple Sclerosis Society Northern Ireland
The Resource Centre 34 Annadale Avenue Belfast BT7 3JJ
Helpline: 0808 800 8000
Tel: 02890 802 802
helpline@mssociety.org.uk
www.mssociety.org.uk

Multiple Sclerosis Therapy Centres (National)
PO Box 126 Whitchurch SY14 7WL
Tel: 0845 3670977
info@msntc.org.uk
www.msntc.org.uk

Multiple Sclerosis Trust
Spirella Building Bridge Road Letchworth Garden City Herts SG6 4ET
Free Phone Information Service: 0800 032 38 39
Tel: 01462 476700
info@mstrust.org.uk
www.mstrust.org.uk

Mumsnet
www.mumsnet.com
Product reviews and parenting advice given by parents

Murder see SAMM

Muscular Dystrophy Campaign
61 Southwark Street London SE1 0HL
Tel: 0800 652 6352 (freephone)
Tel: 020 7803 4800
info@muscular-dystrophy.org
www.muscular-dystrophy.org
Provides support and information

Musculoskeletal Medicine (British Institute of)
PO Box 1116 Bushey Herts WD23 9BY
Tel: 020 8421 9910
deena@bimm.org.uk
www.bimm.org.uk

Museum Net
www.museums.co.uk
Search for museums throughout the UK by keyword or name

Museum of London Docklands
No 1 Warehouse London E14 4AL
Tel: 020 7001 9844
info.docklands@museumoflondon.org.uk
www.museumoflondon.org.uk/docklands

Museum of London Archaeology and Archaeological Archive
Mortimer Wheeler House 46 Eagle Wharf Road London N1 7ED
Tel: 020 7410 2200 (archaeology)
Tel: 020 7490 8447/020 7566 9317 (archive)
email via website
www.museumoflondon.org.uk/archaeology

Museum of Science & Industry see MOSI

Museum of Scotland (National)
Chambers St Edinburgh EH1 1JF
Tel: 0300 123 6789
www.nms.ac.uk

Museums (International Council of)
ICOM Secretariat
Maison de l'UNESCO 1 rue Miollis 75732 Paris Cedex 15 France
Tel: 00 33 1 47 34 05 00
email via website
http://icom.museum

Museums, Libraries & Archives Council now see Arts Council England

Music (Royal Academy of) see Royal Academy of Music

Music and the Deaf
7 Northumberland St Huddersfield HD1 1RL
Tel: 01484 483115
Textphone: 01484 483117
info@matd.org.uk
www.matd.org.uk
Helping deaf people access music and the performing arts through workshops, schools projects & signed theatre performances

Music Council (National)
c/o BASCA British Music House 26 Berners Street London W1T 3LR
Tel: 01707 662 662
info@nationalmusiccouncil.org.uk
www.nationalmusiccouncil.org.uk

Music Educators (National Association of) NAME
Gordon Lodge Snitterton Road Matlock Derbyshire DE4 2JG
admin@name.org.uk
www.name.org.uk
Supports its members in development of highest quality music education accessible to all

Music for Youth MFY
3rd Floor, South Wing Somerset House Strand London WC2R 1LA
Tel: 020 7759 1830
mfy@mfy.org.uk
www.mfy.org.uk
Organises the National Festival of Music for Youth, Regional Festivals and the Schools Proms and promotes performance opportunities for young people.

Music Freedom Day
www.musicfreedomday.org
3rd March annually - marked with events, seminars, exhibitions, radio programmes and newspaper articles on the subject of freedom of expression for musicians all over the world

Music Publishers Association
6th Floor British Music House 26 Berners Street London W1T 3LR
Tel: 020 7580 0126
email via website
www.mpaonline.org.uk
Trade Association supporting UK based music publishers

Music Societies (National Federation Of)
see Making Music

Music Therapy (British Association for)
BAMT
24-27 White Lion Street London N1 9PD
Tel: 020 7837 6100
info@bamt.org
www.bamt.org
Professional body for music therapists. Music therapy is an established clinical discipline which is widely used to help people whose lives have been affected by injury, illness or disability

Musicians (Incorporated Society of)
10 Stratford Place London W1C 1AA
Tel: 020 7629 4413
membership@ism.org
www.ism.org
Professional body for musicians

Musicians Union
60-62 Clapham Road London SW9 0JJ
Tel: 020 7582 5566
info@theMU.org
www.musiciansunion.org.uk
Trade Union for professional musicians

Muslim Schools UK (Association of)
PO Box 14109 Birmingham B6 9BN
Tel: 0844 482 0407
email via website
www.ams-uk.org
Supports & develops excellence in full-time Muslim schools & acts as a voice for Islamic education with government bodies & the media. Gives advice to new Muslim schools

Muslim Welfare House
233 Seven Sisters Rd Finsbury Park London N4 2DA
Tel: 020 7263 3071
info@mwht.org.uk
www.mwht.org.uk
Provides marriage counselling, courses in English for Speakers of Other Languages, IT, crafts, careers, business advice, out of school care for children for whole community

My Supermarket
www.mysupermarket.co.uk
Supermarket price comparison website

Myalgic Encephalomyelitis see also ME (Action for), ME Association, Young People with ME (Association of)

MyBnk My money, our future
MyBnk @ Unit 4 Huguenot Place, Heneage Street London E1 5LN
Tel: 020 7377 8770
info@mybnk.org
www.mybnk.org
Provides young people with the skills to manage their money effectively.

Mycological Society (British)
City View House 5 Union Street Ardwick Manchester M12 4JD
Tel: 0161 277 7638 / 7639
admin@britmycolsoc.info
www.britmycolsoc.org.uk
Promotes study of fungi in all its aspects

Mydaughter.co.uk
Girls' Schools Association 130 Regent Road Leicester LE1 7PG
Tel: 0116 254 1619
www.mydaughter.co.uk
Providing information, expert opinion and useful advice on all aspects of raising and educating happy, fulfilled girls

N

NAACE National Association of Advisers for Computers in Education
PO Box 6511 Nottingham NG11 8TN
Tel: 0115 945 7235
office@naace.co.uk
www.naace.co.uk
Advancing education through ICT

NABSS National Association of Black Supplementary Schools
PO Box 59330 London NW8 1DY
Tel: 07958 348 558
info@nabss.org.uk
www.nabss.org.uk
Central resource for parents, helpers and members of the Afrikan/Caribbean community to find help with their children's education in their locality

Nacro The Crime Reduction Charity
Park Place 10-12 Lawn Lane London SW8
1UD
Tel: 020 7840 7200
Email via website
www.nacro.org.uk/
Runs crime reduction projects including
housing, training, prison projects and youth
work

NAKMAS National Association of Karate
and Martial Art Schools
PO Box 262 Herne Bay Kent CT6 9AW
Tel: 01227 370055
info@nakmas.org.uk
www.nakmas.org.uk
National Governing Body for Traditional and
Modern Martial Arts

NAME see Music Educators (National
Association of)

NAN (National Advocacy Network) see
Advocacy Resource Exchange

NAPE National Association for Primary
Education
Moulton College Management Centre
Moulton Northampton NN3 7RR
Tel 01604 647646
nationaloffice@nape.co.uk
www.nape.org.uk
Independent voice in the world of education
seeking to represent and raise the profile of
the primary phase of education

NAPS see Premenstrual Syndrome
(National Association for)

Narcolepsy UK
PO Box 13842 Penicuik EH26 8WX
Tel: 0845 4500 394
info@narcolepsy.org.uk
www.narcolepsy.org.uk
Narcolepsy causes excessive daytime
sleepiness and attacks of paralysis

Narcotics Anonymous UK
Helpline: 0300 999 1212
email via website
www.ukna.org
A fellowship of recovering addicts who meet
regularly to help each other stay clean

NATE see Teaching of English (National
Association for the)

National Advocacy Network see
Advocacy Resource Exchange

National Archives
Kew Richmond TW9 4DU
Tel: 020 8876 3444
Textphone: 020 8392 9198
email via website
www.nationalarchives.gov.uk

UK national archives with records from 11th
century to today. Includes link to the UK
Government Web Archive

National Archives of Scotland (NAS)
HM General Register House 2 Princes St
Edinburgh EH1 3YY
Tel: 0131 535 1314
enquiries@nas.gov.uk
www.nas.gov.uk
From 1 April 2011, the General Register
Office for Scotland merged with the National
Archives of Scotland to become the National
Records of Scotland (NRS). This website
will remain active until it is replaced in due
course by a new website for NRS

National Childbirth Trust NCT
Alexandra House Oldham Terrace London
W3 6NH
Tel: 0300 3300 770
Tel: 0844 243 6000
email via website
www.nct.org.uk
Information & support for all pregnant
women & parents of young children

National Churches Trust
31 Newbury Street London EC1A 7HU
Tel: 0207 600 6090
email via website
www.nationalchurchestrust.org

National Debtline
Tricorn House 51-53 Hagley Road
Edgbaston Birmingham B16 8TP
Helpline: 0808 808 4000
Email via website
www.nationaldebtline.co.uk
National telephone helpline for people
with debt problems in England, Wales &
Scotland. Free, confidential, independent

National Drama
asknd@nationaldrama.org.uk
www.nationaldrama.co.uk
Professional association for drama
educators

National Energy Action
West 1 Forth Banks Newcastle-upon-Tyne
NE1 3PA
Tel: 0191 261 5677
www.nea.org.uk
Develops and promotes energy efficiency to
tackle the heating and insulation problems of
low income households

National Extension College
Michael Young Centre Purbeck Rd
Cambridge CB2 8HN
Tel: 0800 389 2839
Tel: 01223 400 200
info@nec.ac.uk
www.nec.ac.uk

Specialises in distance learning courses, training materials, open learning packs, open and distance learning consultancy services

National Forest Company
Enterprise Glade Bath Yard Moira Swadlincote Derbyshire DE12 6BA
Tel: 01283 55121
enquiries@nationalforest.org
www.nationalforest.org
A project, blending new and maturing woodland, transforming 200 square miles of central England

National Foundation for Educational Research see NFER

National Gallery
Trafalgar Square London WC2N 5DN
Tel: 020 7747 2885
Education: 020 7747 2424
information@ng-london.org.uk
www.nationalgallery.org.uk

National Gallery (Scottish)
The Mound Edinburgh EH2 2EL
Tel: 0131 624 6200
nginfo@nationalgalleries.org
www.nationalgalleries.org/visit/introduction
www.nationalgalleries.org

National Gallery of Modern Art (Scottish)
75 Belford Road Edinburgh EH4 3DR
Tel: 0131 624 6200
gmainfo@nationalgalleries.org
www.nationalgalleries.org/visit/118-introduction
www.nationalgalleries.org

National Institute for Health and Clinical Excellence NICE
MidCity Place 71 High Holborn London WC1V 6NA
Tel: 0845 003 7780
nice@nice.org.uk
www.nice.org.uk

National Libraries (Friends of the)
c/o Dept of Manuscripts The British Library 96 Euston Rd London NW1 2DB
Tel: 020 7412 7559
email via website
www.friendsofnationallibraries.org.uk
Gives grants to libraries, record offices etc for rare books and manuscripts and archival acquisitions

National Library of Scotland
George IV Bridge Edinburgh EH1 1EW
Tel: 0131 623 3700
enquiries@nls.uk
www.nls.uk

National Library of Wales
Aberystwyth Ceredigion SY23 3BU
Tel: 01970 632 800
Email via website
www.llgc.org.uk

National Media Museum
Bradford West Yorkshire BD1 1NQ
Tel: 0844 856 3797(General & Box Office)
Groups & schools: 0844 856 3799
talk@nationalmediamuseum.org.uk
www.nationalmediamuseum.org.uk

National Museum Cardiff
Cathays Park Cardiff CF10 3NP
Tel: 029 2039 7951
Email via website
www.museumwales.ac.uk

National Museum of Labour History see People's History Museum

National Opera Studio
The Clore Building 2 Chapel Yard Wandsworth High Street London SW18 4HZ
Tel: 020 8874 8811
info@nationaloperastudio.org.uk
www.nationaloperastudio.org.uk

National Parks (Campaign for)
6-7 Barnard Mews London SW11 1QU
Tel: 020 7924 4077
info@cnp.org.uk
www.cnp.org.uk
Campaigning environmental charity

National Portrait Gallery
St Martin's Place London WC2H 0HE
Tel: 020 7306 0055
www.npg.org.uk

National Portrait Gallery (Scottish)
1 Queen Street Edinburgh EH2 1JD
Tel: 0131 624 6200
pginfo@nationalgalleries.org
www.nationalgalleries.org/visit/298-introduction

National Society for the Prevention of Cruelty to Children see NSPCC

National Theatre
South Bank London SE1 9PX
Tel: 020 7452 3000 (Box Office)
Tel: 020 7452 3400 (Info Desk)
info@nationaltheatre.org.uk
www.nationaltheatre.org.uk

National Tidal and Sea Level Facility
Proudman Oceanographic Laboratory Joseph Proudman Building 6 Brownlow Street Liverpool L3 5DA
Tel: 0151 795 4800
Email via website
www.pol.ac.uk/ntslf/
Tidal predictions for selected UK and Irish ports

National Trust
PO Box 39 Warrington WA5 7WD
Tel: 0844 800 1895
Minicom: 0844 800 4410
enquiries@nationaltrust.org.uk
www.nationaltrust.org.uk

National Trust for Ireland see An Taisce

National Trust for Scotland
Hermiston Quay 5 Cultins Road Edinburgh
EH11 4DF
Tel: 0844 493 2100
information@nts.org.uk
www.nts.org.uk
Conservation charity that protects and
promotes Scotland's natural and cultural
heritage

National Trust Holiday Cottages
PO Box 536 Melksham Wiltshire SN12 8SX
Tel: 0844 8002070 (Booking Line)
cottages@nationaltrust.org.uk
www.nationaltrustcottages.co.uk

National Trust Volunteering
National Trust Central Volunteering Team
Heelis Kemble Drive Swindon SN2 2NA
Tel: 01793 817632
volunteers@nationaltrust.org.uk
www.nationaltrust.org.uk/main/w-trust/w-
volunteering.htm

National Trust Working Holidays
Tel: 0844 800 3099
working.holidays@nationaltrust.org.uk
www.nationaltrust.org.uk/workingholidays
Working holidays in beautiful locations
undertaking countryside conservation (min.
age 18)

National Union of Students see NUS

National Youth Ballet of Great Britain
The Old Dairy Wintersell Farm Dwelly Lane
Edenbridge TN8 6QD
info@nyb.org.uk
www.nyb.org.uk
An amateur ballet company for young
people of 8-18 years

Natural Death Centre
In The Hill House Watley Lane Twyford
Winchester SO21 1QX
Tel: 01962 712 690
email via website
www.naturaldeath.org.uk
Info on green, inexpensive, DIY & woodland
funerals and living wills

Natural England
1 East Parade Sheffield S1 2ET
Tel: 0845 600 3078 (enquiries)
enquiries@naturalengland.org.uk
www.naturalengland.gov.uk

Working for people, places and nature now
and in the future

Natural Environment Research Council
Polaris House North Star Ave Swindon SN2
1EU
Tel: 01793 411500
email via website
www.nerc.ac.uk

Natural Heritage (Scottish)
Great Glen House Leachkin Road
Inverness IV3 8NW
Tel: 01463 725000
email via website
www.snh.gov.uk
Concerned with all environmental issues in
Scotland

Natural History Museum
Cromwell Road London SW7 5BD
Tel: 020 7942 5000
Tel: 020 7942 5011 (Main info desk)
Tel: 020 7942 5511 (Customer services)
email via website
www.nhm.ac.uk

Natural Voice Practitioners' Network
Tel: 0114 230 9439
admin@naturalvoice.net
www.naturalvoice.net
Umbrella organisation for local singing
groups that aim to recreate the sense that
singing is natural and open to all

Naturewatch Campaigning Against Animal
Cruelty
14 Hewlett Road Cheltenham GL52 6AA
Tel: 01242 252871
info@naturewatch.org
www.naturewatch.org
Campaigns for vital changes in the law to
help stop animal abuse

Navigation (Royal Institute of)
1 Kensington Gore London SW7 2AT
Tel: 020 7591 3130
admin@rin.org.uk
www.rin.org.uk
To unite in one body those interested in the
science and art of navigation

Navy (US)
www.navy.mil
Official information site

NAWE see Writers in Education (National
Association of)

NBCS National Blind Children's Society
Bradbury House Market Street Highbridge
Somerset TA9 3BW
Freephone: 0800 781 1444 (Family Support
and Information)
Tel: 01278 764764
enquiries@nbcs.org.uk
www.nbcs.org.uk

NCB Children's Bureau (National)
8 Wakley St London EC1V 7QE
Tel: 020 7843 6000
enquiries@ncb.org.uk
www.ncb.org.uk
Promotes interests and wellbeing of all
children and young people

NCDL see Dogs Trust

NCDT see Drama Training (National Council
for)

NCF see Sports Coach UK

NCH (National Children's Homes) now
see Action for Children

NCT see National Childbirth Trust

Neonatal Death see SANDS

NESTA see Science, Technology & the Arts
(National Endowment for)

Netball Association (All England) now
see England Netball

Netdoctor
www.netdoctor.co.uk
Online health advice

Nethouseprices
www.nethouseprices.com
Access to the latest house prices for
England, Scotland and Wales

Netmums
www.netmums.com
Online parenting organisation offering
information, advice, chat and support

Network 81
www.network81.org
www.sen-training.co.uk
For parents of children with special
educational needs

Neuro Foundation UK
Quayside House 38 High Street Kingston
on Thames Surrey KT1 1HL
Tel: 020 8439 1234
info@nfauk.org
www.nfauk.org
Provides help, support and advice to those
affected by Neurofibromatosis, their families
and the professionals working with them

New Bridge Foundation
27a Medway Street London SW1P 2BD
Tel: 020 7976 0779
info@newbridgefoundation.org.uk
www.newbridgefoundation.org.uk
Befriending service for prisoners (prison
visiting and writing) & resettlement service

New Economics Foundation
3 Jonathan St London SE11 5NH
Tel: 0207 820 6300
info@neweconomics.org

www.neweconomics.org
Works to put people and the environment at
the centre of economic thinking

New Internationalist
www.newint.org
New Internationalist Publications is a
communications co-operative. It exists
to report on issues of world poverty and
inequality. Publishes New Internationalist
magazine, films, books and other materials

New Opportunities Fund now see Big
Lottery Fund

Newlife Foundation for Disabled Children
Newlife Centre Hemlock Way Cannock
Staffordshire, WS11 7GF
Tel: 01543 462 777
info@newlifecharity.co.uk
www.newlifecharity.co.uk
Action to help disabled and terminally ill
children in the UK

Newspaper Library (British Library)
http://newspapers.bl.uk/blcs/
UK National Newspaper Archive. Only
available to over 18 years with proof of I.D.

NFER National Foundation for Educational
Research
The Mere Upton Park Slough SL1 2DQ
Tel: 01753 574123
enquiries@nfer.ac.uk
www.nfer.ac.uk
Independent educational research body

NHS Blood and Transplant
Customer Services Collindale Avenue
Collindale London NW9 5BG
Tel: 0300 123 2323
Minicom: 0845 730 0106
Email via website
www.blood.co.uk
Information and statistics on blood and how
to register as a blood or bone marrow donor

NHS Careers
Tel: 0345 60 60 655
Email via website
www.nhscareers.nhs.uk/

NHS Confederation
29 Bressenden Place London SW1E 5DD
Tel: 020 7074 3200
enquiries@nhsconfed.org
www.nhsconfed.org
Dedicated to improving health policy and
practice

NHS Confederation (Welsh)
Unit 3 Waterton Park Bridgend CF31 1PH
Tel: 0845 33 00 499
tegan.williams@welshconfed.org
www.nhsconfed.org

NHS Direct
Helpline: 0845 4647
www.nhsdirect.nhs.uk
Helpline provides direct contact with a
trained nurse

NHS Health Scotland
Woodburn House 54 Canaan Ln Edinburgh
EH10 4SG
Tel: 0131 536 5500
Textphone: 0131 536 5503
nhs.healthscotland-generalenquiries@nhs.
net
www.healthscotland.com

NHS Support Federation
www.nhscampaign.org
A campaign by NHS staff and the public to
ensure the survival of a comprehensive and
adequately funded NHS

NIACE National Institute of Adult
Continuing Education
20 Princess Rd West Leicester LE1 6TP
Tel: 0116 204 4200/1
enquiries@niace.org.uk
www.niace.org.uk
Promoting adult learning

Nicaragua Solidarity Campaign
86 Durham Road London N7 7DT
Tel: 020 7561 4836
email via website
www.nicaraguasc.org.uk

NICON - Northern Ireland Confederation
The Beeches 12 Hampton Manor Drive
Belfast BT7 3EN
Tel: 028 90 644811
info@niconfdhss.org
www.nhsconfed.org
Dedicated to improving health policy and
practice

Nil by Mouth
c/o SCVO 3rd Floor Brunswick House 51
Wilson Street Glasgow G1 1UZ
Tel: 0141 559 5008
mail@nilbymouth.org
www.nilbymouth.org
Campaign against sectarianism in Scotland

NIPPA now see Early Years

No candidate deserves my vote
8 Belmont Court Belmont Hill St Albans
AL1 1RB
Tel: 01727 847370
admin@nocandidate.org.uk
www.nocandidate.org.uk
Political party whose presence on a ballot
paper allows voters to abstain positively

No Panic
93 Brands Farm Way Telford Shropshire
TF3 2JQ

Helpline: 0808 808 0545 Freephone)
Tel: 01952 590005
ceo@nopanic.org.uk
www.nopanic.org.uk
Help on panic attacks, phobias & obsessive/
compulsive disorders

No Sweat
5 Caledonian Road London N1 9DX
Tel: 07904 431959
admin@nosweat.org.uk
www.nosweat.org.uk
Campaigning against sweatshop bosses, in
solidarity with workers, worldwide

NOAH National Organization for Albinism
and Hypopigmentation
www.albinism.org
Volunteer self-help organisation for research
and education. It does not diagnose, treat or
provide genetic counselling

Nobel Prize Internet Archive
www.almaz.com/nobel/peace/
List of prizewinners

NODA National Operatic & Dramatic
Association
58-60 Lincoln Rd Peterborough PE1 2RZ
Tel: 01733 865 790
info@noda.org.uk
www.noda.org.uk

Noise Abatement Society
Suite 2 26 Brunswick Terrace Brighton
East Sussex BN3 1HJ
Free advice helpline: 01273 823850
email via website
www.noiseabatementsociety.com
Raises awareness of noise pollution and
helps to relieve the physical and mental
distress and ill health which noise and
related pollutants cause

Nominet UK
Tel: 01865 332244
Tel: 01865 332211
nominet@nominet.org.uk
www.nominet.org.uk
National registry of all Internet Domain
Names ending in .uk

Non-smokers see also Cleanair, QUIT

Northern Ballet
Quarry Hill Leeds LS2 7PA
Tel: 0113 220 8000
info@northernballet.com
http://northernballet.com
Professional touring ballet company with the
most widespread touring programme of any
UK company

Northern Broadsides
Dean Clough Halifax HX3 5AX
Tel: 01422 369704

www.northern-broadsides.co.uk
National touring theatre company presenting
classic texts

Northern Ireland Environment Link
89 Loopland Drive Belfast BT6 9DW
Tel: 028 9045 5770
iona@nienvironmentlink.org
www.nienvironmentlink.org

Northern Ireland Executive
Stormont Castle Stormont Estate Belfast
BT4 3TT
Tel: 028 9052 8400
www.northernireland.gov.uk

Northern Ireland Office
Stormont House Stormont Estate Belfast
BT4 3SH & 11 Millbank London SW1P 4PN
Tel: 028 9052 0700
Textphone: 028 9052 7668
Email via website
www.nio.gov.uk

Northern Ireland Ombudsman
Progressive House 33 Wellington Place
Belfast BT1 6HN Or Freepost BEL1478
Belfast BT1 6BR
Helpline: 0800 343424
Tel: 028 9023 3821
Textphone: 028 90897789
ombudsman@nl-ombudsman.org.uk
www.ni-ombudsman.org.uk

Northern Stage
Barras Bridge Newcastle upon Tyne NE1
7RH
Tel: 0191 230 5151
info@northernstage.co.uk
www.northernstage.co.uk
Producing theatre company

Norwood
Broadway House 80-82 The Broadway
Stanmore Middlesex HA7 4HB
Tel: 020 8809 8809
info@norwood.org.uk
www.norwood.org.uk
Supports people with learning disabilities
and children and families in need in the
Jewish community and in the wider
community, in London and the South East

NSPCC National Society for the Prevention
of Cruelty to Children
Help for adults concerned about a child:
0808 800 5000
Tel: 020 7825 2500 (headquarters)
Childline: 0800 1111
info@nspcc.org.uk
www.nspcc.org.uk

Nuclear Disarmament see CND, CND
(Scottish)

Nuclear Society (European)
www.euronuclear.org
Largest nuclear society for science and
industry

Nuclear Tourist (Virtual)
www.nucleartourist.com
Independent website on nuclear power &
nuclear power stations

Nursing & Midwifery Council
23 Portland Place London W1B 1PZ
Tel: 020 7637 7181
communications@nmc-uk.org
www.nmc-uk.org

& Scotland
Ground Floor 114-116 George Street
Edinburgh EH2 4LH
Tel: 0131 624 5000
scotland@nmc-uk.org
www.nmc-uk.org

Nurture Group Network Helping young
people
CAN Mezzanine 49-51 East Road Old
Street London N1 6AH
Tel: 020 7250 8300
info@nurturegroups.org
www.nurturegroups.org
International umbrella organisation for
nurture groups. Supports members in their
work to improve the life chances of the most
vulnerable and disadvantaged children and
young people

NUS National Union of Students
4th Floor 184-192 Drummond Street
London NW1 3HP
Tel: 0207 380 6600
Text phone: 0207 380 6600
www.nus.org.uk

& Scotland
29 Forth Street Edinburgh EH1 3LE
Tel: 0131 556 6598
mail@nus-scotland.org.uk
www.nus.org.uk/scotland

& Ireland NUS-USI
42 Dublin Road Belfast BT2 7HN
Tel: 028 90 244 641
info@nistudents.org
www.nistudents.org

& Wales
2nd floor Cambrian Buildings Mount Stuart
Square Cardiff CF10 5FL
Tel: 02920 435 390
office@nus-wales.org.uk
www.nus.org.uk/en/About-NUS/Who-We-
Are/Nations/NUS-Wales/

Nutrition Foundation (British)
High Holborn House 52-54 High Holborn
London WC1V 6RQ
Tel: 020 7404 6504
postbox@nutrition.org.uk
www.nutrition.org.uk

Nutrition Society
10 Cambridge Court 210 Shepherds Bush
Road London W6 7NJ
Tel: 0207 602 0228
office@nutsoc.org.uk
www.nutritionsociety.org
Aims to advance the scientific study
of nutrition and its application to the
maintenance of human and animal health

NWR see Women's Register (National)

NYAS see Youth Advocacy Service
(National)

O

OASIS Overseas Adoption Support and
Information Service
email via website
www.adoptionoverseas.org
For people who want to adopt children from
orphanages abroad

Obesity see also International Association
for the Study of Obesity

**Obesity (International Association for
the Study of) & Obesity TaskForce
(International)** IASO & IOTF
Charles Darwin House 12 Roger Street
London WC1N 2JU
Tel: 020 7685 2580
enquiries@iaso.org
www.iaso.org
Works with WHO to alert the world to the
growing problem of obesity

Obesity Forum (National)
PO Box 10131 Nottingham NG2 9NH
Tel: 0115 846 2109
info@nof.uk.com
www.nationalobesityforum.org.uk
Raises awareness of the growing impact of
obesity and being overweight on patients
and our National Health Service

Occupational Hygiene Society (British)
5-6 Melbourne Business Court Millennium
Way Pride Park Derby DE24 8LZ
Tel: 01332 298101
admin@bohs.org
www.bohs.org

**Occupational Safety & Health (Institution
of)** IOSH
The Grange Highfield Drive Wigston Leics
LE18 1NN
Tel: 0116 257 3100
reception@iosh.co.uk
www.iosh.co.uk
Professional body

OCD Action
Suite 506-509 Davina House 137-149
Goswell Road London EC1V 7ET
Support & information helpline: 0845 390
6232 or 020 7253 2664
Tel: 020 7253 5272 (Office)
support@ocdation.org.uk
support@ocdaction.org.uk
www.ocdaction.org.uk
Promoting recovery from obsessive
compulsive disorders

Ocean Mammal Institute
www.oceanmammalinst.com
Helps individuals understand and feel their
connection to nature and give them courage
to act responsibly for the planet and its
inhabitants

Ocean Youth Trust Adventure under Sail
www.oyt.org.uk
Offshore sail training

**OCR/Oxford Cambridge and RSA
Examinations**
1 Hills Road Cambridge CB1 2EU
Tel: 01223 553311
info@cambridgeassessment.org.uk
www.cambridgeassessment.org.uk

ODL QC see Open & Distance Learning
Quality Council

OFCOM
Riverside House 2A Southwark Bridge Rd
London SE1 9HA
Tel: 020 7981 3040
Tel: 0300 123 3333
Textphone: 020 7981 3043
www.ofcom.org.uk/
Regulator of UK communication
Industries encompassing television,
radio, telecommunications & wireless
communication services

Offenders see UNLOCK, Nacro, SACRO

Office for National Statistics ONS
Room 1.101
Government Buildings Cardiff Road
Newport South Wales NP10 8XG
Tel: 0845 601 3034
info@statistics.gov.uk
www.ons.gov.uk

Official Residences of the Queen now see British Monarchy (The official website of)

Ofgem Gas & Electricity Markets (Office of)
9 Millbank London SW1P 3GE
Tel: 020 7901 7295
consumeraffairs@ofgem.gov.uk
www.ofgem.gov.uk
Regulatory body for gas and electricity markets, protects customers' interests and encourages competition. Independent advisors to the UK Government on tackling and preparing for climate change

Ofqual Office of Qualifications and Examinations Regulation
Spring Place Coventry Business Park Herald Avenue Coventry CV5 6UB
Helpline: 0300 303 3346
Tel: 0300 303 3344
Textphone: 0300 303 3345
info@ofqual.gov.uk
www.ofqual.gov.uk
Regulates general and vocational qualifications in England and vocational qualifications in Northern Ireland

Ofsted Office for Standards in Education
Piccadilly Gate Store Street Manchester M1 2WD
Tel: 0300 123 4234 (education or adult skills)
Children's services: 0300 123 1231
Textphone/Minicom: 0161 618 8524
enquiries@ofsted.gov.uk
www.ofsted.gov.uk
Inspection of schools, local education authorities, teacher training institutions and youth work and registration of early years childcare

OFWAT see Water Services (Office of)

Old Bailey, London (Proceedings of) 1674 to 1834
www.oldbaileyonline.org
Accounts of over 100,000 criminal trials held at London's central criminal court

Olympic Association (British)
60 Charlotte Street London W1T 2NU
Tel: 0207 842 5700
boa@boa.org.uk
www.olympics.org.uk

Olympic Committee (International) see International Olympic Committee

Ombudsman Public Services Ombudsman for Wales
1 Ffordd yr Hen Gae Pencoed CF35 5LJ
Tel: 0845 601 0987
email via website
www.ombudsman-wales.org.uk

Ombudsman Association (British & Irish) BIOA
PO Box 308 Twickenham London TW1 9BE
Tel: 020 8894 9272
secretary@bioa.org.uk
www.bioa.org.uk
Lists the ombudsmen and other complaint-handling bodies

ONE International
151 Wardour Street London W1F 8WE
Tel: 0207 434 7550
email via website
www.one.org
Aims to raise awareness about, and spark response to the crises swamping Africa: unpayable Debts, uncontrolled spread of AIDS, and unfair Trade rules which keep Africans poor

One parent families see also Families Need Fathers, Friendship Works, Gingerbread, HELP, One Plus One

One Plus One
1 Benjamin Street London EC1M 5QG
Tel: 020 7553 9530
info@oneplusone.org.uk
www.oneplusone.org.uk
To enhance understanding of how family relationships contribute to the well being of adults and children

Onekind
10 Queensferry St Edinburgh EH2 4PG
Tel: 0131 225 6039
email via website
www.onekind.org
Campaigns against all animal abuse

Online National Register of Hypnotherapists see Hypnotherapy Organisations (UK Confederation of)

ONS see Office for National Statistics

Open & Distance Learning Quality Council
79 Barnfield Wood Road Beckenham Kent BR3 6ST
Tel: 020 8658 83373
info@odlqc.org.uk
www.odlqc.org.uk
Accreditation of open and distance learning providers

Open College of the Arts
Michael Young Arts Centre Redbrook Business Park Wilthorpe Rd Barnsley S75 1JN
Freephone: 0800 731 2116
enquiries@oca-uk.com
www.oca-uk.com
Providing high quality arts courses by distance learning

Open Museum
200 Woodhead Road South Nitshill
Industrial Estate Glasgow G53 7NN
Tel: 0141 276 9368
Text Phone: 0141 276 9428
OpenMuseumEnquiries@glasgowlife.org.uk
www.glasgowlife.org.uk/museums/our-museums/open-museum/Pages/home.aspx
Offers a free service that allows groups,
venues and community event organisers in
Glasgow to borrow museum objects and
create displays

Open Spaces Society
25A Bell St Henley-on-Thames RG9 2BA
Tel: 01491 573535
hq@oss.org.uk
www.oss.org.uk
Preserves commons & protects footpaths
and public open spaces

Open University
PO Box 197 Milton Keynes MK7 6BJ
Tel: 0845 300 6090
email via website
www.open.ac.uk

Open-City
44-46 Scrutton Street London EC2A 4HH
Tel: 020 3006 7008
admin@open-city.org.uk
www.open-city.org.uk
Architectural education charity

Opera see English National Opera, NODA,
Royal Opera, Scottish Opera, Welsh
National Opera, Youth Opera (British)

Operation Black Vote
18A Victoria Park Square Bethnal Green
London E2 9PB
Tel: 020 8983 5430/5426
info@obv.org.uk
www.obv.org.uk
To raise the profile of the democratic rights
of the black community in the UK

Operation Smile UK
Unit 15, The Coda Centre 189 Munster
Road London SW6 6AW
Tel: 0844 581 1110
Tel: 020 7386 9386
info@operationsmile.org.uk
www.operationsmile.org.uk
Medical charity providing reconstructive
surgery to young people with facial
disfigurements in developing countries

Opportunity International UK
Angel Court 81 St Clements Oxford OX4
1AW
Tel: 01865 725304
impact@opportunity.org.uk
www.opportunity.org.uk
A charity working to create income-raising
opportunities with the world's poor people

& Scottish Office
43 Charlotte Square Edinburgh EH2 4HQ
scotland@opportunity.org.uk
www.opportunity.org.uk
A charity working to create income-raising
opportunities with the world's poor people

Opportunity Now
137 Shepherdess Walk London N1 7RQ
Tel: 0207 566 8650
email via website
www.opportunitynow.org.uk
Business-led campaign for recruitment,
retention and development of women
employees

Optimum Nutrition (Institute for)
Avalon House 72 Lower Mortlake Road
Richmond Surrey TW9 2JY
Tel: 020 8614 7800
ionreception@ion.ac.uk
www.ion.ac.uk
Educational trust for the study, research &
practice of nutritional therapy

Oral History Society
Unit 8, The Old Silk Mill Brook Street Tring
Herts HP23 5EF
Tel: 01422 820585
ohs@webscribe.co.uk
www.ohs.org.uk

Orangutan Foundation
7 Kent Terrace London NW1 4RP
Tel: 020 7724 2912
email via website
www.orangutan.org.uk

Orchestras (Association of British)
32 Rose Street London WC2E 9ET
Tel: 020 7557 6770
info@abo.org.uk
www.abo.org.uk

Orchid Cancer Appeal
St Bartholomew's Hospital London EC1A
7BE
Tel: 0203 465 5766
info@orchid-cancer.org.uk
www.orchid-cancer.org.uk
Dedicated to funding research into
diagnosis, prevention and treatment of
prostate and testicular cancer as well as
promoting awareness of these previously
neglected diseases.

Ordnance Survey
Adanac Drive Southampton SO16 0AS
Tel: 08456 050505
customerservices@ordnancesurvey.co.uk
www.ordnancesurvey.co.uk
National mapping organisation

Organ Donation
NHS Blood and Transplant Organ Donation
and Transplantation Directorate Fox Den Rd
Stoke Gifford Bristol BS34 8RR
Organ Donor Line: 0300 123 2323
Tel: 0117 975 7575
email via website
www.uktransplant.org.uk

**Organ Donation and Transplantation
(International Registry of)** IRODAT
www.tpm.org/secciones/irodat.swf
A complete database that provides
the annual values of the donation and
transplantation activity from the countries
that dispose of them

Organic Research Centre
Elm Farm Hamstead Marshall Nr Newbury
Berks RG20 0HR
Tel: 01488 658298
elmfarm@organicresearchcentre.com
www.efrc.com
Organic farming centre, advisory & research
body

Orienteering Federation (British)
8a Stancliffe House Whitworth Road Darley
Dale Matlock DE4 2HJ
Tel: 01629 734 042
info@britishorienteering.org.uk
www.britishorienteering.org.uk

Ornithology (British Trust for)
The Nunnery Thetford Norfolk IP24 2PU
Tel: 01842 750050
info@bto.org
www.bto.org

Osteopathic Council (General)
176 Tower Bridge Rd London SE1 3LU
Tel: 020 7357 6655
contactus@osteopathy.org.uk
www.osteopathy.org.uk
Statutory regulatory body for osteopaths

Osteoporosis Society (National)
Camerton Bath BA2 0PJ
Helpline: 0845 450 0230
Tel: 01761 471 771 / 0845 130 3076
info@nos.org.uk
www.nos.org.uk

Our Dynamic Earth
Holyrood Rd Edinburgh EH8 8AS
Tel: 0131 550 7800
Email via website
www.dynamicearth.co.uk
Interactive visitor attraction showing the
story of the Earth

Out of Joint
7 Thane Works Thane Villas London N7
7NU
Tel: 020 7609 0207

ojo@outofjoint.co.uk
www.outofjoint.co.uk
Theatre company touring primarily new work
nationally and internationally

Out of trouble
Prison Reform Trust 15 Northburgh Street
London EC1V 0JR
outoftrouble@prisonreformtrust.org.uk
www.outoftrouble.org.uk
Prison Reform Trust campaign working to
reduce the number of children and young
people who are imprisoned in the UK

Outdoor Learning (Institute for)
Warwick Mill Business Centre Warwick
Bridge Carlisle CA4 8RR
Tel: 01228 564 580
email via website
www.outdoor-learning.org
Learning through outdoor experience

Outward Bound Trust
Hackthorpe Hall Hackthorpe Penrith
Cumbria CA10 2HX
Tel: 01931 740000
enquiries@outwardbound.org.uk
www.theoutwardboundtrust.org.uk
Inspiring young people through challenging
outdoor experiences

Overeaters Anonymous of Great Britain
483 Green Lanes London N13 4BS
Tel: 07000 784985
email via website
www.oagb.org.uk

**Overseas Adoption Support and
Information Service** see OASIS

Overseas Development Institute
111 Westminster Bridge Rd London SE1
7JD
Tel: 020 7922 0300
odi@odi.org.uk
www.odi.org.uk
Independent think-tank on international
development and humanitarian issues

Oxfam
Oxfam House John Smith Drive Cowley
Oxford OX4 2JY
Tel: 0300 200 1292
Email via website
www.oxfam.org.uk

Oxfam International
www.oxfam.org/en

P

PACE
34 Hartham Rd London N7 9JL
Tel: 020 7700 1323
info@pacehealth.org.uk
www.pacehealth.org.uk
Lesbian and gay counselling, groups,
advocacy, employment, HIV prevention and
youthwork services and family therapy

PACT (Parents & Abducted Children Together)
22 The Vineyard Richmond Surrey TW10
6AN
Tel: 07506 448 116
support@pact-online.org
www.pact-online.org
To fight parental child abduction across
borders and to locate and retrieve missing
children

PACT (Parents and Children Together)
7 Southern Court South Street Reading
Berkshire RG1 4QS
Tel: 0800 731 1845 (freephone)
Tel: 0118 938 7600
info@pactcharity.org
www.pactcharity.org

PACT (Prison Advice & Care Trust)
Park Place 12 Lawn Lane Vauxhall London
SW8 1UD
Offenders family helpline:
0808 808 2003
Tel: 020 7735 9535
info@prisonadvice.org.uk
www.prisonadvice.org.uk
Works with prisoners who have mental
health needs and support prisoners' families

Pain Relief Foundation
Clinical Sciences Centre University Hospital
Aintree Lower Lane Liverpool L9 7AL
Tel: 0151 529 5820
secretary@painrelieffoundation.org.uk
www.painrelieffoundation.org.uk
Researches the causes & treatment of
chronic pain

Pain Society (British)
3rd Floor, Churchill House 35 Red Lion
Square London WC1R 4SG
Tel: 020 7269 7840
info@britishpainsociety.org
www.britishpainsociety.org

Pain Support
www.painsupport.co.uk

Palliative Care (National Council for)
The Fitzpatrick Building 188-194 York Way
London N7 9AS
Tel: 020 7697 1520

enquiries@ncpc.org.uk
www.ncpc.org.uk
Umbrella body

Panos Institute
9 White Lion St London N1 9PD
Tel: 020 7278 1111
info@panos.org.uk
www.panos.org.uk
Non-profit institute providing information
on global issues with a developing country
perspective

Paperboy
www.thepaperboy.com
Web site with links to more than 5,000
newspapers worldwide

Papworth Trust
Bernard Sunley Centre Papworth Everard
Cambridge CB23 3RG
Freephone 0800 952 5000
Tel: 01480 357200
info@papworth.org.uk
www.papworth.org.uk
Helps disabled people progress to greater
independence

PAPYRUS Prevention of young suicide
67 Bewsey Street Warrington Cheshire
WA2 7JQ
HOPELineUK 0800 068 41 41
Tel: 01925 572 444
admin@papyrus-uk.org
www.papyrus-uk.org
Founded by parents who have lost a young
person through suicide & wish to reduce
such tragedies in the future

Parachute Association (British)
5 Wharf Way Glen Parva Leicester LE2 9TF
Tel: 0116 2785271
skydive@bpa.org.uk
www.bpa.org.uk
Governing body of sport parachuting
(skydiving) in UK

Paralympic GB
60 Charlotte Street, London W1T 2NU
Tel: 020 7842 5789
info@paralympics.org.uk
www.paralympics.org.uk
Organisation responsible for GB Team
competing at Paralympic Games

Parent Teacher Associations (National Confederation of) now see PTA-UK

Parenting UK
Unit 431 Highgate Studios 53-79 Highgate
Road London NW5 1TL
Tel: 020 7284 8370
email via website
www.parentinguk.org

The national organisation for people working with parents

Parentline Plus now see Family Lives

Parents & Abducted Children Together see PACT (Parents & Abducted Children Together)

Parents and Children Together see PACT (Parents and Children Together)

Parents for Children now see TACT

Parents for Inclusion
336 Brixton Road London SW9 7AA
Helpline: 0800 652 3145
Tel: 020 7738 3888
info@parentsforinclusion.org
www.parentsforinclusion.org
Supports parents of disabled children who want to be included in mainstream school & society as a whole

Parkinson's Disease Society
215 Vauxhall Bridge Road London SW1V 1EJ
Helpline: 0808 800 0303
Tel: 020 7931 8080
hello@parkinsons.org.uk
www.parkinsons.org.uk

Parliament
www.parliament.uk/
UK parliament website - includes all aspects of Westminster

Parliamentary and Health Service Ombudsman
Millbank Tower Millbank London SW1P 4QP
Complaints Helpline: 0345 015 4033
Tel: 07624 813 005 'call back' with your name and your mobile number
phso.enquiries@ombudsman.org.uk
www.ombudsman.org.uk
Carries out independent investigations into complaints about UK government departments and their agencies, and the NHS in England

Parliamentary Education Unit
www.parliament.uk/education
Information about the work of parliament for students & teachers

Parliaments (Websites of National)
www.ipu.org/english/parlweb.htm
Portal opening to worldwide parliaments

Partially Sighted Society
7-9 Bennetthorpe Doncaster DN2 6AA
Tel: 0844 477 4966
info@partsight.org.uk
www.partsight.org.uk
Provides information, advice, equipment and clear print material to Help visually impaired

people make the best use of their remaining vision

Passenger Focus
FREEPOST (RRRE-ETTC-LEET)
PO Box 4257 Manchester M60 3AR
Tel: 0300 123 2350
info@passengerfocus.org.uk
www.passengerfocus.org.uk
Official, independent watchdog for rail passengers

Passenger Transport UK (Confederation of) CPT
Drury House 34-43 Russell Street London WC2B 5HA
Tel: 020 7240 3131
www.cpt-uk.org
National trade association for bus, coach & light rail operators

Passion for Jazz
www.apassion4jazz.net
History of Jazz music origins, styles and musicians featuring timeline, photos, festivals, glossary, guitar & piano chords, scales & online lessons.

Passport Office now see Identity & Passport Service

Pastoral Care in Education (National Association for)
PO Box 6005 Nuneaton CV11 9GY
Tel: 07531 453 670
Email via website
www.napce.org.uk

Patent Office (European)
www.epo.org

Patient Safety Agency (National)
4-8 Maple Street London W1T 5HD
Tel: 020 7927 9500
enquiries@npsa.nhs.uk
www.npsa.nhs.uk
Improving the safety and quality of care in the NHS

Patient UK
www.patient.co.uk
Medical website

Patients Association
PO Box 935 Harrow Middlesex HA1 3YJ
Helpline: 0845 608 4455
Tel: 020 8423 9111 (Admin)
helpline@patients-association.com
www.patients-association.com
Represents the needs & wishes of patients in the NHS

Paul Mellon Centre for Studies in British Art see Studies in British Art (Paul Mellon Centre for)

Paul's Cancer Support Centre
3rd Floor Woburn House 155 Falcon Road
London SW11 2PD
Tel: 020 7924 3924
email via website
www.paulscancersupportcentre.org.uk
Providers of information and support,
complementary therapies and educational
programmes

Pax Christi International Catholic
Movement for Peace
Christian Peace Education Centre St
Joseph's Watford Way Hendon London
NW4 4TY
Tel: 020 8203 4884
info@paxchristi.org.uk
www.paxchristi.org.uk
International workcamps, peace education,
campaigning on arms trade and nuclear
disarmament issues

Payplan
Kempton House Dysart Road Grantham
NG31 7LE
Freephone: 0800 280 2816
Email via website
www.payplan.com
A not-for-profit organisation which
works closely with charities who are
involved in assisting individuals who have
unmanageable debts

PDSA People's Dispensary for Sick Animals
Whitechapel Way Priorslee Telford TF2 9PQ
Helpline: 0800 7312502
Tel: 01952 290999
Email via website
www.pdsa.org.uk
Free veterinary services for sick & injured
animals of needy owners

**Peace & Freedom (Women's
International League for)** WILPF
1 rue de Varembé Case Postale 28 1211
Geneva 20 Switzerland
Tel: 00 41 22 919 7080
infoquest@wilpf.ch
www.wilpfinternational.org
Works for peace, disarmament and gender
equality

Peace Alliance
Tottenham Town Hall Town Hall Approach
Seven Sisters N15 4RY
Tel: 0208 808 9439
info@peacealliance.org.uk
www.peacealliance.org.uk
Independent voluntary organisation working
to reduce crime and the fear of crime and
promote peace

Peace Brigades International
Development House 56-64 Leonard Street
London EC2A 4LT
Tel: 020 7065 0775
Email via website
www.peacebrigades.org
Humanitarian organisation working for non-
violent transformation of conflict & to raise
awareness of human rights

Peace Pledge Union
1 Peace Passage London N7 0BT
Tel: 020 7424 9444
email via website
www.ppu.org.uk
www.learnpeace.org.uk
Provides a wide range of teaching and study
resources on peace and war

Pedestrians see Living Streets

PEN see English PEN

Penal Reform see also Howard League for
Penal Reform

Penal Reform International
60-62 Commercial Street London E1 6LT
Tel: 020 7247 6515
info@penalreform.org
www.penalreform.org
Works for penal reform and against the
death penalty

Pensioners Convention (National)
Walkden House 10 Melton Street London
NW1 2EJ
Tel: 020 7383 0388
info@npcuk.org
www.npcuk.org
Campaigns for better pensions, health
services and other services for older people

Pensions Ombudsman
11 Belgrave Rd London SW1V 1RB
Tel: 020 7630 2200
enquiries@pensions–ombudsman.org.uk
www.pensions-ombudsman.org.uk
Investigates and decides complaints
and disputes concerning occupational &
personal pension schemes

People & Planet
51 Union St Oxford OX4 1JP
Tel: 01865 245678
people@peopleandplanet.org
www.peopleandplanet.org
Network of UK students campaigning on
issues of world poverty, human rights and
the environment

People First
F173 Riverside Business Park Haldane
Place London SW18 4UQ
Tel: 0208 874 1377
general@peoplefirstltd.com

www.peoplefirstltd.com
Run for and by people with learning difficulties to help them speak up for themselves

People for the Ethical Treatment of Animals see PETA Foundation

People with Learning Disabilities (National Development Team for) now see Inclusion (National Development Team for)

People's Dispensary for Sick Animals see PDSA

People's History Museum
Left Bank
Spinningfields Manchester M3 3ER
Tel: 0161 838 9190
info@phm.org.uk
www.phm.org.uk

People's Network
The Museums, Libraries and Archives Council Grosvenor House 14 Bennetts Hill Birmingham B2 5RS
Tel: 0121 345 7300
info@mla.gov.uk
www.peoplesnetwork.gov.uk
Access to a wide range of software and digital content, in public libraries already with a trained and supportive staff

People's Palace and Winter Gardens
Glasgow Green Glasgow G40 1AT
Tel: 0141 276 0788
Text Phone: 0141 276 0795
museums@glasgowlife.org.uk
www.glasgowlife.org.uk/museums/our-museums/peoples-palace/Pages/home.aspx
Tells the story of the people and city of Glasgow from 1750 to the end of the 20th century

People's Trust for Endangered Species
15 Cloisters House 8 Battersea Park Road London SW8 4BG
Tel: 020 7498 4533
enquiries@ptes.org
www.ptes.org
Ensures a future for endangered species throughout the world

Peoples Close to Nature see Friends of Peoples Close to Nature

Performing Arts and Technology see BRIT School for Performing Arts and Technology

Performing Arts Medicine (British Association for)
Totara Park House, 4th Floor 34-36 Gray's Inn Road London WC1X 8HR
Tel: 020 7404 5888
Tel: 020 7404 8444 (Clinic)

enquiries@bapam.org.uk
www.bapam.org.uk
Diagnosis and treatment for medical problems encountered by performers of all kinds

Performing Rights Society see PRS for music

Permaculture Association (Britain)
BCM Permaculture Association London WC1N 3XX
Tel: 0845 458 1805
Email via website
www.permaculture.org.uk
Provides information about courses, groups and projects concerned with a sustainable life style

Personal Finance Education Group pfeg
Fifth Floor 14 Bonhill Street London EC2A 4BX
Tel: 020 7330 9470
Tel: 0845 241 0925
Info@pfeg.org
www.pfeg.org
Helps schools to teach personal finance

Personal Injury Lawyers (Association of) APIL
3 Alder Court Rennie Hogg Road
Nottingham NG2 1RX
Tel: 0115 958 0585
Email via website
www.apil.org.uk
Dedicated to improving the service provided to victims of accidents and clinical negligence

Personnel & Development (Chartered Institute of)
151 The Broadway London SW19 1JQ
Tel: 020 8612 6200
email via website
www.cipd.co.uk
Professional body

Pesticide Action Network UK
54-64 Leonard Street Development House London EC2A 4LT
Tel: 020 7065 0905
Email via website
www.pan-uk.org
Independent health and ecological charity working to eliminate the hazards of pesticides

Pet Advisory Committee
PO Box 574 Dorking RH4 9GW
Tel: 01306 628136
email via website
www.petadvisory.org.uk
Makes recommendations to central and local government to encourage responsible pet ownership in society

Pet Behaviour Counsellors (Association of)
PO Box 46 Worcester WR8 9YS
Tel: 01386 751151
info@apbc.org.uk
www.apbc.org.uk

Pet Care Trust
Pet Care Trade Association Bedford
Business Centre 170 Mile Rd Bedford
MK42 9TW
Tel: 01234 273933
Email via website
www.petcare.org.uk
Association promoting responsible pet
ownership and professionalism in the trade

Pet Health Council
4th Floor 6 Catherine Street London WC2B
5JJ
enquiries@pethealthcouncil.co.uk
www.pethealthcouncil.co.uk
Promotes health & welfare of pet animals

Pet Month (National)
3 Crossfield Chambers Gladbeck Way
Enfield EN2 7HF
Tel: 020 8370 3688
info@nationalpetmonth.org.uk
www.nationalpetmonth.org.uk
Encourages responsible pet ownership via
National Pet Week annually

PETA Foundation People for the Ethical
Treatment of Animals
PO Box 36678 London SE1 1YE
Tel: 020 7357 9229
info@peta.org.uk
www.peta.org.uk
UK-based charity dedicated to establishing
and protecting the rights of all animals
through public education, research,
legislation, special events, celebrity
involvement and protest campaigns

PetLog Database (National)
The Kennel Club
4A Alton House Gatehouse Way Aylesbury
Bucks HP19 8XU
Tel: 0844 4633 999
Minicom: 01296 337 517
petlogadmin@thekennelclub.org.uk
www.petlog.org.uk
The National Pet Identification Scheme
using microchips

Pets as Therapy
14a High Street Wendover Aylesbury
Buckinghamshire HP22 6EA
Tel: 01844 345 445
reception@petsastherapy.org
www.petsastherapy.org
Provides therapeutic visits to hospitals,
hospices, nursing and care homes, special
needs schools etc by volunteers with their
own friendly temperament tested and
vaccinated dogs and cats

Phab Physically Disabled & Able Bodied
(England)
Summit House 50 Wandle Rd Croydon
CR0 1DF
Tel: 020 8667 9443
info@phab.org.uk
www.phab.org.uk
Brings together people with & without
physical disabilities

Pharmaceutical Society (Royal)
1 Lambeth High St London SE1 7JN
Tel: 0207 572 2737
Tel: 0845 257 2570
support@rpharms.com
www.rpsgb.org
Professional, regulatory and statutory body
of Britain's practising pharmacists

& Scottish Office
Holyrood Park House 106 Holyrood Road
Edinburgh EH8 8AS
Tel: 0131 556 4386
scotinfo@rpharms.com
www.rpsgb.org

& Welsh Office
Unit 2, Ashtree Court Woodsy Close Cardiff
Gate Business Park Cardiff CF23 8RW
Tel: 029 2073 0310
wales@rpharms.com
www.rpsgb.org

Philip Lawrence Awards Network PLAnet
c/o Nacro Park Place 10-12 Lawn Lane
London SW8 1UD
Tel: 020 7840 7222
philiplawrenceawards@nacro.org.uk
www.philiplawrenceawards.net
Award scheme which acclaims and
rewards outstanding achievements in good
citizenship by young people of 11-20 years

Phonebrain
www.phonebrain.org.uk/
Interactive website providing a young
person's guide to the real cost of premium
phone lines

Phonepay Plus formerly Independent
Committee for the Supervision of Standards
of Telephone Information Services
Clove Building 4 Maguire Street London
SE1 2NQ
Free Helpline: 0800 500212
Tel: 020 7940 7474
email via website
www.phonepayplus.org.uk
Regulates the premium rate goods and
services that you can buy by phone and
pre-pay account

Photographic Society (Royal)
Fenton House 122 Wells Road Bath BA2 3AH
Tel: 01225 325733
reception@rps.org
www.rps.org

photoLondon
www.photolondon.org.uk
Gateway to London's public photographic collections

Physical Education (Association for)
Room 117
  Bredon University of Worcester Henwick Grove Worcester WR2 6AJ
Tel: 01905 855 584
enquiries@afpe.org.uk
www.afpe.org.uk
Professional association for teachers of physical education

Physical Recreation (Central Council of)
see Sport & Recreation Alliance

Physically Disabled & Able Bodied (England) see Phab

Physics (Institute of)
76 Portland Place London W1B 1NT
Tel: 020 7470 4800
physics@iop.org
www.iop.org

Physiotherapy (Chartered Society of)
14 Bedford Row London WC1R 4ED
Tel: 020 7306 6666
Email via website
www.csp.org.uk
Professional, educational and trade union body for chartered physiotherapists, students and assistants

Pilates Foundation
PO Box 58235 London N1 5UY
Tel: 020 7033 0078
admin@pilatesfoundation.com
www.pilatesfoundation.com
Promotes & develops body awareness

Pipedown
1 The Row Berwick St James Salisbury SP3 4TP
Tel: 01722 790622
Tel: 07971 518976
Email via website
www.pipedown.info
Campaigns for the right to freedom from piped music in public places

Pituitary Foundation
PO Box 1944 Bristol BS99 2UB
Tel: 0845 450 0375 (Support and Information HelpLine)
Tel: 0845 450 0376
Email via website
www.pituitary.org.uk
Provides information and support to sufferers of pituitary disorders and their relatives, friends and carers

Placement Survival Guide
www.placementsurvivalguide.com
Skills for life for 14-19 years, comprising work experience, community involvement and personal challenge

Plaid Cymru - The Party of Wales
Ty Gwynfor Anson Court Atlantic Wharf Cardiff CF10 4AL
Tel: 029 2047 2272
post@plaidcymru.org
www.plaidcymru.org

Plain English Campaign
PO Box 3 New Mills High Peak SK22 4QP
Tel: 01663 744409
info@plainenglish.co.uk
www.plainenglish.co.uk
Campaigning for clarity of official communications, edits documents & does training in plain English

Plan UK
Finsgate 5-7 Cranwood Street London EC1V 9LH
Tel: 0300 777 9777
email via website
www.plan-uk.org
Humanitarian child-focused organisation working with families and their communities to meet the needs of children around the world

Planned Parenthood Federation (International) IPPF
4 Newhams Row London SE1 3UZ
Tel: 020 7939 8200
info@ippf.org
www.ippf.org
Global network of family planning associations in 182 countries

Plantlife
14 Rollestone Street Salisbury Wiltshire SP1 1DX
Tel: 01722 342730
enquiries@plantlife.org.uk
www.plantlife.org.uk
The UK's leading plant conservation charity

& Cymru
Unit 14, Llys Castan Ffordd Y Parc Parc
Menai Bangor LL57 4FD
Tel: 01248 670691
cymru@plantlife.org.uk
www.plantlife.org.uk

& Scotland
Balallan House Allan Park Stirling FK8 2QG
Tel: 01786 478509/479382
scotland@plantlife.org.uk
www.plantlife.org.uk

Platform see GFS Platform for Young
Women

Platform 51
Clarendon House 52 Cornmarket St Oxford
OX1 3EJ
Tel: 01865 304200
info@plastform51.org
www.platform51.org
Supports girls and women as they take
control of their lives

Play see also thematic guide - Children &
Young People

Play England
8 Wakley St London EC1V 7QE
Tel: 020 7843 6300
playengland@ncb.org.uk
www.playengland.org.uk
Aims for all children and young people in
England to have regular access to and
opportunity for free, inclusive, local play
provision and play space

Play Wales
Baltic House Mount Stuart Sq Cardiff CF10
5FH
Tel: 029 2048 6050
email via website
www.playwales.org.uk
Aims to influence the policy of all
organisations that have an interest in
children's play

Playbus Association (National) now see
Working on Wheels

PLAYLINK
72 Albert Palace Mansions Lurline Gardens
London SW11 4DQ
Tel: 020 7720 2452
info@playlink.org
www.playlink.org
Works to improve opportunities for children's
free play in quality environments

Plus
Email via website
www.plusgroups.org.uk
Voluntary social activities organisation for
18-36 year olds

PMS see Premenstrual Syndrome (National
Association for)

Pod Charitable Trust
Mount Hall Llanfair Caereinion Welshpool
SY21 0BH
Tel: 01938 810374
pod@podcharity.org.uk
www.podcharity.org.uk
Magicians, musicians, puppeteers,
storytellers and clowns give monthly
shows in children's hospitals, hospices and
children's wards throughout the UK

Podiatrists see Chiropodists & Podiatrists

Poetry Library
Level 5 Royal Festival Hall London SE1 8XX
Tel: 020 7921 0943/0664
Email via website
www.poetrylibrary.org.uk
www.poetrymagazines.org.uk
The most comprehensive and accessible
collection of poetry from 1912 in Britain and
home to a full-text database for UK poetry
magazines of the 20th and 21st centuries

Poetry Society
22 Betterton St London WC2H 9BX
Tel: 020 7420 9880
info@poetrysociety.org.uk
www.poetrysociety.org.uk

Police see also Ask The Police, Black
Police Association (National), Human
Independent Police Complaints
Commission, INQUEST, Metropolitan Police

Police Federation (Scottish) The Voice of
Scotland's Police Service
5 Woodside Place Glasgow G3 7QF
Tel: 0141 332 5234
gensec@spf.org.uk
www.spf.org.uk

Police Federation of England & Wales
Federation House Highbury Drive
Leatherhead Surrey KT22 7UY
Tel: 01372 352000
gensec@polfed.org
www.polfed.org

Policy on Ageing (Centre for)
25-31 Ironmonger Row London EC1V 3QP
Tel: 020 7553 6500
cpa@cpa.org.uk
www.cpa.org.uk
Policy formation, library and information
services on all aspects of aging and later life

Policy Studies (Centre for)
57 Tufton St London SW1P 3QL
Tel: 020 7222 4488
tim@cps.org.uk
www.cps.org.uk
Centre-right independent think tank

Policy Studies Institute
50 Hanson Street London W1W 6UP
Tel: 020 7911 7500
admin@policystudiesinstitute.org.uk
www.psi.org.uk
Non-politically affiliated independent
research institute concerned with
government policy

Polio Fellowship (British)
Eagle Office Centre The Runway South
Ruislip HA4 6SE
Freephone: 0800 018 0586
info@britishpolio.org.uk
www.britishpolio.org.uk

Political Studies Association
Department of Politics University of
Newcastle Newcastle-upon-Tyne NE1 7RU
Tel: 0191 222 8021
psa@ncl.ac.uk
www.psa.ac.uk
Links academics in political science and
current affairs, theorists and practitioners,
policy-makers, journalists, researchers and
students in higher education

Polka Theatre World-class theatre for
children
240 The Broadway Wimbledon London
SW19 1SB
Box Office: 020 8543 4888
www.polkatheatre.com

Pony Club
Stoneleigh Park Kenilworth Warwicks CV8
2RW
Tel: 02476 698300
enquiries@pcuk.org
www.pcuk.org
International youth organisation for those
interested in ponies & riding

Pool Association (English)
www.epa.org.uk

Poppy Project
Tel: 020 7735 2062
www.eaves4women.co.uk/POPPY_Project/
POPPY_Project.php
Eaves project which provides
accommodation and support to women
who have been trafficked into prostitution or
domestic servitude

Popular Astronomy (Society for) SPA
www.popastro.com/
Aims to help beginners, and those who like
a less technical approach, to learn about
astronomy

Population Concern see Interact
Worldwide

Population Services International PSI
www.psi.org
Global health organisation targeting malaria,
child survival, HIV, reproductive health and
non-communicable disease to help the most
vulnerable populations lead healthier lives

Port of London Authority
London River House Royal Pier Road
Gravesend Kent DA12 2BG
Tel: 01474 562200
Email via website
www.pla.co.uk
Ensuring navigational safety along the Tidal
Thames, promoting use of the River and
safeguarding the environment.

Portman Group
4th Floor, 20 Conduit Street London W1S
2XW
Tel: 020 7290 1460
info@portmangroup.org.uk
www.portmangroup.org.uk
Funded by the drinks industry to promote
responsible drinking

Positively UK
347-349 City Road London EC1V 1LR
Peer support helpline: 020 7713 0222
Tel: 020 7713 0444
info@positivelyuk.org
www.positivelyuk.org
National charity championing the rights of
people living with HIV

Post Natal Illness
www.pni.org.uk
Community site and forum offering support
and information

Post Office
Tel: 08457 223344
Textphone: 08457 22 33 55
Email via website
www.postoffice.co.uk

Post-Adoption Centre
5 Torriano Mews Torriano Avenue London
NW5 2RZ
Advice Line: 020 7284 5879

Tel: 020 7284 0555
advice@postadoptioncentre.org.uk
www.postadoptioncentre.org.uk
Offers support, counselling, family work &
advice to anyone involved in adoption

Post-Natal Illness (Association for)
145 Dawes Rd Fulham London SW6 7EB
Tel: 020 7386 0868
Email via website
www.apni.org

Postcode Finder
www.royalmail.com
Find postcodes online, or find addresses if
you only have the postcode and other useful
information about postal services

**Postcomm (Postal Services
Commission)**
Hercules House 6 Hercules Road London
SE1 7DB
Tel: 020 7593 2100
info@psc.gov.uk
www.psc.gov.uk

Postwatch now see Consumer Focus

Practical Action
The Schumacher Centre for Technology &
Development Bourton on Dunsmore Rugby
CV23 9QZ
Tel: 01926 634400
enquiries@practicalaction.org.uk
www.practicalaction.org
Specialises in helping people to use
technology for practical answers to poverty

Prader-Willi Syndrome Association UK
PWSA (UK)

Pre-school Learning Alliance
The Fitzpatrick Building 188 York Way
London N7 9AD
Tel: 020 7697 2500
email via website
www.pre-school.org.uk
Educational charity providing support,
information & training for people working
with under 5s & their families

Pre-school Play Association (Scottish)
SPPA
21-23 Granville Street Glasgow G3 7EE
Tel: 0141 221 4148
info@sppa.org.uk
www.sppa.org.uk
Works to improve pre-school provision

**Pre-School Providers Association
(Wales)**
Unit 1 The Lofts 9 Hunter Street Cardiff Bay
Cardiff CF10 5GX
Tel: 029 2045 1242
cardiffoffice@walesppa.org
www.walesppa.org
Educational charity. Largest provider of
community based pre-school childcare in
Wales

**Premenstrual Syndrome (National
Association for)** NAPS
41 Old Rd East Peckham Kent TN12 5AP
Tel: 0844 8157311
contact@pms.org.uk

www.pms.org.uk
Information, advice & support for PMS
sufferers & their families

Preservation Trusts (UK Association of)
APT
9th Floor, Alhambra House 27-31 Charing
Cross Road London WC2H 0AU
Tel: 020 7930 1629
director.apt@ahfund.org.uk
www.ukapt.org.uk
Representative body for building
preservation trusts in UK, offering support
and advice

President USA see White House

**Press and Broadcasting Freedom
(Campaign for)**
2nd Floor, Vi & Garner Smith House 23
Orford Rd Walthamstow London E17 9NL
Tel: 020 8521 5932
freepress@cpbf.org.uk
www.cpbf.org.uk
Campaigns for a diverse, democratic &
accountable media

Press Association
292 Vauxhall Bridge Rd London SW1V 1AE
Tel: 0870 120 3200
Email via website
www.pressassociation.com
UK national news agency

Press Association Ireland
Scottish Provident Building 7 Donegall
Square West Belfast BT1 6JH
Tel: 028 9024 5008
Email via website
www.pressassociation.com

Press Association Scotland
One Central Quay Glasgow G3 8DA
Tel: 0870 830 6725
Email via website
www.pressassociation.com

Press Complaints Commission
Halton House 20/23 Holborn London EC1N
2JD
Tel: 020 7831 0022
Textphone: 020 7831 0123
complaints@pcc.org.uk
www.pcc.org.uk
Investigates written complaints concerning
the editorial content of newspapers &
magazines in the UK

**Prevention of Accidents (Royal Society
for the)** see RoSPA

Prevention of Cruelty to Animals see
RSPCA

Prevention of Cruelty to Animals see
RSPCA and Scottish SPCA

Prevention of Cruelty to Children see
CHILDREN 1ST, NSPCC

Primary Education (Association for the Study of) see ASPE

Primary Education (National Association for) see NAPE

Primary School Science see SCIcentre

Primate Protection League (International) see IPPL (UK)

Prince's Trust – Cymru
Baltic House Mount Stuart Square Cardiff CF10 5FH
Freephone: 0800 842 842
Tel: 029 2043 7000
webinfowa@princes-trust.org.uk
www.princes-trust.org.uk

Prince's Trust – Northern Ireland
Block 5, Jennymount Court North Derby Street Belfast BT15 3HN
Freephone: 0800 842 842
Tel: 028 9074 5454
webinfoni@princes-trust.org.uk
www.princes-trust.org.uk

Prince's Trust – Pembrokeshire Adventure Centre
Cleddau Reach Pembroke Dock Pembrokeshire SA72 6UJ
Tel: 01646 622013
adventure@princes-trust.org.uk
www.princes-trust.org.uk/pembrokeshire_adventure_centre/centre.aspx
Offers a wide range of adventure sports, based on both land and water

Prince's Trust – Scotland
1st Floor, The Guildhall 57 Queen Street Glasgow G1 3EN
Freephone: 0800 842 842
Tel: 0141 204 4409
webinfosc@princes-trust.org.uk
www.princes-trust.org.uk

Prince's Trust (Head Office)
18 Park Sq East London NW1 4LH
Freephone: 0800 842 842
Tel: 020 7543 1234
Minicom: 020 7543 1374
webinfops@princes-trust.org.uk
www.princes-trust.org.uk
Practical solutions to help young people get their lives working

Princess Royal Trust for Carers see
Carers (The Princess Royal Trust For)

Prison Advice & Care Trust see PACT
(Prison Advice & Care Trust)

Prison Reform Trust
15 Northburgh St London EC1V 0JR
Tel: 020 7251 5070

email via website
www.prisonreformtrust.org.uk
Wide range of publications on penal issues and information and advice to prisoners and their families & campaign for reform

Prison Service NI
Dundonald House Upper Newtownards Road Belfast BT4 3SU
Tel: 028 9052 5065
info@niprisonservice.gov.uk
www.niprisonservice.gov.uk/

Prison Studies (International Centre for)
ICPS
1st Floor, The Merchant Centre 1 New Street Square London EC4A 3BF
Tel: 020 7842 8505
admin@icps.essex.ac.uk
www.prisonstudies.org
Seeks to assist governments & other relevant agencies to develop appropriate policies on prisons & the use of imprisonment

Prison Visitors (National Association of Official)
info@naopv.com
www.naopv.com

Prisoners Abroad
89-93 Fonthill Rd Finsbury Park London N4 3JH
Family freephone 0808 172 0098
Tel: 020 7561 6820
info@prisonersabroad.org.uk
www.prisonersabroad.org.uk
Charity providing practical support to British Citizens imprisoned abroad. Also provide assistance to those affected by imprisonment, and help ex-prisoners start a new life free of crime after their release

Prisoners of Conscience Appeal Fund
PO Box 61044 London SE1 1UP
Tel: 020 7407 6644
info@prisonersofconscience.org
www.prisonersofconscience.org
Helps those persecuted for conscientiously-held beliefs, provided they have not used or advocated violence

Prisoners' Advice Service
PO Box 46199 London EC1M 4XA
Tel: 0207 253 3323
email via website
www.prisonersadvice.org.uk
Provides free and confidential legal advice to all adult prisoners in England & Wales

Prisoners' Families (Action for)
Unit 21, Carlson Court 116 Putney Bridge
Road London SW15 2NQ
Tel: 020 8812 3600
email via website
www.prisonersfamilies.org.uk
Info on local support services and lobby on
behalf of prisoners' families

Prisoners' Families & Friends Service
20 Trinity St London SE1 1DB
Freephone for prisoners' families and
friends: 0808 808 3444
Tel: 020 7403 4091 (Admin)
info@pffs.org.uk
www.pffs.org.uk
Independent voluntary agency providing
support, friendship and advice to the
families and friends of anyone sentenced to
imprisonment or remanded in custody

**Prisons and Probation Ombudsman for
England and Wales**
Ashley House 2 Monck St London SW1P
2BQ
Tel: 020 7035 2876 or 0845 010 7938
mail@ppo.gsi.gov.uk
www.ppo.gov.uk
Investigates complaints from prisoners,
people on probation and immigration
detainees held at immigration removal
centres and deaths of prisoners, residents of
probation service Approved Premises, and
those held in immigration removal centres

Privacy International
265 Strand London WC2R 1BH
Tel: 0208 123 7933
privacyint@privacy.org
www.privacyinternational.org
Human rights group formed as a watchdog
on surveillance by governments &
corporations

Probation Service (National) now see
directgov for public information or
Justice for practitioner or corporate
information

**Professional and Career Development
Loans** see Career Development Loans

Professional Footballers Association
www.givemefootball.com
The union for professional footballers

Professional Golfers' Association
Centenary House
The Belfry
Sutton Coldfield West Midlands B76 9PT
Tel: 01675 470 333
email via website
www.pga.info

**Professional Music Therapists
(Association of)** now see Music Therapy
(British Association for)

**Professional Theatre for Children and
Young People (Association of)** now see
Theatre for Children and Young People
(International Association of)

Project Gutenberg
www.gutenberg.org
American website providing texts of
literature which is out of copyright

Project Trust
The Hebridean Centre Isle of Coll Argyll
PA78 6TE
Tel: 01879 230444
info@projecttrust.org.uk
www.projecttrust.org.uk
Gap year placements abroad, teaching or
social projects

Proofreaders see Editors and Proofreaders
(Society for)

Prospects
www.prospects.ac.uk
UK's official graduate careers website

Prostate Cancer Charity
Cambridge House 100 Cambridge Grove
London W6 0LE
Confidential Helpline: 0800 074 8383
Tel: 020 8222 7622
info@prostate-cancer.org.uk
www.prostate-cancer.org.uk
Research, support, information and
campaigning work

Protection of Animals (World Society for)
see WSPA

Protection of Birds see RSPB

**Protection of Horses (International
League for the)** now see World Horse
Welfare

**Protection of Rural Wales (Campaign for
the)** Ymgyrch Diogelu Cymru Wledig
Ty Gwyn 31 High St Welshpool Powys
SY21 7YD
Tel: 01938 552 525 / 556 212
info@cprwmail.org.uk
www.cprw.org.uk

Provands Lordship
3 Castle Street Glasgow G4 0RB
Tel: 0141 276 1625
museums@glasgowlife.org.uk
www.glasgowlife.org.uk/museums/our-
museums/provands-lordship/Pages/home.
aspx
Dating from the Middle Ages, this museum
gives a glimpse of historical Scotland

PRS for Music
Copyright House 29-33 Berners St London
W1T 3AB
Tel: 020 7580 5544
Email via website
www.prsformusic.com

Psoriasis Association
Dick Coles House 2 Queensbridge
Northampton NN4 7BF
Tel: 01604 251620
Local rate: 0845 676 0076
mail@psoriasis-association.org.uk
www.psoriasis-association.org.uk
Help & support for sufferers

Psychiatrists (Royal College of)
17 Belgrave Square London SW1X 8PG
Tel: 020 7235 2351
email via website
www.rcpsych.ac.uk

Psychical Research (Society for) SPR
49 Marloes Rd London W8 6LA
Tel: 020 7937 8984
Email via website
www.spr.ac.uk
For anyone interested in the paranormal,
have a library, publish a journal and
fund university research into paranormal
phenomena

Psychological Society (British)
St Andrews House 48 Princess Rd East
Leicester LE1 7DR
Tel: 0116 254 9568
enquiries@bps.org.uk
www.bps.org.uk
Professional and regulatory body of
psychologists

Psychotherapists (British Association of)
37 Mapesbury Rd London NW2 4HJ
Tel: 020 8452 9823
admin@bap-psychotherapy.org
www.bap-psychotherapy.org

Psychotherapy see thematic guide -
Counselling & Mental Health

Psychotherapy (UK Council for) UKCP
2nd Floor Edward House 2 Wakley Street
London EC1V 7LT
Tel: 020 7014 9955
info@ukcp.org.uk
www.psychotherapy.org.uk
Umbrella body and voluntary regulatory
organisation. Promotes psychotherapy
for public benefit & provides a register of
suitably trained psychotherapists

PTA-UK
39 Shipbourne Road Tonbridge Kent TN10
3DS
Advice Line: 0845 850 5460
info@pta.org.uk
www.pta.org.uk
Encourages formation of PTAs and
involvement of parents in their children's
education

Public Art Forum now see IXIA

Public Concern at Work
3rd Floor, Bank Chambers 6 - 10 Borough
High Street London SE1 9QQ
Tel: 020 7404 6609
whistle@pcaw.co.uk
www.pcaw.co.uk
Leading authority on whistleblowing in
the workplace offering advice/services to
employees and organisations

Public Health Agency
18 Ormeau Avenue Belfast BT2 8HS
Tel: 028 9031 1611
email via website
www.publichealth.hscni.net
Supports those working in the areas of
health promotion and public health in
Northern Ireland

**Public Management and Policy
Association** PMPA
3 Robert St London WC2N 6RL
Tel: 0207 543 5679
info.pmpa@cipfa.org
www.cipfa.org.uk/pmpa/
Networking organisation for workers in
central & local government

**Public Monuments & Sculpture
Association**
70 Cowcross Street London EC1M 6EJ
Tel: 020 7490 5001
pmsa@btconnect.com
www.pmsa.org.uk
For the promotion and protection of public
monuments and sculpture in UK. Website
contains details of National Recording
Project which is surveying all public
monuments & sculpture in the UK

Public Policy Research (Institute for) see
IPPR

Public Record Office now see National
Archives

Public Sector Information (Office of) now
see legislation.gov.uk

Public Service Excellence (Association for)
2nd Floor, Washbrook House Lancastrian Office Centre Talbot Rd Old Trafford Manchester M32 0FP
Tel: 0161 772 1810
enquiries@apse.org.uk
www.apse.org.uk
Advises local councils on best practice in delivery of public services

Public Services Ombudsman (Scottish)
SPSO
4 Melville Street Edinburgh EH3 7NS
Tel: 0800 377 7330
Text: 0790 049 4372
Email via website
www.spso.org.uk
Investigates complaints about maladministration and service failure in public services in Scotland

Public Whip
www.publicwhip.org.uk/
A searchable site providing the complete voting record of every MP

PWSA (UK) Prader-Willi Syndrome Association UK
125a London Road Derby DE1 2QQ
Tel: 01332 365 676
admin@pwsa.co.uk
www.pwsa.co.uk
Supports those affected by this chromosomal disorder

Pyramid
www.continyou.org.uk/children_and_families/pyramid/home
Helps primary-school children build self-esteem and confidence

Q

Quaker Voluntary Action
1 Holt Lane Holmfirth West Yorkshire HD9 3BW
Tel: 01484 687139
mail@qva.org.uk
www.qva.org.uk
Volunteer projects in the UK and abroad

Quakers in Britain
Friends House 173-177 Euston Rd London NW1 2BJ
Tel: 020 7663 1000
enquiries@quaker.org.uk
www.quaker.org.uk

Qualifications Authority (Scottish) see Scottish Qualifications Authority

Quality in Study Support and Extended Services
www.canterbury.ac.uk/education/quality-in-study-support
Provides consultancy, professional development and an accredited recognition scheme for study support

Queen's House
Greenwich London SE10 9NF
Museum switchboard: 020 8858 4422
Recorded information line: 020 8312 6565
Bookings;: 020 8312 6608
bookings@nmm.ac.uk
www.nmm.ac.uk/places/queens-house/
The 17th-century House showcases the Museum's fine-art collection and provides a unique venue for weddings, corporate and private events

Questionpoint
http://questionpoint.org
US virtual reference service and set of administrative tools for libraries of all sizes

Quilters' Guild of the British Isles
St Anthony's Hall York YO1 7PW
Tel: 01904 613 242
info@quiltersguild.org.uk
www.quiltersguild.org.uk
Independent registered educational charity which is dedicated to preserving the heritage and craft of quilting and patchwork in the UK

QUIT National Society of Non Smokers
63 Saint Mary Axe London EC3A 8AA
Quit line: 0800 002200
Tel: 0207 469 0400
info@quit.org.uk
www.quit.org.uk
Helping smokers to quit

R

Rabbit Council (British)
Purefoy House 7 Kirkgate Newark Notts NG24 1AD
Tel: 01636 676042
info@thebrc.org
www.thebrc.org
Governing body for exhibition rabbit fancying

RAC
www.rac.co.uk
Motoring services

Race Equality Foundation
Unit 35 Tileyard Studios Tileyard Road London N7 9AH
Tel: 0207 619 6220
email via website

www.raceequalityfoundation.org.uk/
Seeks to explore what is known about
discrimination and disadvantage, and to
use this evidence to develop interventions
that overcome barriers and promote race
equality in health, housing and social care

Race Relations (Institute of)
2-6 Leeke St London WC1X 9HS
Tel: 020 7837 0041
Tel: 020 7833 2010
info@irr.org.uk
www.irr.org.uk

Racial Equality (Commission for)
now see Equality and Human Rights
Commission

Racism see also thematic guide Race

Racism in Europe (Youth Against)
PO Box 858 London E11 1YG
Tel: 020 8558 7947
yrehq@yahoo.co.uk
www.yre.org.uk

RAD see Royal Academy of Dance

RADA Royal Academy of Dramatic Art
62-64 Gower St London WC1E 6ED
Tel: 020 7636 7076
enquiries@rada.ac.uk
www.rada.org
Vocational training for actors and theatre
technicians

RADAR Royal Association for Disability
Rights
12 City Forum 250 City Road London EC1V
8AF
Tel: 020 7250 3222
Tel: 020 7250 4119 (Minicom)
radar@radar.org.uk
www.radar.org.uk
Umbrella organisation of 500 member
groups, campaigning for disabled people's
right to social inclusion

Radio see also BBC

Radio Authority now see OFCOM

Radio Communications Agency now see
OFCOM

Radio Society of Great Britain
3 Abbey Court Fraser Road Priory Business
Park Bedford MK44 3WH
Tel: 01234 832 700
email via website
www.rsgb.org
Supports and promotes amateur (or ham)
radio

Rail Enquiries (National)
www.nationalrail.co.uk
Rail timetables, fares etc for all national rail
services in UK

Rail Europe
34 Tower View Kings Hill West Malling
Kent ME19 4ED
General Reservations: 08448 484 064
email via website
www.raileurope.co.uk
Information for travellers and rail fans. Gives
links to national timetables

Rail Regulation (Office of)
1 Kemble Street London WC2B 4AN
Tel: 020 7282 2000
contact.cct@orr.gsi.gov.uk
www.rail-reg.gov.uk

Railfuture
www.railfuture.org.uk
Independent campaign for a better
passenger and freight rail network

Railway Children
1st Floor 1 The Commons Sandbach
Cheshire CW11 1EG
Tel: 01270 757596
enquiries@railwaychildren.org.uk
www.railwaychildren.org.uk
Helps runaway and abandoned children in
the UK & internationally

Railway Crime (Partners Against) now
see Trackoff

Railway Museum (National)
Leeman Road York YO26 4XJ
Tel: 08448 15 3 139
School bookings enquiries: 01904 686230
nrm@nrm.org.uk
www.nrm.org.uk

Railways see also Better Transport
(Campaign for), Community Rail
Partnerships (Association of), Rail
Europe, Heritage Railway Association,
Passenger Focus, Passenger Transport
UK (Confederation of), Sustrans, Trainline,
WalesRails

Rainer now see Catch22

Rainforest see also thematic guide
Environment & Countryside

Rainforest Concern
8 Clanricarde Gardens London W2 4NA
Tel: 020 7229 2093
info@rainforestconcern.org
www.rainforestconcern.org
Conservation & protection of rainforests in
Central and South America & Asia

Rainforest Foundation
2nd Floor, Imperial Works Perren Street
London NW5 3ED
Tel: 020 7485 0193
info@rainforestuk.com
www.rainforestfoundationuk.org
Protects the world's rainforests and their
inhabitants

Raleigh
3rd Floor 207 Waterloo Road London SE1 8XD
Tel: 020 7183 1270
info@raleigh.org.uk
www.raleighinternational.org
Youth development charity running community, environmental and adventure projects in developing countries

Rambert Dance Company
94 Chiswick High Rd London W4 1SH
Tel: 020 8630 0600
rdc@rambert.org.uk
www.rambert.org.uk
Contemporary dance with education and community units

Ramblers
2nd Floor Camelford House 87-90 Albert Embankment London SE1 7TW
Tel: 020 7339 8500
ramblers@ramblers.org.uk
www.ramblers.org.uk
Britain's biggest charity working on behalf of walkers

Ramblers Scotland
Kingfisher House Auld Mart Business Park Milnathort Kinross KY13 9DA
Tel: 01577 861222
cerddwyr@ramblers.org.uk
www.ramblers.org.uk/scotland

Ramblers' Association Wales Cymdeithas y Cerddwyr
3 Coopers Yard Curran Road Cardiff CF10 5NB
Tel: 029 2064 4308
ramblers@ramblers.org.uk
www.ramblers.org.uk/wales
Representative body for walkers in Wales. Aims to encourage walking and public understanding of the outdoors

Rape see also Crossroads Women's Centre, Mankind UK, Roofie Foundation, SurvivorsUK

Rape Crisis England and Wales
BCM Box 4444 London WC1N 3XX
Freephone Helpline: 0808 802 9999
info@rapecrisis.org.uk
www.rapecrisis.co.uk
Gives contact information about rape crisis centres throughout the UK

RAPt Rehabilitation for Addicted Prisoners Trust
Riverside House 27-29 Vauxhall Grove London SW8 1SY
Tel: 0207 582 4677
info@rapt.org.uk
www.rapt.org.uk

Works to help people with drug and alcohol dependence, both in prison and in the community, move towards, achieve and maintain positive and fulfilling drug-free and crime-free lives

Rare Breeds Survival Trust RBST
Stoneleigh Park Nr Kenilworth Warwickshire CV8 2LG
Tel: 024 7669 6551
email via website
www.rbst.org.uk
Works to conserve endangered breeds of British farm livestock

Rathbone
4th Floor Churchgate House 56 Oxford St Manchester M1 6EU
Free Phone: 0800 731 5321
Tel: 0161 236 5358
Email via website
www.rathboneuk.org
Charity helping people with special educational and training needs. Helpline advises parents on special education procedures

Raw Material
2 Robsart St London SW9 0DJ
Tel: 0207 737 6103
info@rawmaterial.org
www.rawmusicmedia.co.uk
Getting young Londoners active in professional music, creative arts and media development

Raynaud's & Scleroderma Association
112 Crewe Rd Alsager Cheshire ST7 2JA
Tel: 01270 872776
Tel: 0800 9172494
info@raynauds.org.uk
www.raynauds.org.uk
Offers support to sufferers of both conditions and raises funds for research and welfare

RDA see Riding for the Disabled Association

RE Today Services
1020 Bristol Rd Selly Oak Birmingham B29 6LB
Tel: 0121 472 4242
admin@retoday.org.uk
www.natre.org.uk
Works nationally and internationally to support religious education in schools

Re-Cycle Bicycle Aid for Africa
www.re-cycle.org
Collects secondhand bicycles to send to Africa, some help health/AIDS workers reach remote villages and even provide an ambulance service

Reach Skilled volunteers
89 Albert Embankment London SE1 7TP
Tel: 020 7582 6543
email via website
www.reachskills.org.uk
Job placement for managerial and
professional people available to offer
part-time services as unpaid volunteers to
voluntary organisations

React Rapid Effective Assistance for
Children with Potentially Terminal illness
St Luke's House 270 Sandycombe Rd Kew
Surrey TW9 3NP
Tel: 020 8940 2575
Email via website
www.reactcharity.org
Helps families facing the financial burden of
caring for a potentially terminally ill child

Read The Reading Agency
60 Farringdon Road London EC1R 3GA
Tel: 0871 750 1207
info@readingagency.org.uk
www.readingagency.org.uk
A charity aiming to inspire a reading nation
by working with readers, writers, libraries
and their partners

Reading see also BookCrossing, Book
Power, BOOKTRUST, Listening Books,
Literacy Association (National), People's
Network, Volunteer Reading Help

Reading Agency now see Read

Real Ale (Campaign for) see CAMRA

Real Education (Campaign for)
18 Westlands Grove York YO31 1EF
Tel: 01904 424134
cred@cre.org.uk
www.cre.org.uk
For higher standards and more choice in
state schools

Recording Association (Professional)
see APRS – The Professional Recording
Association

Recycle for London
Helpline: 0845 600 0323
www.recycleforlondon.com

recycle more
Valpak Ltd Stratford Business Park
Banbury Road
  Stratford-Upon-Avon CV37 7GW
Tel: 08450 682 572
recycle-more@valpak.co.uk
www.recycle-more.co.uk
Encourages homes, businesses and schools
to recycle more waste

Recycle-IT! Ethical solutions
Unit 7 92 Chorlton Road Old Trafford
Manchester M15 4AL
Tel: 0161 226 0637
info@recycle-it.uk.com
www.recycle-it.uk.com
Community Interest Company providing
training, paid work experience and real
jobs for homeless and other long term
unemployed people

RecycleNow
Helpline: 0845 600 0323
Email via website
www.recyclenow.com

Recycling see also Access Space,
Aluminium Packaging Recycling
Organisation, Computer Aid International,
Freecycle, Furniture Re-use Network,
Garden Organic, Save A Cup, Steel Can
Recycling Information Bureau, Waste
Watch, WRAP

Recycling Appeal
31-37 Etna Road Falkirk FK2 9EG
Tel: 08451 30 20 10
info@recyclingappeal.com
www.recyclingappeal.com
Collects mobile phones, PDAs and printer
cartridges for reuse and recycling, raising
funds and helping the environment.

Red Cross (British)
44 Moorfields London EC2Y 9AL
Tel: 0844 871 1111
Tel: 0844 412 2804
Textphone: 020 7562 2050
information@redcross.org.uk
www.redcross.org.uk

**Red Cross (International Committee of
the)**
19 Avenue de la Paix CH-1202 Geneva
Tel: 00 41 22 734 6001
email via website
www.icrc.org

Red List of Endangered Species
www.iucnredlist.org
The World Conservation Union assesses the
threat to species

Red Ribbon International see AIDS Trust
(National)

REDRESS
87 Vauxhall Walk London SE11 5HJ
Tel: 020 7793 1777
info@redress.org
www.redress.org
Charity seeking reparation for torture
survivors

Redwings Horse Sanctuary
Hapton Norwich NR15 1SP
Tel: 01508 481000
info@redwings.co.uk
www.redwings.org.uk
To provide and promote the welfare, care
and protection of horses, ponies, donkeys
and mules

Reflexology Association (British)
Monks Orchard Whitbourne Worcester
WR6 5RB
Tel: 01886 821207
bra@britreflex.co.uk
www.britreflex.co.uk
Representative body for reflexology
practitioners and students

Reform Judaism (Movement for)
The Sternberg Centre for Judaism 80 East
End Rd London N3 2SY
Tel: 020 8349 5724
Email via website
www.reformjudaism.org.uk

**Reformed Offenders (National
Association of)** see UNLOCK

Refuge
4th Floor International House 1 St
Katharine's Way London E1W 1UN
24 hr national domestic violence helpline:
0808 2000 247 run in partnership between
Women's Aid and Refuge
Tel: 020 7395 7700
info@refuge.org.uk
www.refuge.org.uk
www.womensaid.org.uk
Provides safe accommodation for women
& children experiencing domestic violence.
Support, advice and referrals

Refugee Agency (United Nations) see
UNHCR

Refugee Council
240-250 Ferndale Road Brixton London
SW9 8BB
Advice Line: 0808 808 2255
Tel: 020 7346 6700
Text phone: 0808 808 2259
email via website
www.refugeecouncil.org.uk
Promotes refugees' rights in the UK and
abroad and advocate on their behalf

Refugees (Student Action for) STAR
Oxford House Derbyshire Street London
E2 6HG
Tel: 020 7729 8880
email via website
www.star-network.org.uk

Network of university based students
and young people aged 16-25 supporting
refugees locally and nationally

Refugees (US Committee for)
www.refugees.org

**Refugees and Exiles (European Council
on)**
Secretariat Rue Royale 146, 1st Floor 1000
Brussels Belgium
Tel: +32 (0)2 234 3800
ecre@ecre.org
www.ecre.org
Umbrella organisation of over 70 agencies
working in 30 countries to assist refugees

**Register Office for Northern Ireland
(General)**
Oxford House 49-55 Chichester St Belfast
BT1 4HL
Tel: 028 9151 3101
GRO_NISRA@dfpni.gov.uk
www.nidirect.gov.uk/gro
Administers marriage law and the
registration of births, deaths, marriages, civil
partnerships and adoption

Register Office for Scotland (General)
New Register House 3 West Register Street
Edinburgh EH1 3YT
Tel: 0131 334 0380
Email via website
www.gro-scotland.gov.uk
Responsible for registration of births,
marriages, deaths, divorces & adoptions,
censuses of population

Registering life events
www.direct.gov.uk/en/
Governmentcitizensandrights/
Registeringlifeevents/index.htm
Order birth, marriage, death, civil
partnership, stillbirth or adoption certificates
through the General Register Office

Relate The relationship people
Tel: 0300 100 1234
www.relate.org.uk
Supports family life. Provides counselling
& therapy for couples with relationship
problems

Relationships Scotland
18 York Place Edinburgh EH1 3EP
Tel: 0845 1192020
email via website
www.relationships-scotland.org.uk
Helps separating and divorcing parents,
children, young people and families

Relatives & Residents Association
1 The Ivories 6-18 Northampton Street
London N1 2HY
Advice Line: 020 7359 8136
Tel: 020 7359 8148 (Admin)
info@relres.org
www.relres.org
Promotes the well being of older people in
homes and long stay hospitals

Release National drugs and legal helpline
124-128 City Road London EC1V 2NJ
Advice Line: 0845 4500 215
Tel: 020 7324 2989
ask@release.org.uk
www.release.org.uk

**Religious Education (Professional
Council for)** now see Teachers of Religious
Education (National Association of)

Religious Society of Friends see Quakers
in Britain

REMAP
D9 Chaucer Business Park Kemsing
Sevenoaks TN15 6YU
Tel: 0845 1300 456
email via website
www.remap.org.uk
UK-wide charity with panels of local
voluntary engineers who help disabled
people by making specialist equipment for
free

Remploy
18c Meridian East Meridian Business Park
Leicester LE19 1WZ
Tel:0845 155 2700
Minicom: 0845 155 0532
info@remploy.co.uk
www.remploy.co.uk
Provides employment services and
employment to people with disabilities and
complex barriers to work

RenewableUK
Greencoat House Francis Street London
SW1P 1DH
Tel: 020 7901 3000
info@renewable-uk.com
www.bwea.com
Professional body for the UK wind industry

REonline
www.reonline.org.uk
Providing information for all those working
and interested in religious education in
England

Reporters sans Frontières see Reporters
Without Borders

Reporters Without Borders
http://en.rsf.org
Defends jailed journalists and press freedom
throughout the world. Fights against
censorship and laws and works to improve
the safety of journalists, especially those
reporting in war zones

Research Into Ageing now see Age
Cymru, Age UK, Age NI, Age Scotland

Resolution First for family law
PO Box 302 Orpington BR6 8QX
Tel: 01689 820272
info@resolution.org.uk
www.resolution.org.uk
Organisation of lawyers who believe in a
constructive, non-confrontational approach
to family law matters. Also campaigns for
improvements to the family justice system

ReSolv The Society for the Prevention of
Solvent & Volatile Substance Abuse
30A High St Stone Staffs ST15 8AW
Tel: 01785 817885
office@re-solv.org
www.re-solv.org
National charity solely dedicated to the
prevention of solvent and volatile substance
abuse

& Scotland
Tel: 07505 000024
scotland@re-solv.org
www.re-solv.org

& Wales
Tel: 01938 556790
wales@re-solv.org
www.re-solv.org

Resource Information Service now see
Homeless Link

Respect
4th Floor, Development House 56-64
Leonard Street London EC2A 4LT
Repsect phoneline: 0808 802 4040 (free
from landlines and most mobiles)
Tel: 020 7549 0578
textphone: 18001 0808 802 4040
info@respect.uk.net
www.respect.uk.net
UK membership association for domestic
violence perpetrator programmes and
associated support services

Respect for Animals
PO Box 6500 Nottingham NG4 3GB
Tel: 0115 952 5440
info@respectforanimals.org
www.respectforanimals.co.uk
Campaign against the international fur trade

Restless Development
7 Tufton Street London SW1P 3QB
Tel: 020 7976 8070
info@restlessdevelopment.org
www.restlessdevelopment.org
An international development charity that
recruits and trains young adults as volunteer
Peer Educators, to lead programmes that
address urgent health and environmental
issues in Africa and Asia

Restricted Growth Association
PO Box 15755 Solihull B93 3FY
RGA Office & Helpline: 0300 111 1970
office@restrictedgrowth.co.uk
www.restrictedgrowth.co.uk
Support and information for people with
restricted growth, families, professionals and
other interested parties

Rethink Severe Mental Illness Charity
15th Floor 89 Albert Embankment London
SE1 7TP
Tel: 020 7840 3188 (advice)
Tel: 0845 456 0455
info@rethink.org
www.rethink.org
Working to improve the lives of everyone
affected by schizophrenia and other severe
mental illnesses

Retired and Senior Volunteer Programme
RSVP
237 Pentonville Rd London N1 9NJ
Tel: 020 7643 1385
rsvpinfo@csv.org.uk
www.csv-rsvp.org.uk
Enables people aged 50+ to become
actively involved in voluntary work of their
choice

reunite International Child Abduction
Centre
PO Box 7124 Leicester LE1 7XX
Advice Line: 01162 556 234
Tel: 01162 555 345 (Admin)
reunite@dircon.co.uk
www.reunite.org
Information & support for parents who fear
or have experienced the abduction of a child

Revision see Bitesize: BBC revision web
site

RIBA see Architects (Royal Institute of
British)

Ricability
Unit G03 The Wenlock Business Centre 50-
52 Wharf Road London N1 7EU
Tel: 020 7427 2460 (voice)
Textphone: 020 7427 2469
mail@ricability.org.uk
www.ricability.org.uk

Provides consumer information for elderly
and disabled consumers about useful
products and services

RICS see Chartered Surveyors (Royal
Institute of)

Riding for the Disabled Association RDA
Norfolk House 1A Tournament Court
Edgehill Drive Warwicks CV34 6LG
Tel: 0845 658 1082
Email via website
www.rda.org.uk

**Rifle Association (National) of United
Kingdom**
Bisley Brookwood Surrey GU24 0PB
Tel: 01483 797777
Email via website
www.nra.org.uk

Rights of Women
52-54 Featherstone St London EC1Y 8RT
Advice line: 020 7251 6577
Tel: 020 7251 6575 (Admin)
Textphone: 020 7490 2562
info@row.org.uk
www.rightsofwomen.org.uk
Research into the law affecting women &
free legal advice line for women

Rising Tide
62 Fieldgate Street London E1 1ES
info@risingtide.org.uk
www.risingtide.org.uk
UK coalition of groups committed to a
grassroots approach to fighting climate
change

**Riverside Museum: Scotland's Museum
of Transport and Travel**
100 Pointhouse Place Glasgow G3 8RS
Tel: 0141 287 2720
museums@glasgowlife.org.uk
www.glasgowlife.org.uk/museums/our-
museums/riverside-museum/Pages/default.
aspx

RNIB
Royal National Institute of Blind People 105
Judd Street London WC1H 9NE
Helpline: 0303 123 9999
Tel: 020 7388 1266
email via website
www.rnib.org.uk
UK's leading charity offering information,
support and advice to almost two million
people with sight loss

RNIB see Blind (Royal National Institute of
the)

RNIB National Library Service
Royal National Institute of Blind People 105
Judd Street London WC1H 9NE
Helpline: 0303 123 9999

Tel: 020 7388 1266
library@rnib.org.uk
www.rnib.org.uk/livingwithsightloss/
readingwriting/rnibnationallibrary/Pages/
national_library_service.aspx
largest specialist library in the UK for readers
with sight loss.

RNID Action on Hearing Loss
19-23 Featherstone St London EC1Y 8SL
Information Line (Freephone): 0808 808 0123
& 0808 808 9000 (text)
Tel: 020 7296 8000 & 020 7296 8001
(textphone)
informationline@rnid.org.uk
www.rnid.org.uk
Largest charity in the UK tackling hearing
loss and making hearing matter

Road Haulage Association
Roadway House Bretton Way Bretton
Peterborough PE3 8DD
email via website
www.rha.uk.net

Road Runners Club
www.roadrunnersclub.org.uk
Represents road runners nationwide

RoadPeace UK National Charity for Road
Crash Victims
Shakespeare Business Centre 245a
Coldharbour Lane Brixton London SW9
8RR
Helpline: 0845 4500355
Tel: 020 7733 1603
info@roadpeace.org
www.roadpeace.org
For bereaved & injured road traffic victims

Roller Hockey (England)
42 Croft Avenue Letchworth Hertfordshire
SG6 1AP
email via website
www.englandrollerhockey.com

Roller Hockey Association (National)
now see Roller Hockey (England)

Roller Skating see Artistic Roller Skating
(Federation of)

Roman Legion Museum (National)
High Street Caerleon NP18 1AE
Tel: 01633 423134
email via website
www.museumwales.ac.uk/en/roman/
Researches, preserves and displays half a
million objects from Roman fortresses.

Rona Sailing Project
Universal Marina Crableck Lane Sarisbury
Green Southampton SO31 7ZN
Tel: 01489 885098
ann@ronatrust.com
www.ronasailingproject.org
Provides voyages for underprivileged and
disadvantaged youngsters aged 14-25
years and for young people and adults with
special needs

Roofie Foundation
1 Prime Parkway Prime Enterprise Park
Derby DE1 3QB
Tel: 01723 367251
email via website
www.roofie.com
For people who have been drug raped or
sexually abused through drink spiking

Room to Read World Change Starts with
Educated Children
www.roomtoread.org
Seeks to transform the lives of millions of
children in developing countries by focusing
on literacy and gender equality in education

RoSPA Royal Society for the Prevention of
Accidents
RoSPA House 28 Calthorpe Road
Edgbaston Birmingham B15 1RP
Tel: 0121 248 2000
help@rospa.co.uk
www.rospa.com

Roundhouse
Chalk Farm Rd London NW1 8EH
Tel: 0844 482 8008
Tel: 020 7424 9991
info@roundhouse.org.uk
www.roundhouse.org.uk
Performing arts venue

Rowing see British Rowing

Rowntree see Joseph Rowntree
Foundation

Roy Castle Lung Cancer Foundation
4-6 Enterprise Way Wavertree Technology
Park Liverpool L13 1FB
Tel: 0151 254 7200
foundation@roycastle.org
www.roycastle.org
The only charity in the world wholly
dedicated to defeating lung cancer, the
biggest cancer killer in the world

Royal Academy of Arts
Burlington House Piccadilly London W1J
0BD
Tel: 020 7300 8000
Education: 020 7300 5995
Tickets: 0844 209 0051
email via website
www.royalacademy.org.uk
independent, privately funded institution.
Promotes the creation, enjoyment and
appreciation of the visual arts through
exhibitions, education and debate

Royal Academy of Dance
36 Battersea Sq London SW11 3RA
Tel: 020 7326 8000
info@rad.org.uk
www.rad.org.uk
Exists to promote knowledge, understanding
and practice of dance internationally

Royal Academy of Dramatic Art see
RADA

Royal Academy of Music
Marylebone Rd London NW1 5HT
Tel: 020 7873 7373
go@ram.ac.uk
www.ram.ac.uk
Britain's senior music conservatoire, training
performers and composers. Part of the
University of London

Royal Air Force
www.raf.mod.uk

Royal Airforce Museum Cosford
Shifnal Shropshire TF11 8UP
Tel: 01902 376 200
cosford@rafmuseum.org
www.rafmuseum.org.uk/cosford/

Royal Airforce Museum London
Grahame Park Way London NW9 5LL
Tel: 020 8205 2266
london@rafmuseum.org
www.rafmuseum.org.uk/london/

Royal Armouries National museum of
arms and armour Fort Nelson
Portsdown Hill Road Fareham PO17 6AN
Tel: 01329 233 734
fnenquiries@armouries.org.uk
www.royalarmouries.org/visit-us/fort-nelson
Trace the development of artillery from pre-
gunpowder siege machines to modern-day
super guns. There are over 350 big guns on
display

& HM Tower of London
London EC3N 4AB
Tel: 020 3166 6660
www.royalarmouries.org/visit-us/fort-nelson

Trace the development of artillery from pre-
gunpowder siege machines to modern-day
super guns. There are over 350 big guns on
display

& National Museum of Arms and Armour
Leeds
Armouries Drive Leeds LS10 1LT
Tel: 0113 220 1999
enquiries@armouries.org.uk
www.royalarmouries.org

Royal Ballet
Royal Opera House Covent Garden London
WC2E 9DD
Tel: 020 7240 1200 (Admin)
Tel: 020 7304 4000 (Box Office & Info)
Email via website
www.roh.org.uk

Royal Botanic Garden Edinburgh
20a Inverleith Row Edinburgh EH3 5LR
Tel: 0131 552 7171
Email via website
www.rbge.org.uk
Made up of four gardens, together
representing one of the world's largest living
collection of plants

Royal Botanic Gardens, Kew
Richmond Surrey TW9 3AB
Tel: 020 8332 5655
Tel: 020 8332 5655 (24-hour visitor
information line)
info@kew.org
www.kew.org
Saving plants for life

Royal College of Veterinary Surgeons
RCVS
Belgravia House 62-64 Horseferry Rd
London SW1P 2AF
Tel: 020 7222 2001
info@rcvs.org.uk
www.rcvs.org.uk

Royal Geographical Society with The
Institute of British Geographers
1 Kensington Gore London SW7 2AR
Tel: 020 7591 3000
Email via website
www.rgs.org
Promotes, supports and enhances
geographical research, education, fieldwork
and expeditions and the professional
accreditation of geographers

Royal Horticultural Society
80 Vincent Square London SW1P 2PE
Tel: 0845 260 5000
Email via website
www.rhs.org.uk

Royal Institution of Great Britain
21 Albemarle Street London W1S 4BS
Tel: 020 7409 2992
ri@ri.ac.uk
www.rigb.org
Independent charity dedicated to connecting people with the world of science. Also an events space and museum

Royal Mail see Post Office

Royal Mint (British)
Freepost NAT23496 PO Box 500 Llantrisant
  Pontyclun CF72 8YT
Tel: 01443 222111
Email via website
www.royalmint.com
World's leading export mint. Makes and distributes United Kingdom coins as well as supplying blanks and official medals

Royal National Lifeboat Institution
West Quay Road Poole Dorset BH15 1HZ
Tel: 0845 045 6999
email via website
www.rnli.org.uk
Charity that saves lives at sea and provides sea safety and educational resources

Royal Naval Museum
HM Naval Base (PP66) Portsmouth PO1 3NH
023 9272 7562
email via website
www.royalnavalmuseum.org
Making the story of the Royal Navy and its people, from earliest times to the present, accessible to all

Royal Navy
www.royalnavy.mod.uk

Royal Observatory, Greenwich
Blackheath Avenue Greenwich SE10 8XJ
National Maritime Museum switchboard: 020 8858 4422
Recorded information line: 020 8312 6565
Bookings: 020 8312 6608
www.nmm.ac.uk/places/royal-observatory/
Home of Greenwich Mean Time and the Prime Meridian of the World, making it the official starting point for each new day and year. Also home to London's only planetarium, the Harrison timekeepers and the UK's largest refracting telescope

Royal Opera
Royal Opera House Covent Garden London WC2E 9DD
Tel: 020 7240 1200 (Admin)
Tel: 020 7304 4000 (Box Office & Info)
email via website
www.roh.org.uk

Royal Parks
The Old Police House Hyde Park London W2 2UH
Tel: 0300 061 2000
hq@royalparks.gsi.gov.uk
www.royalparks.org.uk
Locations and history

Royal School for the Blind see SeeAbility

Royal Scottish Academy
The Mound Edinburgh EH2 2EL
Tel: 0131 225 6671
Email via website
www.royalscottishacademy.org
Promotes living artists in Scotland through its annual and student shows, scholarships, awards and other exhibitions

Royal Shakespeare Theatre see RSC

Royal Society
6-9 Carlton House Terrace London SW1Y 5AG
Tel: 020 7451 2500
Email via website
http://royalsociety.org/
Fellowship of the world's most eminent scientists and is the oldest scientific academy in continuous existence. Aims to expand the frontiers of knowledge by championing the development and use of science, mathematics, engineering and medicine for the benefit of humanity and the good of the planet

Royal Society of Medicine RSM
1 Wimpole Street London W1G 0AE
Tel: 020 7290 2900
www.rsm.ac.uk
Educational activities and opportunities for doctors, dentists, veterinary surgeons and allied professions

Royalty see British Monarchy (The official website of)

RSA Royal Society for the Encouragement of Arts, Manufactures and Commerce
8 John Adam St London WC2N 6EZ
Tel: 020 7930 5115
general@rsa.org.uk
www.thersa.org
To develop and promote new ways of thinking about human fulfilment and social progress

RSA Exams see OCR/Oxford Cambridge and RSA Examinations

RSC Royal Shakespeare Company
Royal Shakespeare Theatre Waterside
Stratford-upon-Avon Warwickshire CV37
6BB
Tel: 0844 800 1110 (General and tickets)
Tel: 0844 800 1113 (School tickets)
Email via website
www.rsc.org.uk

RSM see Royal Society of Medicine

RSPB Royal Society for the Protection of
Birds
The Lodge Potton Road Sandy
Bedfordshire SG19 2DL
Tel: 01767 680551
Email via website
www.rspb.org.uk

RSPCA Royal Society for the Prevention of
Cruelty to Animals
Wilberforce Way Southwater Horsham W
Sussex RH13 9RS
Cruelty Line: 0300 1234 999 (24 hrs)
Advice Line: 0300 1234 555
www.rspca.org.uk
Animal welfare charity

RSSPCC see CHILDREN 1ST

RSVP see Retired and Senior Volunteer
Programme

RTPI see Town Planning Institute (Royal)

Rugby see also Scrum.com, World Rugby
Museum

Rugby Football League
Red Hall Red Hall Lane Leeds LS17 8NB
Tel: 0844 477 7113
enquiries@rfl.uk.com
www.rfl.uk.com

Rugby Football Union
Rugby House Twickenham Stadium 200
Whitton Road
Twickenham Middlesex TW2 7BA
Tel: 0871 222 2120
enquiries@therfu.com
www.rfu.com

Rugby Football Union (Irish)
10/12 Lansdowne Rd Dublin 4 Ireland
Tel: 00 353 1 647 3800
info@irishrugby.ie
www.irishrugby.ie

Rugby Football Union for Women
Rugby House Twickenham Stadium 200
Whitton Road Twickenham Middlesex TW2
7BA
Tel: 0871 222 2120
enquiries@therfu.com
www.rfu.com/womensRugbyPortal/
Co-ordinating body for women's rugby in
the UK

Runaway Helpline see also Missing
People and Message Home
Helpline: 0808 800 70 70 (free, confidential
and 24/7)
Text 80234 (can text even if no credit left on
mobile phone)
runaway@missingpeople.org.uk
info@missingpeople.org.uk
www.runawayhelpline.org.uk
National, free, confidential service, provided
by the charity Missing People, for anyone
who has run away from home or care, or
been forced to leave home

Runnymede Trust
7 Plough Yard Shoreditch London EC2A
3LP
Tel: 020 7377 9222
info@runnymedetrust.org
www.runnymedetrust.org
Conducts research & policy analysis in racial
equality and cultural diversity

Rural affairs see CLA, Communities in
Rural England (Action with), Countryside
Alliance, CPRE: Campaign to Protect Rural
England, Defra, Natural England, Protection
of Rural Wales (Campaign for the), Self
Unlimited

Rural Communities (Commission for)
Unit 1 Saw Mill End Corinium Avenue
Gloucester GL4 3DE
Tel: 08459 33 55 77
info@ruralcommunities.gov.uk
www.ruralcommunities.gov.uk
To promote awareness of the social and
economic needs of people who live and
work in rural areas and help decision-makers
across and beyond government identify how
those needs can best be addressed

Rural Research (Centre for)
Institute of Science and the Environment
University of Worcester Henwick Road
Worcester WR2 6AJ
Tel: 01905 855185
crr@worc.ac.uk
www.worc.ac.uk/crr
An academic research unit specialising
in economic, social, agricultural and
environmental change in the countryside

**Rural Scotland (Association for the
Protection of)** APRS
Gladstone's Land (3rd Floor) 483
Lawnmarket Edinburgh EH1 2NT
Tel: 0131 225 7012
info@ruralscotland.org
www.ruralscotland.btik.com
Scotland's countryside champion

Ruskin College
Walton St Oxford OX1 2HE
Tel: 01865 554331
enquiries@ruskin.ac.uk
www.ruskin.ac.uk
To enable mature students with little or no qualifications to study

RYA Sailability
RYA House Ensign Way Hamble
Southampton SO31 4YA
Tel: 0844 556 9550
Text: 07823559018
sailability@rya.org.uk
www.rya.org.uk/programmes/ryasailability/
Pages/RYASailability.aspx
National body for all forms of boating, including dinghy and yacht racing, motor and sail cruising, sports boats, powerboat racing, windsurfing, inland cruising and narrowboats. Offers training, advice and support to those with disabilities to take up the sport

S

S4C
Parc Ty Glas Llanishen Cardiff CF14 5DU
Tel: 0870 600 4141
Email via website
www.s4c.co.uk
www.s4c.co.uk/e_index.shtml
Welsh fourth TV channel

SACRO Safeguarding Communities - Reducing Offending in Scotland
29 Albany Street Edinburgh EH1 3QN
Tel: 0131 624 7270
info@national.sacro.org.uk
www.sacro.org.uk
Services to reduce conflict and offending, to make communities safer

SAD see Seasonal Affective Disorder Association

Safe Standing see Football Supporters' Federation

Safer Medicines Campaign
PO Box 62720 London SW2 9FQ
Tel: 020 8265 2880
info@safermedicines.org
www.curedisease.net
Scientists and medical professionals who question the value of testing human drugs on animals

Saferworld
The Grayston Centre 28 Charles Square
London N1 6HT
Tel: 020 7324 4646
general@saferworld.org.uk
www.saferworld.co.uk
Independent foreign affairs think tank working for prevention of armed conflict

Safety Council (British)
70 Chancellors Rd London W6 9RS
Tel: 020 8741 1231
mail@britsafe.org
www.britsafe.org
Corporate membership organisation that provides health, safety and environmental training, auditing, information and publications

Sailing see also Cirdan Sailing Trust, Ellen MacArthur Trust, Historical Maritime Society, Jubilee Sailing Trust, Marine Leisure Association, Ocean Youth Trust, Rona Sailing Project, RYA Sailability, Sea Ranger Association, Tall Ships Youth Trust

Salvation Army
101 Newington Causeway London SE1 6BN
Tel: 020 7367 4500
Email via website
www2.salvationarmy.org.uk

SALVO Architectural Salvage Listings
www.salvo.co.uk

Samaritans
PO Box 9090 Stirling FK8 2SA
Tel: 08457 909090
jo@samaritans.org
www.samaritans.org
See website for local branches. Samaritans offer 24 hour emotional support to anyone in distress in the UK and Republic of Ireland. See Befrienders Worldwide for international centres and support

Samaritans International
www.samaritansinternational.org
Charitable non-profit corporation whose sole purpose is feeding and helping destitute children

SAMH see Mental Health (Scottish Association for)

SAMM Support After Murder & Manslaughter
Pershore Road Edgbaston Birmingham B5 7RN
Hotline: 0845 872 3440
Tel: 0121 471 1200 (enquiries)
info@samm.org.uk
www.samm.org.uk
Offers support and understanding to families bereaved through murder and manslaughter

Sand & Land Yacht Clubs (British Federation of)
www.bfslyc.org.uk

SANDS Stillbirth & Neonatal Death Charity
28 Portland Place London W1B 1LY
Helpline: 020 7436 5881
Tel: 020 7436 7940
support@uk-sands.org
www.uk-sands.org
Supporting anyone affected by the death of a baby and promoting research to reduce the loss of babies' lives

SANE Meeting the challenge of mental illness
First Floor Cityside House 40 Adler St
London E1 1EE
Helpline: 0845 767 8000
Tel: 020 7375 1002
info@sane.org.uk
www.sane.org.uk
Works to raise mental health awareness; combat stigma and increase understanding

Sargent Cancer Care for Children now see CLICSargent

Save A Cup
Falcon Point Park Plaza Heath Hayes
Cannock Staffs WS12 2DE
Tel: 01543 505210
sales@save-a-cup.co.uk
www.save-a-cup.co.uk

Save the Children UK
1 St John's Lane London EC1M 4AR
Tel: 020 7012 6400
supporter.care@savethechildren.org.uk
www.savethechildren.org.uk
Emergency relief runs alongside long-term development & prevention work

Saving Faces
St Bartholomew's Hospital West Smithfield
London EC1A 7BE
Tel: 0203 46 55755
Email via website
www.savingfaces.co.uk
Raises awareness about facial disfigurement through art. Fundraising charity for research into the causes of facial cancers and other conditions leading to disfigurement

Scarlet Centre
Tel; 020 7840 7142 from Tuesdays-Saturdays 10am-5.30pm
www.eaves4women.co.uk/Scarlet_Centre/Scarlet_centre.php
Eaves project providing advice and drop-in support to women who are affected by domestic violence, rape or sexual abuse, homelessness, prostitution, mental health and/or substance misuse problems

Schizophrenia see also Rethink

School Councils UK
The Old Dairy Victoria Street Felixstowe
IP11 7EW
Tel: 0845 4569428
email via website
www.schoolcouncils.org
Charity training teachers & pupils to set up effective structures for pupil involvement

School Food Trust
3rd Floor
2 St Paul's Place
125 Norfolk St
Sheffield S1 2JF
Tel: 0114 2742318
info@sft.gsi.gov.uk
www.schoolfoodtrust.org.uk
National charity and specialist adviser to government on school meals, children's food and related skills

School Governors (National Association of) see Governors' Association (National)

School Journey Association
48 Cavendish Rd London SW12 0DH
Tel: 020 8675 6636
thesja@btconnect.com
www.sjatours.org
Educational tours for school groups and young people

School Librarianship (International Association of) IASL
www.iasl-online.org
Provides an international forum for those interested in promoting school library programmes worldwide

School Library Association
Unit 2 Lotmead Business Village
Wanborough Swindon SN4 0UY
Tel: 01793 791787
info@sla.org.uk
www.sla.org.uk
Committed to promotion and development of libraries and information literacy in schools

Schools Adjudicator (Office of the)
Mowden Hall Staindrop Road Darlington
DL3 9BG
Tel: 01325 735303
osa.team@osa.gsi.gov.uk
www.schoolsadjudicator.gov.uk
Decides on schools organisation issues & admission arrangements which can't be resolved locally

Schools Health Education Unit
3 Manaton Court Manaton Park Exeter EX2 8PF
Tel: 01392 667272
sheu@sheu.org.uk
www.sheu.org.uk

Schools Music Association of Great Britain
24 Royston Street Potton Bedfordshire
SG19 2LP
email via website
www.schoolsmusic.org.uk
SMA provides a vital link between school music teachers and the education policy makers

Schumacher see also Practical Action

Schumacher UK
Create Environment Centre Smeaton Rd
Bristol BS1 6XN
Tel: 0117 903 1081
admin@schumacher.org.uk
www.schumacher.org.uk
Promotes human scale sustainable development "as though people matter" in the UK and abroad

SCIAF Scottish Catholic International Aid Fund
19 Park Circus Glasgow G3 6BE
Tel: 0141 354 5555
sciaf@sciaf.org.uk
www.sciaf.org.uk
Works in over 16 countries across Asia, Africa and Latin America, to help some of the poorest people in the world, regardless of religion, to work their way out of poverty

SCIcentre The National Centre for Initial Teacher Training in Primary School Science
School of Education University of Leicester
21 University Road Leicester LE1 7RF
Tel: 0116 252 3659
iab6@le.ac.uk
www.le.ac.uk/se/centres/sci/SCIcentre.html
Produces resources to help with the training of student teachers in the teaching of science

Science Association (British)
Wellcome Wolfson Building 165 Queen's Gate London SW7 5HD
Tel: 0870 770 7101
email via website
www.britishscienceassociation.org
Nationwide organisation dedicated to public engagement with science through programmes and membership

Science Centre (Glasgow)
50 Pacific Quay Glasgow G51 1EA
Tel: 0141 420 5000
Email via website
www.gsc.org.uk
Visitor attraction presenting concepts of science and technology in unique and inspiring ways

Science Education (Association for)
College Lane Hatfield Herts AL10 9AA
Tel: 01707 283000
info@ase.org.uk
www.ase.org.uk
The subject association for teachers, technicians and others involved in science education

Science Education (Centre for)
Sheffield Hallam University City Campus
Howard St Sheffield S1 1WB
Tel: 0114 225 4870
email via website
www.shu.ac.uk/research/cse/

Science in the Public Interest (Center for)
www.cspinet.org
US organisation that focuses on food and alcohol & on reducing the carnage caused by alcoholic beverages

Science Museum
Exhibition Road London SW7 2DD
Tel: 0870 870 4868
Email via website
www.sciencemuseum.org.uk

Science, Technology & the Arts (National Endowment for) NESTA
1 Plough Place London EC4A 1DE
Tel: 020 7438 2500
information@nesta.org.uk
www.nesta.org.uk
Promotes talent, innovation and creativity

Scientific Exploration Society
Expedition Base Motcombe Nr Shaftesbury Dorset SP7 9PB
Tel: 01747 853353
Email via website
www.ses-explore.org
Expeditions for ordinary people to do extraordinary things for conservation and the environment

Scientists for Global Responsibility
Ingles Manor Castle Hill Avenue Folkestone
CT20 2RD
Tel: 01303 851965
info@sgr.org.uk
www.sgr.org.uk/
Promotes ethical science and technology

Scoliosis Association (UK)
4 Ivebury Court 325 Latimer Rd London
W10 6RA
Helpline: 020 8964 1166
Tel: 020 8964 5343
info@sauk.org.uk
www.sauk.org.uk
Links sufferers from curvature of the spine

Scope
6 Market Rd London N7 9PW
Helpline: 0808 800 3333
Office tel: 020 7619 7100
response@scope.org.uk
www.scope.org.uk
Disability organisation whose focus is people
with cerebral palsy

Scotland Office
Dover House Whitehall London SW1A 2AU
Tel: 020 7270 6754
Email via website
www.scotlandoffice.gov.uk

Scotland Street School Museum
225 Scotland Street Glasgow G5 8QB
Tel: 0141 287 0500
Text Phone: 0141 287 0513
museums@glasgowlife.org.uk
www.glasgowlife.org.uk/museums/our-
museums/scotland-street-school/Pages/
home.aspx
Tells the story of education in Scotland over
a hundred years, from the late 19th century
to the late 20th century

Scots Language Centre
A K Bell Library York Place Perth PH2 8EP
Tel: 01738 440199
info@scotslanguage.com
www.scotslanguage.com

Scottish Arts Council now see Creative
Scotland

Scottish Awards Agency now see Student
Awards Agency for Scotland

Scottish Ballet
Tramway 25 Albert Drive Glasgow G41 2PE
Tel: 0141 331 2931
email via website
www.scottishballet.co.uk
Scotland's National Dance Company

**Scottish Cultural Resources Access
Network** now see SCRAN

Scottish Cycle Union now see Scottish
Cycling

Scottish Cycling
Caledonia House South Gyle Edinburgh
EH12 9DQ
Tel: 0131 317 9704
info@scottishcycling.org.uk
http://new.britishcycling.org.uk/scotland

Scottish Environment LINK
2 Grosvenor House Shore Rd Perth PH2
8BD
Tel: 01738 630804
Email via website
www.scotlink.org
Umbrella organisation providing forum and
network for voluntary environmental groups

Scottish Government
St Andrew's House Regent Road Edinburgh
EH1 3DG
Tel: 0131 556 8400
Tel: 08457 741 741
Minicom: 0131 244 1829
ceu@scotland.gsi.gov.uk
www.scotland.gov.uk

**Scottish National Disability Information
Service** see UPDATE

Scottish National Gallery
The Mound Edinburgh EH2 2EL
Tel: 0131 624 6200
nginfo@nationalgalleries.org
www.nationalgalleries.org

Scottish National Gallery of Modern Art
75 Belford Rd Edinburgh EH4 3DR
Tel: 0131 624 6200
gmainfo@nationalgalleries.org
www.nationalgalleries.org
Collection of modern and contemporary art

Scottish National Party see SNP

Scottish Opera
39 Elmbank Crescent Glasgow G2 4PT
Tel: 0141 248 4567
information@scottishopera.org.uk
www.scottishopera.org.uk

Scottish Parliament
Edinburgh EH99 1SP
Tel: 0131 348 5000
Tel: 0800 092 7500
Textphone: 0800 092 7100
sp.info@scottish.parliament.uk
www.scottish.parliament.uk

Scottish Qualifications Authority SQA
Ironmills Road Dalkeith Midlothian EH22
1LE
Tel: 0845 279 1000
customer@sqa.org.uk
www.sqa.org.uk
Main body in Scotland, responsible for all
qualifications except degrees and some
professional qualifications

**Scottish Society for the Prevention of
Cruelty to Animals** see Scottish SPCA

Scottish SPCA
Kingseat Road Halbeath Dunfermline KY11
8RY
Tel: 03000 999 999
Email via website
www.scottishspca.org
Animal welfare charity

Scottish Tourist Board now see
VisitScotland

Scottish Youth Theatre
The Old Sheriff Court 105 Brunswick Street
Glasgow G1 1TF
Tel: 0141 552 3988
info@scottishyouththeatre.org
www.scottishyouththeatre.org
Scotland's national theatre 'for and by'
young people

scottishathletics
Caledonia House South Gyle Edinburgh
EH12 9DQ
Tel: 0131 539 7320
admin@scottishathletics.org.uk
www.scottishathletics.org.uk
Governing body for athletics in Scotland

Scout Association
Gilwell Park Chingford London E4 7QW
Tel: 0845 300 1818
info.centre@scouts.org.uk
www.scouts.org.uk

SCRAN
John Sinclair House   16 Bernard Terrace
Edinburgh EH8 9NX
Tel: 0131 662 1456
Email via website
www.scran.ac.uk
Part of the Royal Commission on the Ancient
and Historical Monuments of Scotland –
aims to provide educational access to digital
materials representing our material culture
and history

Scrum.com
www.espnscrum.com/
Rugby website

Sea Ranger Association
'Lord Amory' 631 Manchester Road Dollar
Bay London E14 3NU
info@searangers.org.uk
www.searangers.org.uk
For girls aged 10-21, all forms of boating

Seafish
18 Logie Mill Logie Green Rd Edinburgh
EH7 4HS
Tel: 0131 558 3331
seafish@seafish.co.uk
www.seafish.org
Supports the seafood industry for a
sustainable, profitable future

Sealed Knot Ltd
Burlington House Botleigh Grange Business
Park Southampton SO30 2DF
Email via website
www.thesealedknot.org.uk
Charity teaching about the 17th century by
re-enacting civil war battles

Searchlight Magazine Ltd
PO Box 1576 Ilford IG5 0NG
Tel: 020 7681 8660
email via website
www.searchlightmagazine.com
Anti-racism and fascism monthly magazine

Seasonal Affective Disorder Association
SAD
PO Box 989 Steyning West Sussex BN44
3HG
Tel: 01903 814942
www.sada.org.uk
Advises sufferers. Informs public & health
professions

SEBDA Social, Emotional & Behavioural
Difficulties Association
Room 211 The Triangle Exchange Square
Manchester M4 3TR
Tel: 0161 240 2418
admin@sebda.org
www.sebda.org

Secular Society (National)
25 Red Lion Square London WC1R 4RL
Tel: 020 7404 3126
enquiries@secularism.org.uk
www.secularism.org.uk
Fights religious privilege & upholds the
rights of those without religion. Works for
separation of Church and State

SeeAbility
SeeAbility House 1a Hook Rd Epsom
Surrey KT19 8SQ
Tel: 01372 755 000
enquiries@seeability.org
www.seeability.org
Supports adults who are visually impaired
with multiple disabilities including; learning,
physical and mental health disabilities,
acquired brain injuries and degenerative
conditions, to explore their potential

Self Unlimited
14 Nursery Court Kibworth Business Park
Harborough Road Kibworth Leicester LE8
0EX
Tel: 0116 279 3225
info@selfunlimited.co.uk
www.selfunlimited.co.uk
Maintains a network of support services
for people with learning disabilities across
the country. Assisting people to live as
independently as possible and to realise
their full potential

Self-Injury Guidance & Network Support
see FirstSigns

Sickle Cell Society
54 Station Rd London NW10 4UA
Tel: 020 8961 7795
info@sicklecellsociety.org
www.sicklecellsociety.org
Provides info, counselling & care for people with sickle cell disorder

Sightsavers
Grosvenor Hall Bolnore Rd Haywards Heath RH16 4BX
Tel: 01444 446600
info@sightsavers.org
www.sightsavers.org
Projects to prevent & cure blindness in the developing world and train incurably blind people

Signature Excellence in communication with deaf people
Mersey House Mandale Business Park Belmont Durham DH1 1TH
Tel: 0191 383 1155
Tel: 0191 383 7915 (Textphone Answerphone)
durham@signature.org.uk
www.signature.org.uk
Promotes communication between deaf & hearing people. National examination board of British Sign Language

Signed Performances in Theatre see SPIT

Sikh Organisations (Network of) NSO
Suite 405 Highland House 165 The Broadway Wimbledon SW19 1NE
Tel: 020 8544 8037
sikhmessenger@aol.com
www.nsouk.co.uk
Addresses issues of common concern and organises celebration of Sikh activities

Simon Community
St. Joseph's House 129 Malden Road London NW5 4HS
Tel: 020 7485 6639
Tel: 020 7482 0447
info@simoncommunity.org.uk
www.simoncommunity.org.uk
Provides caring & campaigns for London's street homeless

Simon Jones Memorial Campaign
Community Base 113 Queens Road Brighton BN1 3XG
action@simonjones.org.uk
www.simonjones.org.uk
Campaigns against the dangers of casualisation of the workforce, following the death of Simon Jones in 1998

Simon Wiesenthal Centre
www.wiesenthal.com
International Jewish human rights organisation dedicated to preserving the memory of the Holocaust

Simple Free Law Advisor
www.sfla.co.uk

Siobhan Dowd Trust
c/o DFB 31 Beaumont Street Oxford OX1 2NP
Email via website
www.siobhandowdtrust.com/
Bringing books and reading to disadvantaged young people in the UK through the legacy of an award winning writer

Ski Club of Great Britain
The White House 57-63 Church Rd Wimbledon London SW19 5SB
Tel: 0845 45 807 80
Tel: 020 8410 2000
skiers@skiclub.co.uk
www.skiclub.co.uk

Skill: National Bureau for Students with Disabilities see Disability Alliance

Skills for Care
West Gate 6 Grace Street Leeds LS1 2RP
Tel: 0113 245 1716
info@skillsforcare.org.uk
www.skillsforcare.org.uk
Aiming to modernise adult social care in England, by ensuring qualifications and standards continually adapt to meet the changing needs of people who use care services

Skills for Justice Developing skills for safer communities
Centre Court Atlas Way Sheffield S4 7QQ
Tel: 0114 261 1499
info@skillsforjustice.com
www.skillsforjustice.com
Works with employers to raise skills across the Justice Sector

Skills Funding Agency
Cheylesmore House Quinton Road Coventry CV1 2WT
Tel: 0845 377 5000
info@skillsfundingagency.bis.gov.uk
http://skillsfundingagency.bis.gov.uk
Funds and regulates adult further education and skills training in England

Skillshare International
126 New Walk Leicester LE1 7JA
Tel: 0116 254 1862
info@skillshare.org
www.skillshare.org
Development agency working in Africa and Asia

Skin Care Campaign SCC
www.skincarecampaign.org

Working to improve the quality of life for more than 15 million people in the UK with skin conditions

Skin Foundation (British)
Tel: 0207 391 6341
email via website
www.britishskinfoundation.org.uk

Sky British Sky Broadcasting
www.sky.com

Skylight Circus Arts
email via website
www.skylightcircusarts.com
Circus skills workshops and projects for young people, can lead to performances

Slate Museum (National)
Llanberis Gwynedd LL55 4TY
Tel: 01286 870630
email via website
www.museumwales.ac.uk/en/slate/

Slavery see Anti-Slavery International

Slavery Museum (International)
Dock Traffic Office Albert Dock Liverpool L3 4AX
Tel: 0151 478 4499
email via website
www.liverpoolmuseums.org.uk/ism
Hear the untold stories of enslaved people and learn about historical and contemporary slavery

Sleep Council
High Corn Mill Chapel Hill Skipton N Yorkshire BD23 1NL
Freephone leaflet line: 0800 018 7923
Tel: 0845 058 4595
info@sleepcouncil.org.uk
www.sleepcouncil.org.uk
Promotes the benefits to health of a good night's sleep. Non-profit organisation funded by bed manufacturers & retailers.

Slivers of Time
www.sliversoftime.com
Social enterprise running online marketplaces where anyone can sell spare hours, on their own terms, to multiple employers.

Slow Food UK
6 Neal's Yard Covent Garden London WC2H 9DP
Tel: 020 7099 1132
info@slowfood.org.uk
www.slowfood.org.uk
To save & protect small-scale quality specialist food production from industrial standardisation & to list & protect threatened varieties of foodstuffs

Small Animal Veterinary Association (British)
Woodrow House 1 Telford Way Waterwells Business Park Quedgeley Gloucester GL2 2AB
Tel: 01452 726700
administration@bsava.com
www.bsava.com

Small Businesses (Federation of)
Sir Frank Whittle Way Blackpool Business Park Blackpool FY4 2FE
Tel: 01253 336000
email via website
www.fsb.org.uk
UK's largest campaigning pressure group promoting and protecting the interests of the self-employed and owners of small firms

Smallpeice Trust
Holly House 74 Upper Holly Walk Leamington Spa Warwickshire CV32 4JL
Tel: 01926 333200
info@smallpeicetrust.org.uk
www.smallpeicetrust.org.uk
Engineering awareness courses for students 13 - 18 years old

Smith Institute
Somerset House South Wing Strand London WC2R 1LA
Tel: 020 7845 5845
info@smith-institute.org.uk
www.smith-institute.org.uk
Independent think-tank undertaking research/education in issues arising from interaction of equality and enterprise

Smokefree (NHS)
NHS Smoking Helpline: 0800 022 4332
http://smokefree.nhs.uk/

Snow and Ice Data Center (National)
http://nsidc.org/
Support scientific research that informs the world about our planet and our climate systems

SNP Scottish National Party
3 Jackson's Entry Edinburgh EH8 8PJ
Tel: 0800 633 5432
info@snp.org
www2.snp.org

SOCA Serious Organised Crime Agency
PO Box 8000 London SE11 5EN
Tel: 0370 496 7622
www.soca.gov.uk
Tackles crime that affects the UK and our citizens including Class A drugs, people smuggling and human trafficking, major gun crime, fraud, computer crime and money laundering

Social & Economic Research (Institute for)
University of Essex Wivenhoe Park
Colchester CO4 3SQ
Tel: 01206 872957
iser@essex.ac.uk
www.iser.essex.ac.uk
Production and analysis of longitudinal data – evidence tracking changes in the lives of the same individuals over time

Social Care Association
350 West Barnes Lane Motspur Park New Malden KT3 6NB
Tel: 020 8949 5837
email via website
www.socialcaring.co.uk
Professional membership association for all staff in the social care service

Social Democratic & Labour Party
121 Ormeau Rd Belfast BT7 1SH
Tel: 028 9024 7700
info@sdlp.ie
www.sdlp.ie

Social Entrepreneurs (School for)
18 Victoria Park Sq Bethnal Green London E2 9PF
Tel: 020 8981 0300
email via website
www.sse.org.uk
Provide training and opportunities to enable people to use their creative and entrepreneurial abilities more fully for social benefit. Supports individuals to set up new charities, social enterprises and social businesses across the UK

Social Issues Research Centre
27/28 St Clements Oxford OX4 1AB
Tel: 01865 262255
group@sirc.org
www.sirc.org
Independent, non-profit organisation conducting research on social & lifestyle issues

Social Market Foundation
11 Tufton St Westminster London SW1P 3QB
Tel: 020 7222 7060
enquiries@smf.co.uk
www.smf.co.uk
Social policy think tank

Social Sciences (Association for the Teaching of the) ATSS
C/o The British Sociological Association
Palatine House Belmont Business Park
Durham DH1 1TW
Tel: 0191 383 0839
atss@britsoc.org.uk
www.atss.org.uk

Voluntary group of teachers who have joined together to further the interests of Social Science teaching in secondary schools

Social Workers (British Association of)
16 Kent St Birmingham B5 6RD
Tel: 0121 622 3911
email via website
www.basw.co.uk

Socialism see also Christian Socialist Movement

Socialist Health Association
22 Blair Road Manchester M16 8NS
Tel: 0161 286 1926
admin@sochealth.co.uk
www.sochealth.co.uk
Campaigning membership organisation which promotes health and well-being and the eradication of inequalities

Socialist Labour Party
PO Box 706 Barnsley S70 9LE
Tel: 01226 212951
slpscot@btinternet.com
www.socialist-labour-party.org.uk
Aims to end capitalism & replace it with socialism

Soil Association
South Plaza Malborough Street Bristol BS1 3NX
Tel: 0117 314 5000
email via website
www.soilassociation.org
Campaigning for organic food and farming and sustainable forestry

Sojourner Project
Tel: 0207 840 7147
www.eaves4women.co.uk/Sojourner/Sojourner.php
Eaves project for women with no recourse to public funds, who entered the UK on a spousal or partner visa and are eligible to apply for Indefinite Leave to Remain (ILR) under the Domestic Violence Rule

Solar Energy Society UK-ISES
PO Box 489 Abingdon OX14 4WY
Tel: 0776 016 3559
info@uk-ises.org
www.uk-ises.org

Solicitors Family Law Association see Resolution

Solicitors for the Elderly
Suite 17 Conbar House Mead Lane
Hertford SG13 7AD
admin@solicitorsfortheelderly.com
www.solicitorsfortheelderly.com
National association committed to providing high quality legal services for older people, their family and carers

Solidar
Rue de Commerce 22 B-1000 Brussels
Belgium
Tel: 00 322 500 1020
email via website
www.solidar.org
Lobbying for trade union rights,
development and humanitarian aid

Solo Clubs (National Federation of)
PO Box 2278 Nuneaton CV11 5PA
Tel: 02476 736 499
national@federation-solo-clubs.co.uk
www.federation-solo-clubs.co.uk
For widowed, divorced, separated and
single people

**Songwriters, Composers and Authors
(British Academy of)** see BASCA

Sorted In 10
www.sortedin10.co.uk
Practical information and advice on erectile
difficulties

SOS Children's Villages
Terrington House 13-15 Hills Road
Cambridge CB2 1NL
Tel: 01223 365589
info@soschildrensvillages.org.uk
www.soschildrensvillages.org.uk
A child welfare organisation providing
families for orphaned and abandoned
children

Sound and Music SAM
Somerset House The Strand London
WC2R 1LA
Tel: 020 7759 1800
info@soundandmusic.org
www.soundandmusic.org
UK's landmark agency for new music and
sound

Sound Seekers Improving the lives of the
hearing impaired
34 Buckingham Palace Rd London SW1W
0RE
Tel: 020 7233 5700
admin@sound-seekers.org.uk
www.sound-seekers.org.uk
Charity supporting the needs of deaf
children in the developing countries of the
Commonwealth

Sound Sense
www.soundsense.org
Offers comprehensive advice and
information on all aspects of community
music and music and disability

SoundJunction
www.soundjunction.org
Interactive site about exploring, discovering
and creating music. Produced by the

Associated Board of the Royal Schools of
Music

Southbank Centre
Belvedere Road London SE1 8XX
Tel: 020 7960 4200
www.southbankcentre.co.uk
Largest single-run arts centre in the world
and includes Royal Festival Hall, Haywards
Gallery, Queen Elizabeth Hall, Purcell Room,
Poetry Library and 21 acres of creative arts

SOVA Supporting Others Through
Volunteer Action
Unit 201 Lincoln House 1-3 Brixton Road
London SW9 6DE
Tel: 020 7793 0404
email via website
www.sova.org.uk
Recruits & supports volunteers working with
offenders and socially excluded people

Space Agency (European)
www.esa.int

Space Agency (UK)
Polaris House North Star Avenue Swindon
Wiltshire SN2 1SZ
Tel: 020 7215 5000
email via website
www.ukspaceagency.bis.gov.uk
At the heart of the UK efforts to explore and
benefit from space

Space Centre (National)
Exploration Drive Leicester LE4 5NS
Tel: 0116 2610261
info@spacecentre.co.uk
www.spacecentre.co.uk

Spanish Embassy Education Office
20 Peel St London W8 7PD
Tel: 020 7727 2462
consejeria.uk@mec.es
www.educacion.gob.es/exterior/uk/en/
home/index.shtml

Spanish Institute Instituto Cervantes
102 Eaton Sq London SW1W 9AN &
326/330 Deansgate Campfield Avenue
Arcade Manchester M3 4FN
Tel: 020 7235 0353 (London)
Tel: 0161 661 4200 (Manchester)
cenlon@cervantes.es cenman@cervantes.es
http://londres.cervantes.es
http://manchester.cervantes.es
Spanish courses, lectures, cultural activities
and library

Sparks
Heron House 10 Dean Farrar Street
LondonSW1H 0DX
Tel: 020 7799 2111
www.sparks.org.uk
The Children's Medical Research Charity.
Funds pioneering research that has a
practical and positive impact on the lives of
babies and children

Spartacus Educational
www.spartacus.schoolnet.co.uk
History website

Speakability Rebuilding communication
1 Royal Street London SE1 7LL
Tel: 080 8808 9572
Tel: 020 7261 9572
speakability@speakability.org.uk
www.speakability.org.uk
National charity dedicated to supporting and
empowering people with Aphasia and their
carers

Speakers Clubs (Association of)
www.the-asc.org.uk
Exists to promote effective speaking,
communication, and the conduct of
meetings

Speaking up now see Voiceability

**Special Educational Advice (Independent
Parental)** see IPSEA

**Special Educational Needs (National
Association for)** nasen
nasen House 4/5 Amber Business Village
Amber Close Amington Tamworth B77 4RP
Tel: 01827 311500
welcome@nasen.org.uk
www.nasen.org.uk

**Special Educational Needs & Disability
Tribunal** now see Justice

**Special Needs Education (European
Agency for Development in)**
Østre Stationsvej 33 DK-5500 Odense C
Denmark
Tel: 00 45 64 41 00 20
secretariat@european-agency.org
www.european-agency.org

Special Olympics Great Britain
Corinthian House 1st Floor 6-8 Great
Eastern Street London EC2A 3NT
Tel: 020 7247 8891
email via website
www.specialolympicsgb.org
For people with learning disabilities

Specialist Schools and Academies Trust
16th Floor Millbank Tower 21-24 Millbank
London SW1P 4QP
Tel: 020 7802 2300

info@ssatrust.org.uk
www.ssatrust.org.uk
Charity working with schools throughout
England, and in 36 countries across the
world, to raise achievement for all students
(3-19 years)

Speech see also Afasic, Cued Speech
Association UK, Stammering Association
(British), Stammering Children (Michael
Palin Centre for)

**Speech and Language Therapists (Royal
College of)**
2 White Hart Yard London SE1 1NX
Tel: 020 7378 1200
info@rcslt.org
www.rcslt.org
Professional body for UK speech and
language therapists. Sets standards of
practice. Provides careers information to the
public

Spelling Society (The English) TESS
www.spellingsociety.org
Raising awareness of the problems caused
by the irregularity of English spelling and
to promote remedies to improve literacy,
including spelling reform

Spina Bifida see Shine

Spinal Injuries Association SIA
SIA House 2 Trueman Place Oldbrook
Milton Keynes MK6 2HH
Freephone advice line: 0800 980 0501
Tel: 0845 678 6633
email via website
www.spinal.co.uk
Represents spinal cord injured people
regardless of how the impairment occurred

Spinal injury see Aspire

SPIT Signed Performances in Theatre
6 Thirlmere Drive Lymm Cheshire WA13
9PE
email via website
www.spit.org.uk
Charity promoting BSL interpreted
performances of mainstream theatre

Sport & Recreation Alliance
Burwood House 14 Caxton Street London
SW1H 0QT
Tel: 020 7976 3900
info@sportandrecreation.org.uk
www.sportandrecreation.org.uk
Umbrella organisation to which all sport &
recreation governing bodies in the UK are
affiliated

Sport England
3rd Floor Victoria House Bloomsbury
Square London WC1B 4SE
Tel: 08458 508508
info@sportengland.org
www.sportengland.org
To lead the development of sport in England

Sport Northern Ireland
House of Sport 2a Upper Malone Rd
Belfast BT9 5LA
Tel: 028 90 381 222
info@sportni.net
www.sportni.net

Sport Wales
Sophia Gardens Cardiff CF11 9SW
Tel: 0845 045 0904
info@sportwales.co.uk
www.sportwales.org.uk/
Fostering excellence and quality in both
grassroots and elite sports provision

Sports Aid Foundation now see SportsAid

**Sports Association for People with
Learning Disability (UK)** UKSA
1st Floor, 12 City Forum 250 City Road
London EC1V 2PU
Tel: 020 7490 3057
info@uksportsassociation.org
www.uksportsassociation.org
Co-ordinates and develops sporting
opportunities

Sports Centre (Lilleshall National)
Lilleshall National Sports & Conferencing
Centre Near Newport Shropshire TF10 9AT
Tel: 01952 603003
email via website
www.lilleshallnsc.co.uk
Sports and conference centre run on behalf
of Sport England

Sports Coach UK National Coaching
Foundation
114 Cardigan Rd Headingley Leeds LS6
3BJ
Tel: 0113 274 4802
email via website
www.sportscoachuk.org
To help develop sports coaching

Sports Council (Northern Ireland) now
see Sport Northern Ireland

Sports Council UK see UK Sport

Sports Leaders UK
The British Sports Trust 23-25 Linford
Forum Rockingham Drive Linford Wood
Milton Keynes MK14 6LY
Tel: 01908 689180
contact@sportsleaders.org
www.sportsleaders.org
Funds and administers the Sports Leader
awards

SportsAid
3rd Floor Victoria House Bloomsbury
Square London WC1B 4SE
Tel: 020 7273 1975
email via website
www.sportsaid.org.uk
Charity for sports people, helping the next
generation of young British sportsmen and
women to succeed

sportscotland
Doges Templeton on the Green 62
Templeton Street Glasgow G40 1DA
Tel: 0141 534 6500
sportscotland.enquiries@sportscotland.org.
uk
www.sportscotland.org.uk
National agency for sport

**sportscotland Avalanche Information
Service**
www.sais.gov.uk
Daily forecasts on web of avalanche and
climbing conditions in 5 main Scottish
climbing areas from mid December - mid
April

SPPA see Pre-school Play Association
(Scottish)

SPR see Psychical Research (Society for)

SQA see Scottish Qualifications Authority

Squatters (Advisory Service for)
Angel Alley 84b Whitechapel High Street
London E1 7QX
Tel: 020 3216 0099
advice@squatter.org.uk
www.squatter.org.uk

St Fagans: National History Museum
Cardiff CF5 6XB
Tel: 029 2057 3500
email via website
www.museumwales.ac.uk/en/stfagans/
Open-air museum and heritage attraction

St John Ambulance
27 St. John's Lane London EC1M 4BU
Tel: 08700 10 49 50
Email via website
www.sja.org.uk

St Mungo Museum of Religious Life and Art

2 Castle Street Glasgow G4 0RH
Tel: 0141 276 1625
Text Phone: 0141 276 1629
museums@glasgowlife.org.uk
www.glasgowlife.org.uk/museums/our-museums/st-mungo-museum/Pages/home.aspx
Explores the importance of religion in peoples' lives across the world and across time. Aims to promote understanding and respect between people of different faiths and of none

Stakeholder Forum

3 Bloomsbury Place London WC1A 2QL
Tel: 0207 580 6912
info@stakeholderforum.org
www.stakeholderforum.org
International organisation working to advance sustainable development and promote democracy at a global level

Stammering Association (British)

15 Old Ford Rd London E2 9PJ
Helpline:
0845 603 2001
Tel: 020 8983 1003
mail@stammering.org
www.stammering.org

Stammering Children (Michael Palin Centre for) The Association for Research into Stammering in Childhood

Finsbury Health Centre Pine St London EC1R OLP
Tel: 020 7530 4238
email via website
www.stammeringcentre.org
Provides a specialist advice and assessment service for children from all over the UK

STAR see Refugees (Student Action for)

State Education (Campaign for)

98 Erlanger Road London SE14 5TH
Tel: 07932 149942
contact@campaignforstateeducation.org.uk
www.campaignforstateeducation.org.uk
Campaigns for the best in state education for all children

State of the Ocean (International Programme on the)

Tel: 020 7449 6669
email via website
www.stateoftheocean.org
Established by scientists with the aim of saving the Earth and all life on it

Statewatch

PO Box 1516 London N16 0EW
Tel: 020 8802 1882
office@statewatch.org
www.statewatch.org
Monitors the state and civil liberties in the UK and the EU

Statistics see also Australian Bureau of Statistics, Education Statistics (National Center for), General Register Office, Indian Census, National Archives, Office for National Statistics, Register Office for N. Ireland, Register Office for Scotland, World Gazetteer, Worldometers

Statistics New Zealand

www.stats.govt.nz

Steel Can Recycling Information Bureau

c/o Tata Steel Packaging Recycling Trostre Llanelli Carmarthenshire SA14 9SD
Tel: 01554 741111
admin@scrib.org.uk
www.scrib.org
www.tatasteeleurope.com
Offers free resources to everyone, supporting the development of steel can recycling and environmental awareness. Aligned with the curriculum, the Recycling Matters publication is an aid to teaching and learning

Steiner Waldorf Education (European Council for) ECSWE

Kidbrooke Park Forest Row East Sussex RH18 5JA
ecswe@steinerwaldorf.org
www.steinerwaldorfeurope.org
Comprises 26 national Waldorf Associations, representing over 680 schools in Europe. Work in active partnership with other organisations who are concerned with the social emotional education and well being of children

Steiner Waldorf Schools Fellowship

Kidbrooke Park Forest Row East Sussex RH18 5JA
Tel: 01342 822115
office@steinerwaldorf.org
www.steinerwaldorf.org.uk
Serving Steiner Education in the UK & Ireland

Stephen Lawrence Charitable Trust

39 Brookmill Road London SE8 4HU
Tel: 020 8100 2800
information@stephenlawrence.org.uk
www.stephenlawrence.org.uk/
Established in memory of Stephen Lawrence to provide young black people with opportunities to study architecture and associated arts

STEPS Centre
Brighton BN1 9RE
Tel: 01273 915673
steps-centre@ids.ac.uk
www.steps-centre.org
STEPS (Social Technological and
Environmental Pathway to Sustainability)
links environmental sustainability and
technology with poverty reduction and social
justice

Stillbirth & Neonatal Death Charity see
SANDS

Stock Exchange (London)
10 Paternoster Square London EC4M 7LS
Tel: 020 7797 1000
www.londonstockexchange.com

Stonewall
Tower Building York Road London SE1 7NX
Tel: 08000 50 20 20
Minicom: 020 7633 0759
info@stonewall.org.uk
www.stonewall.org.uk
Equality and justice for lesbians, gay men
and bisexuals

Stop Climate Chaos Coalition
c/o Oxfam 232-242 Vauxhall Bridge Road
London SW1V 1AU
Tel: 020 7802 9989
admin@stopclimatechaos.org
www.stopclimatechaos.org
The UK's largest group of people dedicated
to action on climate change and limiting its
impact on the world's poorest communities

Stop Climate Chaos Scotland
Ground Floor 2 Lochside View Edinburgh
EH12 9DH
Tel: 0131 317 4112
info@stopclimatechaosscotland.org
www.stopclimatechaos.org/scotland

Storytelling (Society for)
Morgan Library Aston St Wem SY4 5AU
Tel: 07534 578 386
email via website
www.sfs.org.uk

**Stress Management Association UK
(International)** ISMA UK
PO Box 491 Bradley Stoke Bristol BS34
9AH
Tel: 01179 697284
Tel:0845 680 7 083
stress@isma.org.uk
www.isma.org.uk
Promotes sound knowledge and best
practice

Stroke Association
Stroke House 240 City Road London EC1V
2PR
Helpline: 0303 303 3100
Tel: 020 7566 0300
Textphone: 020 7251 9096
info@stroke.org.uk
www.stroke.org.uk
Helps stroke sufferers and their families to
fight stroke which is the third biggest killer
and most serious disabler in the UK

Strokes see also Different Strokes

Student Awards Agency for Scotland
Gyleview House 3 Redheughs Rigg
Edinburgh EH12 9HH
Tel: 0300 555 0505
Email via website
www.saas.gov.uk
Processes applications from Scottish
students for higher education courses
throughout the UK

Student Drama Festival (National)
Woolyard 54 Bermondsey Street London
SE1 3UD
Tel: 020 7036 9027
info@nsdf.org.uk
www.nsdf.org.uk
Britain's premier festival of the finest student
theatre

Student Loans Company Ltd
100 Bothwell Street Glasgow G2 7JD
Tel: 0141 306 2000 (Admin)
www.slc.co.uk
Administers the Government's student loans
schemes for undergraduates in the UK

Students see also thematic guide -
Education

Students in Europe see ESU

Students Partnership Worldwide now see
Restless Development

**Studies in British Art (Paul Mellon Centre
for)**
16 Bedford Sq London WC1B 3JA
Tel: 020 7580 0311
info@paul-mellon-centre.ac.uk
www.paul-mellon-centre.ac.uk

Study Support see Quality in Study
Support and Extended Services

Sub Aqua Club (British)
Telford's Quay South Pier Road Ellesmere
Port CH65 4FL
Tel: 0151 350 6200
info@bsac.com
www.bsac.com

Substance abuse see thematic guide for Addiction, Alcohol and for Drugs and Substance Abuse

Sudley House
Mossley Hill Road Aigburth Liverpool L18 8BX
Tel: 0151 724 3245
email via website
www.liverpoolmuseums.org.uk/sudley
Explore a Victorian merchant's house with its period furniture and beautiful paintings

Suicide see PAPYRUS (Prevention of Suicides), Survivors of Bereavement by Suicide

Sundial Society (British)
www.sundialsoc.org.uk
Concerned with art & science of gnomonics

SunSmart Campaign
www.sunsmart.com.au
Australian website providing sun protection advice

Support After Murder & Manslaughter see SAMM

Support Dogs
21 Jessops Riverside Brightside Lane Sheffield S9 2RX
Tel: 0114 261 7800
supportdogs@btconnect.com
www.support-dogs.org.uk
Trains dogs for people with epilepsy, physical disabilities and other specific medical conditions

Surf Life Saving GB
1st Floor 19 Southernhay West Exeter EX1 1PJ
Tel: 01392 218007
mail@slsgb.org.uk
www.slsgb.org.uk
Teaching, sport & patrolling of surf beaches

Surfers Against Sewage
Unit 2 Wheal Kitty Workshops St Agnes Cornwall TR5 0RD
Tel: 01872 553001
email via website
www.sas.org.uk
Campaigns for cessation of marine sewage and toxic waste discharge

Surgery Door
www.surgerydoor.co.uk
UK health website

Surname Profiler
www.publicprofiler.org/index.php
Maps the distribution of surnames in Great Britain, both current and historic

Survival International
6 Charterhouse Buildings London EC1M 7ET
Tel: 020 7687 8700
info@survivalinternational.org
www.survivalinternational.org
Supports tribal peoples and helps them protect their lives, lands and human rights

Survivors of Bereavement by Suicide
The Flamsteed Centre Albert Street Ilkeston Derby DE7 5GU
National Helpline: 0844 561 6855
Tel: 0115 944 1117
sobs.admin@care4free.net
www.uk-sobs.org.uk
Charity. Self-help organisation. Offers emotional and practical support to those bereaved by the suicide of a close relative or friend

SurvivorsUK
Ground Floor 34 Great James St London WC1N 3HB
Helpline: 0845 122 1201
Tel: 0207 404 6234
info@survivorsuk.org
www.survivorsuk.org/
Counselling for male rape and sexual abuse

Sustain The Alliance for Better Food & Farming
94 White Lion St London N1 9PF
Tel: 020 7837 1228
sustain@sustainweb.org
www.sustainweb.org
Promoting food and agriculture policies and practices that enhance the health and welfare of people and animals, improve the working and living environment, promote equity and enrich society and culture

SustainAbility
20-22 Bedford Row London WC1R 4EB
Tel: 020 7269 6900
email via website
www.sustainability.com
Specialises in business strategy & sustainable development

Sustrans
2 Cathedral Square College Green Bristol BS1 5DD
Infoline: 0845 113 0065
Tel: 0117 926 8893
info@sustrans.org.uk
www.sustrans.org.uk
UK charity enabling people to travel by foot, bike or public transport for more of the journeys we make every day

& Cymru
123 Bute Street   Cardiff CF10 5AE
sustranscymru@sustrans.org.uk
www.sustrans.org.uk

& Northern Ireland
Ground Floor Premier Business Centres 20
Adelaide Street Belfast BT2 8GD
Tel: 028 9043 4569
belfast@sustrans.org.uk
www.sustrans.org.uk

& Scotland
Glenorchy House 20 Union Street
Edinburgh EH1 3LR
Tel: 0131 539 8122
scotland@sustrans.org.uk
www.sustrans.org.uk

Suzuki Institute (British)
Unit 1.01 The Lightbox 111 Power Road
Chiswick London W4 5PY
Tel: 020 3176 4170
info@britishsuzuki.com
www.britishsuzuki.com
Charity promoting the Suzuki method of
music education

Suzy Lamplugh Trust
National Centre for Personal Safety 218
Strand London WC2R 1AT
Tel: 020 7091 0014
info@suzylamplugh.org
www.suzylamplugh.org
Aims to raise awareness of the importance
of personal safety and to provide solutions
that effect change in order to help people to
avoid violence and aggression and live safer,
more confident lives

Swimming
www.swimming.org
Also gives access to British Swimming,
Amateur Swimming Association and the
Institute of Swimming

Swimming see also Lifeguard Skills,
Lifesavers, Surf Life Saving GB

**Swimming Clubs for people with
Disabilities (National Association for)**
The Willows Mayles Lane Wickham Hants
PO17 5ND
Tel: 01329 833689
naschswim-willows@yahoo.co.uk
www.nasch.org.uk

SYHA Hostelling Scotland
7 Glebe Crescent Stirling FK8 2JA
Tel: 01786 891400
info@syha.org.uk
www.syha.org.uk
Provider of budget accommodation across
all of Scotland from rural areas to cities

T

Table Tennis Association (English)
Queensbury House Havelock Rd Hastings
Road Hastings TN34 1HF
Tel: 01424 722525
admin@etta.co.uk
www.englishtabletennis.org.uk

Tacade
Old Exchange Buildings 6 St Ann's Passage
Manchester M2 6AD
Tel: 0161 836 6850
ho@tacade.co.uk
www.tacade.com
Consultancy, training service, publications,
projects concerned with citizenship, sexual
health & relationships, drugs & alcohol
education & other health related issues

TACT The Adolescent and Children's Trust
The Courtyard 303 Hither Green Lane
Hither Green London SE13 6TJ
Tel: 020 8695 8142
Tel: 0800 232 1157
enquiries@tactcare.org.uk
www.tactcare.org.uk
Finds new families for adoption & fostering
of children with special needs

TAG
info@deaftag.org.uk
www.deaftag.org.uk
Charity promoting access to
electronic communications, including
telecommunications and broadcasting for
deaf and hard of hearing people

Tai Chi Finder
www.taichifinder.co.uk
Locates classes and organisations

Tai Chi Union for Great Britain
5 Corrunna Dr Horsham West Sussex
RH13 5HG
Tel: 01403 257918
email via website
www.taichiunion.com

Talk Adoption
Unit 5 Citygate 5 Blantyre Street
Manchester M15 4JJ
Helpline: 0800 0568 578
Tel: 0161 839 4932
information@afteradoption.org.uk
www.afteradoption.org.uk
Telephone helpline for any young person
who has any issues about adoption

Talking Newspapers and Magazines (National)
National Recording Centre Browning Road Heathfield East Sussex TN21 8DB
Tel: 01435 866102
info@tnauk.org.uk
www.tnauk.org.uk
Subscription service supplying, in alternative format, newspapers and magazines to blind, visually impaired and disabled people

Tall Persons Club (GB & Ireland)
88-90 Hatton Gardens London EC1N 8PN
Tel: 07000 825512
email via website
www.tallclub.co.uk
Promotes interest of tall people and gives practical, medical and social information

Tall Ships Youth Trust
2A The Hard Portsmouth PO1 3PT
Tel: 023 9283 2055
info@tallships.org
www.tallships.org
Dedicated to the personal development of young people aged 12 to 25 through the crewing of their vessels

Tampon Alert (Alice Kilvert)
16 Blinco Rd Urmston Manchester M41 9NF
Tel: 0161 748 3123
enquiries@tamponalert.org.uk
www.tamponalert.org.uk
Provides information about tampon related toxic shock syndrome and support for those affected

Tandem Club
email via website
www.tandem-club.org.uk
To promote and help tandem riding

TAPOL The Indonesia Human Rights Campaign
111 Northwood Rd Thornton Heath Surrey CR7 8HW
Tel: 020 8771 2904
info@tapol.org
www.tapol.org
Campaigns to expose human rights violations in Indonesia, East Timor, West Papua and Aceh

Taskforce for the Rural Poor (International)
12 Eastleigh Ave Harrow Middlesex HA2 0UF
Tel: 020 8864 4740
enquiries@vri-online.org.uk
www.ivcs.org.uk/intaf
Network of development workers, researchers and organisations working for the rural poor in the Third World

Tate Britain
Millbank London SW1P 4RG
Tel: 020 7887 8888
visiting.britain@tate.org.uk
www.tate.org.uk

Tate Liverpool
Albert Dock Liverpool L3 4BB
Tel: 0151 702 7400
visiting.liverpool@tate.org.uk
www.tate.org.uk/liverpool
One of the largest galleries of modern art outside London

Tate Modern
Bankside London SE1 9TG
Tel: 020 7887 8888
visiting.modern@tate.org.uk
www.tate.org.uk/modern

Tate St Ives
Porthmeor Beach St Ives Cornwall TR26 1TG
Tel: 01736 796226
visiting.stives@tate.org.uk
www.tate.org.uk/stives

Tax see also Conscience, HM Revenue and Customs

TaxAid
164-180 Union Street Southwark SE1 0LH
Helpline: 0345 120 3779
email via website
www.taxaid.org.uk
Charity providing free tax advice to people in financial need

TB Alert
FREEPOST LON12815 London NW10 1YS
Helpline: 0845 456 0995
Tel: 01273 234029
info@tbalert.org
www.tbalert.org

Tea Council (UK) Ltd.
Suite 10, 4th Floor Crown House One Crown Square Woking GU21 6HR
Tel: 01483 750599
info@teacouncil.co.uk
www.tea.co.uk

Teacher Support Network
Support lines: England - 08000 562 561
Wales - 08000 855 088
Scotland - 0800 564 2270
email via website
www.teachersupport.info
Counselling, support and services for trainees, working teachers and retired teachers, plus free and confidential 24hr telephone support line

Teacher Training in Primary School Science see SCIcentre

TeacherNet now see Education (Department for)

Teachers of Mathematics (Association of)
Unit 7 Prime Industrial Park Shaftesbury St Derby DE23 8YB
Tel: 01332 346599
admin@atm.org.uk
www.atm.org.uk

Teachers of Religious Education (National Association of) NATRE
1020 Bristol Rd Selly Oak Birmingham B29 6LB
Tel: 0121 472 4242
admin@natre.org.uk
www.natre.org.uk
For RE professionals in primary and secondary schools and higher education

Teaching Council for England (General)
Victoria Square House Victoria Square Birmingham B2 4AJ
Tel: 0370 001 0308
info@gtce.org.uk
www.gtce.org.uk
Aim is to work in the public interest to help improve standards of teaching and learning. October 2011: The government confirmed its intention to have completed closure of the GTC and any transfer of functions by 31 March 2012 – responsibility for teacher regulation will be transferred to the Secretary of State

Teaching Council for Wales (General)
9th Floor Eastgate House 35-43 Newport Road Cardiff CF24 0AB
Tel: 029 20 46 00 99
information@gtcw.org.uk
www.gtcw.org.uk
Protects the public by ensuring that teachers are appropriately qualified and that they maintain high standards of conduct and practice. It works on behalf of teachers to advise government and others on teaching and learning issues

Teaching English & Other Community Languages to Adults (National Association for) NATECLA
South Birmingham College Room HA205, Hall Green Campus Cole Bank Road Hall Green Birmingham B28 8ES
Tel: 0121 688 8121
co-ordinator@natecla.fsnet.co.uk
www.natecla.org.uk
National forum and professional organisation for ESOL teachers

Teaching of Drama (National Association for the) NATD
www.natd.eu

Teaching of English (National Association for the) NATE
50 Broadfield Rd Sheffield S8 0XJ
Tel: 0114 255 5419
info@nate.org.uk
www.nate.org.uk

Tearfund
100 Church Rd Teddington Middlesex TW11 8QE
Tel: 0845 355 8355
enquiry@tearfund.org
www.tearfund.org
Evangelical Christian relief and development charity

Technology Colleges Trust now see Specialist Schools and Academies Trust

Teenage Cancer Trust
3rd Floor 93 Newman Street London W1T 3EZ
Tel: 020 7612 0370
email via website
www.teenagecancertrust.org
Helping young people fight cancer

Telecommunications Action Group now see TAG

Telephone Directories On Web
www.infobel.com/en/world
Telephone directories of various types for most countries of the world, including UK

Telephone Preference Service TPS
DMA House 70 Margaret St London W1W 8SS
Tel: 020 7291 3300
Resgistration Line: 0845 070 0707
tps@dma.org.uk
www.tpsonline.org.uk
Free opt-out facility to avoid cold-call phone sales

Telephone Standards see Phonepay Plus

Telescope (Bradford Robotic)
www.telescope.org/
Collection of telescopes and other instruments on Mount Teide, Tenerife

Television see also thematic guide - Media

Telework Association
61 Charterhouse Road Orpington Kent BR6 9EN
Tel: 0800 616008
email via website
www.telework.org.uk
Encourages take up of telework - providing information and advice to employers and employees

Temperance League (British National) now see BNTL-Freeway

Tenant Participation Advisory Service for England
5th Floor Trafford House Chester Rd Manchester M32 0RS
Tel: 0161 868 3500
info@tpas.org.uk
www.tpas.org.uk
Non-profit organisation providing information, advice, training on all aspects of involving tenants in their housing management

Tenovus
Gleider House Ty Glas Road Cardiff CF14 5BD
Cancer support line: 0808 808 10 10
Tel: 029 2076 8850
post@tenovus.org.uk
www.tenovus.org.uk
Helps patients and their families with essential support

Terrence Higgins Trust
314-320 Gray's Inn Rd London WC1X 8DP
Helpline: 0845 1221 200
Tel: 020 7812 1600
info@tht.org.uk
www.tht.org.uk
www.myhiv.org.uk
Largest HIV and sexual health charity in the UK

Thalidomide Society (UK)
Tel: 01462 438212
info@thalsoc.demon.co.uk
www.thalidomidesociety.co.uk
User-led organisation offering support, information and advice to people affected by Thalidomide and similarly disabled

The Deep
Tower Street Hull HU1 4DP
Tel: 01482 381000
info@thedeep.co.uk
www.thedeep.co.uk
Aquarium telling the story of the world's oceans

The Sikh Way
Sikh Education Council 27 Old Gloucester Street London WC1N 3XX
Tel: 07870 138 616
Email via website
www.thesikhway.com
To raise cultural awareness of Sikh people through workshops and educational activities

Theatre see also thematic guide - Arts, Dance & Music. Refer also to the Dance, Drama, Music & Performing Arts Schools section

Theatre Council (Independent)
12 The Leathermarket Weston St London SE1 3ER
Tel: 020 7089 6821
email via website
www.itc-arts.org
Management association for performing arts organisations

Théâtre de Complicité
14 Anglers Lane London NW5 3DG
Tel: 020 7485 7700
email@complicite.org
www.complicite.org

Theatre for Children and Young People (International Association of)
www.assitej-international.org
Networking, training, advocacy, regular magazine 'Theatre First' and website

Theatre Network (The Amateur)
email via website
http://amdram.co.uk
Promotes amateur theatre

Theatrenet
www.theatrenet.com
News, events and links

Theatres Trust
22 Charing Cross Rd London WC2H 0QL
Tel: 020 7836 8591
info@theatrestrust.org.uk
www.theatrestrust.org.uk
Protecting our theatres and making them better. October 2010 no longer a public body with funding from government but continuing as a charitable trust.

Thesite.org Your guide to the real world
www.thesite.org
Aims to be the first place all young adults turn to when they need support and guidance through life. Provides factsheets and articles on all the key issues facing young people including: sex and relationships; drinking and drugs; work and study; housing, legal and finances; and health and wellbeing

TheyWorkForYou.com
www.theyworkforyou.com
Not for profit organisation to help keep tabs on MPs

Think Global Development Education Association
Can Mezzanine 32-36 Loman Street London SE1 0EH
Tel: 020 7922 7930
info@think-global.org.uk
www.think-global.org.uk
Membership based charity. Works to educate and engage the UK public on global issues

Third Age Trust University of the Third Age (U3A)
National Office Old Municipal Buildings 19 East Street Bromley BR1 1QE
Tel: 020 8466 6139
email via website
www.u3a.org.uk
National representative body. Self-help, self-managed lifelong learning for older people no longer in full time work, pursuing learning not for qualifications, but for fun

Third World First now see People & Planet

Thrive
The Geoffrey Udall Centre Beech Hill Reading RG7 2AT
Tel: 0118 988 5688
email via website
www.thrive.org.uk
www.carryongardening.org.uk
Research, educate and promote the use and advantages of gardening for people with a disability

Tibet see also Free Tibet

Tibet Society UK
Unit 9 139 Fonthill Road Finsbury Park London N4 3HF
Tel: 020 7272 1414
info@tibetsociety.com
www.tibetsociety.com
Works for the freedom of the Tibetan people

Tibetan Nuns Project
www.tnp.org
Helps to support 3 nunneries in NW India through sponsorship and fundraising in the UK

Tim Parry and Johnathan Ball see Foundation for Peace

Time for God
Community House 46-50 East Parade Harrogate N Yorkshire HG1 5RR
Tel: 020 8883 1504
Tel: 01423 536248
office@timeforgod.org
www.timeforgod.org
Christian organisation arranging volunteering opportunities for 18-25 year olds in the UK, Europe and worldwide

Tinnitus Association (British)
Ground Floor Unit 5 Acorn Business Park Woodseats Close Sheffield S8 0TB
Enquiry Line: 0800 018 0527
Tel: 0114 250 9922
Minicom: 0114 258 5694
info@tinnitus.org.uk
www.tinnitus.org.uk
Support and information for people with tinnitus in the UK to help them achieve an improved quality of life

Toc H
The Coach House The Firs High Street Whitchurch Bucks HP22 4JU
Tel: 01296 640055
accounts@toch.org.uk
www.toch.org.uk
Short-term residential volunteering opportunities

Tommy's, the baby charity
Nicholas House 3 Laurence Pountney Hill London EC4R 0BB
PregnancyLine information service: 0800 0147 80 (For advice and information about pregnancy-related issues, contact the Tommy's midwives)
Tel: 0207 398 3400
mailbox@tommys.org
www.tommys.org
Funds medical research on causes and prevention of miscarriage, stillbirth, premature birth and pregnancy health.

Tools for Self Reliance
Ringwood Road Netley Marsh Southampton SO40 7GY
Tel: 023 8086 9697
info@tfsr.org
www.tfsr.org
Volunteers throughout the UK collect and refurbish handtools for grassroots development projects in Africa

Topmarks
contact@topmarks.co.uk
www.topmarks.co.uk
Free website to help teachers, parents and pupils to use the internet effectively for learning

Torture see Amnesty International UK, Medical Foundation for the Care of Victims of Torture, REDRESS

Torture (Association for the Prevention of)
Case postale 2267 CH-1211 Geneva 2
Tel: 00 41 22 919 2170
apt@apt.ch
www.apt.ch
Independent non-governmental organisation committed to working internationally to tackle the global problem of torture and ill-treatment

Torture (The World Organisation Against)
PO Box 21 8, rue du Vieux-Billard CH-1211 Geneva 8 Switzerland
Tel: 00 41 22 809 4939
omct@omct.org
www.omct.org

Tour de France
http://www.letour.fr/indexTDF_us.html
This official website is multilingual

Tour Operators (Association of Independent) AITO
133A St Margaret's Rd Twickenham
Middlesex TW1 1RG
Tel: 020 8744 9280
info@aito.com
www.aito.co.uk
Represents around 160 specialist tour operators

Tourism Concern
Stapleton House 277-281 Holloway Rd
London N7 8HN
Tel: 020 7133 3800
email via website
www.tourismconcern.org.uk
Campaigning for fairly traded and ethical tourism.

Tourism for All
c/o Vitalise Shap Road Industrial Estate
Kendal Cumbria L9 6NZ
Tel: 0845 124 9971
info@tourismforall.org.uk
www.tourismforall.org.uk
Provides information to the public, especially to older or disabled people, on where their specific access needs can be met so that they can fully participate in travel and leisure

Tourism Offices Worldwide Directory
www.towd.com
Provides information about tourist offices in most countries of the world

Town & Country Planning Association
17 Carlton House Terrace London SW1Y 5AS
Tel: 020 7930 8903
tcpa@tcpa.org.uk
www.tcpa.org.uk
Registered charity providing independent comment on planning and environmental policy in the UK and Europe

Town Planning Institute (Royal) RTPI
41 Botolph Lane London EC3R 8DL
Tel: 020 7929 9494
www.rtpi.org.uk
Chartered professional body for town planning in the UK

Trackoff
If you see someone behaving in an unsafe way on the railway or putting other people in danger, report it.
Call free on 0800 40 50 40
email via website
www.trackoff.org/

Britain's rail industry initiative to help educate children and teenagers about safe conduct on the railway

Trade Union see also European Trade Union Confederation, Friedrich Ebert Foundation, Liberal Democrat Trade Unionists (Association of), Simon Jones Memorial Campaign, Solidar

Trade Union Confederation (International) ITUC
Boulevard du Roi Albert II, 5, Bte 1 1210
Brussels Belgium
Tel: 00 32 2 224 0211
info@ituc-csi.org
www.ituc-csi.org

Trade Union Rights (International Centre for)
UCATT House 177 Abbeville Rd London SW4 9RL
Tel: 020 7498 4700
ictur@ictur.org
www.ictur.org

Trades Union Congress
Congress House Great Russell St London WC1B 3LS
Tel: 020 7636 4030
email via website
www.tuc.org.uk

Trading Standards Institute
www.tradingstandards.gov.uk
A one stop shop for consumer protection information

Traffic Statistics (Global) from UK Road Safety Ltd
www.uk-roadsafety.co.uk/Rs_Documents/accident_count.htm
Live updating road safety statistics

Traffic Victims see Roadpeace

Traidcraft
Kingsway Team Valley Trading Estate
Gateshead NE11 0NE
Tel: 0191 491 0591
email via website
www.traidcraft.co.uk
Fighting poverty through fair trade with the developing world. Mail order catalogue available free

Training & Development Agency for Schools TDA
Freephone: 0800 389 2500 (for English speakers)
Freephone: 0800 085 0971 (for Welsh speakers)
Minicom: 0117 915 8161
email via website
www.tda.gov.uk

National agency and recognised sector body responsible for the training and development of the school workforce

Trainline
www.thetrainline.com
Website providing information about train times and tickets for routes on mainland UK and a booking service

Tranquillisers, Antidepressants and Painkillers (Council for Information on)
The JDI Centre 3-11 Mersey View Waterloo Liverpool L22 6QA
Helpline: 0151 932 0102
Tel: 0151 474 9626
cita@citap.org.uk
www.citawithdrawal.org.uk
National helpline, support and information service

Transform Drug Policy Foundation
9-10 King Street Bristol BS1 4EQ
Tel: 0117 325 0295
info@tdpf.org.uk
www.tdpf.org.uk
Advocates an effective system of regulation and control of drugs at national & international levels

Transforming Conflict
National Centre for Restorative Justice in Youth Settings Mortimer Hill Mortimer Berkshire RG7 3PW
Tel: 0118 933 1520
info@transformingconflict.org
www.transformingconflict.org
Citizenship and human rights education

Transparency International
International Secretariat Alt Moabit 96 10559 Berlin Germany
Tel: 00 49 30 3438 20 0
email via website
www.transparency.org
Fights bribery & corruption worldwide. Collects and makes available information about corruption and anti-corruption measures

Transport (Department for)
Great Minster House 76 Marsham St London SW1P 4DR
Tel: 0300 330 3000
FAX9643@dft.gsi.gov.uk
www.dft.gov.uk

Transport & Environment (European Federation for)
Rue d'Edinbourg, 26 1050 Brussels Belgium
Tel: 0032 2 893 0841
info@transportenvironment.org
www.transportenvironment.org

Co-ordinates European groups on transport related environmental campaigning

Transport for London
London Travel 24hr Info Line: 0843 222 1234
Textphone: 020 7918 3015
email via website
www.tfl.gov.uk

Transport Safety (Parliamentary Advisory Council for)
Clutha House 10 Storey's Gate London SW1P 3AY
Tel: 020 7222 7732
admin@pacts.org.uk
www.pacts.org.uk
Registered charity advising parliament on air, rail and road safety issues

Travel advice see Foreign and Commonwealth Office Travel Advice

Travel and Tourism (Institute of)
PO Box 217 Ware Herts SG12 8WY
Tel: 0844 4995 653
enquiries@itt.co.uk
www.itt.co.uk

Travel Warnings (US State Department)
www.travel.state.gov

Travellers see Foreign and Commonwealth Office Travel Advice, Friends, Families and Travellers, MASTA

Treasury see HM Treasury

Tree Council
71 Newcomen Street London SE1 1YT
Tel: 020 7407 9992
info@treecouncil.org.uk
www.treecouncil.org.uk
Promotes improvement of environment through planting and conservation of trees

Treloar Trust
Upper Froyle Alton Hampshire GU34 4JX
Tel: 01420 526526
email via website
www.treloar.org.uk
Provides residential education, care & independence training for young people aged 7-25 with severe physical disabilities

Triathlon Association (British)
PO Box 25 Loughborough Leicestershire LE11 3WX
Tel: 01509 226161
info@britishtriathlon.org
www.britishtriathlon.org

Triumph over Phobia (TOP UK)
PO Box 3760 Bath BA2 3WY
Tel: 0845 6009601
info@topuk.org
www.topuk.org
Network of self-help groups for phobia and
obsessive compulsive disorder sufferers

TRóCAIRE
Maynooth Co. Kildare Ireland
Tel: 00 353 1 6293333
email via website
www.trocaire.org
Irish Catholic agency for world development

Tropical Diseases (Hospital for)
Mortimer Market Building Capper Street
Tottenham Court Road London WC1E 6JB
Tel: 020 7388 9600 (Travel clinic)
email via website
www.thehtd.org
Travel health advice

Tuberous Sclerosis Association UK
www.tuberous-sclerosis.org
Group of parents, affected individuals and
doctors interested in promoting greater
understanding of the condition and providing
mutual support for affected families

Turn2us To access benefits & grants
www.turn2us.org.uk
Helps people in financial need gain access
to welfare benefits, charitable grants and
other financial help

Turning Point
Standon House 21 Mansell Street E1 8AA
Tel: 020 7481 7600
info@turning-point.co.uk
www.turning-point.co.uk
Drug, alcohol-related & mental health
problems & learning disabilities

Twentieth Century Society
70 Cowcross St London EC1M 6EJ
Tel: 020 7250 3857
caseworker@c20society.org.uk
www.c20society.org.uk
Exists to safeguard the heritage of
architecture & design in Britain from 1914
onwards

Twins & Multiple Births Association
(TAMBA)
2 The Willows Gardner Rd Guildford
Surrey GU1 4PG
Twinline: 0800 138 0509
Tel: 01483 304 442
enquiries@tamba.org.uk
www.tamba.org.uk
Information and support for families
with twins, triplets and more and for
professionals involved with their care

U

U3A see Third Age Trust

UCAS
Rosehill New Barn Lane Cheltenham GL52
3LZ
Customer services: 0871 468 0 468
Tel: 01242 222 444
enquiries@ucas.ac.uk
www.ucas.com
Handles all applications for entry to UK
universities and other higher education
institutions

UEFA
Route de Genève 46 Case postale CH-
1260 Nyon 2 Switzerland
Tel: 00 41 848 00 2727
www.uefa.com

UJIA
37 Kentish Town Road London NW1 8NX
Tel: 020 7424 6400
central@ijia.org
To help guarantee a sustainable and positive
future for the people of the Galil and the
Jewish community of the UK

UK Border Agency
www.ind.homeoffice.gov.uk
Responsible for securing the United
Kingdom borders and controlling migration
in

UK Climate Projections UKCP09
http://ukcp09.defra.gov.uk/
Provide UK climate information designed
to help those needing to plan how they will
adapt to a changing climate

UK Islamic Education Waqf UKIEW
17 Brendon Road Nottingham NG8 1HW
Tel: 0115 8602048
info@ukiew.org
www.ukiew.org
Subsidises fees for children of families in
financial need to attend Islamic schools
which are members of Association of Muslim
Schools of UK

UK New Citizen
Tel: 07946 80 89 76
info@uknewcitizen.org
www.uknewcitizen.org
Promotes the social integration of refugees,
immigrants and their descendants through
citizenship and a sense of democracy

UK Parents Lounge
www.ukparents.co.uk
Online magazine and forum for parents

UK Sport
40 Bernard St London WC1N 1ST
Tel: 020 7211 5100
info@uksport.gov.uk
www.uksport.gov.uk
Governing body for whole of UK for elite
athletics

UK Theatre Web
www.uktw.co.uk
Database of information on people, plays,
venues, performances etc. and extensive
archive

UK Youth
Avon Tyrrell Braggers Lane Bransgore
Hampshire BH23 8EE
Tel: 01425 672347
info@ukyouth.org
www.ukyouth.org
National youth work charity, helping young
people to develop skills and interests

UKDPC see Disabled People's Council (UK)

UKERNA see JANET

UKRC Advancing Gender Equality in
Science, Engineering and Technology
Listerhills Park of Science and Commerce
40-42 Campus Road Bradford BD7 1HR
Tel: 01274 436485
email via website
www.theukrc.org
Provision of advice, services and policy
consultation regarding the under-
representation of women in science,
engineering, technology and the built
environment (SET)

**UN High Commissioner for Human
Rights (Office of the)**
www.ohchr.org

unbiased.co.uk
2nd Floor 117 Farringdon Rd London EC1R
3BX
Tel: 0330 303 0025
contact@ifap.org.uk
www.unbiased.co.uk
Promotes the value and accessibility of
independent financial advice to the public

**Unborn Children (Society for the
Protection of)**
3 Whitacre Mews Stannary Street London
SE11 4AB
Tel: 020 7091 7091
information@spuc.org.uk
www.spuc.org.uk
Defending human life, through education
and political lobbying, from conception until
natural death

Uncaged Campaigns
5th Floor, Alliance House 9 Leopold Street
Sheffield S1 2GY
Tel: 0114 283 1155
info@uncaged.co.uk
www.uncaged.co.uk
Pressure group campaigning to abolish
animal experiments and for animal rights

Undercurrents
Old Exchange Pier Street Swansea SA1
1RY
Tel: 01792 455900
info@undercurrents.org
www.undercurrents.org
Video support and training and archive
materials for the use of social and
environmental groups

Understanding Animal Research
25 Shaftesbury Avenue London W1D 7EG
Tel: 020 7287 2818
Email via website
www.understandinganimalresearch.org.uk
Information about the use of animals in
medical research

UNESCO United Nations Educational,
Scientific & Cultural Organisation
1 rue Miollis 75732 Paris Cedex 15 France
Tel: 00 331 45 68 1000
Email via website
www.unesco.org

UNHCR The UN Refugee Agency
Strand Bridge House 138 - 142 Strand
London WC2R 1HH
Tel: 020 7759 8090
gbrloea@unhcr.org
www.unhcr.org.uk
Safeguards the rights and well-being of
refugees

Uni4me
www.aimhigher.ac.uk/uni4me/home/
Answers questions about what it is like to be
a university student. Website developed by
all the universities in Greater Manchester

UNICEF UK
2 Kingfisher House Woodbrook Crescent
Billericay CM12 0EQ
Tel: 0844 801 2414
Email via website
www.unicef.org.uk
United Nations children's fund

Unicorn Theatre for Children
147 Tooley Street More London Southwark
London SE1 2HZ
Tel: 020 7645 0500
admin@unicorntheatre.com
www.unicorntheatre.com

Union Cycliste Internationale see Cycling Union (International)

Unistats
http://unistats.direct.gov.uk/
Brings information about universities and their courses together in one place

Unite
35 King Street Covent Garden London WC2E 8JG
Tel: 020 7420 8900
email via website
www.unitetheunion.org
Unite was formed by a merger between two of Britain's' leading unions, the T&G and Amicus

Unite Against Fascism
PO Box 36871 London WC1X 9XT
Tel: 020 7801 2782
email via website
www.uaf.org.uk
New national campaign against the extreme right

United Nations Association of the UK
3 Whitehall Court London SW1A 2EL
Tel: 020 7766 3454
Email via website
www.una-uk.org
Membership organisation, campaigning and educating to turn the ideals of the UN into a reality

United Nations Development Programme (UNDP)
www.undp.org
The UN's global development network

United Nations Educational, Scientific & Cultural Organisation see UNESCO

United Nations Environment Programme
www.unep.org

United Nations High Commissioner for Refugees see UNHCR

United Nations Volunteers
www.unvolunteers.org
Volunteer arm of the United Nations

United Reformed Church
86 Tavistock Place London WC1H 9RT
Tel: 020 7916 2020
urc@urc.org.uk
www.urc.org.uk

Universities and Colleges Sport (British)
20-24 Kings Bench Street London SE1 0QX
Tel: 020 7633 5080
email via website
www.bucs.org.uk
Organises inter-university championships and GB team for World University Championships

University of the First Age
St Paul's Cottages 59-60 Water Street The Jewellery Quarter Birmingham B3 1EP
Tel: 0121 212 9838
ufa@ufa.org.uk
www.ufa.org.uk
National educational charity working in partnership to develop the confidence and achievement of young people

University of the Third Age Trust see Third Age Trust

UNLOCK National Association of Reformed Offenders
35A High St Snodland Kent ME6 5AG
Tel: 01634 247350
enquiries@unlock.org.uk
www.unlock.org.uk
Aims to overcome the social exclusion and discrimination which currently exists and which prevents reformed offenders from re-integrating into society and leading crime-free lives

Unlock Democracy incorporating Charter 88
9 Cynthia Street Islington London N1 9JF
Tel: 020 7278 4443
info@unlockdemocracy.org.uk
www.unlockdemocracy.org.uk
Campaigns for a modern democracy and human rights

UPDATE Disability Information Scotland
Hays Community Business Centre 4 Hay Avenue Edinburgh EH16 4AQ
Helpline: 0131 669 1600
info@update.org.uk
www.update.org.uk

Urban Saints
Kestin House 45 Crescent Rd Luton LU2 0AH
Tel: 01582 589 850
email@urbansaints.org
www.urbansaints.org
Christian youth organisation with weekly groups and summer holidays

US Department of State
www.state.gov

US Educational Advisory Service see Fulbright Commission

V

Values Education for Life (The Collegiate Centre for)
College House Albion Place Hockley Hill
Birmingham B18 5AQ
Tel: 0121 523 0222
info@vefl.org.uk
http://birmingham.schooljotter.com/valueseducation
Working with young people who are at risk of social exclusion

Vatican
www.vatican.va
Website giving information on many aspects of the Vatican in many European languages

Vatican Museums & Sistine Chapel
www.christusrex.org/www1/vaticano/0-Musei.html
Information on various Vatican museums including opening dates and times

Vegan Society
21 Hylton Street Hockley Birmingham B18 6HJ
Tel: 0121 523 1730
email via website
www.vegansociety.com
Advocating lifestyle free from animal products

Vegetarian & Vegan Foundation
8 York Court Wilder St Bristol BS2 8QH
Tel: 0117 970 5190
info@vegetarian.org.uk
www.vegetarian.org.uk
Provides free information on becoming vegetarian/vegan. Researches health & nutrition issues relating to diet

Vegetarian Society
Parkdale Dunham Rd Altrincham Cheshire WA14 4QG
Tel: 0161 925 2000
info@vegsoc.org
www.vegsoc.org

Vegetarians International Voice for Animals see Viva!

Venice in Peril Fund
Unit 4, Hurlingham Studios Ranelagh Gardens London SW6 3PA
Tel: 020 7736 6891
info@veniceinperil.org
www.veniceinperil.org
British charity for restoration and preservation of Venice

Venture Trust A chance for change...
6d Bruntsfield Terrace Edinburgh EH1 4EX
or Applecross Strathcarron IV54 8ND
Tel: 0131 228 7700
info@venguretrust.org.uk
www.venturetrust.org.uk
Exploring new ways to help young people make positive changes in their lives

Venuemasters
Enquiry hotline: 0114 249 3090
info@venuemasters.co.uk
www.venuemasters.co.uk
Offers free venue finding service for meeting and accommodation facilities at UK academic venues

Victim Support
Supportline: 0845 30 30 900
supportline@victimsupport.org.uk
www.victimsupport.org
National charity providing help and information to people affected by crime

Victorian Society
1 Priory Gardens London W4 1TT
Tel: 020 8994 1019
admin@victoriansociety.org.uk
www.victoriansociety.org.uk
Provides advice to owners and public authorities regarding preservation and repair of Victorian and Edwardian buildings. Aims to involve and educating the public to increase the likelihood of conserving buildings

Video Standards Council
Kinetic Business Centre Theobald St
Borehamwood Herts WD6 4PJ
Tel: 020 8387 4020
vsc@videostandards.org.uk
www.videostandards.org.uk
Advises shops on legality of video sales and rental

Vision Aid Overseas
12 The Bell Centre Newton Rd Crawley W Sussex RH10 2FZ
Tel: 01293 535016
info@vao.org.uk
www.vao.org.uk
Provides spectacles and training in eye care in developing countries.

Visit London
2 More London Riverside London SE1 2RR
Tel: 08701 566 366
email via website
www.visitlondon.com
The official tourism organisation for London

Visit Wales
Tel: 08708 300 306
Minicom: 08701 211255
info@visitwales.co.uk
www.visitwales.com

VisitBritain
Headquarters 1 Palace Street London
SW1E 5HX
Tel: 020 7578 1000
email via website
www.visitbritain.org
www.visitbritain.com
Marketing Britain overseas and developing
the visitor economy

VisitEngland The England Tourist Board
1 Palace Street London SW1E 5HX
Tel: 020 7578 1400
email via website
www.enjoyengland.com
National organisation for marketing England
overseas and in the UK

VisitScotland
Ocean Point 1 94 Ocean Drive Edinburgh
EH6 6JH
Tel: 0845 225 5121 (brochures)
info@visitscotland.com
www.visitscotland.com
The official site of Scotland's national
tourism organisation

Visual Arts & Galleries Association
The Old Village School Witcham Ely CB6
2LQ
Tel: 01353 776356
admin@vaga.co.uk
www.vaga.co.uk
Network & voice for the visual arts world

Vitiligo Society
125 Kennington Road London SE11 6SF
Freephone: 0800 018 2631
www.vitiligosociety.org.uk/
Promotes and funds research projects

Viva! Vegetarians International Voice for
Animals
8 York Court Wilder St Bristol BS2 8QH
Tel: 0117 944 1000
info@viva.org.uk
www.viva.org.uk
Campaigning organisation working to end
factory farming and educate people on
vegetarian and vegan diets

Vivisection see also Anti-Vivisection
Society (National), BUAV, Humane
Research Trust, PETA Foundation, Respect
for Animals, Uncaged Campaigns, Viva!

**Vivisection (British Union for the
Abolition of)** see BUAV

Voice Getting young voices heard
320 City Road London EC1V 2NZ
Freefone: 0808 800 5792
Tel: 020 7833 5792
info@voiceyp.org
www.voiceyp.org
Working and campaigning for children and
young people in public care

Voice for Choice
www.vfc.org.uk
Campaigning for abortion on request
throughout the UK

Voice of the Listener and Viewer
PO Box 401 Gravesend Kent DA12 9FY
Tel: 01474 338711 or 01474 338716
info@vlv.org.uk
www.vlv.org.uk
Represents the citizen and consumer on all
broadcasting issues and works for quality
and diversity

Voice UK
Rooms 100-106 Kelvin House RTC
Business Centre London Road Derby DE24
8UP
Helpline: 0808 802 8686
email via website
/www.voiceuk.org.uk
National charity supporting people with
learning disabilities and other vulnerable
people who have experience crime or abuse

VoiceAbility
Mount Pleasant House Huntingdon Road
Cambridge CB3 0RN
Tel: 01223 555800
Email via website
www.voiceability.org
Gives a voice to vulnerable people and
supports them to take control of their lives

Voices Foundation Transforming children
through singing
34 Grosvenor Gardens London SW1W 0DH
Tel: 020 7730 6677
vf@voices.org.uk
www.voices.org.uk
Music education

Volleyball Association (English)
SportPark Loughborough University 3
Oakwood Drive Loughborough LE11 3QF
Tel: 01509 227722
info@volleyballengland.org
www.volleyballengland.org

Volleyball Association (Scottish)
48 The Pleasance Edinburgh EH8 9TJ
Tel: 0131 556 4633
www.scottishvolleyball.org

Voluntary Action (Wales Council for) see
WCVA

Voluntary Agencies (International Council of) ICVA
26-28 avenue Guiseppe Motta 1202 Geneva Switzerland
Tel: 00 41 22 950 96 00
secretariat@icva.ch
www.icva.ch
Advocacy network of non-governmental organisations

Voluntary and Community Action (National Association for) NAVCA
The Tower 2 Furnival Square Sheffield S1 4QL
Tel: 0114 2786636
Textphone: 0114 278 7025
navca@navca.org.uk
www.navca.org.uk
The England-wide organisation which provides services to local councils for voluntary service

Voluntary Arts Network VAN
121 Cathedral Road Pontcanna Cardiff CF11 9PH
Tel: 029 20 395395
info@voluntaryarts.org
www.voluntaryarts.org
To help people, irrespective of age, participate in the arts

Voluntary Euthanasia Society see Dignity in Dying

Voluntary Organisations (National Council for) (NCVO)
Regent's Wharf 8 All Saints St London N1 9RL
Tel: 020 7713 6161
ncvo@ncvo-vol.org.uk
www.ncvo-vol.org.uk
Umbrella body. Giving voice and support to civil society

Voluntary Organisations (Scottish Council for)
Mansfield Traquair Centre 15 Mansfield Place Edinburgh EH3 6BB
Freephone: 0800 169 0022 (Free information and advice for anyone involved in the voluntary sector)
Tel: 0131 556 3882
enquiries@scvo.org.uk
www.scvo.org.uk
Umbrella body for all voluntary organisations in Scotland

Voluntary Service Overseas see VSO

Voluntary Youth Services (National Council for)
3rd Floor Lancaster House 33 Islington High Street London N1 9LH
Tel: 020 7278 1041

mail@ncvys.org.uk
www.ncvys.org.uk
Represents voluntary organisations working with young people and volunteers

Volunteer Action for Peace
16 Overhill Road East Dulwich London SE22 0PH
Tel: 0844 20 90 927
action@vap.org.uk
www.vap.org.uk
UK based charity organisation that works towards creating and preserving international peace, justice and human solidarity for people and their communities

Volunteer Development Scotland
Jubilee House Forthside Way Stirling FK8 1QZ
Tel: 01786 479593
vds@vds.org.uk
www.vds.org.uk
Support organisations in Scotland who involve volunteers

Volunteer Now
129 Ormeau Road Belfast Northern Ireland BT7 1SH
Tel: 028 9023 6100
info@volunteernow.co.uk
www.volunteernow.co.uk
Promotes and develops volunteering in Northern Ireland

Volunteer Reading Help
14-15 Perseverance Works 38 Kingsland Rd London E2 8DD
Tel: 020 7729 4087
info@vrh.org.uk
www.vrh.org.uk
Supports volunteers to help primary school children

Volunteering England
Regent's Wharf 8 All Saints St London N1 9RL
Tel: 020 7520 8900
volunteering@volunteeringengland.org.uk
www.volunteering.org.uk
Promotes volunteering as a force for change for volunteers and the community as a whole

Volunteers For Rural India
12 Eastleigh Avenue South Harrow HA2 0UF
Tel: 020 8864 4740
enquiries@vri-online.org.uk
www.vri-online.org.uk
DRIVE scheme - opportunity to live in rural India

VSO (Voluntary Service Overseas)
Carlton House 27A Carlton Drive Putney
London SW15 2BS
Volunteering advice line: 020 8780 7500
enquiry@vso.org.uk
www.vso.org.uk
International development charity that works
through volunteers

W

W.I. see Women's Institutes (National
Federation of)

Wales Environment Link
27 Pier Street Aberystwyth Ceredigion
SY23 2LN
Tel: 01970 611621
Email via website
www.waleslink.org

Wales Office
Discovery House Scott Harbour Cardiff
CF10 4HA
Tel: 020 7270 0534
wales.office@walesoffice.gsi.gov.uk
www.walesoffice.gov.uk

Wales PPA see Pre-School Providers
Association (Wales)

WalesRails
www.walesrails.co.uk
Independent survey of railways & the
attractions they serve

Walk to School see Living Streets

Walker Art Gallery
William Brown Street Liverpool L3 8EL
Tel: 0151 478 4199
email via website
www.liverpoolmuseums.org.uk/walker

Walking see also Backpackers Club,
Byways & Bridleways Trust, Long Distance
Walkers Association

Walking Federation (British)
Ground Floor 5 Windsor Square Silver
Street Reading RG1 2TH
info@bwf-ivv.org.uk
www.bwf-ivv.org.uk
Member clubs organising events designed
for people of all ages and abilities

Walkit
www.walkit.com
The urban walking route planner

WalkScotland
www.walkscotland.com
Scottish outdoor & countryside news
updated weekly

WAMT see Women and Manual Trades

War on Want
44-48 Shepherdess Walk London N1 7JP
Tel: 020 7324 5040
support@waronwant.org
www.waronwant.org
Campaign against world poverty

War Resisters League
339 Lafayette St New York NY 10012
Tel: 001 212 228 0450
wrl@warresisters.org
www.warresisters.org

Waste Watch
56-64 Leonard Street London EC2A 4LT
Tel: 020 7549 0300
email via website
www.wastewatch.org.uk
Deals with methods of reduction, reuse and
recycling of waste

WATCh? see What about the Children?

Water Aid
2nd Floor, 47-49 Durham Street London
SE11 5JD
Tel: 020 7793 4594
Email via website
www.wateraid.org
Sustainable provision of safe water,
sanitation and hygiene education to the
world's poorest

Water Services (Office of) OFWAT
Centre City Tower 7 Hill St Birmingham B5
4UA
Tel: 0121 644 7500
enquiries@ofwat.gsi.gov.uk
www.ofwat.gov.uk
Protecting consumers, promoting value and
safeguarding the future

Water Ski & Wakeboard (British)
Unit 3 The Forum Hanworth Lane Chertsey
Surrey KT16 9JX
Tel: 01932 560 007
Email via website
www.britishwaterski.org.uk
Governing body

Waterfront Museum (National)
Oystermouth Road Maritime Quarter
Swansea SA1 3RD
Tel: 01792 638950
email via website
www.museumwales.ac.uk/en/swansea/
Industry and innovation in Wales, now and
over the last 300 years

Waterway Recovery Group
Island House Moor Road Chesham HP5
1WA
Tel: 01494 783 453
enquiries@wrg.org.uk
www.wrg.org.uk
Restores derelict canals

Waterways (British)
64 Clarendon Road Watford WD17 1DA
Tel: 01923 201120
enquiries.hq@britishwaterways.co.uk
www.britishwaterways.co.uk
Manages canals and navigable rivers in
UK. October 2010 Government announced
its intention to transfer British Waterways'
functions into a new charitable body, similar
to National Trust, by April 2012

Waterways Museum (National)
South Pier Road Ellesmere Port Cheshire
CH65 4FW
Tel: 0151 355 5017
ellesmereport@thewaterwaystrust.org.uk
www.nwm.org.uk

WCVA Voluntary Action (Wales Council for)
Baltic House Mount Stuart Square Cardiff
CF10 5FH
Helpdesk: 0800 2888 329
Minicom: 0808 1804 080
help@wcva.org.uk
www.wcva.org.uk
Voice of the voluntary sector

We Are What We Do
71 St John Street London EC1M 4NJ
Tel: 020 7148 7666
info@wearewhatwedo.org
www.wearewhatwedo.org
Not-for-profit behaviour change company
that creates ways for millions of people to
do more small, good things

Weather Centre (BBC Online)
www.bbc.co.uk/weather

**Weights & Measures Association
(British)**
EG8 Panther House 39 Mount Pleasant
London WC1X 0AN
bwma@email.com
www.bwmaonline.com
Promotion of traditional weights and
measures and opposition to compulsory
metrication

Wellbeing of Women
27 Sussex Place Regent's Park London
NW1 4SP
Tel: 020 7772 6400
wellbeingofwomen@rcog.org.uk
www.wellbeingofwomen.org.uk
Medical research charity concerned with
women's reproductive health

Welsh Government Llywodraeth Cymru
Cathays Park Cardiff CF10 3NQ
Tel: 0300 0603300 or 0845 010 3300
Tel: Welsh: 0300 0604400 or 0845 010 4400
wag-en@mailuk.custhelp.com
www.wales.gov.uk

Welsh Athletics
Cardiff International Sports Stadium
Leckwith Road Cardiff CF11 8AZ
Tel: 02920 644870
office@welshathletics.org
www.welshathletics.org
Official governing body for athletics in Wales

**Welsh Language Board (Bwrdd yr Iaith
Gymraeg)**
Market Chambers 5/7 St Mary Street
Cardiff CF10 1AT
Tel: 029 2087 8000
Email via website
www.welsh-language-board.org.uk

Welsh Language Society see Cymdeithas
yr Iaith Gymraeg

Welsh National Opera
Wales Millennium Centre Bute Place Cardiff
CF10 5AL
Tel: 029 2063 5000
email via website
www.wno.org.uk

Welsh Sports Council see Sport Wales

Wessex Cancer Trust
Bellis House 11 Westwood Road
Southampton Hampshire SO17 1DL
Tel: 023 8067 2200
wct@wessexcancer.org
www.wessexcancer.org
Independent charity. Supports many
aspects of cancer care, including leading
edge research, the improvement of patient
facilities, purchase of much needed
equipment, patient grants, complementary
therapy and counselling services

Whale & Dolphin Conservation Society
Brookfield House 38 St Paul St
Chippenham Wiltshire SN15 1LY
Tel: 01249 449 500
info@wdcs.org
www.wdcs.org

What About The Children?
Ebrington Grove Lane Uxbridge UB8 3RG
Tel: 0845 602 7145
enquiries@whataboutthechildren.org.uk
www.whataboutthechildren.org.uk
National charity. Information, research
& education on the emotional needs of
children under 3

Wheelchair Sports Foundation (British)
see WheelPower

WheelPower
Stoke Mandeville Stadium Guttmann Rd
Stoke Mandeville Bucks HP21 9PP
Tel: 01296 395995
info@wheelpower.org.uk
www.wheelpower.org.uk
British wheelchair sport. Promotes and
develops sports for both adults and children
with disabilities

Wheels for All see Cycling Projects

Which?
Castlemead Gascoyne Way Hertford SG14
1LH
Tel: 01992 822800
email via web
www.which.co.uk
Campaign to protect consumer rights,
review products and offer independent
advice

White House
1600 Pennsylvania Avenue NW Washington
DC 20500
Tel: 001 202 456 1414
email via website
www.whitehouse.gov

White Ribbon Alliance For safe
motherhood
2nd Floor, 138 Portobello Road London
W11 2DZ
Tel: 0207 965 6060
info-uk@whiteribbonalliance.org
www.whiteribbonalliance.org
Aims to ensure that pregnancy and childbirth
are safe for all women and newborns in
every country around the world.

Whizz-Kidz
4th Floor Portland House Bressenden
Place London SW1E 5BH
Tel: 020 7233 6600
Email via website
www.whizz-kidz.org.uk
Provides mobility equipment to disabled
children

Who Cares? Trust
Kemp House 152-160 City Rd London
EC1V 2NP
Tel: 020 7251 3117
mailbox@thewhocarestrust.org.uk
www.thewhocarestrust.org.uk
Improving education, employment, health,
counselling & information services for young
people in public care

Wild Flower Society
www.thewildflowersociety.com
Identifies and records wild flowers in Britain

Wildfowl & Wetlands Trust (WWT) Saving
wetlands for wildlife & people
Slimbridge Gloucs GL2 7BT
Tel: 01453 891900
enquiries@wwt.org.uk
www.wwt.org.uk
Leading conservation organisation saving
wetlands for wildlife and people across the
world

Wildlife Aid
Randalls Farm House Randalls Rd
Leatherhead Surrey KT22 0AL
Helpline: 09061 800 132
Tel: 01372 377332 (Admin only)
Email via website
www.wildlifeaid.org.uk
Rescue, rehabilitation, care of sick, injured
and orphaned British wildlife and strong
educational emphasis

Wildlife and Countryside Link
89 Albert Embankment London SE1 7TP
Tel: 020 7820 8600
enquiry@wcl.org.uk
www.wcl.org.uk
Brings together voluntary organisations
in the UK to protect and enhance wildlife,
landscape and the marine environment,
and to further the quiet enjoyment and
appreciation of the countryside

Wildlife Trusts (Royal Society of)
The Kiln Waterside Mather Rd Newark
NG24 1WT
Tel: 01636 677711
enquiry@wildlifetrusts.org
www.wildlifetrusts.org
Administers lottery funding to provide grants
to communities for various environmental
projects. The 47 regional Wildlife Trusts are
dedicated to protecting wildlife for the future

Williams Syndrome Foundation (UK)
161 High Street Tonbridge Kent TN9 1BX
Tel: 01732 365152
email via website
www.williams-syndrome.org.uk
Supports those affected by this non-
hereditary chromosomal disorder

Willow Foundation
Willow House 18 Salisbury Square Hatfield
Hertfordshire AL9 5BE
Tel: 01707 259777
info@willowfoundation.orguk
www.willowfoundation.org.uk
Charity dedicated to improving the quality of
life of seriously ill young people aged 16-40
through the provision of special days

WILPF see Peace & Freedom (Women's
International League for)

Wimbledon
www.wimbledon.com
Official site of the tennis tournament

Wind Energy Association (European)
EWEA
Rue d'Arlon 80 B-1040 Brussels Belgium
Tel: 0032 2 213 1811
ewea@ewea.org
www.ewea.org

Wind Sand & Stars
PO Box 4322 Bath BA1 2BU
Tel: 01225 320 839
office@windsandstars.co.uk
www.windsandstars.co.uk
School journeys and expeditions for young
people to the desert and mountains of Sinai,
Egypt

Windsurfing Association (UK) UKWA
PO Box 703 Haywards Heath RH16 9EE
admin@ukwindsurfing.com
www.ukwindsurfing.com
Organises & provides first class national
competition

Winston Churchill Memorial Trust
South Door 29 Great Smith Street London
SW1P 3BL
Tel: 0207 799 1660
office@wcmt.org.uk
www.wcmt.org.uk
Offers Fellowships to acquire knowledge
and experience abroad.

Winston's Wish The charity for bereaved
children
4th Floor St James's House St James
Square Cheltenham Gloucestershire GL50
3PR
Helpline: 08452 03 04 05
Tel: 01242 515157
info@winstonswish.org.uk
www.winstonswish.org.uk
Offers practical support and guidance
to families, professionals and anyone
concerned about a grieving child

**Winvisible (Women with visible &
invisible disabilities)** contact Crossroads
Women's Centre
www.allwomencount.net

Wired Safety
www.wiredsafety.org
Dedicated to helping protect children in
cyberspace

Wireless for the Blind Fund (British)
10 Albion Place Maidstone Kent ME14 5DZ
Tel: 01622 754 757
Email via website
www.blind.org.uk

Provides radio equipment on free permanent
loan to registered blind & partially-sighted
people in need

Womankind Worldwide
2nd Floor, Development House 56-64
Leonard Street London EC2A 4LT
Tel: 020 7549 0360
info@womankind.org.uk
www.womankind.org.uk
Working with women in the developing world
and the UK in the field of human rights

Women (National Assembly of)
92 Wansbeck Avenue Cullercoats Tyne &
Wear NE30 3DJ
Tel: 0191 2520961
naw@sisters.org.uk
www.sisters.org.uk
Campaigning for full social, economic, legal,
political & cultural equality for women

Women and Manual Trades WAMT
52-54 Featherstone St London EC1Y 8RT
Tel: 020 7251 9192
info@wamt.org
www.wamt.org
The national organisation for tradeswomen
and women training in skilled craft trades

**Women Entrepreneurs (British
Association of)**
Tel: 01827 312 812
president@bawe-uk.org
www.bawe-uk.org
British Affiliate to the World Association
of Women Entrepreneurs (FCEM) with 40
countries and 80,000 members founded in
France 1945

Women in Prison
Unit 10, The Ivories 6 Northampton Street
London N1 2HY
Freephone advice line: 0800 953 0125
(offenders and ex-offenders seeking help
only)
Tel: 020 7359 6674
Email via website
www.womeninprison.org.uk
Campaigns on issues affecting women in
prison and provides education, support
and welfare. NB Do not have the capacity
to respond to enquiries from students and
researchers. Please refer to website

Women in Publishing
info@womeninpublishing.org.uk
www.womeninpublishing.org.uk
Website of information designed to promote
the status of women working in publishing

Women Into Science & Engineering (WISE)
The UKRC Listerhills Park of Science & Commerce 40-42 Campus Road Bradford BD7 1HR
Tel: 01274 436485
wise@theukrc.org
www.wisecampaign.org.uk

Women living under Muslim laws
PO Box 28455 London N19 5JT
www.wluml.org
An international network that provides information, solidarity and support for all women whose lives are shaped, conditioned or governed by laws and customs said to derive from Islam

Women of Great Britain (National Council of) Giving women a voice
72 Victoria Road Darlington Co. Durham DL1 5JG
Tel: 01325 367375
info@ncwgb.org
www.ncwgb.org
Work nationally and internationally on issues of concern to women

Women Solicitors (Association of)
Email via website
www.womensolicitors.org.uk
Network helping to promote the potential and success of each women solicitor at every stage of her career

Women Working Worldwide
MMU Manton Building Rosamond St West Manchester M15 6LL
Tel: 0161 247 1760 or 247 6171
contact@women-ww.org
www.women-ww.org
Supports the struggles of women workers throughout the world

Women's Aid (Scottish)
2nd Floor 132 Rose Street Edinburgh EH2 3JD
24 hr Domestic Abuse Helpline: 0800 027 1234
Tel: 0131 226 6606
contact@scottishwomensaid.org.uk
www.scottishwomensaid.org.uk
National office for 40 affiliated Women's Aid groups in Scotland who provide information, refuge and support for women, children and young people experiencing domestic abuse

Women's Aid (Welsh)
Wales Domestic Abuse Helpline: 0808 8010800
email via website
www.welshwomensaid.org
National umbrella organisation for women's aid groups throughout Wales

Women's Aid Federation (N. Ireland)
129 University St Belfast BT7 1HP
24 hr domestic violence helpline: 0800 917 1414
Tel: 028 9024 9041
info@womensaidni.org
www.womensaidni.org
Provides help for women and children experiencing domestic violence in N. Ireland

Women's Aid Federation of England
PO Box 391 Bristol BS99 7WS
24hr National Domestic Violence Helpline: 0808 2000 247
Tel: 0117 944 4411 (general enquiries only)
info@womensaid.org.uk helpline@womensaid.org.uk
www.womensaid.org.uk
www.thehideout.org.uk
National charity working to end domestic violence against women and children. We support a network of over 500 domestic and sexual violence services across the UK

Women's Archive of Wales
South Wales Miners' Library Hendrefoelan Campus Gower Road Swansea SA2 7NB
info@womensarchivewales.org
www.womensarchivewales.org
Collecting, preserving and publicising sources for women's history in Wales

Women's Bowling Federation (English)
www.fedbowls.co.uk

Women's Clubs (National Association of)
5 Vernon Rise King's Cross Rd London WC1X 9EP
Tel: 020 7837 1434
www.nawc.org.uk
Clubs to promote education, recreation and friendship for the benefit of women

Women's Cricket see Cricket Board (England & Wales)

Women's Engineering Society
The IET Michael Faraday House Six Hills Way Stevenage Hertfordshire SG1 2AY
Tel: 01483 765506
Email via website
www.wes.org.uk
Inspiring women as engineers, scientists and technical leaders

Women's Environmental Network
Ground Floor 20 Club Row London E2 7EY
Tel: 020 7481 9004
info@wen.org.uk
www.wen.org.uk
Campaigns on issues which link women, the environment and health

Women's Food & Farming Union
Cargill plc Witham St Hughs Lincoln LN6 9TN
Tel: 0844 3350 342
secretary@wfu.org.uk
www.wfu.org.uk

Women's Golf Association (English)
11 Highfield Rd Edgbaston Birmingham B15 3EB
Tel: 0121 456 2088
office@englishwomensgolf.org
www.englishwomensgolf.org

Women's Institutes (National Federation of) NFWI
104 New Kings Rd London SW6 4LY
Tel: 020 7371 9300
Email via website
www.thewi.org.uk
Largest voluntary organisation for women in the UK

Women's Library Celebrating and recording women's lives
London Metropolitan University 25 Old Castle St London E1 7NT
Tel: 020 7320 2222
moreinfo@thewomenslibrary.ac.uk
www.thewomenslibrary.ac.uk
The most extensive collection of women's history in the UK

Women's Register (National)
Unit 23 Vulcan House Vulcan Rd North Norwich NR6 6AQ
Tel: 0845 450 0287
Email via website
www.nwr.org
Coordinates women's groups to enable women to find new friends and widen their horizons

Women's Resource Centre
Ground Floor East 33-41 Dallington Street London EC1V 0BB
Tel: 020 7324 3030
Email via website
www.wrc.org.uk
Co-ordinating and support body for non-profit groups working for and with women

Women's Royal Voluntary Service see WRVS

Women's Sports & Fitness Foundation
Victoria House Bloomsbury Square London WC1B 4SE
Tel: 0207 273 1740
email via website
www.wsf.org.uk
Charity that campaigns to make physical activity an everyday part of life for women and girls. Aims to create a nation of active women

Women's Therapy Centre
10 Manor Gardens London N7 6JS
Tel: 020 7263 6200
Tel: 020 7263 7860 (General enquiries)
enquiries@womenstherapycentre.co.uk
www.womenstherapycentre.co.uk
Individual and group psychotherapy advice and information, training and education to professionals

Wood Green Animal Shelters
601 Lordship Lane Wood Green London N22 5LG
Tel: 0844 248 8181
info@woodgreen.org.uk
www.woodgreen.org.uk
Take in unwanted and lost animals, provide shelter and care, find secure and loving homes, provide advice, support and guidance for pet owners and increase the public's awareness of its responsibility towards animals in society

Woodcraft Folk
Units 9-10 83 Crampton Street London SE17 3BQ
Tel: 020 7703 4173
info@woodcraft.org.uk
www.woodcraft.org.uk
Develop children's self-confidence and build their awareness of society around them, through activities, outings and camps. Help members understand important issues like the environment, world debt and global conflict etc

Woodland Trust
Kempton Way Grantham Lincolnshire NG31 6LL
Tel: 01476 581111
enquiries@woodland-trust.org.uk
www.woodland-trust.org.uk
Protects native woodland heritage

Woodworking Federation (British)
Royal London House 22-25 Finsbury Square London EC2A 1DX
Tel: 0844 209 2610
bwf@bwf.org.uk
www.bwf.org.uk
Trade association for the woodworking and joinery manufacturing industry in the UK

Wool Museum (National)
Dre-Fach Felindre Llandysul Carmarthenshire SA44 5UP
Tel: 01559 370929
email via website
www.museumwales.ac.uk/en/wool/

Work & Pensions (Department for) DWP
www.dwp.gov.uk
Government agency responsible for benefit & pension claims

Work Foundation
21 Palmer Street London SW1H 0AD
Tel: 020 7976 3565
email via website
www.theworkfoundation.com
Campaign to make a better working life for
employees

Workaholics Anonymous
www.workaholics-anonymous.org
Self help groups with international coverage

Workers Educational Association WEA
4 Luke Street London EC2A 4XW
Tel: 020 7426 3450
national@wea.org.uk
www.wea.org.uk
Provides education for adults who are not
full-time students

Working Class Movement Library
51 The Crescent Salford M5 4WX
Tel: 0161 736 3601
Email via website
www.wcml.org.uk
A unique collection capturing the stories
and struggles of ordinary people's efforts
to improve their world - Access by
appointment only

Working Families
1-3 Berry St London EC1V 0AA
Helpline: 0800 013 0313
Tel: 020 7253 7243
advice@workingfamilies.org.uk
www.workingfamilies.org.uk
Information & support & campaigns on
issues of concern for working parents

Working For A Charity
NCVO Regent's Wharf 8 All Saints Street
London N1 9RL
Tel: 020 7520 2512
www.workingforacharity.org.uk
Offers training courses aimed at people
wanting to move into the voluntary sector

**Working Men's College for Women &
Men**
44 Crowndale Rd London NW1 1TR
Tel: 020 7255 4700
info@wmcollege.ac.uk
www.wmcollege.ac.uk
Europe's longest established college for
adult learning

Working on Wheels
Brunswick Court Brunswick Square Bristol
BS2 8PE
Tel: 0117 916 6580
info@workingonwheels.org
www.workingonwheels.org
Promotes effective use of community work
on converted vehicles throughout the UK

& Scotland
Gilmerton Community Centre 4 Drum Street
Edinburgh EH17 8QG
Tel: 0131 664 4922
lesley@workingonwheels.org
www.workingonwheels.org
Promotes effective use of community work
on converted vehicles throughout the UK

Working with men
Unit K308 Tower Bridge Business Complex
100 Clements Road London SE16 4DG
Tel: 020 7237 5353
info@workingwithmen.org
www.workingwithmen.org
Develop and implement support projects
that benefit the development of men and
boys. Raise awareness of issues impacting
upon men and boys in addition to trying
to gain a greater understanding of the
underlying issues behind male behaviour

WorkLife Support Limited
Suite G, Maples Business Centre 144
Liverpool Road London N1 1LA
Tel: 0845 873 5680
Email via website
www.worklifesupport.com
Provides employee assistance programmes
for LEAs and schools and also programmes
where staff feedback to management ideas
of what works in a school to improve its
atmosphere and culture

World AIDS Day
www.worldaidsday.org
Takes place on 1st December every year

World Bank
www.worldbank.org
Committed to helping achieve the MDGs.
Source of financial and technical assistance
to developing countries around the world.
Fighting poverty and helping people help
themselves and their environment by
providing resources and sharing knowledge

**World Cancer Research Fund
International** WCRF International –
Stopping cancer before it starts
22 Bedford Square London WC1B 3HH
Tel: 020 734 34200
international@wcrf.org
http://wcrf.org
Not-for-profit umbrella association that leads
a global network of cancer charities based
in the US, UK, Netherlands, Hong Kong and
France. Dedicated to funding research and
education programmes into the link between
food, nutrition, physical activity, weight
maintenance and cancer risk

World Challenge Expeditions
17-21 Queens Road High Wycombe
Buckinghamshire HP13 6AQ
Tel: 01494 427600
email via website
www.world-challenge.co.uk
Provides leadership, teamwork & personal
development training for young people

World Cup
www.fifa.com
The official site for the Football World Cup

World Development Movement
66 Offley Road London SW9 0LS
Tel: 020 7820 4900
wdm@wdm.org.uk
www.wdm.org.uk
Campaigns to tackle the root causes of
poverty

World Food Programme (United Nations)
Via C.G.Viola 68 Parco dei Medici 00148
Rome Italy
Tel: 00 39 06 65131
Email via website
www.wfp.org

World Gazetteer
www.world-gazetteer.com
World population statistics

World Health Organisation
Avenue Appia 20 1211 Geneva 27
Switzerland
Tel: 00 41 22 791 21 11
info@who.int
www.who.int

World Horse Welfare
Anne Colvin House Ada Cole Avenue
Snetterton Norwich NR16 2LR
UK Welfare Hotline: 08000 480180
Tel: 01953 498682
info@worldhorsewelfare.org
www.ilph.org
Charity dedicated to giving abused and
neglected horses a second chance in life

World Jewish Relief
Oscar Joseph House 54 Crewys Road
London NW2 2AD
Tel: 020 8736 1250
info@wjr.org.uk
www.wjr.org.uk
Acts on behalf of the UK Jewish community
to provide emergency and development
aid to those in need throughout the world
regardless of race, religion or ethnic origin

World Ju-Jitsu Federation (Ireland)
PO Box 142 Ballymena BT43 7YB
Tel: 028 2565 1502
wjjf@jujitsuireland.com
www.jujitsuireland.com

World Land Trust
FREEPOST ANG20000 PO Box 27
Halesworth Suffolk IP19 8ZT
Tel: 0845 054 4422
info@worldlandtrust.org
www.worldlandtrust.org
Purchases and protects critically threatened
wilderness areas

World Monuments Fund Britain
2 Grosvenor Gardens London SW1W 0DH
Tel: 020 7730 5344
enquiries@wmf.org.uk
www.wmf.org.uk
Charity that promotes on-site conservation
of cultural landmarks and supports
educational activities

World Museum
William Brown Street Liverpool L3 8EN
Tel: 0151 478 4393
Learning department: 0151 478 4296
email via website
www.liverpoolmuseums.org.uk/wml
Discover treasures from around the world,
explore outer space and meet live creatures!

World Rugby Museum
Twickenham Stadium Rugby Road
Twickenham Middlesex TW1 1DZ
Tel: 020 8892 8877
Email via website
www.rfu.com/microsites/museum

**World Society for the Protection of
Animals** see WSPA International

World Space Week
www.worldspaceweek.org
The Largest Public Space Event on Earth –
celebrated in over 55 Nations every October
4-10

World Tourism Organization WTO
Capitán Haya 42 28020 Madrid Spain
Tel: 00 34 91 567 81 00
omt@unwto.org
www.world-tourism.org
Inter-governmental body for the promotion
and development of tourism

World Trade Organisation WTO
www.wto.org
Administers multilateral trade agreements,
acts as a forum for negotiations, and
handles international trade disputes

World Travel & Tourism Council
1-2 Queen Victoria Terrace Sovereign Court
London E1W 3HA
Tel: 0870 727 9882/ 020 7481 8007
enquiries@wttc.org
www.wttc.org

World Vision UK
Opal Drive Fox Milne Milton Keynes MK15 0ZR
Tel: 01908 84 10 00
info@worldvision.org.uk
www.worldvision.org.uk
Humanitarian aid and development agency

World Wide Fund for Nature see WWF-UK

World Wide Opportunities on Organic Farms see WWOOF

Worldometers
www.worldometers.info
World statistics updated in real time

WorldWide Volunteering
7 North St Workshops Stoke sub Hamdon Somerset TA14 6QR
Tel: 01935 825588
wwv@wwv.org.uk
www.wwv.org.uk
Search and match database of 350,000 UK and worldwide volunteering opportunities for all ages

WRAP
The Old Academy 21 Horse Fair Banbury OX16 0AH
Resource Efficiency Helpline: 0808 100 2040
Switchboard: 01295 819 900
Envirowise advice line: 0800 585 794
Email via website
www.wrap.org.uk
Works in partnership, helping businesses and the general public to reduce waste, to use more recycled material and recycle more things more often

Writers in Education (National Association of) NAWE
PO Box 1 Sheriff Hutton York YO60 7YU
Tel: 01653 618 429
Email via website
www.nawe.co.uk
Supports development of creative writing

Writers' Guild of Great Britain
40 Rosebery Avenue London EC1R 4RX
Tel: 020 7833 0777
erik@writersguild.org.uk
www.writersguild.org.uk

WriteToThem.com
Email via website
www.writetothem.com
Allows you to contact your MP even if you don't know their name or your constituency

WRVS
Beck Court Cardiff Gate Business Park Cardiff CF23 8RP
Tel: 0845 600 5885
Email via website
www.wrvs.org.uk
Registered charity helping people maintain independence and dignity in their homes and communities, particularly in later life

WSPA International World Society for the Protection of Animals
5th Floor 222 Grays Inn Road London WC1X 8HB
Tel: 020 7587 0500
wspa@wspa.org.uk
www.wspa.org.uk
Promoting animal welfare. Concentrate on regions of the world where few, if any, measures exist to protect animals

WWF-UK
Panda House Weyside Park Godalming Surrey GU7 1XR
Tel: 01483 426 444
Email via website
www.wwf.org.uk
www.panda.org (international)
Charity conserving and protecting endangered species & habitats, for the benefit of people & nature

WWOOF UK World Wide Opportunities on Organic Farms
PO Box 2154 Winslow Buckinghamshire MK18 3WS
Email via website
www.wwoof.org.uk
www.wwoof.org (international)
Membership charity teaching people about organic growing and low-impact lifestyles through hands-on experience in the UK. Holds a list of organic farms, gardens and smallholdings, all offering food and accommodation in exchange for practical help on their land

Y

Y Care International
Kemp House 152-160 City Road London EC1V 2NP
Tel: 020 7549 3150
enquiries@ycareinternational.org
www.ycareinternational.org
YMCA's international relief and development agency. Work in partnership with YMCAs across the developing world to respond to the needs of the most disadvantaged young people

Yachting Association (Royal)
RYA House Ensign Way Hamble Southampton SO31 4YA
Tel: 023 8060 4100
enquiries@rya.org.uk
www.rya.org.uk
National body for all forms of boating, including dinghy and yacht racing, motor and sail cruising

Year Out Group
Queensfield 28 Kings Road Easterton Wiltshire SN10 4PX
email via website
www.yearoutgroup.org

YHA see Youth Hostel Association (UK)

YMCA England
45 Beech Street
London, EC2Y 8AD
Tel: 020 7070 2160
enquiries@ymca.org.uk
www.ymca.org.uk
Committed to helping young people, particularly at times of need

Ymgyrch Diogelu Cymru Wledig see Protection of Rural Wales (Campaign for the)

Yoga (British Wheel of)
25 Jermyn St Sleaford Lincs NG34 7RU
Tel: 01529 306851
office@bwy.org.uk
www.bwy.org.uk

Yoga (Iyengar Institute)
223a Randolph Ave Maida Vale London W9 1NL
Tel: 020 7624 3080
office@iyi.org.uk
www.iyi.org.uk

Young Christian Workers
St Josephs, off St Joseph's Grove Watford Way London NW4 4TY
Tel: 020 8203 6290
info@ycwimpact.com
www.ycwimpact.com

Young Concert Artists Trust
23 Garrick St London WC2E 9BN
Tel: 020 7379 8477
info@ycat.co.uk
www.ycat.co.uk
Identifies, nurtures and promotes outstanding young classical soloists and chamber ensembles trained in the UK

Young Engineers
Chiltlee Manor Liphook Hampshire GU30 7AZ
Tel: 01428 727265
Email via website
www.youngeng.org
National network of engineering, electronics & technology clubs and run engineering competitions in schools and colleges

Young Enterprise
Peterley House Peterley Rd Oxford OX4 2TZ
Tel: 01865 776845
Info@young-enterprise.org.uk
www.young-enterprise.org.uk
Practical enterprise activities for young people aged 4-25, supported by business and industry volunteers

Young Farmers' Clubs (National Federation of)
YFC Centre 10th Street Stoneleigh Park Kenilworth Warwickshire CV8 2LG
Tel: 024 7685 7200
post@nfyfc.org.uk
www.nfyfc.org.uk

Young Father's Initiative
Working with Men Unit K401 Tower Bridge Business Complex 100 Clements Road London SE16 4DG
Tel: 020 7237 5353
info@workingwithmen.org
www.young-fathers.org.uk
Information and advice about fatherhood

Young Men's Christian Association see YMCA England

Young People in Focus
23 New Rd Brighton BN1 1WZ
Tel: 01273 693311
info@youngpeopleinfocus.org.uk
www.youngpeopleinfocus.org.uk
Enable the organisations and individuals that work with young people and their families to improve what they do, through research and evaluation, training and publications

Young People with ME (Association of)
10 Vermont Place Tongwell Milton Keynes
MK15 8JA
Tel: 08451 232389
info@ayme.org.uk
www.ayme.org.uk
Offers cheerful support for all children and
young people with ME aged 5 to 25. Free
membership to eligible applicants

Young People's Learning Agency
Cheylesmore House Quinton Road
Coventry CV1 2WT
Learner Support helpline: 0800 121 8989
Tel: 0845 337 2000
enquiries@ypla.gov.uk
www.ypla.gov.uk
October 2010: under review

Young Scot
InfoLine: 0808 801 0338 or text 'callback' to
07781 484 317
infoline@youngscot.org
www.youngscot.org
Scottish youth information for 11 - 26 year
olds

Young Women's Christian Association
now see Platform 51

YoungMinds
48-50 St John Street London EC1M 4DG
Parents helpline: 0808 802 5544
Tel: 020 7336 8445
Email via website
www.youngminds.org.uk
National charity committed to improving
the mental health of all children and young
people

Your Life
www.your-life.com
Accurate information related to reproductive
and sexual health

Youth Access
1 - 2 Taylors Yard 67 Alderbrook Rd
London SW12 8AD
Tel: 020 8772 9900
admin@youthaccess.org.uk
www.youthaccess.org.uk
Provides referral service to youth
information, advice & counselling services
across the country

Youth Advocacy Service (National) NYAS
Egerton House Tower Road Birkenhead
Wirral CH41 1FN
Tel: 0800 616101
Tel: 0151 649 8700
help@nyas.net
www.nyas.net
Help and guidance for all young people

Youth Agency (National)
Eastgate House 19-23 Humberstone Road
Leicester LE5 3GJ
Tel: 0116 242 7350
Email via website
www.nya.org.uk
Aims to advance youth work to promote
young people's development and their voice
in public life

Youth Arts Network (English National)
see ENYAN

Youth Arts Wales (National)
245 Western Ave Cardiff CF5 2YX
Tel: 02920 265 060
nyaw@nyaw.co.uk
www.nyaw.co.uk
Representing the National Youth Brass
Band, Chamber Ensemble, Choir, Orchestra
and Theatre of Wales and National Youth
Dance, Wales

Youth at Risk
The Old Warehouse 31 Upper King St
Royston Herts SG8 9AZ
Tel: 01763 241120
Email via website
www.youthatrisk.org.uk
Support and mentors for disadvantaged 15
-19 year olds

Youth Award Scheme see ASDAN

Youth Cancer Trust
Tracy Ann House 5 Studland Road Alum
Chine Bournemouth BH4 8HZ
Tel: 01202 763591
admin@yct.org.uk
www.yct.org.uk
Provide free, fun activity based holidays
for young people (aged 14 to 30) suffering
with cancer or any malignant disease, from
anywhere in the UK and the Irish Republic,
or who are patients of any UK hospital. You
can also come on a holiday if you have been
in remission for up to five years or are living
with the effects of having had cancer as a
teenager

Youth Choir of Great Britain (National)
NYCBG
Pelaw House University of Durham Leazes
Road Durham DH1 1TA
Tel: 0191 3348110
office@nycgb.net
www.nycgb.net
Nurtures exceptional young musical talent.
Offers residential courses and concerts

Youth Clubs (UK) see UK Youth

Youth Council (British)
6th Floor Hillgate House 26 Old Bailey London EC4M 7HW
Tel: 0845 458 1489
email via website
www.byc.org.uk
National voice for young people in the UK

Youth Council for N. Ireland
Forestview Purdy's Lane Belfast BT8 7AR
Tel: 028 9064 3882
info@ycni.org
www.ycni.org
Advisory body on quality of life for children and young people

Youth for Christ
Business Park East Unit D2, Coombswood Way Halesowen West Midlands B62 8BH
Tel: 0121 502 9620
email via website
www.yfc.co.uk
Christian outreach

Youth Hostel see also Hostelling International, Hostelling International (N. Ireland), Hostels.com, SYHA Hostelling Scotland

Youth Hostel Association (N. Ireland)
now see Hostelling International (N. Ireland)

Youth Hostel Association (UK) YHA
Trevelyan House Dimple Road Matlock Derbyshire DE4 3YH
Tel: 01629 592600 or 0800 0191700
customerservices@yha.org.uk
www.yha.org.uk
Accommodation and activity provider. All ages, families and groups welcome

Youth Hostel Federation (International)
now see Hostelling International

Youth Hostels Association (Scottish)
now see SYHA Hostelling Scotland

Youth in Action
British Council 10 Spring Gardens London SW1A 2BN
Tel: 0116 242 7400 (if you are based in England)
Tel: 0131 313 2488 (if you are based in Scotland)
Tel: 0300 062 5604 (if you are based in Wales)
yia@nya.org.uk
www.britishcouncil.org/youthinaction
UK National Agency for the European Commission's YOUTH programme eg youth exchange, voluntary service etc

Youth Information The information toolkit for Young People
www.youthinformation.com
Information for young people from the National Youth Agency

Youth Justice Board for England and Wales now see Justice

Youth Music
One America St London SE1 0NE
Tel: 020 7902 1060
info@youthmusic.org.uk
www.youthmusic.org.uk
UK charity using music to transform the lives of disadvantaged children and young people

Youth Music Theatre (National)
Adrian House 27 Vincent Square London SW1P 2NN
Tel: 020 7802 0386
enquiries@nymt.org.uk
www.nymt.org.uk

Youth Opera (British)
LSBU 103 Borough Road London SE1 0AA
Tel: 020 7815 6090
info@byo.org.uk
www.byo.org.uk

Youth Orchestra (National of GB)
Somerset House South Building London WC2R 1LA
Tel: 020 7759 1880
info@nyo.org.uk
www.nyo.org.uk

Youth Sport Trust
SportPark Loughborough University 3 Oakwood Drive Loughborough LE11 3QF
Tel: 01509 226600
info@youthsporttrust.org
www.youthsporttrust.org
Quality physical education and sport programmes for all young people

Youth Theatre see Scottish Youth Theatre, Youth Music Theatre (National)

Youth Theatre of GB (National)
Woolyard 52 Bermondsey Street London SE1 3UD
Tel: 020 7281 3863
info@nyt.org.uk
www.nyt.org.uk
Acting, administration, costume making, lighting and sound, scenery and prop making or stage management for 14 - 21 year olds

Youth Theatres (National Association of)
NAYT
Arts Centre Vane Terrace Darlington DL3
7AX
Tel: 01325 363 330
Email via website
www.nayt.org.uk
Umbrella organisation for youth theatres

Youthhealthtalk
DIPEx PO Box 428 Witney Oxon OX28
9EU
Tel: 01865 744209
info@youthhealthtalk.org
www.youthhealthtalk.org
Young people's real life experiences of
health and lifestyle

YouthNet UK
First Floor 50 Featherstone Street London
EC1Y 8RT
Tel: 020 7250 5700
email via website
www.youthnet.org
Website directs young people to where they
can obtain information about organisations
and publications

YWCA now see Platform 51

Z

Zoo Check see Born Free Foundation

Zoos (London & Whipsnade) now see
ZSL London Zoo and ZSL Whipsnade Zoo

ZSL London Zoo
Outer Circle Regent's Park London NW1
4RY
Tel: 0844 225 1826
Email via website
www.zsl.org

ZSL Whipsnade Zoo
Dunstable Bedfordshire LU6 2LF
Tel: 0844 225 1826
Email via website
www.zsl.org

Universities & Colleges

The majority of institutions accept applications via UCAS, but some, particularly specialist dance, drama, music and art institutions, require a direct application.

The institutions are arranged in alphabetical order by place name wherever possible.

UCAS
(Universities & Colleges Admissions Service)
www.ucas.ac.uk

Unistats
unistats.direct.gov.uk

Aberdeen
www.abdn.ac.uk/sras

Abertay
www.abertay.ac.uk

Aberystwyth
www.aber.ac.uk

Accrington & Rossendale College
www.accrosshighereducation.co.uk

American InterContinental University - London
www.aiulondon.ac.uk

Anglia Ruskin University
www.anglia.ac.uk

Anglo European College of Chiropractic
www.aecc.ac.uk

Askham Bryan College
www.askham-bryan.ac.uk

Aston
Birmingham
www.aston.ac.uk

Bangor
www.bangor.ac.uk

Barking and Dagenham College
www.barkingdagenhamcollege.ac.uk

Barony College
www.barony.ac.uk

Basingstoke College of Technology
www.bcot.ac.uk

Bath
www.bath.ac.uk

Bath College (City of)
www.citybathcoll.ac.uk

Bath Spa
www.bathspa.ac.uk

Bedford College
www.bedford.ac.uk

Bedfordshire
www.beds.ac.uk

Belfast
see Queen's University, St. Mary's University College & Stranmillis University College

Birkbeck
University of London
www.bbk.ac.uk

Birmingham
www.birmingham.ac.uk

Birmingham (City College)
www.citycol.ac.uk

Birmingham City University
www.bcu.ac.uk

Birmingham Metropolitan College
www.bmetc.ac.uk

Birmingham, University College
www.ucb.ac.uk

Bishop Burton College
Beverley, East Yorkshire
www.bishopburton.ac.uk

Bishop Grosseteste College
Lincoln
www.bishopg.ac.uk

Blackburn College
www.blackburn.ac.uk

Blackpool and The Fylde College
www.blackpool.ac.uk

Bolton
www.bolton.ac.uk

Bournemouth
www.bournemouth.ac.uk

Bournemouth
The Arts University College at
www.aucb.ac.uk

BPP University College
www.bpp.com

Bradford
www.bradford.ac.uk

Bradford College
www.bradfordcollege.ac.uk

Bridgwater College
www.bridgwater.ac.uk

Brighton
www.brighton.ac.uk

Brighton & Sussex Medical School
www.bsms.ac.uk

Bristol
www.bristol.ac.uk

Bristol College (City of)
www.cityofbristol.ac.uk

Bristol Filton College
www.filton.ac.uk

British Institute of Technology &
E-commerce
London
www.bite.ac.uk

British School of Osteopathy
www.bso.ac.uk

Brooklands College
www.brooklands.ac.uk

Brooksby Melton College
www.brooksbymelton.ac.uk

Brunel University
www.brunel.ac.uk

Buckingham
www.buckingham.ac.uk

Buckinghamshire New University
www.bucks.ac.uk

Cambridge
www.cam.ac.uk

Canterbury Christ Church University
www.canterbury.ac.uk

Cardiff
www.cardiff.ac.uk

Cardiff see also UWIC
www.uwic.ac.uk

Carmarthenshire College
see Coleg Sir Gar

Castle College Nottingham
now see South Nottingham College

Central Lancashire
www.uclan.ac.uk

Central School of Speech & Drama
www.cssd.ac.uk

Chester (University College)
www.chester.ac.uk

Chichester
www.chiuni.ac.uk

Chichester College
www.chichester.ac.uk

City University
www.city.ac.uk

Cleveland College of Art and Design
www.ccad.ac.uk

Cliff College
www.cliffcollege.ac.uk

Colchester Institute
www.colchester.ac.uk

Coleg Llandrillo, Cymru
www.llandrillo.ac.uk

Coleg Menai
www.menai.ac.uk

Coleg Sir Gar/Carmarthenshire College
www.colegsirgar.ac.uk

College of Agriculture, Food and Rural
Enterprise
Antrim
www.cafre.ac.uk

Cornwall College
www.cornwall.ac.uk

Courtauld Institute of Art
(University of London)
www.courtauld.ac.uk

Coventry
www.coventry.ac.uk

Coventry (City College)
www.covcollege.ac.uk

Craven College
www.craven-college.ac.uk

Creative Arts, University for the
www.ucreative.ac.uk

Croydon College
www.croydon.ac.uk

Cumbria University
www.cumbria.ac.uk

Dartington College of Arts
Now see Falmouth

Dearne Valley College
www.dearne-coll.ac.uk

Derby
www.derby.ac.uk

Dewsbury College
now see Kirklees College

Doncaster College
www.don.ac.uk

Duchy College
www.duchy.ac.uk

Dudley College of Technology
www.dudleycol.ac.uk

Dundee
www.dundee.ac.uk

Durham
www.dur.ac.uk

Durham (New College)
www.newdur.ac.uk

Ealing, Hammersmith & West London
College
www.wlc.ac.uk

East Anglia
www.uea.ac.uk

East London
www.uel.ac.uk

Easton College
www.easton-college.ac.uk

East Riding College
www.eastridingcollege.ac.uk

East Surrey College
(Incorporating Reigate School of Art and Design)
www.esc.ac.uk

Edge Hill University
www.edgehill.ac.uk

Edinburgh
www.ed.ac.uk

Edinburgh
see also Heriot-Watt, Napier, Queen Margaret

Edinburgh College of Art
www.eca.ac.uk

Edinburgh: Queen Margaret University
www.qmu.ac.uk

Essex
www.essex.ac.uk

European Business School, London
www.ebslondon.ac.uk

European School of Economics
www.eselondon.ac.uk

European School of Osteopathy
www.eso.ac.uk

Exeter
www.exeter.ac.uk

Exeter College
www.exe-coll.ac.uk /he

Falmouth (University College)
www.falmouth.ac.uk

Farnborough College of Technology
www.farn-ct.ac.uk

Glamorgan, Cardiff and Pontypridd
www.glam.ac.uk

Glasgow
www.gla.ac.uk

Glasgow Caledonian University
www.gcu.ac.uk

Glasgow School of Art
www.gsa.ac.uk

Gloucestershire
www.glos.ac.uk

Gloucestershire College
www.gloscol.ac.uk

Glyndwr University
formerly North East Wales Institute of Higher Education
www.glyndwr.ac.uk

Goldsmiths College
(University of London)
www.gold.ac.uk

Gower College Swansea
www.gowercollegeswansea.ac.uk

Greenmount and Enniskillen Colleges
see College of Agriculture, Food and Rural Enterprise

Greenwich
www.gre.ac.uk

Greenwich School of Management
www.greenwich-college.ac.uk

Grimsby Institute of Further and Higher Education
www.grimsby.ac.uk

Guildford College of Further and Higher Education
www.guildford.ac.uk

Harper Adams University College
www.harper-adams.ac.uk

Havering College of Further and Higher Education
www.havering-college.ac.uk

Hereford College of Arts
www.hca.ac.uk

Heriot-Watt
www.hw.ac.uk

Hertfordshire
www.herts.ac.uk

Heythrop College
(University of London)
www.heythrop.ac.uk/

Highbury College
www.highbury.ac.uk

Highlands & Islands
see UHI Millennium Institute

Holborn College
www.holborncollege.ac.uk

Hopwood Hall College
www.hopwood.ac.uk/

Huddersfield
www.hud.ac.uk

Huddersfield Technical College
now see Kirklees College

Hull
www.hull.ac.uk

Hull College
www.hull-college.ac.uk/HE

Hull York Medical School
www.hyms.ac.uk

ifs School of Finance
www.ifslearning.ac.uk

Imperial College
(University of London)
www.imperial.ac.uk

Islamic College for Advanced Studies
www.islamic-college.ac.uk

Keele
www.keele.ac.uk

Kensington College of Business
www.kensingtoncoll.ac.uk

Kent
www.kent.ac.uk

Kent Institute of Art and Design
see University College for the Creative Arts

King Alfred's Winchester
see Winchester (University College)

King's College London
www.kcl.ac.uk

Kingston
www.kingston.ac.uk

Kirklees College
www.kirkleescollege.ac.uk

LCA Business School
London
www.lcabusinessschoo.com

Lakes College West Cumbria
www.lcwc.ac.uk

Lampeter
now see Trinity Saint David

Lancaster
www.lancs.ac.uk

Leeds
www.leeds.ac.uk

Leeds City College
www.leedscitycollege.ac.uk

Leeds College of Art
www.leeds-art.ac.uk

Leeds College of Music
www.lcm.ac.uk

Leeds Metropolitan University
www.leedsmet.ac.uk

Leeds: Trinity University
(formerly Leeds Trinity and All Saints)
www.leedstrinity.ac.uk

Leicester
www.le.ac.uk

Leicester College
www.leicester.ac.uk

Leicester: De Montfort
www.dmu.ac.uk

Lincoln
www.lincoln.ac.uk

Lincoln College
www.lincolncollege.ac.uk

Liverpool
www.liv.ac.uk

Liverpool Community College
www.liv-coll.ac.uk

Liverpool Hope University College
www.hope.ac.uk

Liverpool Institute for Performing Arts
www.lipa.ac.uk

Liverpool John Moores University
www.ljmu.ac.uk

Llandrillo College
see Coleg Llandrillo

London College, UCK
www.lcuck.ac.uk

London Electronics College
www.lec.ac.uk

London Guildhall University
see London Metropolitan University

London Metropolitan University
www.londonmet.ac.uk

London: Queen Mary
(University of London)
www.qmul.ac.uk

London School of Commerce
www.lsclondon.co.uk

London School of Economics and Political Science
(University of London)
www.lse.ac.uk

London School of Science and Technology
www.lsst.com

London South Bank University
www.lsbu.ac.uk

London: University of West London
www.uwl.ac.uk

Loughborough
www.lboro.ac.uk

Loughborough College
www.loucoll.ac.uk

Manchester
www.manchester.ac.uk

Manchester College, The
formerly Manchester City College and The
Manchester College of Art and Technology
www.themanchestercollege.ac.uk

Manchester Metropolitan University
www.mmu.ac.uk

Matthew Boulton College of Further and
Higher Education
Now see Birmingham Metropolitan

Medway School of Pharmacy
www.msp.ac.uk

Menai
see Coleg Menai

Mid-Cheshire College
www.midchesh.ac.uk

Middlesex
www.mdx.ac.uk

Moulton College
www.moulton.ac.uk

Mountview Academy of Theatre Arts
www.mountview.org.uk

Myerscough College
www.myerscough.ac.uk

Napier
Edinburgh
www.napier.ac.uk

Nazarene Theological College
www.nazarene.ac.uk

Neath Port Talbot College
www.nptc.ac.uk

NESCOT
North East Surrey College of Technology
www.nescot.ac.uk

New College Telford
www.nct.ac.uk

Newcastle
www.ncl.ac.uk

Newcastle College
www.ncl-coll.ac.uk

Newham College of Further Education
www.newham.ac.uk

Newman University College Birmingham
www.newman.ac.uk

Newport
www.newport.ac.uk

North East Surrey College of Technology
see NESCOT

North East Worcestershire College
www.ne-worcs.ac.uk

North Glasgow College
northglasgowcollege.ac.uk

North Lindsey College
www.northlindsey.ac.uk

North London
see London Metropolitan University

North Warwickshire and Hinckley
College
www.nwhc.ac.uk

Northampton
www.northampton.ac.uk

Northbrook College Sussex
www.northbrook.ac.uk

Northumberland College
www.northland.ac.uk

Northumbria
www.northumbria.ac.uk

Norwich: City College of Further &
Higher Education
www.ccn.ac.uk

Norwich University College of the Arts
www.nuca.ac.uk

Nottingham
www.nottingham.ac.uk

Nottingham (New College)
www.ncn.ac.uk

Nottingham Trent University
www.ntu.ac.uk

Open University
www.open.ac.uk

Oxford
www.ox.ac.uk

Oxford and Cherwell Valley College
www.ocvc.ac.uk/

Oxford Brookes
www.brookes.ac.uk

Paisley
now see West of Scotland

Paris (University of London Institute in)
www.ulip.lon.ac.uk

Pembrokeshire College
www.pembrokeshire.ac.uk

Peninsula College of Medicine and
Dentistry
Universities of Exeter & Plymouth
www.pmmd.ac.uk

Peterborough - University Centre
www.anglia.ac.uk/ucp

Petroc
www.petroc.ac.uk

Plymouth
www.plymouth.ac.uk

Plymouth College of Art
www.plymouthart.ac.uk

Portsmouth
www.port.ac.uk

Queen's University
Belfast
www.qub.ac.uk

Ravensbourne
www.rave.ac.uk

Reading
www.reading.ac.uk

Regents Business School London
www.regents.ac.uk

Richmond, The American International
University in London
www.richmond.ac.uk

Riverside College Halton
Widnes
www.riversidecollege.ac.uk

Robert Gordon
Aberdeen
www.rgu.ac.uk

Roehampton
(University of Surrey)
www.roehampton.ac.uk

Rose Bruford
Sidcup
www.bruford.ac.uk

Rotherham College of Arts and
Technology
www.rotherham.ac.uk

Royal Academy of Dance
London
www.rad.org.uk

Royal Agricultural College
Gloucester
www.rac.ac.uk

Royal College of Art
London (Post graduate only)
www.rca.ac.uk

Royal Holloway
London
www.rhul.ac.uk

Royal Veterinary College
London
www.rvc.ac.uk

Royal Welsh College of Music & Drama
Cardiff
www.rwcmd.ac.uk

Ruskin College Oxford
www.ruskin.ac.uk

SAE Institute
(School of Audio Engineering) Glasgow,
Liverpool & London
www.sae.edu

Salford
www.salford.ac.uk

Salisbury College
now see Wiltshire College

Sandwell College
www.sandwell.ac.uk

School of Oriental and African Studies
(University of London)
www.soas.ac.uk

School of Pharmacy
(University of London)
www.pharmacy.ac.uk

Scottish Agricultural College
(The National College for Food, Land and
Environmental Studies)
www.sac.ac.uk

Sheffield
www.sheffield.ac.uk

Sheffield College
www.sheffcol.ac.uk

Sheffield Hallam
www.shu.ac.uk

Solihull College
www.solihull.ac.uk

Somerset College of Arts and
Technology
www.somerset.ac.uk

South Cheshire College
www.s-cheshire.ac.uk

South Devon College
www.southdevon.ac.uk

South Downs College
www.southdowns.ac.uk

South Essex College
www.southessex.ac.uk

South Nottingham College
www.snc.ac.uk

South Tyneside College
www.stc.ac.uk

Southampton
www.southampton.ac.uk

Southampton Solent University
www.solent.ac.uk

Southport College
www.southport-college.ac.uk/

Sparsholt College Hampshire
www.sparsholt.ac.uk

St Andrews
Fife
www.st-andrews.ac.uk

St George's University of London
Formerly St George's Hospital Medical
School
www.sgul.ac.uk

St Helens College
www.sthelens.ac.uk

St Martin's College, Lancaster:
Ambleside: Carlisle: London
now see Cumbria University

St Mary's University College
Twickenham
www.smuc.ac.uk

St Mary's University College
Belfast
www.smucb.ac.uk

Staffordshire
www.staffs.ac.uk

Stamford New College
www.stamford.ac.uk

Stephenson College Coalville
www.stephensoncoll.ac.uk

Stirling
www.stir.ac.uk

Stockport College
www.stockport.ac.uk

Stourbridge College
www.stourbridge.ac.uk

Stranmillis University College
Belfast
www.stran.ac.uk

Stratford upon Avon College
www.stratford.ac.uk

Strathclyde
www.strath.ac.uk

Suffolk, University Campus
www.ucs.ac.uk

Sunderland
www.sunderland.ac.uk

Sunderland College (City of)
www.citysun.ac.uk

Surrey
www.surrey.ac.uk

Sussex
www.sussex.ac.uk

Sutton Coldfield College
now see Birmingham Metropolitan College

Swansea
www.swansea.ac.uk

Swansea Metropolitan University
formerly Swansea Institute
www.smu.ac.uk

Swindon College
www.swindon-college.ac.uk

Tameside College
www.tameside.ac.uk

Teesside
www.tees.ac.uk

Thames Valley
(The University of West London)
www.tvu.ac.uk

Trinity St David
(University of Wales)
www.trinitysaintdavid.ac.uk

Truro and Penwith College
www.trurocollege.ac.uk

Tyne Metropolitan College
www.tynemet.ac.uk

UCP Marjon
St Mark and St John (The College of),
Plymouth
www.marjon.ac.uk

UHI Millennium Institute
www.uhi.ac.uk

Ulster
www.ulster.ac.uk

University College London
www.ucl.ac.uk

University of the Arts London
Camberwell College of Arts, Central Saint
Martins College of Art and Design, Chelsea
College of Art and Design, London College
of Communication, London College of
Fashion, Wimbledon College of Art
www.arts.ac.uk

University of Wales Institute, Cardiff
(UWIC)
www.uwic.ac.uk

Uxbridge College
www.uxbridgecollege.ac.uk

Wakefield College
www.wakefield.ac.uk

Walsall College
www.walsallcollege.ac.uk

Warrington Collegiate
www.warrington.ac.uk

Warwick
www.warwick.ac.uk

Warwickshire College
www.warwickshire.ac.uk

West Anglia (College of)
www.col-westanglia.ac.uk

West Cheshire College
www.west-cheshire.ac.uk

West of England
Bristol
www.uwe.ac.uk

West of Scotland
formerly Paisley University
www.uws.ac.uk

West London
www.uwl.ac.uk

West Thames College
www.west-thames.ac.uk

Westminster
www.westminster.ac.uk

Westminster Kingsway College
www.westking.ac.uk

Wigan and Leigh College
www.wigan-leigh.ac.uk/

Wiltshire College
www.wiltshire.ac.uk

Winchester
www.winchester.ac.uk

Wirral Metropolitan College
www.wmc.ac.uk

Wolverhampton
www.wlv.ac.uk

Worcester
www.worcester.ac.uk

Worcester College of Technology
www.wortech.ac.uk

Writtle College
www.writtle.ac.uk

York
www.york.ac.uk

York College
www.yorkcollege.ac.uk

York St John University College
w3.yorksj.ac.uk

Yorkshire Coast College of Further and Higher Education
www.yorkshirecoastcollege.ac.uk

Dance, drama, music & performing arts

The institutions listed offer post-16 vocational training. This is different from the theatre, dance, drama and performing arts degrees offered by many universities.

Some institutions accept applications through UCAS but for the majority application will be direct.

Those listed as DADA are accredited to offer Dance and Drama (DADA) Awards. These cover most of the tuition fees for their courses, which are at National Certificate or National Diploma level. See www.direct.gov.uk for full information.

The National Council for Drama Training (NCDT) is a partnership of employers in theatre, broadcast and media industries, employee representatives and training providers which accredits vocational courses.

The Council for Dance Education and Training (CDET) is the national standards body of the professional dance industry. It accredits programmes of training in vocational dance schools.

There are also prestigious institutions which function outside of other systems and administer their own admissions and funding.

Academy of Live and Recorded Arts (Alra)
Studio 24
Royal Victoria Patriotic Building
John Archer Way
London SW18 3SX
Tel: 020 8870 6475
email via website
www.alra.co.uk
ALRA North:
Turner Street
Wigan
WN1 3SU
Telephone, email and website as above
DADA NCDT

Arts Ed London
Cone Ripman House
14 Bath Rd
London W4 1LY
Tel: 020 8987 6666
c.smith@artsed.co.uk
www.artsed.co.uk
CDET DADA NCDT

Bird College – Dance and Drama Theatre Performance
The Centre
27 Station Rd
Sidcup DA15 7EB
Tel: 020 8300 6004
deborah.preston@birdcollege.co.uk
www.birdcollege.co.uk
CDET DADA

Birmingham School of Acting
Millennium Point
Curzon Street
Birmingham B4 7XG
Tel: 0121 331 7220
info@bsa.bcu.ac.uk
www.bcu.ac.uk/pme/school-of-acting
NCDT

Bristol Old Vic Theatre School
2 Downside Road
Clifton
Bristol BS8 2XF
Tel: 0117 973 3535
enquiries@oldvic.ac.uk
www.oldvic.ac.uk
NCDT
Conservatoire for Dance and Drama

Cambridge Performing Arts at Bodyworks
Bodywork Dance Studios
25-29 Glisson Rd
Cambridge CB1 2HA
Tel: 01223 314461
www.bodywork-dance.co.uk
CDET DADA

Central School of Ballet
10 Herbal Hill
Clerkenwell Road
London EC1R 5EG
Tel: 020 7837 6332
info@csbschool.co.uk
www.centralschoolofballet.co.uk
Conservatoire for Dance and Drama

Central School of Speech and Drama
Eton Avenue
London NW3 3HY
Tel: 020 7722 8183
admissions@cssd.ac.uk
www.cssd.ac.uk
NCDT

Circus Space
Coronet Street
London
N! 6HD
Tel: 020 7729 9522
info@circusspace.co.uk
www.circusspace.co.uk

Conservatoire for Dance and Drama
Tavistock House,
Tavistock Square
London
WC1H 0JJ
Tel: 020 7387 5101
info@cdd.ac.uk
www.cdd.ac.uk
The Conservatoire is a Higher Education
Institution comprising eight small, specialist
institutions with international reputations for
high quality delivery in their respective fields:
Bristol Old Vic Theatre School
Central School of Ballet
Circus Space
London Academy of Music and Dramatic Art
London Contemporary Dance School
Northern School of Contemporary Dance
Rambert School of Ballet and Contemporary
Dance

CPA College
The Studios
219b North Street
Romford,
Essex
RM1 4QA
Tel: 01708 766 007
Email via website
www.cpastudios.co.uk
CDET

Drama Centre London
Central Saint Martins College of Arts and
Design
University of the Arts London
Granary Building
1 Granary Square
London
N1C 4AA
Tel: 020 7514 8760
drama@arts.ac.uk
www.csm.arts.ac.uk
NCDT

Drama Studio London
Grange Court
1 Grange Rd
London W5 5QN
Tel: 020 8579 3897
admin@dramastudiolondon.co.uk
www.dramastudiolondon.co.uk
DADA NCDT

East 15 Acting School
Loughton campus:
Hatfields
Rectory Lane
Loughton
Essex IG10 3RY
Tel: 020 8508 5983
Southend Campus:
Elmer Approach
Southend-on-Sea SS1 1LW, UK
Tel: 01702 328200
east15@essex.ac.uk
www.east15.ac.uk
NCDT

Elmhurst School for Dance (in association
with Birmingham Royal Ballet)
249 Bristol Rd
Edgbaston
Birmingham B5 7UH
Tel: 0121 472 6655
enquiries@elmhurstdance.co.uk
www.elmhurstdance.co.uk
CDET DADA

English National Ballet School
Carlyle Building
Hortensia Road
London SW10 0QS
Tel: 020 7376 7076
info@enbschool.org.uk
www.enbschool.org.uk
CDET, DADA

Guildford School of Acting
Stag Hill Campus,
Guildford
Surrey GU2 7X
Tel: 01483 560701
gsaenquiries@gsa.surrey.ac.uk
www.conservatoire.org
DADA NCDT

Guildhall School of Music & Drama
Silk Street
Barbican
London EC2Y 8DT
Tel: 020 7628 2571
registry@gsmd.ac.uk
www.gsmd.ac.uk
NCDT

Hammond School
Hoole Bank
Mannings Lane
Chester CH2 4ES
Tel: 01244 305350
enquiries@thehammondschool.co.uk
www.thehammondschool.co.uk
CDET, DADA

Italia Conti Academy of Theatre Arts Ltd
For BA (Hons) Acting:
'Avondale'
72 Landor Road
London, SW9 9PH
Tel: 020 7733 3210
For Theatre Arts School:
Italia Conti House
23 Goswell Road
London EC1M 7AJ
Tel: 020 7608 0047
admin@italiaconti.com
www.italiaconti.com
CDET DADA NCDT

Laban see Trinity Laban Conservatoire of Music and Dance

Laine Theatre Arts
The Studios
East Street
Epsom
Surrey KT17 1HH
Tel: 01372 724 648
info@laine-theatre-arts.co.uk
www.laine-theatre-arts.co.uk
CDET DADA

LAMDA see London Academy of Music & Dramatic Art

Leeds College of Music
3 Quarry Hill
Leeds LS2 7PD
Tel: 0113 222 3400
enquiries@lcm.ac.uk
www.lcm.ac.uk

Liverpool Institute for Performing Arts
Mount Street
Liverpool L1 9HF
Tel: 0151 330 3000
reception@lipa.ac.uk
www.lipa.ac.uk
CDET

Liverpool Theatre School and College
Performing Arts Centre
19 Aigburth Road
Liverpool L17 4JR
Tel: 0151 728 7800
info@liverpooltheatreschool.co.uk
www.liverpooltheatreschool.co.uk
CDET DADA

London Academy of Music & Dramatic Art (LAMDA)
155 Talgarth Road
London W14 9DA
Tel: 020 8834 0500
enquiries@lamda.org.uk
www.lamda.org.uk
NCDT
Conservatoire for Dance and Drama

London Contemporary Dance School
The Place
17 Dukes Road
London WC1H 9PY
Tel: 020 7121 1111
lcds@theplace.org.uk
www.theplace.org.uk
Conservatoire for Dance and Drama

London Studio Centre
42-50 York Way
London N1 9AB
Tel: 020 7837 7741
info@london-studio-centre.co.uk
www.london-studio-centre.co.uk
CDET

Manchester School of Theatre
Manchester Metropolitan University
Mabel Tylecote Building
Cavendish Street
Manchester
M15 6BG
Tel: 0161 247 1751
artdes.fac@mmu.ac.uk
www.theatre.mmu.ac.uk
NCDT

Midlands Academy of Dance and Drama
Century House, Building B
428 Carlton Hill
Nottingham
NG4 1QA
Tel: 0115 911 0401
admin@maddcollege.supanet.com
www.maddcollege.co.uk
CDET

Millennium Performing Arts
29 Thomas Street
Woolwich
London SE18 6HU
Tel: 020 8301 8744
info@md2000.co.uk
www.md2000.co.uk
CDET, DADA

Mountview Academy of Theatre Arts
Ralph Richardson Memorial Studios
Clarendon Road
Kingfisher Place
London N22 6XF
Tel: 020 8881 2201
enquires@mountview.ac.uk
www.mountview.org.uk
DADA NCDT

Northern Ballet School
The Dancehouse
10 Oxford Road
Manchester M1 5QA
Tel: 0161 237 1406
enquiries@northernballetschool.co.uk
www.northernballetschool.co.uk
CDET DADA

Northern School of Contemporary Dance
98 Chapeltown Road
Leeds LS7 4BH
Tel: 0113 219 3000
info@nscd.ac.uk
www.nscd.ac.uk
Conservatoire for Dance and Drama

Oxford School of Drama
Sansomes Farm Studios
Woodstock
Oxfordshire OX20 1ER
Tel: 01993 812 883
info@oxforddrama.ac.uk
www.oxforddrama.ac.uk
DADA NCDT

Performers College
Southend Road
Corringham
Essex SS17 8JT
Tel: 01375 672 053
lesley@performerscollege.co.uk
www.performerscollege.co.uk
CDET DADA

Rambert School of Ballet & Contemporary Dance
Clifton Lodge
St. Margaret's Drive
Twickenham TW1 1QN
Tel: 0208 892 9960
info@rambertschool.org.uk
www.rambertschool.org.uk
Conservatoire for Dance and Drama

Rose Bruford College
Lamorbey Park
Burnt Oak Lane
Sidcup
Kent DA15 9DF
Tel: 020 8308 2600
enquiries@bruford.ac.uk
www.bruford.ac.uk
NCDT

Royal Academy of Dance (Faculty of Education)
36 Battersea Square
London SW11 3RA
Tel: 020 7326 8000
info@rad.org.uk
www.rad.org.uk

Royal Academy of Dramatic Art (RADA)
62-64 Gower Street
London WC1E 6ED
Tel: 020 7636 7076
enquiries@rada.ac.uk
www.rada.ac.uk
NCDT
Conservatoire for Dance and Drama

Royal Academy of Music
Marylebone Rd
London NW1 5HT
Tel: 020 7873 7373
email via website
www.ram.ac.uk

Royal Ballet School
Upper School:
46 Floral Street
Covent Garden, London, WC2E 9DA
Lower School:
White Lodge
Richmond Park
Richmond
Surrey TW10 5HR
Tel: 020 7836 8899 (Upper School)
Tel: 020 8392 8440 (Lower School)
enquiries@royalballetschool.co.uk
www.royal-ballet-school.org.uk

Royal College of Music
Prince Consort Rd
London SW7 2BS
Tel: 020 7591 4300
info@rcm.ac.uk
www.rcm.ac.uk

Royal Northern College of Music
124 Oxford Rd
Manchester M13 9RD
Tel: 0161 907 5200
info@rncm.ac.uk
www.rncm.ac.uk

Royal Conservatoire of Scotland
100 Renfrew St
Glasgow G2 3DB
Tel: 0141 332 4101
email via website
www.rcs.ac.uk
NCDT

Royal Welsh College of Music & Drama
Castle Grounds
Cathays Park
Cardiff CF10 3ER
Tel: 029 2034 2854
admissions@rwcmd.ac.uk
www.rwcmd.ac.uk
NCDT

SLP College Leeds
5 Chapel Lane
Garforth
Leeds LS25 1AG
Tel: 01332 868 136
info@slpcollege.co.uk
www.slpcollege.co.uk
CDET, DADA

Stella Mann College
10 Linden Road
Bedford MK40 2DA
Tel: 01234 213331
administrator@stellamanncollege.co.uk
www.stellamanncollege.co.uk
CDET

Tring Park School for the Performing Arts
Tring
Hertfordshire
HP23 5LX
Tel: 01442 824 255
info@tringpark.com
www.tringpark.com
CDET DADA

Trinity Laban Conservatoire of Music and Dance
Dance Faculty
Laban
Creekside
London
SE8 3DZ
Tel: 020 8691 8600
email via website

&
Music Faculty
Trinity
King Charles Court
Old Royal Naval College
Greenwich
London SE10 9JF
Tel: 020 8305 4444
email via website
www.trinitylaban.ac.uk

Urdang Academy
The Old Finsbury Town Hall
Rosebery Avenue
London EC1R 4RP
Tel: 0207 713 7710
info@theurdangacademy.com
www.theurdangacademy.com
CDET DADA

WAC Performing Arts and Media College
Hampstead Town Hall Centre
213 Haverstock Hill
London NW3 4QP
Tel: 020 7692 5888
info@wac.co.uk
www.wac.co.uk
DADA

Theatres & touring companies

Access London Theatre
www.officiallondontheatre.co.uk/access
Guide to West End Theatres for
theatregoers with a disability

London theatres: online
www.officiallondontheatre.co.uk

Theatrenet
www.theatrenet.com

UK Theatre Web
www.uktw.co.uk/

Aberdeen: His Majesty's Theatre
Rosemount Viaduct
Aberdeen AB25 1GL
Tel: 01224 641122
www.boxofficeaberdeen.com

Action Transport
Whitby Hall
Stanney Lane
Ellesmere Port CH65 9AE
Tel: 0151 357 2120
www.actiontransporttheatre.org

Arc Theatre
First Floor
The Malthouse Studios
62-76 Abbey Road
Barking
Essex IG11 7BT
Tel: 020 8594 1095
www.arctheatre.com

Basingstoke: Anvil, Forge and Haymarket
Anvil Arts
Churchill Way
Basingstoke RG21 7QR
Tel: 01256 819 797
Box Office: 01256 844244
www.anvilarts.org.uk

Bath: Theatre Royal
Sawclose
Bath BA1 1ET
Box Office: 01225 448844
www.theatreroyal.org.uk

Birmingham Repertory Theatre
Centenary Sq
Broad St
Birmingham B1 2EP
Box Office: 0121 236 4455
www.birmingham-rep.co.uk

Blackpool: Grand Theatre
33 Church Street
Blackpool FY1 1HT
Box Office: 01253 290190
Groups:01253 743232
www.blackpoolgrand.co.uk

Blackpool: Opera House
Church Street
Blackpool FY1 1HW
Box Office: 0845 856 1111
www.blackpoollive.co.uk

Bolton: Octagon Theatre
Howell Croft South
Bolton BL1 1SB
Box Office: 01204 520661
www.octagonbolton.co.uk

Bradford: Alhambra Theatre
Morley Street
Bradford BD7 1AJ
Tel: 01274 432375
Box Office: 01274 432000
www.bradford-theatres.co.uk/alhambra

Bradford: Theatre in the Mill
Shearbridge Rd
Bradford BD7 1DP
Box Office: 01274 233200
www.brad.ac.uk/theatre

Bristol Old Vic
King St
Bristol BS1 4ED
Tel: 0117 949 3993
Box Office: 0117 987 7877
www.bristololdvic.org.uk

Bromley: The Churchill Theatre
High Street
Bromley
Kent BR1 1HA
Box Office: 0844 871 7620
Groups: 0844 871 7636
www.atgtickets.com/The-Churchill

Buxton Opera House
Water St
Buxton SK17 6XN
Tel: 01298 72050
Box Office: 0845 1272190
www.buxtonoperahouse.org.uk/

Cambridge Arts Theatre
6 St Edward's Passage
Cambridge CB2 3PJ
Box Office: 01223 503333
www.cambridgeartstheatre.com

Canterbury: Marlowe Theatre
New theatre under construction. Performances
at various venues
Box Office: 01227 787787
www.marlowetheatre.com

Cardiff: New Theatre
Park Place
Cardiff CF10 3LN
Box Office: 029 2087 8889
www.newtheatrecardiff.co.uk

Cardiff: Sherman Theatre
Senghennydd Rd
Cardiff CF24 4YE
Box Office: 029 2064 6900
www.shermancymru.co.uk

Clwyd Theatr Cymru
Mold
Flintshire CH7 1YA
Box Office: 0845 330 3565
www.clwyd-theatr-cymru.co.uk

Colchester: Mercury Theatre
Balkerne Gate
Colchester CO1 1PT
Box Office: 01206 573948
www.mercurytheatre.co.uk

Coventry: Belgrade Theatre
Belgrade Sq
Coventry CV1 1GS
Box Office: 024 7655 3055
www.belgrade.co.uk

Darlington: Civic Theatre
Parkgate
Darlington DL1 1RR
Box Office: 01325 486555
www.darlingtonarts.gov.uk/arts

Derby Theatre
Eagle Centre
Derby DE1 2NF
Box Office: 01332 255800
www.derbytheatre.co.uk

Dundee Repertory Theatre
Tay Sq
Dundee DD1 1PB
Box Office: 01382 223530
www.dundeereptheatre.co.uk

Edinburgh: FestivalTheatre
13/29 Nicolson Street
Edinburgh EH8 9FT
Tel: 0131 529 6000
www.fctt.org.uk/festivaltheatre

Edinburgh: Kings Theatre
2 Leven Street
Edinburgh EH3 9LQ
Tel: 0131 529 6000
www.fctt.org.uk/kings-theatre

Edinburgh Playhouse
18-22 Greenside Place
Edinburgh EH1 3AA
Tickets: 0844 847 1660
www.edinburghplayhouse.org.uk

Edinburgh: Royal Lyceum Theatre
Grindlay St
Edinburgh EH3 9AX
Box Office: 0131 248 4848
Groups: 0131 248 4949
www.lyceum.org.uk

Edinburgh: Traverse Theatre
Cambridge St
Edinburgh EH1 2ED
Box Office: 0131 228 1404
www.traverse.co.uk

English Touring Theatre
25 Short St
London SE1 8LJ
Tel: 020 7450 1990
www.ett.org.uk

Exeter: Northcott Theatre
Stocker Rd
Exeter EX4 4QB
Box Office: 01392 493493
www.exeternorthcott.co.uk

Glasgow: Citizens Theatre
119 Gorbals St
Glasgow G5 9DS
Box Office: 0141 429 0022
www.citz.co.uk

Glasgow: Tramway
25 Albert Drive
Glasgow G41 2PE
Tel: 0845 330 3501
www.tramway.org

Glasgow: Tron Theatre
63 Trongate
Glasgow G1 5HB
Box Office: 0141 552 4267
www.tron.co.uk

Harrogate Theatre
Oxford St
Harrogate HG1 1QF
Box Office: 01423 502116
www.harrogatetheatre.co.uk

Headlong Theatre
34-35 Berwick Street
London W1F 8RP
Tel: 020 7478 0270
www.headlongtheatre.co.uk

Hornchurch: Queen's Theatre
Billet Ln
Hornchurch RM11 1QT
Box Office: 01708 443333
www.queens-theatre.co.uk

Huddersfield: Lawrence Batley Theatre
Queens Square
Queens St
Huddersfield HD1 2SP
Box Office: 01484 430528
www.thelbt.org

Hull Truck Theatre
50 Ferensway
Hull, HU2 8LB
Box Office: 01482 323638
www.hulltruck.co.uk

Ipswich: Sir John Mills Theatre
Gatacre Rd
Ipswich IP1 2LQ
Box Office: 01473 211498
www.easternangles.co.uk

Kendal: Brewery Arts Centre
122A Highgate
Kendal LA9 4HE
Box Office: 01539 725133
www.breweryarts.co.uk

Keswick: Theatre by the Lake
Lakeside
Keswick CA12 5DJ
Box Office: 01768 774411
www.theatrebythelake.co.uk

Lancaster: Duke's Cinema & Theatre
Moor Lane
Lancaster LA1 1QE
Box Office: 01524 598 500
www.dukes-lancaster.org

Leeds: Grand Theatre
46 New Briggate
Leeds LS1 6NZ
Box Office: 0844 848 2706
www.leedsgrandtheatre.com

Leeds: West Yorkshire Playhouse
Playhouse Sq
Quarry Hill
Leeds LS2 7UP
Box Office: 0113 213 7700
Groups: 0113 213 7212
www.wyp.org.uk

Leicester: Curve
Rutland Street
Leicester LE1 1SB
Tel: 0116 2423595
www.curveonline.co.uk

Lincoln: Theatre Royal
Clasketgate
Lincoln LN2 1JJ
Box Office: 01522 519999
www.lincolntheatreroyal.com

Liverpool: Empire
Lime St
L1 1JE
Box Office: 0844 871 3017
Groups: 0844 871 3037
www.liverpoolempire.org.uk

Liverpool: Everyman Theatre
5-9 Hope St
Liverpool L1 9BH
Box Office: 0151 709 4776
Groups: 0151 708 3733
www.everymanplayhouse.com
Closed for refurbishment in July 2011

Liverpool: Playhouse
Williamson Square
Liverpool L1 1EL
Box Office: 0151 709 4776
Groups: 0151 708 3733
www.everymanplayhouse.com

London: Almeida Theatre
Almeida St
Islington
London N1 1TA
Box Office: 020 7359 4404
www.almeida.co.uk

London: Barbican Centre
Silk St
London EC2Y 8DS
Box Office: 020 7638 8891
www.barbican.org.uk

London: Donmar Warehouse
41 Earlham St
London WC2H 9LD
Box Office: 0844 871 7624
www.donmarwarehouse.com

London: Hampstead Theatre
Eton Ave
Swiss Cottage
London NW3 3EU
Box Office: 020 7722 9301
www.hampsteadtheatre.com

London: Lyric Theatre
King St
London W6 0QL
Box Office: 0871 2211 729
www.lyric.co.uk

London: National Theatre
South Bank
London SE1 9PX
Tel: 020 7452 3000 (Box Office)
www.nationaltheatre.org.uk

London: New Wimbledon Theatre
The Broadway
Wimbledon
London SW19 1QG
Box Office: 0844 871 7646
www.atgtickets.com/New-Wimbledon-Theatre

London: Open Air Theatre
Inner Circle
Regent's Park NW1 4NR
Box Office: 0844826 4242
www.openairtheatre.org

London: Polka Theatre for Children
240 The Broadway
Wimbledon
London SW19 1SB
Box Office: 020 8543 4888
www.polkatheatre.com

London: Royal Court Theatre
Sloane Sq
London SW1W 8AS
Tel: 020 7565 5050
Box Office: 020 7565 5000
www.royalcourttheatre.com

London: Sadler's Wells Theatre
Rosebery Av
London EC1R 4TN
Tel: 020 7863 8198
Box Office: 0844 412 4300
www.sadlerswells.com

London: Shakespeare's Globe Theatre
21 New Globe Walk
Bankside
London SE1 9DT
Box office: 020 7401 9919
www.shakespearesglobe.org

London: Theatre Royal Stratford East
Gerry Raffles Sq
London E15 1BN
Tel: 020 8534 0310
www.stratfordeast.com

London: Tricycle Theatre
269 Kilburn High Rd
London NW6 7JR
Box Office: 020 7328 1000
www.tricycle.co.uk

London: Unicorn Theatre for Children
147 Tooley Street
More London
Southwark
London SE1 2HZ
Tel: 020 7645 0560
www.unicorntheatre.com

London: Young Vic
66 The Cut
London SE1 8LZ
Tel: 020 7922 2922
www.youngvic.org

Manchester: Contact Theatre
Oxford Rd
Manchester MI5 6JA
Box Office: 0161 274 0600
www.contactmcr.com

Manchester: Library Theatre
Moved out of the Manchester Central
Library in July 2010 and will be performing
at alternative venues across the region until
moving into a new permanent home. Most
bookings should be done through the website.
For general enquiries: Tel: 0161 234 1913
www.librarytheatre.com

Manchester: Opera House
Quay Street
Manchester M3 3HP
Tel: 0844 871 3018
www.manchesteroperahouse.org.uk

Manchester: Palace Theatre
Oxford Street
Manchester M1 6FT
Box Office: 0844 871 3018
www.manchesterpalace.org.uk

Manchester: Royal Exchange Theatre Co
St Ann's Sq
Manchester M2 7DH
Box Office: 0161 833 9833
www.royalexchange.org.uk

Manchester: The Green Room
54 Whitworth St West
Manchester M1 5WW
Box Office: 0161 615 0500
www.greenroomarts.org

Milford Haven: Torch Theatre
St Peter's Rd
Milford Haven SA73 2BU
Box Office: 01646 695267
www.torchtheatre.co.uk

Musselburgh: Brunton Theatre
Ladywell Way
Musselburgh EH21 6AA
Box Office: 0131 665 2240
www.bruntontheatre.co.uk

Newbury: Watermill Theatre
Bagnor
Newbury
Berks RG20 8AE
Box Office: 01635 46044
www.watermill.org.uk

Newcastle under Lyme: New Vic Theatre
Etruria Rd
Newcastle under Lyme ST5 0JG
Box Office: 01782 717962
www.newvictheatre.org.uk

Newcastle upon Tyne: Live Theatre Company
27 Broad Chare
Quayside
Newcastle upon Tyne NE1 3DQ
Box Office: 0191 232 1232
www.live.org.uk

Newcastle upon Tyne: Northern Stage
Barras Bridge
Newcastle upon Tyne NE1 7RH
Tel: 0191 230 5151
www.northernstage.co.uk

Northampton Theatres Trust: Royal & Derngate Theatre
Guildhall Rd
Northampton NN1 1DP
Box Office: 01604 624811
www.royalandderngate.co.uk

Northern Broadsides
Dean Clough
Halifax HX3 5AX
Tel: 01422 369704
www.northern-broadsides.co.uk

Norwich Playhouse
42 - 58 St. George's Street
Norwich NR3 1AB
Box office: 01603 598 598
www.norwichplayhouse.co.uk

Norwich: Theatre Royal
Theatre St
Norwich NR2 1RL
Box Office: 01603 630000
www.theatreroyalnorwich.co.uk

Nottingham Playhouse
Wellington Circus
Nottingham NG1 5AF
Box Office: 0115 941 9419
www.nottinghamplayhouse.co.uk

Nottingham: Theatre Royal
Theatre Square
Nottingham NG1 5ND
Box Office: 0115 989 5555
www.royalcentre-nottingham.co.uk

Oldham Coliseum
Fairbottom St
Oldham OL1 3SW
Box Office: 0161 624 2829
www.coliseum.org.uk

Out of Joint
7 Thane Works
London N7 7PH
Tel: 020 7609 0207
www.outofjoint.co.uk

Oxford Playhouse
Beaumont St
Oxford OX1 2LW
Box Office: 01865 305305
www.oxfordplayhouse.com

Perth Theatre
185 High St
Perth PH1 5UW
Tel: 01738 621 031
www.horsecross.co.uk

Pilot Theatre
c/o York Theatre Royal
St Leonard's Place
York YO1 7HD
Tel: 01904 635755
www.pilot-theatre.com

Plymouth: Theatre Royal
Royal Parade
Plymouth PL1 2TR
Box Office: 01752 230440
www.theatreroyal.com

Portsmouth: New Theatre Royal
Guildhall Walk
Portsmouth
Hampshire PO1 2DD
Box Office: 02392 649000
www.newtheatreroyal.com

Royal Opera House
Covent Garden
London WC2E 9DD
Box Office: 020 7304 4000
Switchboard: 020 7240 1200
www.roh.org.uk

Salford: The Lowry
Pier 8, Salford Quays
Manchester M50 3AZ
Tel: 0843 208 6000
www.thelowry.com

Salisbury Playhouse
Malthouse Lane
Salisbury SP2 7RA
Tel: 01722 320117
Box Office: 01722 320333
www.salisburyplayhouse.com

Scarborough: Stephen Joseph Theatre
Westborough
Scarborough YO11 1JW
Tel: 01723 370540
Box Office: 01723 370541
www.sjt.uk.com

Shakespeare at the Tobacco Factory
Raleigh Rd
Southville
Bristol BS3 1TF
Tel: 0117 963 3054
www.sattf.org.uk

Shared Experience Theatre
Oxford Playhouse
11-12 Beaumont Street
Oxford OX1 2LW
Tel: 01865 305321
www.sharedexperience.org.uk/

Sheffield: Crucible Theatre
55 Norfolk St
Sheffield S1 1DA
Tel: 0114 249 5999
Box Office: 0114 249 6000
www.sheffieldtheatres.co.uk

Sheffield: Lyceum Theatre
55 Norfolk St
Sheffield S1 1DA
Tel: 0114 249 5999
Box Office: 0114 249 6000
www.sheffieldtheatres.co.uk

Southampton: Nuffield Theatre
University Rd
Southampton SO17 1TR
Tel: 023 80 315 500
Box Office: 023 80 671 771
www.nuffieldtheatre.co.uk

Southend on Sea: Palace Theatre
Cliffs Pavillion
Station Rd
Southend on Sea
Essex SS0 7RA
Box Office: 01702 351135
HR & Admin: 01702 390657
www.thecliffspavilion.co.uk/

Stoke-on-Trent: Regent Theatre
Piccadilly
Cultural Quarter
Stoke-On-Trent ST1 1AP
Box Office: 0844 871 7649
www.atgtickets.com/Stoke-On-Trent

Stratford-upon-Avon: Royal Shakespeare Theatre
Waterside
Stratford-upon-Avon
Warwickshire CV37 6BB
Box Office: 0844 800 1110
www.rsc.org.uk

Stratford-Upon-Avon: Swan Theatre
Waterside
Stratford-Upon-Avon
Warwickshire CV37 6BB
Box Office:0844 800 1110
www.rsc.org.uk

Stratford-Upon-Avon: The Other Place
Southern Lane
Stratford-Upon-Avon
Tel: 0844 800 1110

TARA ARTS
356 Garratt Lane
London SW18 4ES
Tel: 020 8333 4457
www.tara-arts.com

Théâtre de Complicité
14 Anglers Lane
London NW5 3DG
Tel: 020 7485 7700
www.complicite.org

Tie Tours
TIE Tours Actionwork
PO Box 433
Weston Super Mare
BS24 0WY
Tel: 01934 815163
www.tietours.com

Wakefield: Theatre Royal & Opera House
Drury Lane
Wakefield WF1 2TE
Box Office: 01924 211311
www.wakefieldtheatres.co.uk/

Watford: Palace Theatre
Clarendon Rd
Watford WD17 1JZ
Tel: 01923 235455
Info Line: 01923 225671
www.watfordtheatre.co.uk

Worcester: Swan Theatre
The Moors
Worcester WR1 3ED
Box Office: 01905 611427
www.worcesterlive.co.uk

York Theatre Royal
St Leonards Place
York YO1 7HD
Tel: 01904 658162
Box Office: 01904 623568
www.yorktheatreroyal.co.uk

369 0290580

'ADOLESCENCF' PREGNANCY AND
ЭN

Why, despite evidence to the contrary, does the narrative of the negative consequences of teenage pregnancy, abortion and childbearing persist? This book argues that the negativity surrounding early reproduction is underpinned by a particular understanding of adolescence. It traces the invention of 'adolescence' and the imaginary wall that the notion constructs between young people and adults. Macleod examines the entrenched status of 'adolescence' within a colonialist discourse that equates development of the individual with the development of civilisation, and the consequent threat of degeneration that 'adolescence' implies.

Many important issues are explored, such as the invention of teenage pregnancy and abortion as a social problem; issues of race, culture and tradition in relation to teenage pregnancy; and health service provider practices, specifically in relation to managing risk. In the final chapter, an argument is made for a shift from the signifier 'teenage pregnancy' to 'unwanted pregnancy'.

Using data gathered from studies worldwide, this book highlights central issues in the global debate concerning teenage pregnancy. It is ideal for academics, and students of health psychology, women's studies, nursing and sociology, as well as practitioners in the fields of youth and social work, medicine and counselling.

Catriona Macleod is Professor of Psychology at Rhodes University, South Africa. She has written extensively in national and international journals in the areas of teenage pregnancy, termination of pregnancy, methodological issues, feminist theory, and postcolonialism and psychology

25·99.

WOMEN AND PSYCHOLOGY
Series Editor: Jane Ussher
School of Psychology, University of Western Sydney

This series brings together current theory and research on women and psychology. Drawing on scholarship from a number of different areas of psychology, it bridges the gap between abstract research and the reality of women's lives by integrating theory and practice, research and policy.

Each book addresses a 'cutting edge' issue of research, covering such topics as post-natal depression, eating disorders, theories and methodologies.

The series provides accessible and concise accounts of key issues in the study of women and psychology, and clearly demonstrates the centrality of psychology to debates within women's studies or feminism.

The Series Editor would be pleased to discuss proposals for new books in the series.

Other titles in this series:

THE THIN WOMAN
Helen Malson

THE MENSTRUAL CYCLE
Anne E. Walker

POST-NATAL DEPRESSION
Paula Nicolson

RE-THINKING ABORTION
Mary Boyle

WOMEN AND AGING
Linda R. Gannon

BEING MARRIED. DOING GENDER
Caroline Dryden

UNDERSTANDING DEPRESSION
Janet M. Stoppard

Key Organisations 2012

The up-to-date guide to organisations

REFERENCE ONLY

Complete Issues
articles • opinions • statistics • contacts

Get instant online access to this book by logging on to:
www.completeissues.co.uk

User name: _____

Password: _____

Introduction

Welcome to Key Organisations – the essential, annually updated, contact list.

Always updated

More than 3,000 addresses have been carefully checked and more than 1,000 important changes have been made.

More organisations have been added. In particular, we've included many new websites. 'Dead' sites have been removed. Where we know that an organisation is likely to change in the near future that too has been noted.

Organised with you in mind

We list organisations by the key word in their name eg Adoption and Fostering (British Association for), but we make an exception when reorganising the name would make the details less easy to find or would make a well-known name unfamiliar eg British Museum.

When an organisation changes its name, we include a cross-reference from the previous name eg ASBAH is now known as Shine. When the name of an organisation does not describe what it does, we include a brief description.

The Thematic Guide

When you are interested in a particular area or subject, but do not know any specific names, you can look under the appropriate theme. So the Children's Orchestra appears under both Music and Children/Young People. The themes are listed opposite.

New and improved

With Key Organisations you can access our fantastically helpful, new searchable database. Enter a key word here and generate a list of useful, current, relevant organisations – live and ready to go. See **www.completeissues.co.uk/ko**

You can make this available to everyone with an inexpensive site licence. See **www.carelpress.co.uk/keyorganisations**.

We have now integrated our major publications in the Complete Issues website. Key Organisations is combined with Essential Articles and Fact File to bring you a complete source of opinions, facts, figures and further research. Go to: **www.completeissues.co.uk**

13859072

Learning Resources

Publication information
© 2012 Carel Press Ltd, 4 Hewson Street, Carlisle, CA2 5AU, UK
Tel 01228 538928 Fax: 591816
office@carelpress.co.uk
www.carelpress.co.uk
Editorial team: Anne Louise Kershaw, Debbie Maxwell, Christine A Shepherd, Chas White
Database: Debbie Maxwell
Subscription manager: Ann Batey

Cover design: Anne Louise Kershaw
Logos: Craig Mitchell
Printed by: Finemark, Poland
British Library Cataloguing in Publication Data
Is available for this publication
ISBN-13: 978-1-905600-28-1